INTELLECTUAL PROPERTY AND DEVELOPMENT

Lessons from Recent Economic Research

INTELLECTUAL PROPERTY AND DEVELOPMENT

Lessons from Recent Economic Research

*Edited by Carsten Fink
and Keith E. Maskus*

**A copublication of the World Bank
and Oxford University Press**

A copublication of the World Bank and Oxford University Press.
198 Madison Avenue
New York, NY 10016

This volume is a product of the staff of the International Bank for Reconstruction and Development/ The World Bank. The findings, interpretations, and conclusions expressed here are those of the author(s) and do not necessarily reflect the views of the Executive Directors of The World Bank or the governments they represent.

The World Bank does not guarantee the accuracy of the data included in this work. The boundaries, colors, denominations, and other information shown on any map in this work do not imply any judgement on the part of The World Bank concerning the legal status of any territory or the endorsement or acceptance of such boundaries.

ISBN 0-8213-5772-7

Library of Congress Catologing-in-Publication Data

Intellectual property and development : lessons from recent economic research / edited by
    Carsten Fink, Keith E. Maskus.
        p. cm. – (Trade and development series)
    Includes bibliographical references and index.
    ISBN 0-8213-5772-7 (pbk.)
        1. Intellectual property—Economic aspects. 2. Law and economic development. I. Fink,
Carsten. II. Maskus, Keith E. (Keith Eugene) III. Series.

K1401.I5528 2004
346.04'8–dc22

                                                                2004056350

Cover illustration photos: The World Bank/Curt Carnemark, Tran Thi Hoa, Trevor Samson

CONTENTS

v

EDITORS' PREFACE

Studying and writing about the economic effects of intellectual property protection has occupied a good part of our professional careers, both in academia and at the World Bank. No doubt about it—this is an exciting field of public policy. Every year, new intellectual property laws are passed, international treaties are signed, technologies move to another level, and fresh disputes arise. Policy changes affect the bottom-line profitability of Fortune 500 companies, but they also have an impact on poor people in remote parts of this world.

As trade economists, we both initially set out to answer a simple question: what are the international economic implications of the intellectual property rules mandated by the WTO's Agreement on Trade Related Intellectual Property Rights (TRIPS)? Unfortunately (or fortunately), we soon discovered that there is no easy answer to this question, but we did find ourselves left with a large number of new questions that kept us busy for many years. We also quickly realized that the World Bank would be the perfect place to discuss this topic. Not only were Bank staffers interested in our research, but we met other economists working on related questions, further inspiring our own efforts. The studies presented in this volume bring together research that has been conducted both by the editors and by economic researchers at or affiliated with the World Bank. While we still struggle with too many unanswered questions, we believe that considerable progress has been made and we hope this is reflected in this book.

We wish to thank the authors who have contributed to this volume. Special thanks go to Bernard Hoekman, who originally proposed this book project to us. In addition, we are also grateful to a large number of friends and colleagues whose thoughts and advice have been invaluable over the years, including Frederick Abbott, John Barton, Clive Bell, Denise Konan, Manjula Luthria, James Markusen, Michael Nicholson, Jerome Reichman, Pamela Smith, and Jayashree Watal.

CONTRIBUTORS

Carlos A. Primo Braga, senior trade advisor, World Bank

Yongmin Chen, associate professor of economics, University of Colorado at Boulder

Sean M. Dougherty, Organisation for Economic Co-operation and Development, Paris.

Carsten Fink, Development Research Group, World Bank

Mattias Ganslandt, The Research Institute of Industrial Economics, Stockholm, Sweden

Keith E. Maskus, department of economics, University of Colorado at Boulder

Andrew Mertha, assistant professor of political science, Washington University

Beata Smarzynska Javorcik, Development Research Group, World Bank

Eina V. Wong, economic analyst, Sun Microsystems

Guifang (Lynn) Yang, managing director, KPMG Associates, Atlanta, Georgia

ABBREVIATIONS
AND ACRONYMS

AIC	Administration for Industry and Commerce
ASEAN	Association of South East Asian Nations
CACM	Central American Common Market
CD	compact disc
CES	constant-elasticity-of-substitution
CIF	cost, insurance, and freight
DALYs	disability-adjusted life years
DEFEND	Developing Economies' Fund for Essential New Drugs
EBRD	European Bank for Reconstruction and Development
EC	European Community
ECJ	European Court of Justice
EFTA	European Free Trade Association
EMRs	exclusive marketing rights
EU	European Union
FDI	foreign direct investment
GATT	General Agreement on Trade and Tariffs
GDP	gross domestic product
GLS	generalized least squares
GNP	gross national product
IIPA	International Intellectual Property Alliance
IMF	International Monetary Fund
IPRs	intellectual property rights
LAFTA	Latin American Free Trade Association
LAIA	Latin American Integration Association
LM	Lagrange multiplier

MERCOSUR   Mercado Común del Sur (Southern Cone Common Market)
MLE   maximum likelihood estimation
MNE   multinational enterprise
NAFTA   North American Free Trade Agreement
NTB   nontariff barrier
OECD   Organisation for Economic Co-operation and Development
OLI   ownership-location-internalization
OLS   ordinary least squares
PC   personal computer
R&D   research and development
SIC   Standard Industrial Classification
SITC   Standard International Trade Classification
SOE   state-owned enterprise
TB   tuberculosis
TFP   total factor productivity
TI   Transparency International
TNC   transnational corporation
TRAINS   Trade Analysis and Information System
TRI   Trade Restrictiveness Index
TRIPS   Agreement on Trade-Related Aspects of Intellectual
            Property Rights
UNAIDS   United Nations Programme on AIDS
UNCTAD   United Nations Conference on Trade and Development
VCD   video compact disc
WHO   World Health Organization
WIPO   World Intellectual Property Organization
WTO   World Trade Organization

1

WHY WE STUDY INTELLECTUAL PROPERTY RIGHTS AND WHAT WE HAVE LEARNED

Carsten Fink and Keith E. Maskus

I. Introduction

International policies toward protecting intellectual property rights (IPRs) have seen profound changes over the past two decades. Rules on how to protect patents, copyrights, trademarks, and other forms of IPRs have become a standard component of international trade agreements. Most significantly, during the Uruguay Round of multilateral trade negotiations (1986–94), members of what is today the World Trade Organization (WTO) concluded the Agreement on Trade-Related Aspects of Intellectual Property Rights (TRIPS), which sets out minimum standards of protection that most of the world's economies must respect. Additional international IPR rules have been created in various bilateral and regional trade agreements and in a number of intergovernmental treaties negotiated under the umbrella of the World Intellectual Property Organization.

At a general level, these policy reforms were driven by two related forces. First, the emergence of new technologies has demanded continuous adaptation of IPR instruments. Key examples of areas in which technological developments have raised new intellectual property questions include integrated circuits, computer software, and biotechnology inventions. The advent of the Internet has posed special challenges to the printing and publishing and entertainment industries, because content in digital form can be perfectly reproduced at minimal cost. Second, the

1

process of economic globalization has enabled intellectual property to cross international boundaries more easily. Indeed, for many rich countries, IPR-intensive goods and services constitute a rising share of the income they derive from their presence in foreign markets. It is therefore not surprising to see political economy forces at work in these countries, leading governments to raise IPR protection as a key negotiating issue in international trade agreements.

Spurred by these real-world developments, researchers have sought to understand better the economic underpinnings of different degrees and forms of IPR protection. In particular, economists have tried to assess the effects of stronger standards of protection on various measures of economic and social performance—ranging from innovation, competition, and market structure to trade, investment, and licensing decisions. Such analysis can be useful to policymakers, both in deciding what kinds of IPR standards are in a country's best interest and in designing complementary policy reforms that help minimize the costs and maximize the benefits of new IPR regulations.

This book presents studies conducted by economic researchers at or affiliated with the World Bank. Intellectual property policies can play an important role in efforts to foster development and reduce poverty. The World Bank has had a keen interest in better understanding this role, both to inform public opinion and to equip governments in developing countries with knowledge about the implications of policy reforms. Global requirements that these countries expand and strengthen their IPR systems are both new and complex. Accordingly, relatively few policymakers in developing nations have sufficient experience and knowledge to understand the potential effects of this change. Members of the World Bank trade research team have discussed these issues extensively with authorities in a number of developing countries, encountering a range of attitudes—from outright opposition to reforming IPRs to an unthinking acceptance that doing so will encourage innovation and growth. As we will argue, the truth lies somewhere between these poles, and the effects of awarding stronger rights to protect technology will depend on the underlying circumstances in each country.

In this introductory chapter, we first set the stage by describing why and in what areas economic research can make a useful contribution to our understanding of IPR policies. In particular, we stress that many effects of stronger IPR standards are theoretically ambiguous and thus need to be subjected to empirical analysis. Second, we summarize some of the key conclusions of the studies presented in this book and assess their implications for policy. The discussion also points to areas where research does not yet provide reliable policy guidelines. Thus, we also outline priorities for future research. In the final section we offer some concluding remarks.

Before proceeding, we need to make two important caveats. First, these studies by no means constitute a comprehensive compendium on the economics of IPRs.[1]

There are important studies conducted by university professors and research institutes— many of which are cited in the references to this chapter—that complement the findings presented here. Second, an edited volume on such a complex topic necessarily must be limited in scope. In particular, the studies included here focus on patents, copyrights, and trademarks and ignore questions of traditional knowledge, access to genetic resources, and other topics that are increasingly relevant to policymakers in developing countries. On the latter issues, we refer interested readers to the volume by Finger and Schuler (2003) that is published in this series.

II. Intellectual Property and Economic Analysis: Some Conceptual Guidance

Intellectual property law awards to inventors, artists, and institutions certain exclusive rights to produce, copy, distribute, and license goods and technologies within a country. In principle, when a country strengthens its IPR protection, it must strike a balance among several important tradeoffs. In a closed economy, IPRs provide incentives to inventors to develop new knowledge and to authors and artists to create forms of artistic expression. Thus, over time there are dynamic gains from the introduction of new products, information, and creative activities. But from the perspective of efficiency, they are only a second-best means of encouraging invention, because the market exclusivity conferred by IPRs reduces current competition and may therefore lead to a static distortion in the allocation of resources. Patents and copyrights have a limited term, which minimizes the costs of market exclusivity. The optimal length of protection becomes an empirical question, taking into account the social value of new inventions and artistic creations, preferences of consumers, and the extent to which IPRs raise prices above marginal costs.[2]

Additional tradeoffs come into play once one considers an open economy. How do foreign owners of intellectual property react to the possibility that their goods may or may not be copied in the domestic market? From a static perspective, it is easy to show that the effects of strengthened IPRs on the sales of a foreign firm are ambiguous.[3] The assurance that copycat firms are excluded from the market enlarges the demand for the foreign IPR holder's good, suggesting a positive effect. But at the same time, the market exclusivity conferred by IPRs increases the market power of the foreigner, which may lead to curtailed sales. In short, the net effect of stronger IPRs is an empirical question.

If one considers separately the various ways in which an IPR holder can serve a foreign market—exports, foreign direct investment (FDI), licensing—a further source of ambiguity arises. The approach most commonly used by economists in analyzing why firms may prefer one mode of delivery over another is the so-called ownership-location-internalization (OLI) framework. In a nutshell, the OLI framework suggests that firms that possess ownership advantages—for example, in the form of IPRs—would choose foreign production over export if the attributes of a particular location (for example, lower wages or proximity to international markets) favor production abroad. The choice between FDI and licensing would depend on internalization advantages—for example, the transaction costs of maintaining an arm's-length relationship with an independent foreign firm relative to the costs of establishing a wholly owned subsidiary. IPR policies can have an effect on both location advantages and internalization advantages, such that strengthened protection can lead a firm to invest in different places and switch from wholly owned production to licensing. The strongest theoretical case can probably be made for a positive link between IPRs and international licensing, because the enforceability of licensing contracts relies fundamentally on the security that these rights provide for a firm's technologies and reputation-enhancing assets. But in general, the effect of IPRs on firms' international economic transactions is an empirical question.

From a dynamic perspective, open economies face another tradeoff. A weak IPR regime might allow domestic firms to imitate foreign technologies and thereby contribute to economywide productivity and income growth. That perspective assumes, however, that firms can master all components of new technologies, including both codified knowledge and know-how, without the participation of foreign intellectual property holders. If that were not the case, stronger IPRs could be better suited to promoting technology diffusion, by enhancing access to knowledge-intensive foreign inputs and promoting formal technology transfer through joint ventures and licensing agreements. Assessing which scenario is more realistic in which industry requires careful empirical study.[4]

A special dimension of IPR policy that becomes relevant in open economies is the extent to which rights holders retain control over the distribution of protected goods once they have been placed on a national market for initial sale. In circumstances where such goods vary in price between countries, international arbitragers, called *parallel traders,* could profit by buying the goods in the cheaper location and selling them in the dearer location. An interesting and central question is whether parallel traders should be allowed to perform this task. The legality of parallel importation is determined by the "exhaustion" rule related to patents, copyrights, and trademarks. Under a rule of national exhaustion, after the first sale, firms lose the right to prevent further resale of their goods within a country's territory but are allowed to prevent parallel importation of their goods from outside the territory. Under a rule of international IPR exhaustion, after a good has been put on the market in any location, firms would fully lose control over further distribution, leaving markets open to parallel importation from foreign territories.[5]

From an economic perspective, rules on IPR exhaustion determine the extent to which firms can segment national markets. Economists have demonstrated that the desirability of allowing parallel importation depends, among other things, on what causes parallel trade. One possibility is that IPRs confer market power to firms, which allows them to set prices according to demand elasticities in national markets. The resulting price differences create incentives for arbitrage by parallel traders. Another explanation has centered on the possibility that parallel traders buy goods cheaply in the wholesale market and free ride on the promotional and sales support activities of retailers. Finally, incentives for arbitrage can arise if a firm sells its good to a foreign distributor cheaply in order to encourage efficient vertical pricing in the foreign market (see Maskus and Chen's study, chapter 8). The implications for welfare of restraints on parallel trade vary considerably across these motivations. In the end, empirical research is necessary to determine whether and for whom the permissibility of parallel trade is welfare enhancing.

For many developing countries that traditionally have not provided strong protection for intellectual property and, indeed, host industries that rely on copying foreign technology and products, IPR reforms pose some special questions. For example, how great are the costs of tighter IPRs, in particular if rights holders are predominantly of foreign origin? One such cost relates to higher prices for intermediate and final goods, ranging from pharmaceuticals to computer software. Quantifying potential price effects is important when designing complementary policies and regulations that seek to soften the effect on firms and consumers. Another cost is the loss of employment in copying industries, which must be evaluated against the ease with which laid-off workers can find new jobs. Again, quantifying the potential employment effects is important when predicting possible fiscal implications and developing labor market policies that would facilitate job transition.

Finally, are the traditional intellectual property instruments that were developed in the industrial world really suitable for stimulating innovative and artistic activity in poorer countries? Although the fundamental incentives posed by patents, trademarks, and copyrights should be the same around the world, developing countries differ from their industrial counterparts in their innovative potential, the education of their work force, the structure and funding of research and development (R&D), the management of technological assets, and the existence of complementary intellectual property institutions, such as collection agencies and technology-transfer offices. Empirical research can make an important contribution in identifying the kind of intellectual property instruments that work best for a particular stage of development or a particular set of institutional circumstances.

III. What Have We Learned from Past Research?

The previous section made it clear that most positive and normative effects of IPR reforms are theoretically ambiguous and dependent on circumstances. Thus, they need to be assessed empirically to the extent possible. In this section, we summarize some of the main findings of the studies presented in this volume and what we can say with confidence about the likely effects of IPR policy changes. Where relevant, we point to complementary reforms that studies have identified as maximizing the benefits or minimizing the costs of reformed IPRs. We also identify areas where more research is necessary before reliable conclusions can be reached and outline the nature of future research.

This section follows the sequence of the chapters in the book. We first look at the evidence regarding links between intellectual property and trade, FDI, and international licensing. We then consider the results of studies of how intellectual property exhaustion rules and parallel importation affect prices and welfare, noting important policy conclusions. Finally, we discuss what various studies say about the role of IPRs in affecting market structure and innovation in developing countries.

Intellectual Property Protection, Trade, FDI, and International Licensing

Inward technology transfer remains the primary source of new information for effecting technical change and structural transformation in most developing countries. Thus, a central goal of the literature has been to investigate how market-based technology flows are influenced by variations across countries in the strength of their intellectual property systems. Researchers have sought to shed light on how the decision of a single country to tighten its technology protection might be expected to alter the incentives to undertake such transfers. Furthermore, such research is useful for assessing the potential effects of global agreements, such as TRIPS, on innovation through technology transfer and diffusion.

Recalling that the links between the degree of IPR protection and firms' international economic transactions are theoretically ambiguous, economists have attempted to establish such relationships empirically. Studies that have been conducted in this area exploit the cross-country variation in trade, FDI, and licensing activity to explore whether countries with more stringent IPR regimes participate more or less in international commerce. In virtually all cases, the strength of IPR protection is approximated by rankings of national IPRs, in particular the widely used index of patent rights developed by Ginarte and Park (1997).

The study by Fink and Primo Braga (chapter 2) focuses on international trade flows and finds that stronger IPRs have a significantly positive effect on total trade. However, somewhat surprisingly, the stringency of a country's patent regime is found to be irrelevant to trade in an aggregate of high-technology products. That finding is consistent with similar results in the literature. Maskus and Penubarti (1995) and Smith (1999) confirm a positive trade link, but the former finds no effect for the industries that are most patent sensitive and the latter finds no effect in countries that face no threat of imitation. One may interpret these results in a variety of ways. First, it seems likely that multinational trading firms do not base their export decisions on IPRs in the poorest countries, where the local threats of reverse engineering are weakest. Second, patent rights matter importantly in middle-income, large developing countries, where such imitation is more likely. As these countries reduce the imitation threat through stronger patents, foreign firms are more likely to expand their volumes of trade accordingly. Third, the products of many high-technology industries are inherently difficult to imitate, so those trade flows are less responsive to IPRs than those in medium-technology or mature-technology sectors. Fourth, high-technology firms may decide to serve foreign markets through FDI and licensing, so that exports in such industries may be little affected by variations in the degree of patent protection.

Evidence is less conclusive in the case of FDI. As Maskus (chapter 3) points out, IPRs feature as one among many variables that determine the attractiveness of an FDI location. A poor country hoping to attract inward FDI would be better advised to improve its overall investment climate and business infrastructure than to strengthen its patent regime sharply, an action that would have little effect on its own. However, IPRs are quite important for multinational firms making location decisions among middle-income countries with strong abilities to absorb and learn technology. Maskus also discusses significant data problems in this area. From a researcher's perspective, correctly measuring the activity of foreign affiliates of multinational companies is more challenging than correctly measuring trade flows. The United States is the only country that publishes readily available statistics on the sales of overseas affiliates, a singularity that limits the number of observations that can be used in econometric investigations. Statistics on FDI flows and stocks are only imperfect measures of the activity of multinational firms.

In an analysis of international transactions by U.S. and German multinationals, Fink (chapter 4) cannot identify a noticeable influence of the stringency of the patent regime. One exception is a weakly negative link found between the degree of patent protection and sales of U.S. overseas affiliates in the chemicals industry (including pharmaceuticals). Fink's results confirm that variables other than patent protection account for most of the cross-country variation in the activity of multinationals—except in narrowly defined industries that are highly dependent on legal protection for their intellectual assets. Fink's findings are in line with early results in the literature (Maskus and Konan 1994), although a more recent study was able to find a positive link between the strength of IPRs and sales of U.S. affiliates (Smith 2001). Again, however, this result seems to hold for middle-income and large developing countries, not for smaller and poorer ones.

The study by Smarzynska Javorcik (chapter 6) makes a useful departure from the literature in that it uses survey data of multinational companies investing in Eastern Europe instead of the more aggregate data on the activity of multinational firms that are published by national statistical offices. The results of the study's econometric investigation suggest that weak IPRs have a negative effect on the likelihood of investments being made. In addition, the enforcement of IPRs affects the type of investments made: companies tend to avoid investing in local production if IPRs are weak and concentrate instead on distribution facilities. Similar findings emerge from the case study of IPRs and economic development in China by Maskus, Dougherty, and Mertha (chapter 12). Weak IPR enforcement is found to make foreign companies reluctant to transfer R&D facilities to China.

With regard to international licensing flows, the studies by Fink (chapter 4) of German outward technology flows and by Yang and Maskus (chapter 5) of U.S. licensing receipts from unaffiliated foreign firms both find a significantly positive effect of the strength of IPR protection abroad. These results are consistent with the notion that intellectual property protection stimulates formal technology transfer. As we noted earlier, licensing activity is most likely to be sensitive to changes in IPRs because transparent and reliable technology protection can reduce the cost of agreeing on and enforcing licensing contracts. At the same time, these studies look only at licensers' income from technology contracts and cannot distinguish between price and quantity effects. Recent work by Nicholson (2001) uses data on the number of U.S. firms that are engaged in FDI and licensing; it finds that with stronger IPR protection, firms are more likely to use licensing contracts and move away from FDI.

In sum, existing research suggests that countries that strengthen their IPR regimes are unlikely to experience a sudden boost in inflows of FDI. At the same time, the empirical evidence does point to a positive role for IPRs in stimulating formal technology transfer, through FDI in production and R&D facilities and through cross-border technology licensing.

Although the existing studies on the effects of IPR protection on trade, FDI, and licensing offer valuable insights, more research is needed in several areas. First, it would be helpful to refine the existing work with microlevel data on the activities of specific firms, joint ventures, and affiliates. Such data tend to be more informative than the aggregate statistics used in most of the studies presented in this volume. The study by Smarzynska Javorcik (chapter 6) already offers an example of such an approach. Second, most existing studies rely on cross-country regressions, which are not entirely satisfactory because national rankings of IPRs tend to be correlated with other development-related variables (rule of law, incidence of corruption, and the like). Moreover, although Ginarte and Park (1997) must be commended for their efforts to construct an index of the level of IPR protection, the use of an index variable in econometric research has certain limitations. Combining different aspects of intellectual property law, enforcement, and administration into a single index number relies on ad hoc rules of thumb. The final measure may not adequately capture the often narrow intellectual property concerns of individual industries. Future empirical work should look for natural experiments that explore within one country how economic variables have changed after a regime shift on a well-defined element of the intellectual property system. Time-series analyses should increasingly be possible, because a large number of developing countries have reformed IPR policies over the past decade.

Finally, we still know relatively little about the way technology diffuses internationally. Case studies of firms and industries on international joint venture and licensing arrangements would help shed greater light on the role of intellectual property protection in this process. Such studies should assess how different IPR standards may either promote or forestall access to foreign technologies. It would be useful also to study how the technology transfer and diffusion that may be identified with IPRs works its way into higher productivity growth in developing nations.

Intellectual Property Exhaustion and Parallel Importation

Parallel imports have attracted considerable attention from trade researchers at the World Bank. The subject is complex but fascinating, as demonstrated in the review by Fink (chapter 7). Fink discusses the multiple potential sources of price differences, the prospects for arbitrage, and the implications for welfare and innovation. The only real conclusion is that there are no easy solutions for policy. For example, a country could sensibly choose different exhaustion policies for patented and copyrighted goods and technologies than for trademarked commodities.

Studies in this area have sought to assess empirically the importance of the various determinants of parallel trade. The econometric investigation by Maskus and Chen (chapter 8), focusing on a variety of products in which parallel trade frequently occurs, finds support for the theory that parallel trade is created by firms' vertical pricing decisions. The authors note that the bulk of parallel trade occurs at the wholesaler-distributor level, not at retail outlets. Thus, they construct a model explaining how vertically related manufacturers and wholesalers maximize profits through the joint setting of wholesale and retail prices in two countries. This process sets up profitable opportunities for arbitrage at the wholesale level. Maskus and Chen's econometric study supports the basic model. This finding is important, but it makes the task of deciding on a welfare-maximizing exhaustion policy no easier. Maskus and Chen show that the welfare consequences of permitting parallel importation under these circumstances depend on the extent of international trade costs. Further, the welfare interests of the two countries may not coincide.

Pricing-to-market strategies are probably most relevant in the pharmaceutical industry, where product patents extend significant market power to the research-based pharmaceutical industry and demand influences differ markedly across countries. For policy purposes, this issue has arisen most visibly in global debates over the prices of essential medicines in poor countries.[6] In chapter 9, Ganslandt, Maskus, and Wong take a close look at international prices of drugs for treating HIV/AIDS. Although significant price differentiation has emerged on behalf of poor countries, prices are still high in relation to available incomes. The authors set out a policy suggestion, called the DEFEND Proposal, that could help resolve some of the conflicts between the needs for wide diffusion of new medicines and for encouragement of research into new therapies.[7] Central to any such policy would be restrictions on parallel exports of medicines to areas outside the regions within which low prices are to be sustained.

What do these findings imply for IPR exhaustion policies? First, as pointed out by Fink (chapter 7), the welfare consequences of an exhaustion policy differ across industries and across the various types of intellectual property. For some technologies, such as pharmaceuticals, there are good reasons for restrictions on parallel trade. In others, the case for limiting parallel trade is less clear. Second, a case can be made for a regional approach to parallel trade, whereby parallel trade is allowed within but not from outside a group of countries. This viewpoint follows from the conclusion by Maskus and Chen (chapter 8) that the welfare effects of permitting parallel trade are more likely to be positive if trade costs are small. Another justification for a regional approach emerges from the price discrimination literature, which suggests that countries should be grouped according to similarity in demand elasticities (see Malueg and Schwartz 1994).

Third, countries that opt for a regime of permitting parallel imports would be well advised to lower tariffs and other trade costs. In addition, governments need to promote competition among parallel traders by creating a certain legal framework for parallel trade and by ensuring easy market entry conditions. Otherwise, there is the risk that price reductions will be offset by real resource costs and rents to parallel traders.

Finally, as further discussed by Fink (chapter 7), a well-developed competition policy framework can serve as an important complement to intellectual property exhaustion policies. A regime of competition regulations that scrutinizes the practice by private firms of inserting territorial restraints in licensing and purchasing contracts can offer a more tailor-made approach to the permissibility of parallel trade. At the same time, such an approach may not be practical in many developing countries that have underdeveloped competition policies and in the absence of international cooperation on competition policy matters.

More research is necessary to improve our understanding of the effects of permitting parallel trade. We point to three priority areas for future research. First, although a general case can be made for regional exhaustion regimes, there is little empirical guidance as to which set of countries constitutes an optimal IPR exhaustion region for a particular group of products. For example, can an empirical case be made to free parallel trade within regional trading blocs? Second, no systematic evidence exists to assess the effects of parallel imports and parallel exports in developing countries. Would poor countries benefit from foreign restraints on parallel trade by allowing firms to set cheaper prices in these countries? To what extent can parallel importers increase competition in developing countries' distribution sectors, which often exhibit substantial barriers to entry? Third, it is important to study more completely the effects of parallel imports on the R&D decisions of innovative firms. If such trade restricts incentives to develop new products, the overall welfare effects may be negative in a dynamic sense.

Intellectual Property Protection, Market Structure, and Innovation in Developing Countries

Two studies in this category attempt to simulate the effects of IPR reforms in developing countries on market structure and prices in static partial equilibrium settings. Fink (chapter 10) focuses on the implications of introducing product patent protection in the Indian pharmaceutical market, as required by India's obligations under TRIPS. The study demonstrates the relevance of competition among therapeutic substitute products. If future drug discoveries are mainly new varieties of already-existing therapeutic treatments, the price effects may well be small. However, if newly discovered drugs are medical breakthroughs, prices may be significantly above competitive levels and associated static welfare losses of patents may be quite large.

The study by Maskus (chapter 11) analyzes the effects of more stringent IPR enforcement in Lebanon's pharmaceutical, software, printing and publishing, music, and film industries. The study takes a different approach, by modeling the effect of a change in the IPR regime as raising the costs of imported inputs, under various assumptions about how products are distributed in Lebanon. Overall, price and employment effects are found to be small, even if one assumes that demand does not respond significantly to price increases. Nonetheless, policies to ease the transition of unemployed workers to legitimate production could be beneficial.[8]

These findings point to the need for instituting complementary policy measures that seek to minimize static welfare losses, in particular in sensitive sectors such as pharmaceuticals or educational materials. Examples of such additional measures include establishing price controls, maintaining an option to override exclusive IPRs by issuing compulsory licenses, promoting competition in the distribution of goods and services subject to exclusive rights, considering the freeing of parallel importation (see discussion earlier), and providing for fair-use exemptions in copyright laws.

One central weakness of existing research on the static welfare costs of stronger IPRs has been the lack of reliable estimates of demand elasticities. For example, estimates of demand elasticities from industrial countries' pharmaceutical markets are unlikely to hold in a developing country with vastly lower purchasing power and far less coverage by health insurance. One priority for future research therefore is to estimate country-specific demand functions, so as to provide a more precise quantification of the price effect of stronger IPRs.[9] A second priority is to assess which policy measures are most practical and economically least distorting in cushioning static welfare losses.

The last study in this category focuses on the role IPRs play in stimulating enterprise development and innovation in developing countries. The case study of China's IPR system (by Maskus, Dougherty, and Mertha, in chapter 12) illustrates how inadequate enforcement of IPRs limits incentives to develop products and brand names, especially on the part of small and medium-size enterprises. In particular, interviews with firm managers and IPR experts point to the special importance of trademark protection. Companies that develop copyrighted and patented products typically market and license them under trademark rights. Thus, weak trademark enforcement has a profoundly negative effect on innovative Chinese enterprises. Interestingly, there are strong regional disparities in the enforcement of IPRs—with the effect that firms are reluctant to expand into China's poorer regions, where enforcement is comparatively weaker.

The study's findings support a positive role for IPRs in stimulating enterprise development and innovation in developing countries. At the same time, they also make clear that a reformed legal regime is likely to be a necessary but not sufficient condition for local technology development. In particular, to benefit fully from intellectual property systems, the public and private sectors need to allocate adequate resources to R&D and invest in the development of human capital.

One shortcoming of existing research is that is has focused on the richer middle-income countries. It would be useful to have more case study evidence on least developed countries and lower-middle-income countries, which typically have a less developed legal and institutional infrastructure and in which very few firms, if any, conduct R&D.

IV. Conclusion

The economic research presented in this book suggests that there is an important development dimension to the protection of IPRs. At the same time, in view of the various tradeoffs associated with alternative IPR standards, a "one size fits all" approach is unlikely to work. Developing countries may want to opt for different standards of protection than the ones that prevail in high-income countries that have different technological and financial capabilities. Although the current international framework for the protection of intellectual property provides for some degree of harmonization of global IPR standards, TRIPS, in particular, still leaves important room to adjust IPR norms to domestic needs.

Future trade negotiations may well place pressure on developing countries to sign up for stronger standards of protection. This pressure may not only be in the multilateral context. Indeed, key IPR-producing nations such as the United States and regional blocs such as the European Union are likely to resort to the increasing number of bilateral and regional trade agreements to negotiate additional rules for the protection of IPRs. Developing countries should carefully assess whether the economic benefits of such rules outweigh their costs. They also need to take into account the costs of administering and enforcing a reformed IPR system (which this book does not consider). These costs encompass both the net fiscal expenditure of financing relevant government agencies and the opportunity cost of employing possibly scarce human capital in the administration of the intellectual property system (see, for example, Finger and Schuler 2000).

Although the existing economic literature on IPRs provides some useful guidance to policymakers in developing countries, there is still a lot we do not know. We have offered a number of suggestions for future research. In particular, we believe that there is a need for studies based on firm-level data (such as the study by Smarzynska Javorcik, in chapter 6) as well as on single-country natural experiments. In addition, we believe that there is an important role for firm and industry case studies on effects that cannot easily be measured, such as the nature of technology transfer. Such case studies can usefully complement more formal econometric investigations and can offer helpful guidance to policymakers.

Notes

1. Maskus (2000) provides a recent and comprehensive discussion of positive and normative aspects of international IPR policymaking.

2. The protection of trademarks and geographic indications (or appellations of origin) is typically justified on different grounds. Trademarks and geographic indications primarily aim to minimize consumer confusion about the true origins of goods and services. They do not prevent the copying of goods and services, as long as such goods are sold under different names. Trademarks and geographic indications have less of a competition-reducing effect, which is reflected in the fact that their terms of protection are not limited by time.

3. This point was first described analytically by Maskus and Penubarti (1995).

4. Recent theoretical research by Grossman and Lai (forthcoming) derives dynamically optimal patent policies in a noncooperative Nash equilibrium and finds that countries generally benefit from international cooperation. However, they conclude that harmonization of patent policies is neither necessary nor sufficient for the efficiency of the global IPR regime and that harmonization at an efficient level would typically benefit northern countries but possibly harm southern countries. Scotchmer (2004) also analyzes theoretically why countries fail to choose jointly beneficial IPR regimes and the incentives for nations that do not innovate much to free ride on nations that do.

5. TRIPS leaves WTO members free to adopt their preferred exhaustion rule, except that the chosen rule has to be applied on a nondiscriminatory basis (national treatment and most-favored-nation treatment).

6. A recent paper by Scherer and Watal (2002) provides extensive discussion.

7. Lanjouw (2002) and Kremer (2002) have recently made related proposals that seek to resolve the same conflict over global pharmaceutical patents and their implications for drug prices.

8. More recently, McCalman (2001) has taken a different approach to quantifying the static welfare losses to developing countries caused by stronger IPRs. He assesses empirically the redistribution of income to IPR-producing nations deriving from the international harmonization of patent standards promoted by TRIPS.

9. The recent study by Chaudhuri, Goldberg, and Jia (2003) makes a first step in this direction by estimating key price elasticities and supply-side parameters for the segment of systemic antibiotics in the Indian pharmaceutical market.

References

Chaudhuri, Shubham, Pinelopi K. Goldberg, and Panle Jia. 2003. "Estimating the Effects of Global Patent Protection in Pharmaceuticals: A Case Study of Quinolones in India." Yale University, New Haven, Conn. Processed.

Finger, J. Michael, and Philip Schuler. 2000. "Implementation of Uruguay Round Commitments: The Development Challenge." *World Economy* 23:511–25.

————. 2003. *Poor People's Knowledge: Promoting Intellectual Property in Developing Countries.* Washington, D.C.: World Bank and Oxford University Press.

Ginarte, Juan Carlos, and Walter G. Park. 1997. "Determinants of Patent Rights: A Cross-National Study." *Research Policy* 26(3):283–301.

Grossman, Gene M., and Edwin L.-C. Lai. Forthcoming. "International Protection of Intellectual Property." *American Economic Review.*

Kremer, Michael. 2002. "Pharmaceuticals and the Developing World." *Journal of Economic Perspectives* 16(4):67–90.

Lanjouw, Jean O. 2002. "Beyond TRIPS: A New Global Patent Regime." Policy Brief 3. Center for Global Development, Washington, D.C.

Malueg, David A., and Marius Schwartz. 1994. "Parallel Imports, Demand Dispersion, and International Price Discrimination." *Journal of International Economics* 37:167–95.

Maskus, Keith E. 2000. *Intellectual Property Rights in the Global Economy*. Washington, D.C.: Institute for International Economics.

Maskus, Keith E., and Denise Eby Konan. 1994. "Trade-Related Intellectual Property Rights: Issues and Exploratory Results." In Alan V. Deardorff and Robert M. Stern, eds., *Analytical and Negotiating Issues in the Global Trading System*. Ann Arbor: University of Michigan Press.

Maskus, Keith E., and Mohan Penubarti. 1995. "How Trade Related Are Intellectual Property Rights?" *Journal of International Economics* 39:227–48.

McCalman, Phillip. 2001. "Reaping What You Sow: An Empirical Analysis of International Patent Harmonization." *Journal of International Economics* 51:161–86.

Nicholson, Michael W. 2001. "Intellectual Property Protection and Internalization: An Econometric Investigation." University of Colorado at Boulder. Processed.

Scherer, F. Michael, and Jayashree Watal. 2002. "Post-TRIPS Options for Access to Patented Medicines in Developing Countries." *Journal of International Economic Law* 5:913–39.

Scotchmer, Suzanne. 2004. "The Political Economy of Intellectual Property Treaties." *Journal of Law, Economics, and Organizations* 20:415–37.

Smith, Pamela J. 1999. "Are Weak Patent Rights a Barrier to U.S. Exports?" *Journal of International Economics* 48(1):151–77.

———. 2001. "How Do Foreign Patent Rights Affect U.S. Exports, Affiliate Sales, and Licenses?" *Journal of International Economics* 55:411–39.

PART I

INTELLECTUAL PROPERTY, TRADE, FOREIGN DIRECT INVESTMENT, AND INTERNATIONAL LICENSING

HOW STRONGER PROTECTION OF INTELLECTUAL PROPERTY RIGHTS AFFECTS INTERNATIONAL TRADE FLOWS

Carsten Fink and Carlos A. Primo Braga

I. Introduction

Intellectual property rights (IPRs) affect international trade flows when knowledge-intensive goods move across national boundaries. The importance of IPRs for trade has gained more significance as the share of knowledge-intensive or high-technology products in total world trade has doubled between 1980 and 1994 from 12 percent to 24 percent.[1] At the international level, IPRs have traditionally been governed by several conventions—most prominently the Paris Convention for patents and trademarks and the Berne Convention for copyrights—which are administered by the World Intellectual Property Organization (WIPO). In the 1980s, mounting disputes over IPRs led to the inclusion of trade-related IPRs on the agenda of the Uruguay Round of multilateral trade negotiations. The resulting Agreement on Trade-Related Aspects of Intellectual Property Rights,

This paper is adapted from an earlier version published as Policy Research Working Paper 2051 by the World Bank in 1999. Comments and assistance from Azita Amjadi, Clive Bell, Raed Safadi, and Christoph Schmidt are gratefully acknowledged.

(TRIPS) of 1994 represents the most far-reaching multilateral agreement toward global harmonization of IPRs.[2]

Several studies have attempted to estimate the extent to which IPRs relate to trade. Maskus and Penubarti (1995) use an augmented version of the Helpman-Krugman model of monopolistic competition to estimate the effects of patent protection on international trade flows. Their results indicate that higher levels of protection have a positive effect on bilateral manufacturing imports into both small and large developing economies. These results are confirmed by Primo Braga and Fink (1997), whose results for a similar model showed the same positive link between patent protection and trade flows.

This study provides new evidence regarding the effects of patent protection on international trade. It uses a gravity model of bilateral trade flows and estimates the effects of increased protection on a cross section of 89 by 88 countries. It improves on previous studies in two respects. First, we estimate the gravity model for two different kinds of aggregates: total nonfuel trade and high-technology trade. Moreover, we address the problem of zero trade flows between countries by adopting a bivariate probit model. Second, to measure the strength of IPR regimes, we use a fine-tuned index on national IPR systems developed by Park and Ginarte (1997). Our results confirm previous findings suggesting a positive link between IPR protection and trade flows for the aggregate of nonfuel trade. However, IPRs are not found to be significant for high-technology trade flows.

The next sections provide a summary of theoretical considerations, present the estimation setup, report the results obtained, and compare our results to related studies.

II. A Review of the Economics of Trade-Related IPRs

The conventional economic rationale for the protection of IPRs in closed economies can be found in Arrow (1962). Because knowledge is nonrival in consumption, it should be freely available (apart from the cost of transmitting it). If it were freely available, however, the market would underinvest in the production of new knowledge because innovators would not be able to recover their costs. By granting innovators the exclusive rights to commercialize their intellectual assets over a certain period of time, IPRs offer an incentive for the production of knowledge. In short, IPRs introduce a static distortion (that is, access to proprietary knowledge is sold above its marginal cost), which is rationalized as an effective way to foster the dynamic benefits associated with innovative activities.

IPRs are territorial in character—that is, they are created by national laws and differ across countries. If intellectual property embedded in goods and services originating in country A crosses the border to country B, two questions arise. First, how will IPR protection in country B affect the magnitude of the bilateral trade flow from country A to country B? Second, what are the implications of such protection on the economic welfare of both countries?

Bilateral Trade Flows and Differences in IPR Protection

IPRs affect international trade flows in several ways. For example, a firm may be deterred from exporting its patented good into a foreign market if potential "pirates" can diminish the profitability of the firm's activity in that market because of a weak IPR regime. Accordingly, strengthening a country's patent regime would tend to increase imports as foreign firms face increasing net demand for their products, reflecting the displacement of pirates. A firm might choose to reduce its sales in a foreign market as a response to stronger IPR protection because of its greater market power in an imitation-safe environment. These opposing market expansion and market power effects imply that the overall effect of IPR protection on bilateral trade flows is theoretically ambiguous (Maskus and Penubarti 1995).

A further source of ambiguity stems from the fact that differing levels of IPR protection may affect a firm's decision about its preferred mode of serving a foreign market. A firm may choose to serve a foreign market by foreign direct investment (FDI) or by licensing its intellectual asset to a foreign firm instead of exporting the product in an environment characterized by strong IPRs (Ferrantino 1993).[3] Thus, strengthened IPR protection may have a further negative effect on trade flows in this respect.

Welfare Implications

The implications of tighter IPRs for economic welfare are complex. The simple fact that trade flows rise or fall in response to tighter IPRs is not sufficient for drawing conclusions regarding economic welfare. Both static and dynamic effects need to be considered. Moreover, in this chapter, we are primarily concerned with the effects of IPRs on international trade flows. In a different paper (Primo Braga and Fink 1997), we discuss how tighter IPRs affect economic welfare through FDI, the transfer of technology, and domestic research and development (R&D). The following paragraphs summarize the static and dynamic costs and benefits for two trading economies that may arise only in response to changes in trade flows fostered by stronger IPRs.

From a static partial equilibrium point of view, the source country of the trade flow is likely to gain from tighter protections, because it can capture increased monopoly profits from the sale of its goods abroad. In contrast, the static effects on the welfare of the destination country are likely to be negative: increased market power by foreign title holders generates deadweight losses.[4] Taking this view, many small, innovation-consuming countries fear that increased patent protection will only lead to a rent transfer to industrial, innovation-producing countries.[5]

From a static general equilibrium point of view, tighter IPRs tend to be further detrimental to the destination country of the trade flow because the reallocation of production—that is, the shift of product lines from the destination country to the source country—worsens the terms of trade in favor of the source country. In addition, the reallocation of production may reduce welfare in both countries as efficiency considerations call for an allocation of manufacturing to the region with lower costs.[6] This effect may be of particular relevance if one recalls that most countries that have weak IPRs are low-wage, developing countries. At the same time, the welfare implications resulting from the reallocation of production may be partly offset by increased production through foreign subsidiaries (that is, FDI).

From a dynamic point of view, the introduction of IPRs stimulates innovation in the source country and thus increases future trade flows. That effect is beneficial for both trading economies, assuming that social returns on the innovations exceed private returns.[7] The international recognition of IPRs also can be seen as an adjustment mechanism that guarantees dynamic competition between countries. Through IPRs, innovation-producing countries have an incentive to develop new technologies, which in their next generation are manufactured by follower countries. This mechanism thus leads to continued technological progress and economic growth and, from a dynamic point of view, is beneficial for both leaders and followers (Fisch and Speyer 1995).

In sum, the overall effect of IPR protection on levels of bilateral trade flows is ambiguous. From a static welfare point of view, IPRs can be viewed as a rent transfer mechanism that worsens the international allocation of production. Most studies conclude that the destination country loses from tighter protection, whereas the source country is usually better off (see, for example, Chin and Grossman 1988; Deardorff 1992; and Helpman 1993). However, benefits of a dynamic nature can be identified for both trading partners. On average, it is not clear whether these dynamic benefits can compensate for the static losses in the countries strengthening their IPR systems and whether tighter IPRs improve world economic welfare through their effect on trade flows. It is worth pointing out that these theoretical considerations may be dominated by political economy considerations, which have been clearly in favor of higher standards of protection over the past decades.[8]

III. Empirical Analysis: The Estimation Setup

To empirically estimate the effects of increased patent protection on bilateral trade flows, we use a conventional gravity model. Gravity models have been applied successfully to explain different types of international flows, such as migration, commuting, recreational traffic, and trade. Typically, they specify that a flow from country i to country j can be explained by supply conditions in country i, by demand conditions in country j, and by forces either assisting or resisting the flow's movement.[9]

Our depend variables are bilateral trade flows for 89 by 88 countries, which were extracted from the United Nations (UN) Comtrade database. The data refer to 1989 total nonfuel and high-technology trade. The rationale for using high-technology trade flows in addition to total nonfuel trade is based on the a priori expectation that the effects of IPR protection are stronger for knowledge-intensive trade. For a definition of our high-technology aggregate, see table 2.1.

Following earlier specifications of gravity models, our explanatory variables are the gross domestic product (GDP) and population of countries i and j; the geographic distance between the two countries; a dummy variable, which is one if the two countries share a common border and zero otherwise; and a dummy variable, which is one if the two countries share the same language and zero otherwise.[10] The coefficients on GDP are expected to be positive and close to unity (Anderson 1979); the coefficients on population are expected to be small and negative, representing economies of scales (Linneman 1966). Greater geographic and cultural distances are expected to have a negative influence on bilateral trade flows; that is, the coefficient on geographic distance is expected to be negative, and the coefficients on common border and language are expected to be positive. Appendix 2.A gives more information about the countries included and the sources of all variables.

To capture the effects of preferential trading agreements, we also include separate dummy variables for the European Union (EU), the European Free Trade Association (EFTA), the Latin American Integration Association (LAIA) and Latin American Free Trade Association (LAFTA), the Association of South East Asian Nations (ASEAN), and the Central American Common Market (CACM). We expect positive coefficients on these five dummy variables.

Finally, to capture the effect of IPRs on bilateral trade flows, we use the IPR index developed by Park and Ginarte (1997).[11] This index grades the national IPR regimes of 110 countries on a scale from zero to five. To compute a country's ranking, Park and Ginarte created five categories—extent of coverage, membership in international patent agreements, provisions for loss of protection, enforcement mechanisms, and duration of protection. For each category, they used several

TABLE 2.1   Definition of High-Technology Aggregate

SITC code	Description
513	Inorganic elements
514	Other inorganic chemicals
515	Radioactive materials
533.1	Coloring materials
541	Medicinal products excluding pharmaceuticals
541.9	Pharmaceutical goods
561.3	Potassic fertilizers
571.2	Fuses and detonators
571.4	Hunting and sporting ammunition
581.1	Plastics and products of condensation
581.2	Products of polymerization
651.6	Synthetic fibers
651.7	Yarn and artificial fibers
711.3	Steam engines
711.4	Aircraft engines
711.5	Internal combustion engines
711.6	Gas turbines
711.8	Engines, not elsewhere specified
714	Office machinery
724	Telecommunications apparatus
729.3	Transistors, photocell, and so forth
729.7	Electron accelerators
729.9	Electrical machinery and apparatus
734	Aircraft
861	Scientific instruments
862	Photographic supplies
891.1	Tape recorders
891.2	Recorders of sound
894.3	Nonmilitary arms
899.6	Orthopedic appliances

SITC = Standard International Trade Classification.
Note: Definition is based on SITC Revision 1 classification.
Source: Primo Braga and Yeats (1992).

benchmark criteria (for example, patentability of pharmaceuticals for extent of coverage) and computed the share of "fulfilled" criteria. A country's score is the unweighted sum of these shares over all categories.[12] The United States received the highest score with 4.52; several countries with no patent laws (for example, Angola, Ethiopia, Myanmar, and Papua New Guinea) received a score of zero.

A common problem regarding the estimation of bilateral trade flows is that some flows are reported as zero because countries do not trade with each other. For example, in our data set, on average, about 26 percent of the total nonfuel trade flows and 53 percent of the high-technology trade flows are zero. A standard log-linear model with a log normally distributed error term cannot, by definition, explain these zero trade flows. Simple exclusion of zero trade flows would lead to a potential bias in the sample selection. There are several ways to address this problem. We follow Bikker and de Vos (1992), who propose a bivariate, normally distributed, probit regression.[13] The model consists of an equation for the probability of zero observations and an equation for the magnitude of a positive action:

(2.1)
$$I_{ij} = \begin{cases} 0 & \text{if } z_{ij}\gamma + v_{ij} \leq 0 \\ y_{ij} & \text{if } z_{ij}\gamma + v_{ij} > 0 \end{cases}$$

(2.2)
$$y_{ij} = x_{ij}\beta + u_{ij}$$

I_{ij} is the observed phenomenon, which is zero if the bilateral trade flow from country i to country j is zero and y_{ij}—the log of bilateral trade—if the trade flow is positive; z_{ij} is the log of the variables explaining the probability of a positive observation (the gravity variables without the preferential trading dummies and the Park and Ginarte index), and γ is the corresponding vector of coefficients for these variables.[14] The variable v_{ij} is a normally distributed error term with mean zero; the variance of v_{ij} is normalized to one, as all parameters γ are determined, apart from a constant. The matrix x_{ij} is the logarithm of the explanatory variables for positive trade flows (the gravity variables and the Park and Ginarte index), β is the corresponding vector of coefficients to be estimated, and u_{ij} is a normally distributed error term with mean zero and variance σ^2. The error terms v_{ij} and u_{ij} are correlated with each other and drawn from a bivariate normal distribution with a correlation coefficient equal to ρ. Equations 2.1 and 2.2 can be estimated by the maximum likelihood technique. Appendix 2.B derives the likelihood function.

Besides addressing the problem of sample selectivity, the bivariate probit regression model is attractive because it also estimates the effects of explanatory variables (such as IPRs) on the probability that two countries trade with each other.

Two alternative specifications are estimated: Model I estimates the probit and gravity equations without the Park and Ginarte index, and model II includes the Park and Ginarte index. The rationale for this exercise is to evaluate what effect the inclusion of IPRs has on the other explanatory variables. Moreover, to evaluate the robustness of the results, we estimate these two model specifications for both exports—bilateral trade flows from country i to country j, as reported by country i—and imports—bilateral trade flows from country j to country i, as reported by country i. Because we are primarily interested in the role of IPRs in attracting trade flows and not in creating them, we use only the Park and Ginarte index of the destination country of the trade flow as an explanatory variable (that is, country j in the case of exports and country i in the case of imports).

IV. Empirical Estimates

Our estimation results are presented in tables 2.2 through 2.5. The overall performance of the models is satisfactory. Most gravity variables have the expected signs and are statistically significant. For total nonfuel trade (tables 2.2 and 2.3), there are two exceptions: the coefficient on the border dummy has the wrong sign in the probit equation and is statistically not significant in the gravity equation, and the coefficients on the dummies that indicate EU and EFTA membership in the gravity equation have the wrong signs but are, however, never significant. For the high-technology aggregate (tables 2.4 and 2.5), the exceptions are similar: the coefficients on the border dummy in the probit equation and on the EU and EFTA membership dummies in the gravity equation are statistically not significant and sometimes have the wrong sign. Likelihood ratio tests indicate that, for all alternative specifications estimated, the explanatory variables are jointly significantly different from zero.

The estimated correlation coefficients between the probit and gravity equations $\hat{\rho}$ are always close to zero and are statistically not significant according to a likelihood ratio test for both total nonfuel trade and high-technology trade. That suggests that for our data, it would have been possible to estimate the equations independently and that the exclusion of zero observations in the gravity equation does not lead to a bias stemming from a nonrandom sample selection.

Recalling the theoretical ambiguity of the effect of IPRs on bilateral trade described earlier, we had no expectations regarding the sign of the coefficient on the Park and Ginarte index. For total nonfuel imports and exports, the Park and Ginarte index has only a small effect on the probability of positive trade flows between countries, although the effect is positive and statistically significant at the 5 percent level for total nonfuel exports. Turning to the gravity equation, IPRs have a significantly positive effect on bilateral trade flows for total nonfuel imports and exports. Comparisons of models I and II in tables 2.2 and 2.3 suggests that the inclusion of IPRs leads to relatively small changes in the coefficients of most gravity variables. The biggest changes occur in the coefficients on GDP and on population of the destination country of the trade flow. These changes can be explained by the strong correlation between the strength of IPR protection and the level of economic development, as measured by per capita GDP.[15]

For high-technology trade, as shown in tables 2.4 and 2.5, the evolving pattern is different. For both exports and imports, the Park and Ginarte index has a

TABLE 2.2   Maximum Likelihood Estimates for Total Nonfuel Imports

	Model I		Model II	
	Probit	Gravity	Probit	Gravity
Intercept	−7.000	−10.228	−6.960	−10.956
	(−27.40)	(−29.02)	(26.28)	(−30.58)
GDP$_i$	0.541	1.109	0.545	0.949
	(31.47)	(51.73)	(29.90)	(34.98)
GDP$_j$	0.567	1.341	0.566	1.339
	(32.36)	(61.89)	(32.33)	(62.12)
Population$_i$	−0.194	−0.233	−0.198	−0.082
	(−9.80)	(−8.53)	(−9.17)	(−2.64)
Population$_j$	−0.058	−0.333	−0.058	−0.336
	(−3.03)	(−12.76)	(−3.03)	(−12.97)
Distance	−0.435	−1.109	−0.437	−1.060
	(−12.17)	(−23.87)	(−12.15)	(−23.20)
Border	−0.376	0.179	−0.378	0.239
	(−2.32)	(0.91)	(−2.33)	(1.27)
Language	0.592	0.861	0.591	0.867
	(8.67)	(9.50)	(8.66)	(9.62)
Eu		−0.264		−0.305
		(−0.94)		(−1.08)
EFTA		−0.393		−0.415
		(−0.81)		(−0.86)
LAIA and LAFTA		0.713		0.951
		(3.27)		(4.37)
ASEAN		2.269		2.476
		(4.64)		(5.10)
CACM		2.133		2.414
		(4.32)		(4.91)
IPRs[a]			−0.014	0.369
			(−0.53)	(9.59)
$\hat{\sigma}$		2.100		2.083

(Continued)

TABLE 2.2   Maximum Likelihood Estimates for Total Nonfuel Imports (Continued)

	Model I		Model II	
	Probit	Gravity	Probit	Gravity
Number of observations	7,304	5,492	7,304	5,492
$\hat{\rho}$	-0.034		-0.043	
$-2 \ln \lambda(\rho = 0)^b$	0.853		1.346	
$-2 \ln \lambda(\{\gamma, \beta\} = 0)^b$	8,874.433		8,965.677	

Note: The t-statistics appear in parentheses.
a. Park and Ginarte index of the destination country of the trade flow; that is, country j in the case of exports and country i in the case of imports.
b. For a definition of the likelihood ratio test statistics, see appendix 2.B.
Source: Authors' calculations

significantly negative effect on the probability that countries trade with each other. The impact of IPRs on positive trade flows, in turn, is slightly negative but not statistically significant. This result is somewhat surprising. If IPRs influence trade flows, we would expect this influence to be most visible for trade in knowledge-intensive goods. Several explanations can be posited. First, strong market power effects in the case of high-technology goods may offset positive market expansion effects caused by stronger IPR regimes. Second, stronger IPR regimes may cause high-technology firms to serve foreign markets through FDI, in part substituting for trade flows. Third, it may be that the Park and Ginarte index does not correctly capture the IPR effect (see later discussion) or that development-related effects interplay with stronger IPR protection. Fourth, our high-technology aggregate may include many knowledge-intensive goods that are insensitive to the destination country's IPR regime; for these goods, other means than IPRs may be more important in appropriating investment in R&D (for example, first-mover advantage or rapid movement down the learning curve). Finally, we omitted important explanatory variables in our gravity equation such as tariff and nontariff trade barriers; this type of specification error may bias our estimated results.

V. Comparisons with Related Studies

There are several related studies that also try to estimate the effects of IPRs on bilateral trade flows. An early study by Maskus and Konan (1994) also uses a gravity

TABLE 2.3   Maximum Likelihood Estimates for Total Nonfuel Exports

	Model I		Model II	
	Probit	Gravity	Probit	Gravity
Intercept	−6.631	−10.791	−6.766	−11.170
	(−27.77)	(−29.31)	(−27.10)	(−29.55)
GDP_i	0.556	1.374	0.556	1.374
	(33.86)	(60.26)	(33.85)	(60.38)
GDP_j	0.458	1.017	0.443	0.945
	(29.84)	(46.85)	(25.93)	(35.11)
Population$_i$	−0.052	−0.320	−0.052	−0.320
	(−2.84)	(−12.18)	(−2.83)	(−12.20)
Population$_j$	−0.153	−0.137	−0.137	−0.070
	(−8.15)	(−4.90)	(−6.57)	(−2.17)
Distance	−0.473	−1.114	−0.467	−1.100
	(−13.55)	(−23.69)	(−13.34)	(−23.41)
Border	−0.393	0.301	−0.381	0.328
	(−2.54)	(1.52)	(−2.47)	(1.65)
Language	0.588	0.826	0.588	0.826
	(8.96)	(8.95)	(8.97)	(8.98)
EU		−0.068		−0.096
		(−0.24)		(−0.34)
EFTA		−0.137		−0.152
		(−0.28)		(−0.31)
LAIA and LAFTA		0.822		0.944
		(3.73)		(4.26)
ASEAN		2.352		2.442
		(4.78)		(4.97)
CACM		2.127		2.267
		(4.28)		(4.56)
IPRs[a]			0.047	0.176
			(1.92)	(4.46)
$\hat{\sigma}$		2.113		2.109

(Continued)

TABLE 2.3 Maximum Likelihood Estimates for Total Nonfuel Exports (Continued)

	Model I		Model II	
	Probit	Gravity	Probit	Gravity
Number of observations	7,309	5,294	7,309	5,294
$\hat{\rho}$	0.005		0.002	
$-2 \ln \lambda(\rho = 0)^b$	0.016		0.003	
$-2 \ln \lambda(\{\gamma, \beta\} = 0)^b$	8,520.968		8,544.524	

Note: The t-statistics appear in parentheses.
a. Park and Ginarte index of the destination country of the trade flow; that is, country j in the case of exports and country i in the case of imports.
b. For a definition of the likelihood ratio test statistics, see appendix 2.B.
Source: Authors' calculations

model to estimate the effect of IPR protection on bilateral trade. They regress the index developed by Rapp and Rozek (1990) along with several other development-related variables on the residual of the gravity flow estimation. This approach would be justified if those variables were uncorrelated with the independent variables of the gravity estimation. That may not be the case, because both GDP and population are included in Maskus and Konan's gravity model. Hence, the extent of reliability of their finding of a positive link between IPRs and trade is uncertain.

Maskus and Penubarti (1995) estimate the effect of IPRs on bilateral trade flows in an augmented version of the Helpman-Krugman model of monopolistic competition. Imports of good i by country j from exporter k as a share of aggregate expenditure in country j are explained by the sectoral exporter output, the importer gross national product (GNP) per capita, trade-resistance measures for the importing country (tariff revenue as a percentage of dutiable imports, black-market exchange rate premiums), and the Rapp and Rozek index of patent strength for country j.[16] Dummy variables that indicate whether the importing developing country has a small or large market are interacted with the Rapp and Rozek index.

To address the problem of endogeneity and also potential errors of measurement in the Rapp and Rozek index, Maskus and Penubarti adopt an instrumental variable approach. Their instruments are prior indicators of the level of economic development (GDP per capita, primary exports as a share of total exports, infant mortality rate, and secondary enrollment ratio), as well as dummy variables for

TABLE 2.4   Maximum Likelihood Estimates for High-Technology Imports

	Model I		Model II	
	Probit	Gravity	Probit	Gravity
Intercept	−5.494	−14.487	−4.794	−14.313
	(−27.17)	(−26.21)	(−22.87)	(−26.95)
GDP_i	0.568	0.911	0.717	0.960
	(40.12)	(22.68)	(39.04)	(16.69)
GDP_j	0.495	1.898	0.512	1.897
	(36.36)	(52.12)	(36.45)	(52.38)
$Population_i$	−0.324	−0.086	−0.474	−0.132
	(−18.71)	(−2.06)	(−22.59)	(−2.38)
$Population_j$	−0.170	−0.733	−0.175	−0.731
	(−10.31)	(−20.70)	(−10.43)	(−20.70)
Distance	−0.421	−1.115	−0.466	−1.124
	(−13.56)	(−19.11)	(−14.62)	(−19.00)
Border	0.011	0.157	−0.110	0.141
	(0.08)	(0.64)	(−0.78)	(0.61)
Language	0.480	1.154	1.488	1.154
	(8.54)	(9.53)	(8.43)	(9.49)
EU		0.224		0.227
		(0.74)		(0.76)
EFTA		−0.053		−0.057
		(−0.10)		(−0.11)
LAIA and LAFTA		0.798		0.771
		(3.24)		(3.08)
ASEAN		3.407		3.374
		(6.53)		(6.46)
CACM		2.992		2.959
		(5.63)		(5.55)
IPRs[a]			−0.340	−0.093
			(−14.09)	(−1.50)
$\hat{\sigma}$		2.229		2.228

(Continued)

TABLE 2.4   Maximum Likelihood Estimates for High-Technology Imports (Continued)

	Model I		Model II	
	Probit	Gravity	Probit	Gravity
Number of observations	7,304	3,548	7,304	3,548
$\hat{\rho}$	0.066		0.064	
$-2 \ln \lambda(\rho = 0)^b$	1.354		1.309	
$-2 \ln \lambda(\{\gamma, \beta\} = 0)^b$	7,606.860		7,812.274	

Note: The t-statistics appear in parentheses.

a. Park and Ginarte index of the destination country of the trade flow; that is, country j in the case of exports and country i in the case of imports.

b. For a definition of the likelihood ratio test statistics, see appendix 2.B.

Source: Authors' calculations

former British and French colonies, for membership in the Paris and Berne Conventions, and for the existence of legislative provisions for pharmaceutical and chemical product patents. Maskus and Penubarti find a positive IPR-trade link: countries that have stronger patent regimes import more than is predicted by the Helpman-Krugman model. Moreover, the effect of patent protection on trade flows is found to be bigger in the larger developing countries. At the same time, Maskus and Penubarti do not find a positive IPR-trade link when the estimation is confined to the most patent-sensitive industries—mirroring our result for high-technology trade flows.

As Maskus and Penubarti did, we, too, face the problem that the strength of intellectual property protection may be an endogenous variable. It can be argued, however, that the degree of endogeneity may not be too severe if one takes into account that most countries' IPR regimes were established during or before the 1960s and that the level of protection remained fairly constant until 1989–90 (the years of our estimation).[17] A potential source of bias in Maskus and Penubarti's estimation lies in the way they interact the Rapp and Rozek index with dummy variables for small and large developing countries. As mentioned previously, the strength of patent protection tends to be strongly correlated with the level of economic development.[18] Through interaction with the two dummy variables, the Rapp and Rozek index is allowed a much more flexible effect than GNP per capita. Hence, it may be that the three coefficients estimated for the Rapp and Rozek index pick up a misspecification in the functional form of GNP per capita.[19]

TABLE 2.5   Maximum Likelihood Estimates for High-Technology Exports

	Model I		Model II	
	Probit	Gravity	Probit	Gravity
Intercept	−8.300	−14.272	−8.334	−14.225
	(−32.67)	(−28.75)	(−31.67)	(−28.02)
GDP$_i$	0.987	1.804	0.987	1.803
	(47.17)	(44.86)	(47.15)	(44.85)
GDP$_j$	0.270	0.927	0.265	0.936
	(18.71)	(36.09)	(15.10)	(29.05)
Population$_i$	−0.305	−0.658	−0.305	−0.658
	(−17.00)	(−18.43)	(−17.01)	(−18.41)
Population$_j$	−0.086	−0.097	−0.081	−0.105
	(−4.28)	(−2.67)	(−3.60)	(−2.59)
Distance	−0.596	−1.062	−0.595	−1.064
	(−17.27)	(−18.78)	(17.21)	(−18.76)
Border	−0.121	0.129	−0.116	0.124
	(−0.84)	(0.58)	(−0.810)	(0.565)
Language	0.706	1.225	0.707	1.226
	(11.01)	(10.66)	(11.03)	(10.67)
EU		0.326		0.332
		(1.14)		(1.15)
EFTA		0.086		0.089
		(0.17)		(0.18)
LAIA and LAFTA		0.720		0.702
		(2.96)		(2.86)
ASEAN		3.467		3.455
		(6.97)		(6.93)
CACM		2.661		2.640
		(5.20)		(5.15)
IPRs[a]			0.0132	−0.022
			(0.50)	(−0.45)
$\hat{\sigma}$		2.121		2.121

(Continued)

TABLE 2.5 Maximum Likelihood Estimates for High-Technology Exports (Continued)

	Model I		Model II	
	Probit	Gravity	Probit	Gravity
Number of observations	7,309	3,342	7,309	3,342
$\hat{\rho}$		−0.027		−0.027
$-2 \ln \lambda(\rho = 0)^b$		0.451		0.442
$-2 \ln \lambda(\{\gamma, \beta\} = 0)^b$		8,725.684		8,726.127

Note: The *t*-statistics appear in parentheses.
a. Park and Ginarte index of the destination country of the trade flow; that is, country *j* in the case of exports and country *i* in the case of imports.
b. For a definition of the likelihood ratio test statistics, see appendix 2.B.
Source: Authors' calculations

VI. Summary and Conclusion

With the increasing share of knowledge-intensive products in international trade and the inclusion of trade-related IPRs on the agenda of the multilateral trading system, IPRs have become an important trade issue. Political economy influences—as reflected in TRIPS—have promoted higher standards of IPR protection.

Economic analysis suggests that the effects of IPR protection on bilateral trade flows are theoretically ambiguous. Because of the complex static and dynamic considerations related to a policy of tighter protection, it is difficult to generate normative recommendations. When we estimate the effects of IPR protection in a gravity model of bilateral trade flows, our empirical results suggest that, on average, higher levels of protection have a significantly positive effect on nonfuel trade. However, this result is not confirmed when confining the estimation to high-technology goods, for which we found IPRs to have no significant effect. These results are consistent with the literature, in particular the study by Maskus and Penubarti (1995).

More empirical research is needed to gain more insight regarding the IPR-trade link, especially at the industry and firm levels. The challenge of such research will be to find "natural experiments" to overcome the colinearity and endogeneity problems of cross-country analyses such as the present study. One alternative, for instance, would be to consider a country that at some point in the past significantly changed its system of IPRs and to test for subsequent structural change.

Appendix 2.A. Country Data

Data on bilateral trade flows were extracted from the UN Comtrade database. We collected data for the following 89 countries:

Algeria	Honduras[d]	Papua New Guinea
Argentina[a]	Hong Kong, China	Paraguay[a]
Australia	India	Peru[a]
Austria[b]	Indonesia[e]	Philippines[e]
Bangladesh	Iran, Islamic Rep. of	Portugal
Belgium-Luxembourg[c]	Ireland[c]	Saudi Arabia
Benin	Israel	Senegal
Bolivia[a]	Italy[c]	Singapore[e]
Brazil[a]	Jamaica	Somalia
Cameroon	Japan	Spain
Canada	Jordan	Sri Lanka
Chile[a]	Kenya	Sweden[b]
Colombia[a]	Korea, Rep. of	Switzerland[b]
Congo, Rep. of	Kuwait	Syrian Arab Rep.
Costa Rica[d]	Madagascar	Tanzania
Côte d'Ivoire	Malaysia[e]	Thailand[e]
Denmark[c]	Mauritania	Togo
Dominican Republic	Mauritius	Trinidad and Tobago
Ecuador[a]	Mexico[a]	Tunisia
Egypt, Arab Rep.	Morocco	Turkey
El Salvador[d]	Myanmar	United Arab Emirates
Ethiopia	Netherlands[c]	United Kingdom[c]
Finland[b]	New Zealand	United States
France[c]	Nicaragua[d]	Uruguay[a]
Gabon	Niger	Venezuela, R. B. de[a]
Germany[c]	Nigeria	Yemen, Rep. of
Ghana	Norway[b]	Zaire[f]
Greece[c]	Oman	Zambia
Guatemala[d]	Pakistan	Zimbabwe
Haiti	Panama	

a. Latin American Integration Association (LAIA) and Latin American Free Trade Association (LAFTA).
b. European Free Trade Association (EFTA).
c. European Union (EU). Separate trade flows for Belgium and Luxembourg were not available from Comtrade.
d. Central American Common Market (CACM).
e. Association of South East Asian Nations (ASEAN).
f. Data was collected in 1989, when the Dem. Rep. of Congo was still called Zaire.

All countries except Zambia served as reporter and partner countries of bilateral trade flows. Zambia was not listed as a reporter in the database. These numbers sum to a maximum of $[(89 \times 88) - 88] = 7{,}744$ observations. In the estimation, the data set had to be further reduced, because the Park and Ginarte index did not include rankings for Kuwait, Oman, the United Arab Emirates, and the Republic of Yemen. Belgium-Luxembourg also had to be excluded, because the two countries have different IPR regimes. However, these countries could still serve as source countries of trade flows. This explains the total of 7,309 observation for exports and 7,304 observations for imports. Trade data refer to the 1989 U.S. dollar value of total nonfuel trade (SITC 0 through 9-3) and high-technology trade (see table 2.1).

The data for 1989 GDP (Atlas method) and population were taken from the World Bank's STARS database. Geographic distance is the straight-line distance between the economic centers of the respective countries and was taken from Erzan, Holmes, and Safadi (1992). The languages included in the corresponding dummy variable are Arabic, English, Portuguese, and Spanish. We are most grateful to Raed Safadi for providing the data for the gravity variables.

Appendix 2.B. Description of Likelihood Function and Likelihood Ratio Tests

Following Bikker and de Vos (1992), we can derive the likelihood function as follows. From equation 2.1, the likelihood of zero observations can be written as:

$$(2A.1) \qquad P(I_{ij} = 0) = \Phi(-z_{ij}\gamma)$$

where Φ denotes the standard normal distribution function. Recalling that the conditional density of v_{ij}, given u_{ij}, is given by $u_{ij}\rho/\sigma + \varepsilon_{ij}$, where ε_{ij} is (univariate) normally distributed with mean zero and variance $1 - \rho^2$, the likelihood of nonzero observations is as follows:

$$(2A.2) \qquad \begin{aligned} P(I_{ij} = y_{ij}) &= P(z_{ij}\gamma + v_{ij} > 0 \,|\, u_{ij}) \, \phi\big[(y_{ij} - x_{ij}\beta)/\sigma\big] \\ &= \Phi\big[\big(z_{ij}\gamma + \rho(y_{ij} - x_{ij}\beta)/\sigma\big)/(1 - \rho^2)^{1/2}\big]\frac{1}{\sigma}\phi\big[(y_{ij} - x_{ij}\beta)/\sigma\big] \end{aligned}$$

where ϕ denotes the standard normal distribution function. From equations 2A.1 and 2A.2, the logarithm of the complete likelihood function is as follows:

$$(2A.3) \qquad \begin{aligned} \ln L(\gamma, \beta, \sigma, \rho) &= \sum_{I_{ij}=0} \ln \Phi(-z_{ij}\gamma) + \sum_{I_{ij}=y_{ij}} \Big\{ \ln \Phi\big[\big(z_{ij}\gamma + \rho(y_{ij} - x_{ij}\beta)/\sigma\big)/(1 - \rho^2)^{1/2}\big] \\ &\quad - \ln \sigma + \ln \phi\big[(y_{ij} - x_{ij}\beta)/\sigma\big] \Big\} \end{aligned}$$

The log-likelihood function can be maximized by iterative procedures. To test whether the correlation coefficient ρ is statistically different from zero, we apply a likelihood ratio test. This test involves maximizing the likelihood function in equation 2A.3 under the restriction $\rho = 0$ and computing the likelihood ratio:

$$(2A.4) \qquad \qquad \lambda = L^{**}_{max} / L^{*}_{max}$$

where L^{**}_{max} denotes the maximum of the likelihood function in the restricted model and L^{*}_{max} the maximum of the likelihood function in the unrestricted model. The test statistic $-2\ln \lambda$ (as reported in table 2.1) is asymptotically chi-square distributed.

Similarly, the joint statistical significance of all explanatory variables can be tested by restricting all coefficients (except the coefficients on the intercepts) to zero and computing the corresponding likelihood ratio.

Notes

1. These estimates are based on trade data from the UN Comtrade database. For the definition of high-technology products, see table 2.1.

2. For a detailed review of TRIPS and its economic implications, see Primo Braga (1996).

3. FDI as a mode of serving a foreign country is of special relevance because the existence of intangible assets such as intellectual property is a major rationale for the existence of (horizontally integrated) multinational companies (Caves 1996). The importance of FDI is also highlighted by the fact that in 1992, worldwide sales of foreign affiliates (US\$5.325 trillion) exceeded global exports of goods and services (US\$4.570 trillion). See World Bank (1996) for further details.

4. For example, Deardorff (1992). Maskus and Konan (1994), Nogués (1993), and Subramanian (1995) try to estimate these deadweight losses for the pharmaceutical industry in several developing countries.

5. This scenario assumes that the destination country is able to imitate the source countries' products in the absence of IPRs. If this is not the case—that is, if technology is not freely available— the introduction of IPRs creates consumer surplus in the form of newly available products, which may partly offset the deadweight loss. In this view, tighter IPRs are beneficial in that they transfer technology.

6. See Helpman (1993), who develops these conclusions from a dynamic general equilibrium model with two regions, one product, and one factor.

7. Diwan and Rodrik (1991), for example, show that a southern, innovation-consuming country may have an incentive to protect patent rights if it has a different distribution of preferences over the range of exploitable technologies and if R&D resources in northern, innovation-producing countries are scarce.

8. See, for example, Primo Braga (1996) for a discussion of the political economy in the context of the TRIPS negotiations.

9. Gravity models were developed on the basis of intuitive reasoning rather than economic modeling. Because of their empirical success, there have been numerous attempts to shed some light on the economic underpinnings of the gravity equation. Linneman (1966) showed how the standard gravity equation can be derived from a quasi-Walrasian general equilibrium model of export supply and import demand. Leamer and Stern (1970) showed how a gravity model can be derived from a

probability model of trade patterns. Anderson (1979) suggested a theoretical foundation in terms of an expenditure system, with goods differentiated by countries of origin. Bergstrand (1985, 1989) used a general equilibrium world trade model, assuming utility- and profit-maximizing agent behavior and showed that the gravity model fits in with the Heckscher-Ohlin model of interindustry trade and the Helpman-Krugman-Markusen models of intraindustry trade.

10. Earlier gravity studies include Aitken (1973); Linneman (1966); Pelzman (1977); Primo Braga, Safadi, and Yeats (1994); and Tinbergen (1962).

11. For a short review of alternative indices, see Primo Braga and Fink (1997). The Park and Ginarte index is most attractive in the present context because it has the broadest country coverage and refers to the state of protection as of 1990, which is consistent with our trade data. Moreover, compared with the index developed by Rapp and Rozek (1990), it allows for a much more fine-tuned ranking of national IPR regimes.

12. Park and Ginarte (1997) recognize the possibility that different weights for each category may significantly alter a country's ranking. They examine how sensitive their index is to changes in the weights of the categories and conclude that "the ordering of IPR values by country is not sensitive to the application of equal weighting (or unweighting) of categories."

13. An alternative approach to deal with the problem of zero trade flows is to use a log-linear specification with an additive, normally distributed, error term, which can explain nonpositive flows, and a Tobit limited dependent variable model (see Rohweder 1988). We obtained good estimates with this approach for the total nonfuel aggregate but could not obtain a maximum likelihood for the high-technology aggregate. We attributed this problem to the nonlinear nature of the model and the corresponding undesirable features of the likelihood function.

14. The reason for excluding the preferential trading dummies is that zero trade flows do not occur in (most) preferential trading agreements. Inclusion of these variables in the probit regression would then lead to perfect colinearity.

15. In our data, the Personian correlation coefficient between GNP per capita and the Park and Ginarte index lies at around 65 percent.

16. Sectoral exporter output is used as predicted by a first-stage regression that is designed to address endogeneity problems.

17. Park and Ginarte (1997) compute their IPR ranking quinquennially from 1960 to 1990. The average level of patent protection increased from 2.13 in 1960 to 2.46 in 1990.

18. Maskus and Penubarti (1995) report a correlation coefficient of 0.712 between the Rapp and Rozek index and GNP per capita.

19. We also estimated our gravity model in a way similar to that of Maskus and Penubarti (1995). Instead of the Park and Ginarte index, we used the Rapp and Rozek index interacted with three dummies for high-income countries, large developing countries, and small developing countries. Our estimated coefficients were similar: we find a significantly positive IPR-trade link for large developing countries. However, inclusion of the Rapp and Rozek index interacted with the three dummies led to large changes in the coefficients on GDP and population. We concluded that the relatively more flexible effect of IPRs in our model indeed picks up a misspecification in the functional form of per capita income, and we therefore abandoned this approach.

References

Aitken, Norman D. 1973. "The Effect of the EEC and EFTA on European Trade: A Temporal Cross-Section Analysis." *American Economic Review* 63:881–92.

Anderson, James E. 1979. "A Theoretical Foundation for the Gravity Equation." *American Economic Review* 69:106–16.

Arrow, Kenneth J. 1962. "Economic Welfare and the Allocation of Resources for Invention." In Richard R. Nelson, ed., *The Rate and Direction of Inventive Activity*. Princeton, N.J.: Princeton University Press.

Bergstrand, Jeffrey H. 1985. "The Gravity Equation in International Trade: Some Microeconomic Foundations and Empirical Evidence." *Review of Economics and Statistics* 67:474–81.

———. 1989. "The Generalized Gravity Equation, Monopolistic Competition, and the Factor-Proportions Theory in International Trade." *Review of Economics and Statistics* 71:143–53.

Bikker, Jacob A., and Aart F. de Vos. 1992. "An International Trade Flow Model with Zero Observations: An Extension of the Tobit Model." *Cahiers Economiques de Bruxelles* 135. Nederlandsche Bank, Amsterdam.

Caves, Richard E. 1996. *Multinational Enterprise and Economic Analysis*, 2nd ed. Cambridge, U.K.: Cambridge University Press.

Chin, Judith C., and Gene M. Grossman. 1988. "Intellectual Property Rights and North-South Trade." NBER Working Paper 2769. National Bureau of Economic Research, Cambridge, Mass.

Deardorff, Alan V. 1992. "Welfare Effects of Global Patent Protection." *Economica* 59:35–51.

Diwan, Ishac, and Dani Rodrik. 1991. "Patents, Appropriate Technology, and North-South Trade." *Journal of International Economics* 30:27–47.

Erzan, Refik, Christopher Holmes, and Raed Safadi. 1992. "How Changes in the Former CMEA Area May Affect International Trade in Manufactures." PREM Working Paper 973. World Bank, Washington, D.C.

Ferrantino, Michael J. 1993. "The Effect of Intellectual Property Rights on International Trade and Investment." *Weltwirtschaftliches Archiv* 129(2):300–31.

Fisch, Gerhard, and Bernd Speyer. 1995. "TRIPS as an Adjustment Mechanism in North-South Trade." *Intereconomics* (March–April):65–69.

Helpman, Elhanan. 1993. "Innovation, Imitation, and Intellectual Property Rights." *Econometrica* 61(6):1247–80.

Leamer, Edward E., and Robert M. Stern. 1970. "Quantitative International Economics." Boston: Allyn and Bacon.

Linneman, Hans. 1966. *An Econometric Study of International Trade Flows*. Amsterdam: North-Holland.

Maskus, Keith E., and Denise Eby Konan. 1994. "Trade-Related Intellectual Property Rights: Issues and Exploratory Results." In Alan V. Deardorff and Robert M. Stern, eds., *Analytical and Negotiating Issues in the Global Trading System*. Ann Arbor: University of Michigan Press.

Maskus, Keith E., and Mohan Penubarti. 1995. "How Trade Related Are Intellectual Property Rights?" *Journal of International Economics* 39:227–48.

Nogués, Julio J. 1993. "Social Costs and Benefits of Introducing Patent Protection for Pharmaceutical Drugs in Developing Countries." *Developing Economies* 31(1):24–53.

Park, Walter G., and Juan C. Ginarte. 1997. "Determinants of Patent Rights: A Cross-National Study." *Research Policy* 26:283–301.

Pelzman, Joseph. 1977. "Trade Creation and Trade Diversion in the Council of Mutual Economic Assistance: 1954–70." *American Economic Review* 67:713–22.

Primo Braga, Carlos A. 1996. "Trade-Related Intellectual Property Issues: The Uruguay Round Agreement and Its Economic Implications." In Will J. Martin and L. Alan Winters, eds., *The Uruguay Round and the Developing Economies*. Cambridge, U.K.: Cambridge University Press.

Primo Braga, Carlos A., and Carsten Fink. 1997. "The Economic Justification for the Grant of Intellectual Property Rights: Patterns of Convergence and Conflict." In Frederick M. Abbott and David J. Gerber, eds., *Public Policy and Global Technological Integration*. Dordrecht, Netherlands: Kluwer Academic Publishers.

Primo Braga, Carlos A., and Alexander Yeats. 1992. "How Minilateral Trading Arrangements May Affect the Post–Uruguay Round World." Policy Research Working Paper WPS 974. World Bank, International Economics Department, Washington, D.C.

Primo Braga, Carlos A., Raed Safadi, and Alexander Yeats. 1994. "Regional Integration in the Americas: 'Déjà Vu All over Again?'" *World Economy* 17:577–601.

Rapp, Richard, and Richard Rozek. 1990. "Benefits and Costs of Intellectual Property Protection in Developing Countries." Working Paper 3. National Economic Research Associates, Washington, D.C.

Rohweder, Herold C. 1988. "Ökonometrische Methoden zur Schätzung von Gravitationsmodellen des internationalen Handels-Darstellung, Kritik und Alternativen." *Allgemeines Statistisches Archiv* 72:150–70.

Subramanian, Arvind. 1995. "Putting Some Numbers on the TRIPS Pharmaceutical Debate." *International Journal of Technology Management* 10(2–3):252–68.

Tinbergen, Jan. 1962. *Shaping the World Economy: Suggestions for an International Policy*. New York: Twentieth Century Fund.

World Bank. 1996. *Global Economic Prospects and the Developing Countries 1996*. Washington, D.C.

THE ROLE OF INTELLECTUAL PROPERTY RIGHTS IN ENCOURAGING FOREIGN DIRECT INVESTMENT AND TECHNOLOGY TRANSFER

Keith E. Maskus

I. Introduction

The global system of intellectual property rights (IPRs) is undergoing profound changes. Numerous developing countries recently have undertaken significant strengthening of their IPR regimes. Regional trading arrangements, such as the North American Free Trade Agreement (NAFTA) and a series of partnership agreements under negotiation between the European Union (EU) and various Eastern European and Middle Eastern nations, now pay significant attention to issues of regulatory convergence, with particular emphasis on IPRs. Most important is the introduction of the multilateral Agreement on Trade-Related Aspects of Intellectual Property Rights (TRIPS) within the World Trade Organization

An edited version of this chapter was published in the fall of 1998 in the *Duke Journal of Comparative & International Law* 9(1):109–62.

(WTO). Under the terms of TRIPS, which I discuss further later in the chapter, current and future WTO members must adopt and enforce strong and nondiscriminatory minimum standards of protection for intellectual property. Finally, although considerable controversy persists over international means of protecting key information technologies, including databases and electronic information transfers, there is an evident commitment to achieving strong protection in those areas.

That the international system is moving toward markedly stronger IPRs is not a surprise when viewed in the context of economic globalization, which is the transcendent commercial and political force of this era. Globalization is the process in which national and regional markets are more tightly integrated through the reduction of government and natural barriers to trade, investment, and technology flows. In this global economy, the creation of knowledge and its incorporation in product designs and production techniques are increasingly essential for commercial competitiveness and economic growth. The situation acquires growing political saliency in light of the fact that the international mobility of capital and technology has increased markedly relative to that of most types of labor. Accordingly, globalization tends to vest its largest rewards in creative and technically skilled workers and to place its largest pressures on lower-skilled workers.

Emerging countries have strong and growing interests in attracting trade, foreign direct investment (FDI), and technological expertise, although such encouragements must be tempered with accompanying programs to build local skills and to ensure that the benefits of competition actually arise. In this context, IPRs are an important element in a broader policy package that governments in developing economies should design with a view toward maximizing the benefits of expanded market access and promoting dynamic competition in which local firms take part meaningfully. That broad package would include promoting political stability and economic growth; encouraging flexible labor markets and building labor skills; continuing to liberalize markets; and developing forward-looking regulatory regimes in services, investment, intellectual property, and competition policy.

It is beyond the scope of this chapter to consider in detail all of these issues and their complex interrelationships. Rather, I focus here on relationships between IPRs and technology transfer. In the next section, I give an overview of recent trends in international investment and licensing, using U.S. data as a particular illustration. In the third section, I discuss the role of IPRs in attracting technology flows through FDI and licensing. In the fourth section, I discuss the limited number of econometric studies of these effects. In the fifth section, I present the broad outlines of a pro-competitive strategy for attracting investment and technology. In a final section, I offer concluding remarks.

II. Trends in FDI and Technology Transfer

Multinational enterprises make multifaceted decisions regarding the means by which they can serve foreign markets. Firms may choose simply to export at arm's length to a particular country or region. Alternatively, they may decide to undertake FDI, which requires selecting where to invest, what kind of facilities to invest in, whether to purchase existing operations or construct new plants (so-called greenfield investments), which production techniques to pursue, and how large an equity position to take with potential local partners. Firms may prefer a joint venture with some defined share of input costs, technology provision, and profits or losses. Finally, multinational enterprises may opt to license a technology, product, or service, thus leading to complicated issues of bargaining over license fees and royalty payments. Those decisions are jointly determined and, for any firm, the outcome depends on a host of complex factors regarding local markets and regulations. IPRs clearly play an important role in those processes, though their importance varies by industry and market structure.

I begin with a glance at recent international data on FDI and licensing. Many countries do not compile reliable and comprehensive data on such flows, so the overview is constrained by limited data availability.

Table 3.1 lists aggregate figures on FDI inflows and outflows, in millions of U.S. dollars, for representative countries from the International Monetary Fund's (IMF) Balance of Payments Statistics. One immediate observation is that reported FDI data are quite volatile. For example, while inward FDI into the United States remained fairly steady at between US$48 billion and US$60 billion between 1987 and 1995, outward FDI more than tripled from 1990 to 1995. Japan's outward FDI rose sharply in the late 1980s but fell by more than half between 1990 and 1995. The volatility suggests that one should be cautious about making inferences on the basis of a single year of data.

Despite this problem, it is clear that the period saw sharply rising FDI flows in both the industrial countries and most of the key developing countries.[1] Spain experienced a dramatic increase in inward FDI during the late 1980s after its accession to the EU, but that inflow later moderated. The United Kingdom continued to be a net supplier of FDI, but annual investment in that country doubled over the period. Japan remained, in relation to its gross national product (GNP), a very small recipient of inward FDI but a large supplier of outward FDI. Poland's rapid liberalization and deregulation program, along with its increasing commercial ties with Western Europe, led to a 40-fold increase in inward FDI in the early 1990s.

As is well known, FDI in China mushroomed during these years, rising by a factor of 10 between 1990 and 1995. Its receipt of nearly US$36 billion in FDI in

TABLE 3.1   Total FDI Flows, Selected Countries (US$ million)

Country	1987 Inward	1987 Outward	1990 Inward	1990 Outward	1995 Inward	1995 Outward
Industrial						
Canada	8,040	8,540	7,855	4,725	10,786	5,761
Germany	1,820	9,760	2,530	24,210	8,940	34,890
Japan	1,170	19,520	1,760	48,050	60	22,660
Spain	4,571	745	13,987	3,522	6,250	3,574
United Kingdom	15,696	31,335	32,430	19,320	32,210	40,330
United States	58,220	28,360	47,920	29,950	60,230	95,530
Developing						
Argentina	–19	—	1,836	—	1,319	155
Brazil	1,169	138	989	665	4,859	1,384
Chile	891	6	590	8	1,695	687
China	2,314	645	3,487	830	35,849	2,000
Egypt, Arab Rep. of	948	19	734	12	598	93
Indonesia	385	—	1,093	—	4,348	603
Kenya	39	31	57	—	33	—
Korea, Rep. of	616	540	788	1,056	1,776	3,529
Malaysia	423	—	2,332	—	4,348	—
Mexico	2,621	—	2,634	—	6,963	—
Poland	12	8	89	—	3,659	42
Singapore	2,836	206	5,575	2,034	6,912	3,906
Thailand	352	170	2,444	140	2,068	886
Turkey	115	9	684	16	885	113

— = not available.

Source: IMF Balance of Payment Statistics (1987, 1990, and 1995).

1995 marked China as easily the largest destination for direct investment in the developing world. It received 52 percent of the inward FDI in 1995 among the developing countries listed in table 3.1, a share that rose dramatically from 15 percent in 1990. Indonesia, Malaysia, and Thailand all received rising inward FDI flows between 1987 and 1995, and Thailand's investment abroad rose sharply in the 1990s. Singapore became a significant supplier of FDI in that decade as well.

Two African countries are listed in table 3.1: Kenya and the Arab Republic of Egypt. Both displayed declining trends in inward FDI over the decade, indicating severe economic problems in that continent. In contrast, Mexico experienced a sharp rise in FDI in the 1990s, some of it undoubtedly related to negotiation and passage of NAFTA. Brazil and Chile received similar large increases in FDI since 1990.

From this review, the early 1990s appear to have been a period of substantially rising FDI, with a rising proportion of investment flowing to the emerging economies. China is particularly noteworthy in this context. The one dark spot in this trend is the declining ability of very poor and inward-looking economies, such as those in Africa, to attract investment. Overall, the summary points to rapid growth and increasing openness as key encouraging factors.

Table 3.2 provides figures, also from the IMF's Balance of Payment Statistics, on net receipts (credits less debits) for royalties and license fees, other business services, and direct investment income. Royalties and license fees are the most direct measure available of international earnings on patents, trademarks, copyrights, and trade secrets. However, these fees are imperfect measures of the value of technology exchange. Within a multinational firm, the fees charged a subsidiary may depend on international tax structures. Furthermore, optimal pricing of information is a complex problem, and receipts of license fees and investment income may be poor indicators of the economic value of intellectual assets. Nonetheless, those data are worth considering.

The United States remained, by far, the largest recipient of such fees, earning a net US$20.7 billion in 1995. The United Kingdom was also a net recipient. However, Germany, Japan, and Spain paid out more in royalties and fees than they took in, indicating that they were net purchasers of technologies and product designs. It is no surprise that all of the developing economies for which such data were reported were also net payers of royalties and license fees, as befits their status as technology importers. The interesting fact is that for every such country (except, perhaps, India) there was a marked rise in such net payments over the decade. Thus, it appears that the international exploitation of intellectual property became increasingly important in the process of globalization over that period.

The United States publishes the most extensive data on FDI by country and industry. Table 3.3 lists the stock of U.S.-owned foreign capital (foreign investment position at historical cost) for key countries. The foreign investment position is a more informative measure of investment activity than is current FDI, because the latter flow is so variable. The top row of table 3.3 demonstrates that U.S. ownership of foreign direct capital nearly tripled from 1985 to 1994.[2] Thus, again we find that FDI grew remarkably in this period.

Despite the increasing attractiveness of developing economies as destination countries, the bulk of U.S. investment remained in the industrial countries. The EU (then consisting of 12 countries) actually increased its share of U.S. investment stock from 36 percent to 41 percent over the period, while Japan's share rose

TABLE 3.2 Net Receipts on Royalties, License Fees, Business Services, and Direct Investment Income, Selected Countries (US$ million)

Country	1987			1990			1995		
	Royalties and license fees	Business services	Direct investment income	Royalties and license fees	Business services	Direct investment income	Royalties and license fees	Business services	Direct investment income
Industrial									
Germany	−1,290	−1,670	−1,400	−1,810	−1,980	−510	−2,660	−5,270	−640
Japan	−2,520	−6,630	2,000	−3,550	−11,200	2,550	−3,350	−7,500	6,850
Spain	−350	661	−1,482	−932	−670	−2,098	−1,073	−1,407	−1,179
United Kingdom	16	14,334	6,373	−450	7,010	15,460	1,710	7,160	20,270
United States	8,320	10,200	32,190	13,500	14,810	55,600	20,660	12,870	57,480
Developing									
Brazil	−36	−560	−1,527	−42	−1,151	−1,865	−497	−370	−2,044
Chile	−30	0	−218	−37	−142	−333	−49	22	−890
China	—	630	8	—	575	—	—	−3,190	−9,952
Egypt, Arab Rep. of	—	−482	43	—	−322	233	−50	694	−149
India	−40	−144	—	−71	252	—	−68[a]	−256[a]	—
Korea, Rep. of	−47	−65	−88	−99	−892	−145	−2,086	830	−242
Malaysia	—	−318	−1,077	—	−527	−1,863	—	−1,492	−3,785
Mexico	−212	−371	−794	−307	−636	−2,304	−370	−749	−2,664
Poland	—	178	—	—	−22	—	−40	−231	−1,028
Turkey	—	827	−80	—	1,622	−161	—	2,883	−272

— = not available.

a. Data for 1992.

Source: IMF Balance of Payment Statistics (1987, 1990, 1992, and 1995).

TABLE 3.3 U.S. FDI Position in Selected Countries (US$ million)

Country	1985	Percentage of total	1990	Percentage of total	1994	Percentage of total
World	230,250	100.0	426,958	100.0	612,109	100.0
Europe	105,171	45.7	213,368	50.0	300,177	49.0
EU-12[a]	83,898	36.4	179,102	41.9	251,149	41.0
Germany	16,764	7.3	27,480	6.4	39,886	6.5
Spain	2,281	1.0	7,802	1.8	8,048	1.3
Turkey	234	0.1	515	0.1	1,084	0.2
United Kingdom	33,024	14.3	72,343	16.9	102,244	16.7
Canada	46,909	20.4	69,106	16.2	72,808	11.9
Asia-Pacific	33,983	14.8	63,585	14.9	108,402	17.7
China	—	—	356	0.1	1,699	0.3
Hong Kong, China	3,295	1.4	5,994	1.4	11,988	2.0
India	383	0.2	368	0.1	818	0.1
Japan	9,235	4.0	22,511	5.3	37,027	6.0
Korea, Rep. of	743	0.3	2,677	0.6	3,612	0.6
Malaysia	1,140	0.5	1,513	0.4	2,382	0.4
Latin America	28,261	12.3	70,752	16.6	114,985	18.8
Brazil	8,893	3.9	14,268	3.3	18,977	3.1
Chile	88	0.0	1,876	0.4	4,457	0.7
Mexico	5,088	2.2	10,255	2.4	16,375	2.7
Africa	5,891	2.6	3,592	0.8	5,472	0.9

Notes: Data are on historical cost basis.

— = not available.

a. The EU-12 are Belgium, Denmark, France, Germany, Greece, Ireland, Italy, Luxembourg, the Netherlands, Portugal, Spain, and the United Kingdom.

Source: USDOC/BEA, *Survey of Current Business* (1985, 1990, and 1994).

from 4 percent to 6 percent. It is surprising to note that by 1994 the United Kingdom had supplanted Canada as the host of the largest U.S. foreign investment position, with Canada's share falling considerably over the period. The combined shares of Europe, Canada, and Japan summed to 66.9 percent of the global U.S. foreign capital stock in 1994.

It is likely that recent relative increases in investment will change these shares over time in favor of the emerging countries. As it is, each country or region listed except Africa saw a large increase in U.S.-owned capital stock China's share of the U.S. FDI position tripled, and the investment stock in Hong Kong, (China), doubled in the 1990s. Mexico's share also rose sharply, which was partly a result of NAFTA, as did Chile's. As a continent, Africa experienced an absolute decline in the investment stock (indicating a sizable disinvestment) over the period, with its share falling from 2.6 percent to 0.9 percent.

The African experience points out that the distribution of FDI in developing countries remained uneven. This trend was particularly acute in the 1980s, as documented in Amirahmadi and Wu (1994). In that decade, 15 countries received 80 percent of all FDI inflows to the developing areas. These flows were highly concentrated within regions as well. For example, China, Hong Kong (China), Indonesia, the Republic of Korea, Malaysia, Singapore, Taiwan (China), and Thailand absorbed more than 90 percent of FDI in developing countries over the decade.

Listed in table 3.4 are data on the U.S. foreign investment position in 1994 for major industries in selected nations. The global stock of capital in banking and finance was nearly as large as that in total manufacturing, thus pointing out the importance of financial services in the globalization process. Also significant were investments in wholesale trade, which amounted to US$67.3 billion. These figures indicate an important feature of FDI in today's economy: much investment is complementary across sectors. That is, a strong manufacturing presence in a foreign economy typically goes hand in hand with investments in finance and distribution in order to help with local marketing efforts and the financing of further expansion of facilities. Such investments also are strongly complementary with merchandise trade flows, particularly those within multinational enterprises.

It would be tedious to discuss these figures in detail. A convenient summary is in the bottom two rows of table 3.4, which indicates crudely the breakdown of sectoral investment into stocks in industrial regions and countries (Europe, Canada, and Japan) and stocks in developing countries. The manufacturing sector with the highest representation in emerging countries was electrical equipment, followed by food and kindred products and other manufacturing goods. These are industries in which comparative advantage in important subsectors could be expected to lie in developing economies, with their low-wage labor and abundant agricultural endowments. Thus, FDI between the United States and developing

TABLE 3.4 U.S. FDI Position by Major Sector in Selected Countries, 1994 (US$ million)

Country	Sector											
	TMF	F&K	CHEM	MET	MAC	EEQ	TREQ	OMF	TRD	B&FIN	SVC
World	220,328	28,796	51,638	10,974	30,425	20,922	28,057	49,516	67,303	204,574	22,994
Europe	108,655	13,678	29,239	5,481	16,773	8,631	11,731	23,121	36,435	107,384	14,813
EU-12[a]	101,009	11,453	28,328	5,105	15,527	7,671	11,042	21,883	23,584	86,595	12,825
Germany	22,131	2,103	4,152	1,469	4,359	1,306	5,180	3,562	4,049	8,999	946
Spain	4,512	775	754	171	444	441	1,104	821	824	2,014	413
Turkey	693	139	130	—	—	4	133	86	19	110	—
United Kingdom	27,247	3,327	4,560	1,656	5,022	2,941	3,201	6,539	5,564	47,477	5,034
Canada	35,037	3,600	5,856	2,822	2,024	1,820	8,548	10,369	7,006	12,951	3,509
Asia-Pacific	41,577	4,205	8,870	1,189	9,019	7,915	2,875	7,504	16,829	20,685	3,259
China	765	128	188	10	29	—	—	89	131	—	—
Hong Kong, China	1,902	—	99	—	435	492	—	652	4,209	4,107	698
India	308	25	166	9	84	5	5	14	37	442	23
Japan	15,844	1,121	3,634	298	4,425	1,665	1,842	2,860	6,844	6,820	496
Korea, Rep. of	1,391	261	291	66	40	195	78	460	422	1,630	29
Malaysia	1,582	5	66	—	—	1,209	0	208	142	210	0
Latin America	31,932	6,949	6,534	1,237	2,436	1,989	4,819	7,968	6,574	61,019	885
Brazil	13,681	1,794	2,268	732	1,904	935	2,271	3,777	402	3,657	129
Chile	376	56	154	—	2	—	—	190	262	1,954	—
Mexico	10,697	2,792	2,169	—	—	579	1,949	2,390	994	1,982	261

(Continued)

TABLE 3.4 U.S. Foreign Direct Investment Position by Major Sector in Selected Countries, 1994 (US$ million) (Continued)

Country	Sector										
	TMF	F&K	CHEM	MET	MAC	EEQ	TREQ	OMF	TRD	B&FIN	SVC
Africa	1,274	292	—	207	—	47	82	266	248	922	86
Industrial (percent)	72	64	75	78	76	58	79	73	75	62 (77)	82
Developing (percent)	28	36	25	22	24	42	21	27	25	38 (23)	18

— = not available.

Note: TMF = total manufacturing, F&K = food and kindred products, CHEM = chemicals and allied products, MET = primary and fabricated metals, MAC = industrial machinery, EEQ = electrical equipment, TREQ = transport equipment, OMF = other manufacturing, TRD = wholesale trade, B&FIN = banking and finance, SVC = services.

a. The EU-12 are Belgium, Denmark, France, Germany, Greece, Ireland, Italy, Luxembourg, the Netherlands, Portugal, Spain, and the United Kingdom.

Source: USDOC/BEA, *Survey of Current Business* (1994).

countries does tend to follow comparative advantages based on factor costs.[3] The chemicals sector also had a fairly high presence in emerging countries, which is particularly true of the pharmaceuticals subsector (Maskus and Penubarti 1995). Indeed, the data in table 3.4 show that the chemicals industry had the largest stock of investment in China and was also prominent in Latin America.

The banking and finance sectors had a large presence in developing economies, with some 38 percent of their FDI stocks there in 1994. Much of this investment was in Bermuda and Panama because of special tax and operating advantages, which indicates that some forms of FDI are sensitive to regulatory regimes. Netting out investment in those two countries yields the percentage distribution in parentheses, suggesting that 77 percent of sectoral FDI, based more on long-term microeconomic factors, existed in the industrial countries. Investment in service sectors (largely hotels and engineering and business services) was solidly located in industrial economies. However, a substantial portion (25 percent) of investment in wholesale trade activities existed in developing economies. Again, this finding reflects the complementarities between finance and distribution, on the one hand, and trade and FDI in goods, on the other hand.

Further perspective on the sectoral characteristics of FDI is available in table 3.5, which lists data on U.S. investment abroad by high-technology manufacturing and service industries in 1989. Note first that there was significant variation across industries in the number of foreign affiliates per U.S. parent, which indicates the relative importance of investing in either numerous foreign subsidiaries of fairly small size or fewer foreign facilities of larger size. The pharmaceuticals industry topped this list with 33.8 affiliates per firm. Pharmaceuticals are characterized by having large numbers of foreign affiliates producing under license. Advertising and industrial chemicals had the next largest numbers, with other industries trailing behind.

Second, the stock of foreign assets owned by U.S. firms is shown again to have been sparsely located in emerging countries. The highest proportions of investment in emerging countries were in electric components and circuits and telecommunications equipment. Each of these sectors includes considerable electronics production that is fairly standardized and labor intensive. Health services had unusually high numbers in this context among the service sectors.

Third, the proportion of intrafirm sales, which are largely between the parent and its affiliates, differed considerably across industries. In comparison with the stock of foreign assets, intrafirm trade was quite high in electronic components, office machines and computers, and motor vehicles and parts. This situation reflects substantial trade in inputs among vertically differentiated firms. Intrafirm trade was much smaller in chemicals, pharmaceuticals, and printing and publishing, in which multinational enterprises tend to be horizontally integrated.

TABLE 3.5 Indicators of Multinational Activity in U.S. High-Technology Industries, 1989[a]

Sector	Affiliates per parent	Total assets abroad (US$ billion)	Assets in emerging countries (percent)[b]	Intrafirm sales (percent)[c]	Intrafirm trade with United States (US$ billion)
Manufacturing					
Industrial chemicals and polymers	14.3	63.9	10.6	31.8	5.9
Pharmaceuticals	33.8	40.5	11.0	21.9	2.2
Industrial machinery	6.4	22.4	19.2	29.4	6.4
Office machines and computers	11.1	86.8	23.3	49.8	16.1
Telecommunications equipment	11.3	20.0	34.3	30.1	1.9
Electronic components and circuits	5.2	10.1	41.3	49.4	11.4
Electrical machinery	9.1	11.0	22.9	18.5	2.2
Motor vehicles and parts; aircraft	10.5	122.3	12.2	19.4	50.6
Printing, publishing, and recordings	5.3	5.7	5.5	4.4	0.1
Precision instruments	5.8	21.9	12.0	33.1	4.8
All manufacturing	8.5	593.8	15.6	30.8	114.8

Services					
Advertising	14.9	4.4	15.9	0.1	0.0
Motion pictures	8.9	5.0	10.0	0.1	0.0
Health services	2.9	1.6	31.7	0.0	0.0
Engineering and architectural services	4.6	2.0	18.4	8.5	0.01
Finance, except banking	6.0	171.6	24.6	23.8	0.0
All services[d]	5.0	219.9	21.2	17.7	31.8

a. Data are for majority-owned nonbank affiliates of nonbank U.S. parents.

b. Percentage of assets located in *emerging countries*, defined as nations and regions other than Canada, Europe, Japan, or Australia.

c. Intrafirm sales as a percentage of total sales.

d. Wholesale trade, finance (except banking), and services.

Source: USDOC/BEA 1992.

Unsurprisingly, there was virtually no intrafirm trade in high-technology services, which essentially require direct contact between supplier and customer.

III. The Influences of IPRs on Technology Transfer

The various means by which IPRs affect FDI and other channels of information flows are subtle and complex. Moreover, it must be emphasized that strong IPRs alone are insufficient for generating strong incentives for firms to invest in a country. If that were the case, recent FDI flows to developing economies would have gone largely to Sub-Saharan Africa and Eastern Europe. In contrast, Brazil, China, and other high-growth, large-market developing economies with weak protection would not have attracted nearly as much FDI if investment were heavily dependent solely on IPRs.

Seen in the proper policy context, IPRs are an important component of the general regulatory system, including taxes, investment regulations, production incentives, trade policies, and competition rules. As such, it is joint implementation of a pro-competitive business environment that matters overall for FDI, as I discuss more fully later. This section focuses strictly on mechanisms by which the strength of IPRs could affect FDI decisions.

The obvious point is that FDI is a forward-looking decision, in that it commits a multinational enterprise to long-term operations in a host nation. Therefore, what matters ultimately to the firm is the likelihood that an investment will raise its expected profits. Although there are numerous factors that influence profitability, the issue regarding IPRs is the extent to which the IPR regime affects the firm's perception that it will be able to earn a higher return on its protected knowledge-based assets through FDI, relative to other means of earning such returns.

This is a complex subject that permits few definitive conclusions, at least in theory. To sketch an idea of this complexity, consider that a firm with a knowledge-based asset (reputation for quality, new technology, or new products) has several choices in deciding how to service a particular foreign market. First, it can export the good there through standard, arm's-length trade channels. Second, it can choose to produce locally within the firm by undertaking FDI and controlling the production process. Third, it can choose to license or franchise its knowledge-based asset to an unrelated firm in the host country and allow local production in return for royalties and fees. Finally, it could undertake a joint venture involving some joint production or technology-sharing agreement.[4] These decisions are not made independently, and it is possible to observe more than one mode of supply in certain circumstances.

Exports are likely to be the primary mode of supply when transport costs and tariffs are low in comparison with the costs of FDI and licensing. That the volume of exports could depend on the strength of local IPRs has been discussed most fully by Maskus and Penubarti (1995). Strong IPRs in all forms—patents, trademarks, copyrights, and trade secrets—provide protection for exporting firms against local copying of the product, suggesting that they would increase the market size facing exporters and induce them to sell more. This market expansion effect is likely to be strongest in countries with large markets (either in absolute size or in terms of per capita GNP) that have significant technical capabilities for imitating products and technologies. At the same time, such firms enjoy greater market power, allowing them to charge higher prices, although concerns about this "monopoly effect" are often overstated in light of competitive realities (Maskus and Konan 1994). It is more likely to be important in countries that have small markets and limited technological abilities. Overall, empirical evidence indicates that, other things being equal, countries that have stronger IPR regimes do attract more imports, although the effect varies across industries (Maskus and Penubarti 1995). It is interesting to note that the effect of stronger trademarks seems particularly strong in increasing imports of relatively low-technology goods, such as clothing and other consumer goods, because the ease of knocking off such products under weak trademarks limits foreign firms' incentives to sell them locally. Effectively, stronger trademarks lower the costs of exporting because a firm faces a smaller need to discipline local imitators (through lower prices). This effect is also true of pharmaceuticals, although these goods are more likely to be produced under local license, as discussed earlier, than extensively imported. Trade in goods that are difficult to imitate, such as certain kinds of machinery, or for which trademarks are not as significant, such as basic metal manufactures, is less sensitive to variations in IPRs because there is little threat of losing market share to local infringing firms.[5]

FDI is likely to supplant direct exports of a good where trade and transport costs are high, the fixed costs of building foreign plants are low, local productivity is high relative to wage costs, the size of the host market is large, and the research and development (R&D) or marketing intensity of the product is substantial.[6] The last factor is critical for horizontal FDI in differentiated goods and advanced technologies in that it is generally the knowledge basis—or intellectual component—of the firm's advantage that induces it to become a multinational enterprise.

Thus, FDI exists because firms that own some significant knowledge-based asset prefer to exploit it through internal organization of multinational activity, with the location of that activity depending on local market characteristics. This analysis suggests first that IPRs should take on different levels of importance in different sectors with respect to encouraging FDI. Investment in lower-technology goods and services, such as textiles and apparel, electronic assembly, distribution, and hotels, depends relatively little on the strength of IPRs and relatively much on input costs and market opportunities. Investors in a product or technology that is costly to imitate may also pay little attention to local IPRs in their decisionmaking, although the fact that imitation has become markedly easier over time in many sectors points to the rising importance of IPRs. Firms with products and technologies that can easily be copied, such as pharmaceuticals, chemicals, food additives, and software, are more concerned with the ability of the local IPR system to deter imitation. Firms that are considering investing in a local R&D facility would pay particular attention to local patent protection.

This perspective is consistent with results reported in Mansfield (1994), who surveyed 100 major U.S. firms that had international operations in 1991. Intellectual property executives in firms from six industries were asked to give their opinions of the importance of IPRs in their FDI and licensing decisions and to provide their assessments of the adequacy of IPRs in 16 countries. Table 3.6 reproduces the results regarding type of investment facility. In no industry was there much concern about IPRs protecting the operation of sales and distribution outlets. In the chemical industry, which includes pharmaceuticals, 46 percent of firms were concerned about protection for basic production and assembly facilities, 71 percent for component manufacture, 87 percent for complete product manufacture, and 100 percent for R&D facilities. This tendency to be more concerned with IPRs, the higher the stage of production, carried over to all sectors. Overall, the chemical industry was the most affected in its decisions to invest, whereas in all sectors there was a strong concern about local IPRs in locating R&D operations. In a companion paper, Mansfield (1995) demonstrated that these findings held also for Japanese and German firms that were considering foreign investments.

Table 3.7 presents additional results for selected countries that had weak IPRs at the time of the survey. India elicited the greatest concern about IPRs; fully 80 percent of the chemical firms surveyed indicated that they could not engage in joint ventures or transfer new technologies to subsidiaries or unrelated firms because of weak IPR protection. Interestingly, in chemicals there was little difference between joint ventures and subsidiaries in this regard. Both investments evidently provided foreign firms with approximately the same level of security about their technologies (although there was more concern about joint ventures in Indonesia and Mexico). Across all countries, however, licensing to unrelated firms was seen as riskier because of weak IPRs. This situation seemed to be true as well in machinery. In the other sectors, however, there was little difference in the willingness to transfer technology through various modes according to weakness in IPRs.

TABLE 3.6 Percentage of Firms Claiming that the Strength or Weakness of IPRs Has a Strong Effect on Whether Direct Investments will Be Made, by Type of Facility, 1991

Sector	Sales and distribution	Basic production and assembly	Components manufacture	Complete products manufacture	R&D facilities	Average
Chemicals	19	46	71	87	100	65
Transport equipment	17	17	33	33	80	36
Electrical equipment	15	40	57	74	80	53
Food products	29	29	25	43	60	37
Metals	20	40	50	50	80	48
Machinery	23	23	50	65	77	48
Average	20	32	48	59	80	48

Source: Mansfield (1994).

TABLE 3.7 Percentage of Firms Claiming that Intellectual Property Protection Is Too Weak to Permit Types of Investment, 1991

Country	Chemicals	Transport equipment	Electrical equipment	Food products	Metals	Machinery	Average
Joint ventures with local partners							
Argentina	40	0	29	12	0	27	18
Brazil	47	40	31	12	0	65	32
India	80	40	39	38	20	48	44
Indonesia	50	40	29	25	0	25	28
Mexico	47	20	30	25	0	17	22
Korea, Rep. of	33	20	21	12	25	26	23
Thailand	43	80	32	12	0	20	31
Average over the countries listed	49	34	30	19	6	33	
Transfer of newest or most effective technology to wholly owned subsidiaries							
Argentina	44	20	21	12	0	14	18
Brazil	50	40	24	12	0	39	28
India	81	40	38	38	20	41	43
Indonesia	40	20	31	25	0	23	23
Mexico	31	20	21	25	0	22	20
Korea, Rep of.	31	20	28	12	40	22	26
Thailand	60	80	31	12	0	18	20
Average over the countries listed	48	34	28	19	9	26	

Licensing of newest or most effective technology to unrelated firms

Argentina	62	0	26	12	0	29	22
Brazil	69	40	29	25	0	73	39
India	81	40	38	38	20	50	44
Indonesia	73	20	33	25	0	37	31
Mexico	56	20	28	25	0	36	28
Korea, Rep. of	38	20	34	12	40	29	29
Thailand	73	80	36	12	0	25	38
Average over the countries listed	65	31	32	21	9	40	

Source: Mansfield (1994).

That licensing is seen as insecure relative to investment in the high-technology sectors in countries that have weak IPRs points up a subtle aspect of intellectual property protection. Firms are more likely to undertake FDI than licensing when they have a complex technology and highly differentiated products and when costs of transferring technology through licensing are high (Davidson and McFetridge 1984, 1985; Horstmann and Markusen 1987; Teece 1986). Under these circumstances, it is efficient to internalize the costs of technology transfer through FDI in a wholly owned or majority-owned subsidiary. As IPRs improve, licensing costs should fall, because it becomes easier to discipline licensees against revelation or appropriation of proprietary technology and against misuse of a trademark. Thus, for a given level of complexity of innovations, we would expect to see licensing displace FDI as IPRs are strengthened.

It is useful to summarize the predictions about IPRs, FDI, and technology transfer. First, investment and technology transfer are relatively insensitive to international differences in IPRs in sectors that have old products and standardized, labor-intensive technologies. Here, FDI is influenced by factor costs, market sizes, trade costs, and other location advantages. Second, other things being equal, FDI that represents complex but easily copied technologies is likely to increase as IPRs are strengthened because patents, copyrights, and trademarks increase the value of knowledge-based assets, which may be efficiently exploited through internalized organization. Third, to the extent that stronger IPRs reduce licensing costs, FDI could be displaced over time by efficient licensing. Finally, whatever the mode, the likelihood that the most advanced technologies will be transferred rises with the strength of IPRs.

One interesting implication of this analysis is that rapidly growing developing countries, as they move up the "technology ladder" and attain an ability to absorb and even develop more sophisticated innovations, should have a natural interest in improving their IPRs over time. This is perhaps the strongest argument in favor of adopting stronger protection in such nations as Brazil, the Republic of Korea, Malaysia, and Mexico. In the early stages of their industrial growth, such countries have an interest in being able to imitate imported technologies freely, calling for limited protection. As they develop, however, they should become increasingly interested in tightening IPRs, in order both to attract the most modern technologies and to encourage their own innovation.

Economists cannot be entirely optimistic about the implications of stronger IPRs for technology transfer, however. Technological information is diffused from one firm to another, or from one country to another, through numerous channels. Patents themselves have potentially ambiguous effects. They directly facilitate additional information transfer (if not know-how diffusion) by disclosing the details of inventions in application materials. This information then is available for use by local firms to develop follow-on products that do not violate the scope of the original patent. On the one hand, as more countries provide and enforce patents, there should be additional global innovation and patenting, with a positive effect on follow-on innovation. On the other hand, patents could slow down technology diffusion by limiting the use of key technologies through restrictive licensing arrangements. This view of patents has long been held in numerous developing nations and still commands widespread respect in some quarters.

In fact, theoretical treatments of the effects of IPRs on technology diffusion in growth models bear mixed messages. In some models, technology is transferred through imitation by firms in developing countries. When the global IPR system is strengthened by the adoption of minimum standards, imitation becomes more difficult as foreign patents are enforced. The rate of imitation declines, and contrary to what might be expected, this decline slows down the global rate of innovation also: if innovative firms expect slower loss of their technological advantages, they can earn higher profits per innovation, reducing the need to engage in R&D (Glass and Saggi 2002; Helpman 1993).[7]

This result is sensitive to model assumptions and may not hold up to alternative specifications. Indeed, Lai (1998) found that product innovation and technology diffusion are strengthened under tighter IPRs if production is transferred through FDI, rather than through imitation. This result points clearly to the need for developing economies to remove impediments to inward FDI as they strengthen their intellectual property systems. Vishwasrao (1994) demonstrated in a game-theoretic setting that, although the mode of technology transfer is affected by IPR protection, the quality of technologies transferred rises with stronger IPRs. Taylor (1994) also showed that technology transfer expands with stronger patents when there is competition between a foreign innovator and a domestic innovator. A failure to provide patents removes the incentive for the foreign firm to license its best-practice technologies. Rockett (1990) found that in cases where local imitation requires knowledge that is available only through the licensed use of technology, the foreign licensers make available lower-quality technologies. By doing so, they reduce the licensee's incentive to imitate the technology, lowering both the quality and the extent of knowledge transfer.

Empirically, an optimistic view comes from studies of international patenting behavior. Eaton and Kortum (1996) found that the value of patent rights varies across countries and technology fields but is typically significant in important developing countries. This result suggests that stronger patents would induce further R&D, patent applications, and patent working. There appear to be considerable spillovers of technological knowledge through patenting and trade in patented products. Indeed, Eaton and Kortum claimed that, except for the United States, the countries of the Organisation for Economic Co-operation and Development have derived substantial productivity growth from importing knowledge through patents.

The importance of technology transfer through trade in technologically advanced inputs (machinery, chemicals, software, producer services, and so on) should also be emphasized. There is evidence that such trade is responsible for significant amounts of productivity gains across borders and for a crucial part of the technology convergence that has emerged among the industrial economies in recent decades (Coe and Helpman 1995). This evidence suggests that emerging economies have a joint interest in trade liberalization and in linking their regimes IPR systems with those of the developed countries. The resulting gains in productivity spillovers could outweigh costs associated with additional market power.

A further comment about the emerging system of global IPRs should be made because it is little appreciated in the policy arena. To the extent that *different* levels of IPRs across nations act as a locational determinant of FDI and technology transfer, the trend toward harmonization of IPRs within TRIPS will offset such advantages. That is, it will increase the attractiveness of countries that are strengthening their IPRs but reduce the *relative* attractiveness of those with strong IPRs already in existence. This harmonization of global minimum standards presents great opportunities for firms that develop technologies and products, because they will no longer have to pay as much attention to localized protection and enforcement problems in safeguarding their proprietary information. They can focus their R&D programs on those areas with the highest global payoffs. Ultimately, however, it means that IPRs no longer will play much of a role in determining locational choice.

The discussion so far has focused on a narrow interpretation of how IPRs interact with incentives for FDI and technology transfer. Many analysts, however, claim that strong IPRs play a much larger role in signaling to potential investors that a particular country recognizes and protects the rights of foreign firms to make strategic business decisions with few government impediments (Sherwood 1990). In this view, trade liberalization, or the removal of market restrictions at the border, is insufficient to provide assurances that an economy is becoming more open to international commerce. Market access could remain blocked by inefficient investment regulations, limited rights of establishment, domestic credit, production and marketing controls, arbitrary or punitive taxes, licensing restrictions, and weak IPRs. Indeed, the issue of attaining market access through rationalization of these internal barriers to competition is now at the top of the international trade policy agenda (Hoekman 1997). Some also consider that stronger IPRs convey a commitment to move from opaque to transparent legal systems, from arbitrary pronouncements to unbiased enforcement of commercial laws, and from corruption to professionalism in public management.

Because intellectual property protection has taken on increasing importance to multinational enterprises, the adoption of stronger IPR regimes has become a primary device that governments in emerging economies use to indicate a shift toward a more business-friendly environment. The objective is to attract more FDI through this signal, whatever the particular incentives that may be generated in various sectors by stronger IPRs. To date, there is little evidence supporting the responsiveness of investment to this signal, but in emerging economies there is a widespread and growing belief in its importance. This phenomenon explains why several poor countries that have limited technical capabilities unilaterally strengthened their IPR laws and enforcement in the 1990s, despite serious questions about the wisdom of doing so. They preferred not to be left behind in the global competition for capital and technology. It also helps explain the universal acceptance of TRIPS.

IV. Econometric Evidence on IPRs and Technology Transfer

A few studies have included the strength of IPRs in different countries as a potential determinant of FDI and licensing. The theoretical discussion earlier showed that this is essentially an empirical question. Three early studies (Ferrantino 1993; Mansfield 1993; Maskus and Konan 1994) could not find any relationship between crude measures of intellectual property protection and the international distribution of FDI by U.S. multinational enterprises. These articles suffered from limited specification of models and poor measurements of IPRs.

More recently, Lee and Mansfield (1996) used survey results to develop an index of weakness of IPRs in destination countries, as perceived by U.S. firms. They regressed the volume of U.S. direct investment in various countries over the period 1990–92 on this index, along with measures of market size, the past investment stock, the degree of industrialization, a measure of openness, and a dummy variable for Mexico to control for its special investment relationship with the United States. They found that weakness of IPRs had a significant negative impact on the location of U.S. FDI. Furthermore, in a sample of chemical firms, the proportion of FDI devoted to final production or R&D facilities was negatively and significantly associated with weakness of protection. Moreover, the weakness of IPRs had much less effect on the decisions of firms that had limited ownership (ownership of less than 50 percent) of local affiliates, because such firms would be unlikely to transfer their frontier technologies in any case. From these results, it appears that both the volume and the quality of investment are diminished in countries that have limited property rights.

An extended approach was taken by Maskus (1998). He argued that the literature was incorrectly specified in that it did not recognize the joint decisions made by multinational enterprises. In particular, multinational firms may choose to export, raise sales from existing foreign operations, increase investment, or transfer technology directly in response to stronger patent rights. He estimated a simultaneous set of equations to capture these joint effects, controlling for market size, tariff protection, level of local R&D by affiliates, distance from the United States, and investment incentives and disincentives provided by local authorities. He did so for a panel of 46 destination countries, using annual data from 1989 to 1992. The index of patent strength was taken from Maskus and Penubarti (1995).

Table 3.8 lists the results from the preferred specifications, with coefficients expressed as elasticities. It appears from these calculations that FDI, as measured by the asset stock, reacted positively to patent strength in developing countries. Because these are elasticities, the data suggest that a 1 percent rise in the extent of patent protection would expand the stock of U.S. investment in that country by 0.45 percent, other things equal. This elasticity is significantly positive and,

TABLE 3.8   Elasticities of Modes of Supply with Respect to Domestic Characteristics and Policies

Variable	Asset stock[a]	Affiliate sales[b]	Intrafirm exports to affiliates[c]	Patent applications[d]
Real GDP in US$ billions	0.25	0.30	0.13	0.19
Tariff level[e]	–0.02	–0.00[f]	–0.01	–0.01
Affiliate R&D[g]	0.27	0.29	0.15	0.07
Distance[h]	–0.25	–0.02	–0.03	0.02
Incentives[i]	0.97	0.24	0.13	0.17
Disincentives[j]	–0.25	–0.02	0.02	–0.01
Patent strength in developing countries[k]	0.45	0.05	–0.02	0.69

a. Total assets of foreign nonbank affiliates of U.S. parents in US$ millions.
b. Total sales of foreign affiliates in US$ millions.
c. U.S. exports shipped to affiliates in US$ millions.
d. Number filed in the host country.
e. Tariff revenues divided by total dutiable imports.
f. Coefficient is not significantly different from zero.
g. Expenditure on R&D by foreign affiliates in US$ millions.
h. Kilometers of capital city from Washington, D.C.
i. Number of affiliates that received tax concessions in the host country divided by the number that received tax concessions in all the sample countries.
j. Number of affiliates required to employ a minimum amount of local personnel divided by the number of affiliates that are so constrained in all the sample countries.
k. An endogeneity-corrected index of patent laws and enforcement.
Source: Computed from Maskus (1998).

indeed, trails only the responsiveness of FDI to policy incentives. These results suggest that FDI is sensitive to international variations in patent rights.

This outcome is not universally supported by empirical analysis. For example, Primo Braga and Fink (1998), using a different framework and data set, could not find a significant relationship between an index of patent rights and FDI. Thus, more work is needed on this subject.

One area in which additional empirical research would be particularly valuable is in tracing the effect of IPR reform in developing countries on the relative production levels in FDI-source and FDI-recipient nations. The theoretical work noted above by Glass and Saggi (1995) and Helpman (1993) argued that stronger patent rights in developing countries would restrict imitation there and reinforce profitability of production in industrial countries. As a result, the effect of stronger patents would be to reduce production in the south relative to the north, slowing down the so-called product cycle of international production transfer. However, the article by Lai (1998) found that if technology were transferred through FDI, the effect would be the opposite. Thus, stronger patents would accelerate the shift in production from innovative countries to developing countries. The evidence in Maskus (1998) that was reviewed earlier suggests that stronger patents would tend to increase affiliate sales in developing countries.[8] However, it says nothing about relative levels of production and, indeed, all of the studies reviewed looked only at the one-way flow of activity from north to south. A satisfactory empirical analysis of shifts in production would be difficult to perform because of the problems of directly linking IPR reform in one country to production in another, but such an analysis would be a considerable contribution.[9]

Other Empirical Work on the Effects of IPRs

There is evidence that a policy of weak IPRs in technology-recipient nations reduces the quality of technology transferred. Drawing on a study of collaboration agreements between British and Indian firms, Davies (1977) concluded that difficulties in securing property rights over the profits that accrue to technical information raised powerful barriers to information trades between industrial and developing economies. Contractor (1980) studied a sample of 102 technology licenses provided by U.S. firms, and his regression results supported the hypothesis that returns to a technology supplier increase with patent protection in the recipient nation. He found that technologies transferred to developing countries tend to be significantly older than those transferred to industrial economies. Although these findings are rather dated, they point to the significance of patent regimes in attracting technology through licensing.

Evidence also exists that the effectiveness of IPR protection in inducing technical innovation and technology transfer depends on the trade orientation of an
economy. In a survey of more than 3,000 Brazilian companies, Braga and Willmore
(1991) found that firms' propensities to develop their own technologies or to purchase them from foreign sources were both negatively related to the degree of trade
protection they enjoyed. Thus, in closed economies, protecting IPRs may not
expand innovation much because the competitive conditions are inadequate to
stimulate it. Gould and Gruben (1996) performed cross-country growth regressions using data on patent protection, openness of trade regimes, and country-
specific characteristics. They found that patent strength was an important determinant of economic growth across countries and that this effect was stronger in
relatively open economies. In their preferred specification, estimates suggested that
growth induced by IPR protection (at moderate levels of protection among developing countries) was approximately 0.66 percent higher per year in open
economies than it was in closed economies. This finding bears the important
implication that, as countries liberalize their trade regimes, simultaneous strengthening of IPRs provides a more affirmative path to economic growth.

V. Policies to Attract Beneficial FDI and Technology Transfer

This extensive review indicates that, in theory, investment and licensing flows do
not necessarily increase with a strengthening of IPRs, but there is emerging
empirical evidence in favor of that hypothesis. It seems increasingly to be taken
for granted that FDI and the acquisition of new technologies through FDI and
licensing are beneficial for the recipient country. As discussed in this section, there
is a strong presumption in this direction, but it is not a necessary outcome in all
situations. Rather, it is important that such flows result in stronger competition,
in order to ensure these gains for the long term. After a brief review of the potential benefits and costs of these activities, I discuss components of a coherent policy
approach to enhance the likelihood that stronger IPRs in an emerging economy
will contribute to more dynamic competition.

Benefits and Costs of Inward FDI and Licensing

Although their effects vary across countries and over time, FDI and licensing bear
considerable promise for improving efficiency and growth in developing countries, particularly those that are scarce in capital, use production techniques that
are far from the most productive in the world, and have limited managerial and

entrepreneurial talents. These FDI and licensing flows provide access to the technological and managerial assets of foreign multinational enterprises, and those assets may generate both a direct spur to productivity and significant spillover benefits as they diffuse throughout the economy. This diffusion comes through numerous channels, including the movement of newly trained labor among enterprises, the laying out of patents, product innovation through the legitimate "inventing around" of patents and copyrights, and the adoption of newer and more efficient specialized inputs that reduce production costs (software is particularly important in this context). Furthermore, the introduction of efficient and competitive international enterprises can stimulate local entrepreneurship and innovation by increasing competition and raising demands for subcontracting. There could also be a beneficial demonstration effect for local firms.

Thus, successful adoption of competition-enhancing FDI and licensing should materially improve the knowledge base of the economy and move it toward the globally efficient production frontier. There is undeniable evidence that many developing countries suffer from significantly lagging labor productivity and managerial efficiency, related in part to a failure to adopt the newest technologies (Baumol, Blackman, and Wolff 1992; Trefler 1995). Recent experiences in numerous developing economies indicate that liberalization of trade policies and investment regimes can have significantly positive growth effects in the medium term, even if there is some initial economic adjustment period. Further, there is little doubt that a major determinant of relatively rapid economic growth and industrial restructuring in East Asia has been access to foreign technologies through both licensing and FDI, in addition to importation of advanced machinery and other technical inputs (World Bank 1993). There are good reasons to expect these growth effects to be long-lasting because wider access to knowledge allows economic expansion to continue without necessarily running into diminishing returns. Additional benefits include access to a wider variety of specialized products, inputs, and technologies; a deeper and better-trained skilled labor pool; and rising real wages.

These beneficial effects of inward FDI and technology transfer do not come without costs. If there are only insignificant links to other economic sectors, FDI may operate in enclaves, with limited spillovers into technologies adopted and wages earned by local firms and workers.[10] This limited diffusion could be insufficient to compensate the economy for the profits taken out by the multinational enterprise. That is, because profit repatriation and license fees are the payments that emerging countries make for incoming capital, technology, and advanced producer services, the terms of this exchange could be unfavorable in a social sense, if not in a private sense. This situation is aggravated to the extent that multinational enterprises engage in abusive practices of their protected market positions in exploiting stronger IPRs. Such abuses could emerge in setting restrictive licensing conditions, requiring technology grant-backs, engaging in tied sales, tying up technology fields through cross-licensing agreements, establishing vertical controls through distribution outlets that prevent product competition, and engaging in price discrimination and in predation against local firms. Thus, countries could find certain sectors of their economies coming under increasing control of multinational enterprises through exploitation of such enterprises' specific advantages, including brand names, patented technology, marketing skills, and economies of scale.

Although these are possible and real costs, there is little evidence that they are systematic problems in many countries. More fundamentally, they relate to the failure of an economy to erect a policy system that promotes the maximum gains from FDI. Enclave production, for example, makes sense only when the subsidiary is encouraged to produce solely for export rather than to compete locally as well. Firms that are provided full access to local and regional markets are more likely to erect complementary business systems (production, distribution, and services) that compete more widely in the economy and generate greater spillover benefits. Abusive practices are possible only to the extent that monopoly positions are protected and tolerated. Many developing economies have not yet developed appropriate competition rules to deal with these issues, preferring instead to forgo the benefits of FDI and licensing by claiming an unwillingness to suffer such abuses, at least at the hands of foreign firms.

Intellectual Property Rights

Seen properly, IPRs do not necessarily generate monopoly market positions that result in high prices, limited access, and exclusive use of technologies. They are more similar to standard property rights, in that they define the conditions within which a right owner competes with rivals (UNCTAD 1996). Except in particular sectors, cases are infrequent in which a patent holder or copyright owner becomes a strong monopolist. Rather, there are likely to be competing products and technologies, including new ones that do not infringe the property right. Much depends on the scope of the product and process claims protected and on the technical characteristics of the invention. For example, narrow patent claims are relatively easy to invent around in generating follow-on innovation.

Thus, IPRs may encourage dynamic competition, even if they may sometimes diminish competition among existing products. Advocates of strong IPRs maintain that they create competition with long-run consumer benefits. For example, survey evidence indicates that patent disclosure requirements are significant mechanisms for diffusing technical information to competitors within a short period (Mansfield 1985). The information may then be used to develop a new product or process that competes with the original. This incremental nature of innovation is a key fact in most technical progress. It generally builds dynamic competition rather than vesting unassailable market power in a firm. Thus, patents, copyrights, and other IPRs can raise the costs of imitation but likely do not materially retard competing product introduction. Moreover, patents and trademarks provide greater certainty to firms, lower the costs of transferring technology, and facilitate monitoring of licensee operations. Additional licensing could then result in greater adaptive innovation in user firms.

In this view, stronger IPRs in developing economies promise long-term growth and efficiency benefits as they attract additional FDI and licensing and spur further follow-on innovation and technology spillovers. This outcome is far more likely, however, if the implementation of stronger IPRs is accompanied by complementary policies that promote dynamic competition.

Broader Policy Approaches

Overall, it is wider market access to the local economy, in conjunction with sensible competition rules and related regulatory systems, that promises to procure the greatest net benefits from incoming investment. Thus, emerging economies that wish to increase their attractiveness to foreign investors would be advised first to proceed with significant market liberalization. Although the Uruguay Round committed most countries to cutting trade barriers, further reduction of tariffs and removal of nontariff barriers on a credible and irrevocable schedule would provide an important signal of openness to foreign investors. Regional trade integration, particularly with industrial economies that could be the source of additional FDI, could assist in this process. However, such agreements also bear the potential for trade and investment diversion and should be considered carefully in each instance.

Developing countries need also to expand the rights of foreign firms to establish local facilities in services, in light of the complementarity of merchandise trade with FDI in production and services. Removal or rationalization of various investment regulations, such as local content requirements, equity restrictions, and limitations on profit repatriation, would expand incentives to invest. It is likely that such regulations generate net welfare losses for the countries that impose them, in any case. Finally, continued privatization of state-owned enterprises could attract further capital as it raises domestic competition.

It is important for emerging economies to pursue sound and stable macroeconomic policies. Development of modern and efficient infrastructure is also important and could be instrumental in promoting agglomeration gains that attract cumulatively higher amounts of both domestic and foreign investment. There is also evidence that FDI flows are sensitive to international variations in taxes and incentives. Although this provides some argument for providing fiscal advantages to FDI, it suggests more powerfully the gains that can be made from establishing relatively low tax rates and uniform tax treatment of all investors, domestic and foreign. Certainty and stability in taxes are more effective in promoting investment than are discriminatory and arbitrary policies, and uniform tax schedules can generate considerable efficiencies in resource usage (Konan and Maskus 2000).[11] Similarly, there is no evidence that repression of labor rights aids in attracting FDI or promoting exports. Rather, firms are more interested in market size, stability, and growth. In any case, the technical superiority of any investments that would be so attracted in labor-intensive sectors is likely to be quite limited.

An important component of any program to attract high-quality FDI and technology transfer is the development of a competent indigenous technological capacity. In the first instance, this calls for public and private investments in education and training and the removal of impediments to the acquisition of human capital. It also points toward the development of national innovation systems that promote dynamic competition (UNCTAD 1996). Such development involves support for improving basic research capabilities, removing disincentives for applied R&D and its commercialization, instituting incentive structures that help stimulate local innovation, and taking greater advantage of access to scientific and technical information that exists within the global information infrastructure. To date, governments and firms in many developing countries have made inadequate progress in this regard.

IPRs are an important component of any technology development program. In implementing stronger IPRs, as required by TRIPS, or in other policy initiatives, emerging economies will need to strike a balance between needs for technology acquisition, market access, and diffusion. Most nations will wish to adopt a set of IPR regulations that do not significantly disadvantage follow-on inventors and creators, making use of sensible fair-use exemptions, compensated compulsory licensing under tightly defined conditions, and a carefully defined scope of protection. Furthermore, it will be important to implement effective competition rules to ensure that IPR systems are used advantageously. Each of these policy initiatives requires the development of considerable administrative and judicial expertise. For example, countries may wish to monitor the terms of key technology licensing agreements or to intervene in contracts for the development of indigenous public resources.

VI. Concluding Remarks

This chapter has reviewed recent trends in FDI and licensing and has considered the available evidence on what factors are most important in making these decisions. The fundamental message here is that, although there are indications that strengthening IPRs can be an effective means of inducing additional inward FDI, it is only one component of a far broader set of important influences. Emerging economies should recognize the strong complementarities among IPRs, market liberalization and deregulation, technology development policies, and competition regimes. These are complicated issues, leading to complex tradeoffs for market participants. Governments in emerging economies would do well to devote considerable attention and analysis to means for ensuring that they will achieve net gains from stronger IPRs over time.

Notes

1. These figures are in nominal U.S. dollars and are not adjusted for inflation or changes in real exchange rates.
2. Because these data are in nominal U.S. dollars at historical cost, they should be viewed with caution.
3. A similar finding for U.K. investment was detected in Maskus and Webster (1995).
4. A further option—not supplying the market at all—may pertain in small, poor markets with limited IPRs, but it is not considered further here.
5. These results were refined and strengthened by Smith (1999) in a paper published after this one originally appeared.
6. This is a relative comparison only. It does not mean that raising trade barriers would attract FDI but rather that high tariffs in relation to fixed costs are associated with FDI. In general, however, significant trade liberalization tends to attract FDI, for it encourages the establishment of international production networks.
7. The paper by Glass and Saggi was available in manuscript form at the time of writing of the present chapter. It was subsequently published in 2002.
8. In an article published after this chapter was originally published, Smith (2001) found results that are consistent with this claim.
9. Recently, in work done after this chapter was originally published, He (2004) developed a model in which FDI from north to south would be enhanced by stronger patents, but this would slow down productivity growth in industrial countries because of an outsourcing spillover effect. This area of research remains severely understudied.
10. For example, Aitken, Harrison, and Lipsey (1996) provide evidence that U.S. multinationals operating in Mexico and the República Bolivariana de Venezuela pay significantly higher wages than average to their own employees but that these wage effects have not spread to other parts of the economy.
11. The Konan and Maskus paper was in manuscript form at the time this chapter was published. It was subsequently published in 2000.

References

Aitken, Brian, Ann Harrison, and Robert E. Lipsey. 1996. "Wages and Foreign Ownership: A Comparative Study of Mexico, Venezuela, and the United States." *Journal of International Economics* 40:345–72.

Amirahmadi, Hooshang, and Weiping Wu. 1994. "Foreign Direct Investment in Developing Countries." *Journal of Developing Areas* 28:167–90.

Balance of Payment Statistics [data]. Various years. Statistics Department, International Monetary Fund, Washington, D.C.

Baumol, William J., Sue Anne Batey Blackman, and Edward N. Wolff. 1992. *Productivity and American Leadership: The Long View.* Cambridge, Mass.: MIT Press.

Braga, Helson C., and Larry N. Willmore. 1991. "Technological Imports and Technological Effort: An Analysis of Their Determinants in Brazilian Firms." *Journal of Industrial Economics* 34:421–33.

Coe, David, and Elhanan Helpman. 1995. "International R&D Spillovers." *European Economic Review* 39:859–87.

Contractor, Farok J. 1980. "The 'Profitability' of Technology Licensing by U.S. Multinationals: A Framework for Analysis and an Empirical Study." *Journal of International Business Studies* 11(2):40–63.

Davidson, William H., and Donald G. McFetridge. 1984. "International Technology Transactions and the Theory of the Firm." *Journal of Industrial Economics* 32:253–64.

————. 1985. "Key Characteristics in the Choice of International Technology Transfer Mode." *Journal of International Business Studies* (Summer):5–21.

Davies, Howard. 1977. "Technology Transfer through Commercial Transactions." *Journal of Industrial Economics* 26:161–75.

Eaton, Jonathan, and Samuel J. Kortum. 1996. "Trade in Ideas: Patenting and Productivity in the OECD." *Journal of International Economics* 40:251–78.

Ferrantino, Michael J. 1993. "The Effect of Intellectual Property Rights on International Trade and Investment." *Weltwirtschaftliches Archiv* 129(2):300–31.

Glass, Amy, and Kamal Saggi. 2002. "Intellectual Property Rights and Foreign Direct Investment." *Journal of International Economics* 56:387–410

Gould, David M., and William C. Gruben. 1996. "The Role of Intellectual Property Rights in Economic Growth." *Journal of Development Economics* 48:323–50.

He, Yin. 2004. "Vertical Foreign Direct Investment, Knowledge Spillovers, and Global Growth: Models and Evidence." Ph.D. dissertation, University of Colorado at Boulder. Processed.

Helpman, Elhanan. 1993. "Innovation, Imitation, and Intellectual Property Rights." *Econometrica* 61(6):1247–80.

Hoekman, Bernard. 1997. "Competition Policy and Market Access in Multilateral Trade Negotiations." In Keith E. Maskus, Peter M. Hooper, Edward E. Leamer, and J. David Richardson, eds., *Quiet Pioneering: Robert M. Stern and His International Economic Legacy.* Ann Arbor: University of Michigan Press.

Horstmann, Ignatius, and James R. Markusen. 1987. "Licensing versus Direct Investment: A Model of Internalization by the Multinational Enterprise." *Canadian Journal of Economics* 20:464–81.

Konan, Denise Eby, and Keith E. Maskus. 2000. "Joint Trade Liberalization and Tax Reform in a Small Open Economy: The Case of Egypt." *Journal of Development Economics* 61:365–92.

Lai, Edwin L.-C. 1998. "International Intellectual Property Rights Protection and the Rate of Product Innovation." *Journal of Development Economics* 55(1):133–53.

Lee, Jeong-Yeon, and Edwin Mansfield. 1996. "Intellectual Property Protection and U.S. Foreign Direct Investment." *Review of Economics and Statistics* 78(2):181–86.

Mansfield, Edwin. 1985. "How Rapidly Does Industrial Technology Leak Out?" *Journal of Industrial Economic* 34:217–23.

————. 1993. "Unauthorized Use of Intellectual Property: Effects on Investment, Technology Transfer, and Innovation." In Mitchel B. Wallerstein, Mary Ellen Mogee, and Roberta A. Schoen, eds., *Global Dimensions of Intellectual Property Rights in Science and Technology.* Washington, D.C.: National Academy Press.

————. 1994. *Intellectual Property Protection, Foreign Direct Investment, and Technology Transfer.* IFC Discussion Paper 19. Washington, D.C.: World Bank.

————. 1995. *Intellectual Property Protection, Direct Investment and Technology Transfer: Germany, Japan, and the United States.* Discussion Paper 27. Washington, D.C.: World Bank.

Maskus, Keith E. 1998. "The International Regulation of Intellectual Property." *Weltwirtschaftliches Archiv* 134(2):186–208.

Maskus, Keith E., and Denise Eby Konan. 1994. "Trade-Related Intellectual Property Rights: Issues and Exploratory Results." In Alan V. Deardorff and Robert M. Stern, eds., *Analytical and Negotiating Issues in the Global Trading System.* Ann Arbor: University of Michigan Press.

Maskus, Keith E., and Mohan Penubarti. 1995. "How Trade Related Are Intellectual Property Rights?" *Journal of International Economics* 39:227–48.

Maskus, Keith E., and Allan Webster. 1995. "Comparative Advantage and the Location of Inward Foreign Direct Investment: Evidence from the U.K. and South Korea." *The World Economy* 18:315–28.

Primo Braga, Carlos, and Carsten Fink. 1998. "The Relationship between Intellectual Property Rights and Foreign Direct Investment." *Duke Journal of Comparative and International Law* 9:163–88.

Rockett, Katharine. 1990. "The Quality of Licensed Technology." *International Journal of Industrial Economics* 8:559–74.

Sherwood, Robert M. 1990. *Intellectual Property and Economic Development.* Boulder, Colo.: Westview Press.

Smith, Pamela J. 1999. "Are Weak Patent Rights a Barrier to U.S. Exports?" *Journal of International Economics* 48(1):151–77.

———. 2001. "How Do Foreign Patent Rights Affect U.S. Exports, Affiliate Sales, and Licenses?" *Journal of International Economics* 55:411–39.

Taylor, M. Scott. 1994. "TRIPS, Trade, and Growth." *International Economic Review* 35(2):361–81.

Teece, David J. 1986. *The Multinational Corporation and the Resource Cost of International Technology Transfer.* Cambridge, Mass.: Ballinger.

Trefler, Daniel. 1995. "The Case of the Missing Trade and Other Mysteries." *American Economic Review* 85:1029–46.

UNCTAD (United Nations Conference on Trade and Development). 1996. *The TRIPS Agreement and Developing Countries.* New York: United Nations.

USDOC/BEA (U.S. Department of Commerce, Bureau of Economic Analysis). 1992. *Benchmark Survey of U.S. Direct Investment Abroad: 1989.* Washington, D.C.

———. Monthly editions of various years. *Survey of Current Business.* Washington D.C.: U.S. Department of Commerce.

Vishwasrao, Sharmila. 1994. "Intellectual Property Rights and the Mode of Technology Transfer." *Journal of Development Economics* 44:381–402.

World Bank. 1993. *The East Asian Miracle: Economic Growth and Public Policy.* Oxford: Oxford University Press.

INTELLECTUAL PROPERTY RIGHTS AND U.S. AND GERMAN INTERNATIONAL TRANSACTIONS IN MANUFACTURING INDUSTRIES

Carsten Fink

I. Introduction

The well-known ownership-location-internalization theory relates the formation of transnational corporations (TNCs) to the presence of knowledge-based assets (see Dunning 1979, 1981). TNCs rely extensively on the intellectual property right (IPR) system to protect their intellectual assets. For example, 50 TNCs from industrial countries accounted for 26 percent of all patents granted in the United States between 1990 and 1996 (see World Bank 1998, p. 28). Consequently, one would expect the activity of TNCs in a particular country to be sensitive to the strength or weakness of that country's IPR system.

This chapter investigates the link between IPRs and TNC activity empirically. It econometrically estimates the effect of different IPR regimes on U.S. and German international transactions in various manufacturing industries in a cross section

This chapter is adapted from a chapter published in *Intellectual Property Rights, Market Structure, and Transnational Corporations in Developing Countries* (Berlin: Mensch und Buch Verlag, 2000).

of industrial and developing countries. International transactions in this context are broadly considered to be foreign sales of goods that were produced with knowledge developed by domestic firms. By definition, such international transactions are dominated by TNCs. The empirical investigation focuses on both total international transactions and individual modes of delivery—exporting, foreign production, and licensing arrangements.

Both the United States and Germany are significant producers of knowledge-intensive goods and services. In 1992, the United States spent about US$165 billion on research and development (R&D), or 2.78 percent of its gross domestic product (GDP), and Germany spent about US$37 billion on R&D, or 2.48 percent of its GDP (see OECD 1997, pp. 14–16). However, the importance of R&D and, hence, the significance of knowledge-based assets differ considerably across manufacturing industries. Figure 4.1 shows industrial R&D spending as a percentage of sales in 10 manufacturing industries for Germany and the United States. It is evident that in both countries R&D activities are relatively more important for precision instruments, electrical machinery, general machinery, chemical products, and motor vehicles than for foods and beverages, textiles and apparel, rubber products, ceramics, and primary metals.

Moreover, even though R&D activities may be equally important for two industries, the importance of IPR protection in appropriating R&D outputs may not be the same for these industries. The technical properties of one industry's

Figure 4.1: The Differing Importance of R&D across Industries: Industrial R&D as a Percentage of Sales in Selected Manufacturing Industries

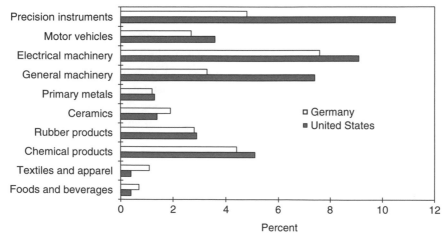

Note: Data refer to the early and mid-1980s.
Source: Grossman and Helpman (1991).

typical R&D output may allow easier imitation than that of another industry. The former industry would be highly dependent on legal protection to appropriate its R&D investments compared with the latter industry, which can rely to some extent on other means of R&D appropriation. Mansfield (1986) reports survey findings across manufacturing industries on the share of inventions that would not have been commercially introduced if patent protection had not been available. Only in the pharmaceutical industry (65 percent) and chemical industry (30 percent) was patent protection found to be highly relevant. For other industries, the share of inventions that would not have been commercially introduced in the absence of patents was consistently below 20 percent and equal to zero in four industries. In view of these differences, the empirical investigation in this study focuses on international transactions at the level of individual industries (although estimates for total manufacturing are also reported).

The next section of this chapter discusses what theoretical models predict about the link between IPRs and international transactions and reviews available empirical evidence in this context. The subsequent sections explain the empirical models and present estimation results. The third section focuses on total U.S. international transactions, and the fourth section considers U.S. arm's-length exports and sales by overseas affiliates. Turning to the German data, the fifth section investigates total German exports and foreign direct investment (FDI) stocks, and the sixth section looks at German receipts from patents, inventions, and processes. The last section summarizes the chapter's main findings.

II. Theoretical Predictions and Available Empirical Evidence

Fink (2000) develops a partial equilibrium model of the decisionmaking process of an IPRs-owning TNC, which points toward a positive link between IPRs and TNC activity. Intuitively, as the southern country moves to a higher level of IPR protection, the TNC's output (supplied directly through home or foreign production or indirectly through a licensee) increases as it faces increasing net demand from the displacement of pirates. The market becomes more concentrated, leading to a higher price for the TNC's product and, therefore, also to an augmented value of the TNC's output.

This unambiguously positive relationship, however, is due to the specific assumptions of the model. Maskus and Penubarti (1993) develop a model of a dominant firm with a competitive fringe industry and demonstrate that a negative "market power effect" caused by stronger IPRs may offset the positive effect caused by increased net demand.[1] Depending on the extent of the price increase, the firm's output value may rise or fall.

Predictions regarding the effects of stronger IPRs become even more ambiguous if one considers individual modes of delivery (exports, FDI, and licensing) instead of total international transactions. As illustrated in Fink (2000), a TNC may choose to switch its preferred mode of serving the foreign market once the southern country strengthens its IPR regime. The nature of such a switch depends both on the initial level of protection and on the extent to which IPRs are strengthened.

In empirical investigations of the link between IPRs and international transactions, one faces the additional problem that available data on international trade flows typically do not distinguish between intermediate goods and goods for final sale.[2] Hence, it may be that trade and FDI (or licensing) are complementary to each other, instead of the substitute relationship implicitly assumed above. If the degree of IPR protection affects the way TNCs vertically integrate their activities across countries, the relationship between a country's IPR regime and international transactions gains an additional level of complexity.

Empirical evidence is available concerning the IPR-trade link. Maskus and Penubarti (1995) use an empirical specification of the Helpman-Krugman trade model of monopolistic competition to examine how a country's imports respond to the degree to which it protects intellectual property. The strength of countries' IPR regimes is represented by the patent index developed by Rapp and Rozek (1990). Maskus and Penubarti find that countries with stronger patent regimes import more than what is predicted by the Helpman-Krugman model, although this result does not hold when the estimation is confined to the most patent-sensitive industries. These results are largely confirmed by Fink and Primo Braga (chapter 2 in this book), who estimate the effects of IPRs in a gravity model of international trade using the patent index developed by Park and Ginarte (1997). Fink and Primo Braga find a significantly positive link between IPRs and total (nonfuel) trade—but, again, this link does not hold when the estimation is confined to high-technology trade.

Some empirical evidence is also available regarding the extent to which IPRs affect FDI and technology licensing. Support for a positive relationship is confirmed by survey evidence from industrial country TNCs. Mansfield (1994) collected data from patent attorneys and executives of major manufacturing firms in the United States. Most industries surveyed regard IPRs as a relevant variable in their foreign investment and technology transfer decisions. In line with existing empirical evidence, the importance of IPRs was found to be most pronounced in the chemical and pharmaceutical industries. Moreover, the survey findings indicate that IPRs are more relevant for knowledge-intensive parts of the production process (such as R&D or technology-intensive product assembly), confirming the risk of technology leakage related to foreign production.[3] Using Mansfield's survey findings as a base, Lee and Mansfield (1996) compiled an index of IPR protection for 16 developing countries and used this index to explain U.S. FDI flows in an ad hoc model of the determinants of TNCs' overseas investment decisions. Their estimation results indicate that countries whose IPR regime is perceived to be stronger generally attract significantly higher flows of FDI.[4]

The most comprehensive empirical investigation on the link between IPRs and international transactions to date is Ferrantino's (1993) study. This study recognizes that trade, FDI, and licensing are simultaneously determined. It explains U.S. arm's-length exports, intrafirm exports, and sales by U.S. overseas affiliates using a gravity model. The strength of IPR protection is approximated by several dummy variables on membership in international IPR conventions and on the term of patent protection. Ferrantino's results indicate a weak association between IPRs and arm's-length U.S. exports, no influence of IPRs on sales by overseas affiliates, and a significantly negative effect with respect to intrafirm trade. Ferrantino interprets these findings as an indication that U.S. TNCs prefer to maintain production within the United States and engage in intrafirm trade rather than risk the loss of proprietary knowledge by locating production in countries that have weak IPRs.

The empirical investigation presented in the following sections takes an approach similar to that of Ferrantino's study—it considers trade, FDI, and licensing as simultaneously determined. It improves on Ferrantino's work in several respects, however. Besides considering the individual modes of delivery, the present study evaluates the effect of IPRs on total international transactions. It employs a much more finely tuned measure of IPR protection and considers the possibility that the selection of countries for which data are available is not random. Recalling the theoretical ambiguity of the relationship between IPRs and TNC activity, the empirical investigation does not presuppose any expectation on the direction (if any) in which countries' IPR regimes influence U.S. and German international transactions.

III. IPRs and Total U.S. International Transactions

The first set of econometric estimations tries to evaluate the effect of IPR protection on U.S. firms' total international transactions in manufacturing as a whole and in four manufacturing industries (chemical and allied products, nonelectrical machinery, electric and electronic equipment, and transportation equipment). Total international transactions for this purpose are defined as the sum of U.S.

arm's-length exports to and overseas sales by U.S. affiliates in a cross section of industrial and developing U.S. partner countries, where arm's-length exports are total U.S. exports less intrafirm exports to overseas affiliates.[5] The relevant data were drawn from the U.S. Department of Commerce and the United Nations (UN) Comtrade database and refer to 1992 (see appendix 4.A).

To explain total international transactions, we use a gravity model. Gravity models have been empirically successful in explaining different types of international or regional flows, such as trade, FDI, migration, and commuting. In general, they specify that a bilateral flow is influenced by supply conditions in the origin country and demand conditions in the destination country, as well as by factors either assisting or resisting the flow's movement (see also chapter 2 in this book). Because the estimation is only performed on one source country, supply-side variables are not of relevance in the present context (that is, there is a uniform fixed effect). Accordingly, the explanatory variables are gross national product (GNP) and GNP per capita of the destination country, geographic distance between the United States and the destination country, the average tariff rate for the industry group in the destination country, a dummy variable that is one if the destination country shares a common border with the United States (Mexico and Canada) and zero otherwise, and a dummy variable that is one if the destination country shares the same language (as a proxy for cultural similarity) with the United States and zero otherwise.[6] The data sources are described in more detail in appendix 4.A. The expected sign of the coefficients is positive for GNP and the two dummies, and negative for geographic distance and the tariff rate. Because one would expect a positive effect of population, the coefficient on GNP per capita can be positive or negative.[7]

The effect of IPR protection is captured by the Park and Ginarte (1997) index of national patent regimes. Fink (2000) describes this index in more detail as well as three alternative IPR rankings that are available in the literature. The choice of the Park and Ginarte index was guided by several factors. First, rankings are available for a large number of countries. Second, the index refers to the state of IPR protection as of 1990, which can be considered as broadly consistent with the other dependent and independent variables.[8] Third, the Park and Ginarte index focuses on patents, which is arguably the most relevant form of IPR in the manufacturing sector. Fourth, the index is more fine-tuned than the index developed by Rapp and Rozek (1990). On the downside, it should be noted that the Park and Ginarte index captures only the strength of IPRs as written "on the books." Hence, the measure may be biased if the practical applications of laws and regulations on the books translate differently into practice. As explained in the previous section, there is no a priori expectation regarding the sign of the coefficient on the Park and Ginarte index.

Turning to the estimation procedure, we find that the U.S. Department of Commerce (USDOC) reports data for 57 U.S. partner countries.[9] Of these 57 countries, 15 had to be excluded because of missing data in other variables (see appendix 4.A for details), which would leave 42 countries for each estimation. However, because of the disclosure policies adopted by the U.S. Department of Commerce, between 4 and 14 observations—depending on the industry group—had to be further excluded.

Given the relatively small number of observations, the likelihood of data availability may be correlated with the error term of the gravity regression.[10] If this were the case, then simple ordinary least squares (OLS) estimates of the gravity model would yield biased coefficients because the countries used would not be a random sample of all countries. To test for this possibility and to obtain consistent estimates in case of an OLS bias, we enlarged the basic data set of 42 countries less disclosed observations by 101 countries and adopted a bivariate normally distributed probit regression analysis. For these 129 to 139 observations (depending on the industry group), basic data on GNP, GNP per capita, and surface area were used to explain the likelihood of data availability in the USDOC listings.[11] The overall model then consists of an equation for the probability of data availability (4.1) and the gravity equation. The former is

$$(4.1) \qquad I_i = \begin{cases} 1 & \text{if } I_i^* = z_i \gamma + v_i > 0, \\ 0 & \text{if } I_i^* = z_i \gamma + v_i \leq 0 \end{cases}$$

where I_i is an observed variable that is one if country i is listed in the USDOC publication and zero otherwise. I_i^* is an unobserved variable describing the process whereby a country is listed or not. This unobserved variable is explained by variables z_i (GNP, GNP per capita, and surface area) with the corresponding coefficients γ to be estimated. The second equation (4.2) is the standard gravity equation

$$(4.2) \qquad y_i = X_i \beta + u_i$$

where y_i indicates U.S. firms' total international transactions in country i; X_i indicates the gravity variables (GNP, GNP per capita, geographic distance, tariffs, the border dummy, the dummy for English language, and the IPR index); and β indicates the coefficients to be estimated. All dependent and independent variables are expressed in natural logarithms, except average tariff rates and the Park and Ginarte index.[12] The two error terms v_i and u_i are bivariate normally distributed with means zero and a correlation coefficient ρ. The variance of v_i is normalized to one; this is no restriction, as the parameters γ and v_i are determined, only up to a constant. The variance of u_i is σ^2.

The bivariate normally distributed probit model defined by equations 4.1 and 4.2 can be estimated by the maximum likelihood estimation (MLE) technique.[13] The contribution to the likelihood function of an observation for which data are not available can be written as

$$(4.3) \qquad P(I_i = 0) = 1 - \Phi(z_i\gamma) = \Phi(-z_i\gamma)$$

where $\Phi(\cdot)$ denotes the cumulative standard normal distribution function. In case data are available, the probability of y_i is given by

$$(4.4) \qquad P(I_i = 1, y_i) = P(I_i = 1 | y_i)P(y_i) = \Phi\left(\frac{z_i\gamma + \dfrac{\rho}{\sigma}(y_i - X_i\beta)}{(1-\rho^2)^{1/2}}\right)\frac{1}{\sigma}\phi\left(\frac{y_i - X_i\beta}{\sigma}\right)$$

where $\Phi(\cdot)$ is the standard normal density function.[14] From equations 4.3 and 4.4, the logarithm of the likelihood function L can be written as

$$\ln L(\gamma, \beta, \rho, \sigma) = \sum_{i \in N} \ln \Phi(-z_i\gamma) +$$

$$(4.5) \qquad \sum_{i \in A}\left[\ln\Phi\left(\frac{z_i\gamma + \dfrac{\rho}{\sigma}(y_i - X_i\beta)}{(1-\rho^2)^{1/2}}\right) - \ln\sigma + \ln\phi\left(\frac{y_i - X_i\beta}{\sigma}\right)\right]$$

where $N = \{\forall i \text{ for which } I_i = 0\}$ and $A = \{\forall i \text{ for which } I_i = 1\}$.

Tables 4.1 and 4.2 present, respectively, OLS estimates using equation 4.2 only and maximum likelihood estimates for equation 4.5 for the total manufacturing aggregate. To better evaluate the influence of the IPR proxy on the estimation, we tested two gravity equations—with and without the Park and Ginarte index. In table 4.1, OLS coefficients of the gravity variables have the expected signs and magnitudes. All variables except the two dummies are statistically significant at the 10 percent level. High F-statistics and adjusted R-squares in the 80th percentile suggest that the explanatory power of the model is quite high. Inclusion of the Park and Ginarte index does not increase the explanatory power of the model, the estimated coefficient being close to zero and statistically not significant. Turning to the maximum likelihood estimates in table 4.2, one finds only small differences in the estimated gravity coefficients compared to the OLS case. As in table 4.1, the MLE coefficient on IPRs is close to zero and is statistically not significant. The estimated correlation coefficients between the error terms in the two model specifications lie between 0.35 and 0.40, but they are statistically not significant

TABLE 4.1   U.S. International Transactions in Total Manufacturing: Ordinary Least Squares Estimates

Model	Without IPRs	With IPRs
Intercept	−2.766 (−1.57)	−2.923 (−1.50)
ln(GNP)	0.910 (9.01)	0.913 (8.77)
ln(GNP per capita)	−0.442 (−2.58)	−0.424 (−2.18)
ln(Distance)	−0.313 (−1.29)	−0.321 (−1.29)
Tariff	−0.065 (−3.54)	−0.065 (−3.42)
Border	0.958 (1.62)	0.914 (1.44)
Language	0.516 (2.12)	0.531 (2.07)
IPRs		−0.032 (−0.21)
Adjusted R-square	0.825	0.819
Number of observations	38	38
F-statistic	30.09	25.00
Variance	0.350	0.361

Note: t-statistics are in parentheses.
Source: Authors' calculations.

based on a likelihood ratio test. This result suggests that the countries used in the gravity regression are indeed a random sample of the extended set of countries. With respect to the probit equation, only GNP contributes significantly to the explanation of data availability; the MLE coefficients on GNP per capita and surface area are statistically not significant. Finally, goodness of fit matrices suggests that the probit model correctly predicts data availability and unavailability for approximately 91 percent of the 139 countries included in this estimation.[15]

Unfortunately, the likelihood function did not generate a maximum in the case of the individual manufacturing industries. It was found that the likelihood

TABLE 4.2 U.S. International Transactions in Total Manufacturing: Maximum Likelihood Estimates

Model	(a) Without IPRs		(b) With IPRs	
	Probit equation	Gravity equation	Probit equation	Gravity equation
Intercept	−19.242	−4.411	−19.307	−4.781
	(−6.19)	(−1.55)	(−6.17)	(−1.61)
ln(GNP)	0.810	0.955	0.811	0.964
	(4.32)	(8.52)	(4.32)	(8.48)
ln(Area)	−0.098		−0.097	
	(−0.76)		(−0.75)	
ln(GNP per capita)	0.081	−0.413	0.085	−0.383
	(0.43)	(−2.58)	(0.45)	(−2.12)
ln(Distance)		−0.244		−0.252
		(−1.01)		(−1.04)
Tariff		−0.064		−0.063
		(−3.83)		(−3.74)
Border		1.080		1.023
		(1.89)		(1.72)
Language		0.502		0.524
		(2.26)		(2.28)
IPRs				−0.050
				(−0.36)
Number of observations	101	38	101	38
Variance		0.549		0.551
−2 ln λ (all coefficients)	164.649		164.778	
		0.367		0.394
		(0.73)		(0.81)
−2 ln λ ($\rho = 0$)	0.452		0.528	

TABLE 4.2   (Continued)

Goodness of Fit Matrices (Probit Model):		
	Frequency of occurrence	
	Data are not available	Data are available
Model (a) without IPRs		
Probit equation predicts that data are not available	96	8
Probit equation predicts that data are available	5	30
Model (b) with IPRs		
Probit equation predicts that data are not available	96	8
Probit equation predicts that data are available	5	30

Notes: t-statistics are in parentheses; $-2 \ln \lambda$ (all coefficients) is the likelihood ratio test statistic with the null hypothesis that all coefficients (except the intercepts) are equal to zero; $-2 \ln \lambda$ $(\rho = 0)$ is the likelihood ratio test statistic with the null hypothesis $\rho = 0$. These test statistics are asymptotically χ^2-distributed.
Source: Authors' calculations.

function was unbounded for values of ρ approaching 1 or -1 and no interior maximum could be found (using a grid search tuned to two decimal digits).[16] Although the maximum likelihood estimates for total manufacturing rejected a sample selection bias in the OLS case, it remains open to what extent this finding justifies the use of OLS estimates for the individual industry aggregates.

Table 4.3 presents the estimation results for the individual manufacturing industries. OLS estimates for chemical and allied products are similar to those for total manufacturing. With the exception of the dummy for Canada and Mexico, all gravity coefficients have the expected signs and are statistically significant. The adjusted R-squares lie in the upper 70th percentile. Inclusion of the Park and Ginarte index does not contribute to the explanatory power of the model; the corresponding coefficient is close to zero and statistically not significant.

OLS estimates for nonelectrical machinery give a slightly different picture. The coefficients on GNP per capita, tariff, and the border dummy are statistically not significant. The adjusted R-square lies in the lower 70th percentile. The coefficient on the Park and Ginarte index shows a negative sign but is statistically not significant. Next, the estimated OLS coefficients for electric and electronic equipment are similar to the results obtained for total manufacturing as well as chemicals and

TABLE 4.3   U.S. International Transactions in Individual Manufacturing Industries: OLS Estimates

Industry	Chemicals and allied products		Nonelectrical machinery		Electric and electronic equipment		Transportation equipment	
Model	(a) Without IPRs	(b) With IPRs	(a) Without IPRs	(b) With IPRs	(a) Without IPRs	(b) With IPRs	(a) Without IPRs	(b) With IPRs
Intercept	-8.846 (-4.78)	-8.966 (-4.31)	-7.396 (-3.06)	-8.280 (-3.26)	-4.094 (-1.80)	-4.644 (-1.78)	-6.849 (-2.15)	-6.941 (-1.95)
ln(GNP)	1.176 (11.72)	1.178 (11.36)	0.849 (7.29)	0.889 (7.32)	0.795 (6.23)	0.819 (5.86)	0.825 (4.35)	0.830 (3.93)
ln(GNP per capita)	-0.665 (-5.26)	-0.652 (-4.04)	0.008 (0.05)	0.078 (0.42)	-0.418 (-1.89)	-0.376 (-1.55)	-0.108 (-0.34)	-0.102 (-0.31)
ln(Distance)	-0.823 (-3.03)	-0.823 (-2.98)	-0.471 (-1.48)	-0.547 (-1.69)	0.737 (2.02)	0.699 (1.84)	0.367 (0.68)	0.354 (0.60)
Tariff	-0.069 (-4.73)	-0.069 (-4.63)	0.015 (0.35)	0.006 (0.15)	-0.080 (-3.53)	-0.081 (-3.50)	-0.040 (-1.12)	-0.040 (-1.08)
Border	-0.111 (-0.18)	-0.130 (-0.20)	0.512 (0.70)	0.192 (0.24)	2.758 (3.44)	2.570 (2.82)	1.953 (1.71)	1.906 (1.40)
Language	0.965 (3.89)	0.969 (3.81)	0.442 (1.48)	0.584 (1.81)	0.673 (2.08)	0.701 (2.10)	-0.080 (-0.18)	-0.067 (-0.13)

IPRs	−0.022 (−0.13)		−0.220 (−1.11)		−0.124 (−0.46)		−0.025 (−0.07)
Adjusted *R*-square	0.839	0.788	0.790	0.794	0.787	0.684	0.668
Number of observations	37	32	32	29	29	28	28
F-statistic	32.31	20.25	17.69	19.02	15.75	10.74	8.77
Variance	0.340	0.502	0.497	0.549	0.569	1.053	1.105

Note: t-statistics are in parentheses.

Source: Author's calculations.

allied products. One exception is the statistically significant positive coefficient on geographic distance. The coefficient on the IPR index is negative but again is statistically not significant.

Finally, OLS estimates for transportation equipment also show a positive sign for geographic distance, although the coefficient is statistically not significant, as are the coefficients on tariff and the language dummy. The coefficient on the Park and Ginarte index has a negative value but is once more statistically not significant.

To check the robustness of the estimated coefficients, we conducted an additional estimation. The data for the four industry aggregates were pooled into one regression and estimated with four intercepts—one for each industry aggregate. That is, the effect of GNP, GNP per capita, geographic distance, tariff, and the two dummies was constrained to be the same across the four manufacturing industries. The advantage of this procedure is to gain degrees of freedom and thus to increase the reliability of the estimates.[17] The estimated coefficients in the specification without IPRs in table 4.4 show that all gravity variables have the expected signs and, except the coefficient on geographic distance, are statistically significant. The adjusted R-square lies in the mid-70th percentile. When the Park and Ginarte index is included across all industries, the corresponding coefficient shows a negative sign, which is statistically significant at the 10 percent level. In the third model specification, the Park and Ginarte index is allowed to differ across the four industry aggregates by interacting the four dummy intercepts with the IPR proxy. The corresponding coefficients uniformly show a negative sign and are significant at the 10 percent level in the case of chemical and allied products as well as electric and electronic equipment.

In sum, the econometric results presented in this section suggest no link—or at best a weakly negative link—between the strength of countries' IPR regimes and U.S. international transactions in manufacturing. For the total manufacturing aggregate, this result holds when accounting for a potential bias stemming from a nonrandom selection of countries for which data on international transactions are available. For the individual manufacturing industries, statistically negative coefficients could be found only for chemicals and allied products and electric and electronic equipment, and then only when pooling the four industries into one regression.

IV. IPRs and U.S. Arm's-Length Exports and Sales by Overseas Affiliates

Following the examination of the effect of IPR protection on the overall service of U.S. firms to foreign countries, this section investigates how different IPR regimes affect the different modes of delivery individually—U.S. arm's-length trade and

**TABLE 4.4   U.S. International Transactions in Four Manufacturing
Industries: Pooled Ordinary Least Squares Estimates**

Model	(a) Without IPRs	(b) With IPRs	(c) With IPRs
Chemicals and allied products	−6.334 (−5.20)	−7.209 (−5.44)	−7.198 (−5.14)
Nonelectrical machinery	−6.315 (−5.19)	−7.195 (−5.43)	−7.398 (−5.30)
Electric and electronic equipment	−6.755 (−5.52)	−7.608 (−5.75)	−7.338 (−5.30)
Transportation equipment	−6.471 (−5.31)	−7.329 (−5.55)	−7.466 (−5.45)
ln(GNP)	0.902 (13.52)	0.934 (13.52)	0.936 (13.13)
ln(GNP per capita)	−0.302 (−3.06)	−0.225 (−2.06)	−0.227 (−2.04)
ln(Distance)	0.041 (−0.22)	−0.098 (−0.52)	−0.096 (−0.50)
Tariff	−0.051 (−4.36)	−0.053 (−4.49)	−0.053 (−4.37)
Border	1.333 (3.20)	1.056 (2.36)	1.047 (2.29)
Language	0.428 (2.59)	0.512 (2.97)	0.502 (2.87)
IPRs		−0.192 (−1.62)	
IPRs* (Chemicals and allied products)			−0.211 (−1.36)
IPRs* (Nonelectrical machinery)			−0.132 (−0.81)
IPRs* (Electric and electronic equipment)			−0.298 (−1.54)
IPRs* (Transportation equipment)			−0.155 (−0.79)

(Continued)

TABLE 4.4   U.S. International Transactions in Four Manufacturing Industries: Pooled Ordinary Least Squares Estimates (Continued)

Model	(a) Without IPRs	(b) With IPRs	(c) With IPRs
Adjusted R-square	0.758	0.761	0.756
Number of observations	126	126	126
F-statistic	44.46	40.84	30.84
Variance	0.619	0.610	0.623

Note: t-statistics are in parentheses.
Source: Author's calculations.

sales by overseas affiliates. This investigation is carried out by estimating a two-equation gravity model similar to the model specified in the previous section. Because the previous section did not find a bias related to a potentially nonrandom sample selection, the probit regression is omitted. The model estimated in this section is given by

$$(4.6) \qquad y_i^1 = X_i \beta^1 + u_i^1$$

$$(4.7) \qquad y_i^2 = X_i \beta^2 + u_i^2$$

where y_i^1 denotes the natural logarithm of U.S. arm's-length exports (defined as total U.S. exports less intrafirm exports to overseas affiliates); y_i^2, the natural logarithm of overseas sales by U.S. affiliates; X_i, the same set of gravity variables as in the previous section; and β^1 and β^2a the coefficients to be estimated. The disturbance terms u_i^1 and u_i^2 are normally distributed but not necessarily independent of each other. From an economic perspective, the sign of the covariance between u_i^1 and u_i^2 indicates whether arm's-length trade and FDI are complements (positive sign) or substitutes (negative sign).

The data sources and definitions are the same as in the previous section (see appendix 4.A), and the basic data set includes the same 42 countries less disclosed observations. However, in three industry groups (nonelectrical machinery, electric and electronic equipment, and transportation equipment), some observations on sales by U.S. overseas affiliates were reported as zero. These observations cannot, by definition, be explained by the log-linear model specification in equation 4.7. Hence, the zero observations had to be dropped.[18] Of course, the exclusion of zero observations adds to the problem of a nonrandom sample selection caused by nonreported observations and disclosed observations. For transportation equipment, the remaining number of usable observations was too low to permit meaningful estimations; for nonelectrical machinery as well as electric and electronic equipment, the estimated coefficients should be treated with great caution.

Because the explanatory variables are the same in both equations, there is no efficiency loss from estimating the two equations separately by OLS and computing the covariance from the estimated residuals (see, for example, Johnston 1984, pp. 330–38). The gravity equations were again estimated first without and then with the IPR index.

Table 4.5 presents the estimation results for the total manufacturing aggregate. Most gravity variables have the expected signs and are significant at least at the 10 percent level. Exceptions are the positive sign on geographic distance in the arm's-length trade equation and the negative sign on the border dummy in the sales by affiliates equation; neither coefficient, however, is statistically significant. The R-squares lie around 70 percent for arm's-length trade and around 80 percent for sales by affiliates. The covariance assumes a small, positive value, suggesting a weakly complementary relationship between the two dependent variables. The coefficient on the Park and Ginarte index is close to zero and statistically not significant for both arm's-length trade and sales by affiliates.

Table 4.6 presents the estimation results for the individual manufacturing industries. In the case of chemical and allied products, the coefficients on geographic distance for arm's-length trade (correct signs) and on the border dummy for sales by affiliates (wrong signs) are both statistically not significant. The R-squares for arm's-length trade are somewhat lower and lie in the mid-50th percentile. The estimated covariances are close to zero, suggesting an independent relationship between the two modes of delivery. The coefficients on the IPR index are again very close to zero and statistically not significant for both arm's-length trade and sales by U.S. affiliates.

As mentioned above, estimates for nonelectrical machinery should be treated with great care because the estimation is based on only 21 observations. Most of the coefficients are not significant, and some coefficients have the wrong sign. The estimated coefficient on the Park and Ginarte index for arm's-length trade is negative and statistically significant at the 10 percent level; for sales by overseas affiliates, the coefficient is also negative but is not significant.

Similar caveats hold for the estimated coefficients for electric and electronic equipment, which are based on only 26 observations. Many coefficients are not statistically significant; the coefficient on geographic distance has the wrong sign for both modes of delivery. The estimated covariance between the two regressions takes a positive value, suggesting a complementary relationship between exports and sales by affiliates. The coefficient on the IPR index is close to zero for

TABLE 4.5   U.S. Arm's-Length Exports and Sales by Affiliates in Total Manufacturing: OLS Estimates

Model	(a) Without IPRs		(b) With IPRs	
Dependent variable	Arm's-length exports	Sales by affiliates	Arm's-length exports	Sales by affiliates
Intercept	2.129	–9.698	1.810	–9.409
	(1.16)	(–3.83)	(0.90)	(–3.37)
ln(GNP)	0.627	1.311	0.634	1.305
	(6.00)	(9.05)	(5.90)	(8.76)
ln(GNP per capita)	–0.360	–0.754	–0.322	–0.788
	(–2.05)	(–3.10)	(–1.61)	(–2.83)
ln(Distance)	0.193	–1.141	0.176	–1.126
	(0.76)	(–3.26)	(0.68)	(–3.13)
Tariff	–0.051	–0.111	–0.050	–0.112
	(–2.66)	(–4.17)	(–2.55)	(–4.11)
Border	2.000	–0.278	1.910	–0.197
	(3.26)	(–0.33)	(2.90)	(–0.22)
Language	0.338	1.057	0.366	1.031
	(1.35)	(3.03)	(1.39)	(2.81)
IPRs			–0.065	0.059
			(–0.40)	(0.26)
Adjusted R-square	0.705	0.806	0.697	0.801
Number of observations	39	39	39	39
F-statistic	16.15	27.38	13.51	22.80
Variance	0.379	0.727	0.389	0.749
Covariance	0.106		0.111	

Note: t-statistics are in parentheses.
Source: Author's calculations.

arm's-length trade and negative for sales by affiliates, but neither coefficient is significant.

Finally, table 4.7 presents pooled regression estimates across the three industries with industry-specific intercepts.[19] The first model specification is the standard gravity equation without IPRs. All coefficients except the one on geographic

TABLE 4.6 U.S. Arm's-Length Exports and Sales by Affiliates in Individual Manufacturing Industries: OLS Estimates

Industry	Chemicals and allied products				Nonelectrical machinery				Electric and electronic equipment			
Model	(a) Without IPRs		(b) With IPRs		(a) Without IPRs		(b) With IPRs		(a) Without IPRs		(b) With IPRs	
Dependent variable	Arm's-length exports	Sales by affiliates	Arm's-length exports	Sales by affiliates	Arm's-length exports	Sales by affiliates	Arm's-length exports	Sales by affiliates	Arm's-length exports	Sales by affiliates	Arm's-length exports	Sales by affiliates
Intercept	-2.811 (-1.03)	-13.342 (-5.93)	-2.851 (-0.93)	-13.341 (-5.27)	1.436 (0.34)	-31.37 (-4.59)	-0.881 (-0.21)	-34.24 (-4.81)	-0.242 (-0.08)	-11.233 (-2.06)	0.038 (0.01)	-15.578 (-2.47)
ln(GNP)	0.781 (5.29)	1.432 (11.76)	0.781 (5.13)	1.432 (11.38)	0.491 (3.14)	1.707 (6.76)	0.537 (3.57)	1.764 (6.98)	0.578 (3.77)	1.054 (3.94)	0.567 (3.25)	1.218 (4.18)
ln(GNP per capita)	-0.475 (-2.58)	-0.870 (-5.72)	-0.471 (-2.00)	-0.870 (-4.46)	-0.035 (-0.11)	-0.077 (-0.15)	0.265 (0.74)	0.295 (0.49)	-0.340 (-1.25)	-0.401 (-0.85)	-0.355 (-1.19)	-0.164 (-0.33)
ln(Distance)	-0.147 (-0.37)	-1.250 (-3.79)	-0.147 (-0.36)	-1.250 (-3.73)	-0.148 (-0.31)	-0.268 (-0.34)	-0.210 (-0.46)	-0.345 (-1.21)	1.037 (2.16)	0.490 (0.59)	1.032 (2.09)	0.555 (0.67)
Tariff	-0.043 (-2.03)	-0.098 (-5.54)	-0.043 (-1.99)	-0.098 (-5.43)	0.005 (0.07)	0.017 (0.15)	-0.013 (-0.20)	-0.006 (-0.05)	-0.068 (-2.51)	-0.161 (-3.40)	-0.068 (-2.41)	-0.168 (-3.60)
Border	1.339 (1.47)	-0.699 (-0.93)	1.333 (1.41)	-0.699 (-0.89)	1.459 (1.62)	-0.216 (-0.15)	1.051 (1.18)	-0.722 (-0.48)	3.597 (3.79)	2.217 (1.34)	3.638 (3.58)	1.574 (0.93)
Language	0.799 (2.20)	1.001 (3.33)	0.801 (2.15)	1.001 (3.26)	0.350 (0.87)	1.926 (2.96)	0.275 (0.72)	1.832 (2.84)	0.562 (1.55)	0.582 (0.92)	0.560 (1.50)	0.619 (1.00)
IPRs			-0.008 (-0.03)	0.000 (0.00)			-0.467 (-1.64)	-0.580 (-1.21)			0.044 (0.14)	-0.689 (-1.31)

(Continued)

TABLE 4.6 U.S. Arm's-Length Exports and Sales by Affiliates in Individual Manufacturing Industries: OLS Estimates (Continued)

Industry	Chemicals and allied products				Nonelectrical machinery				Electric and electronic equipment			
Model	(a) Without IPRs		(b) With IPRs		(a) Without IPRs		(b) With IPRs		(a) Without IPRs		(b) With IPRs	
Dependent variable	Arm's-length exports	Sales by affiliates	Arm's-length exports	Sales by affiliates	Arm's-length exports	Sales by affiliates	Arm's-length exports	Sales by affiliates	Arm's-length exports	Sales by affiliates	Arm's-length exports	Sales by affiliates
Adjusted R-square	0.550	0.829	0.535	0.823	0.527	0.764	0.578	0.772	0.644	0.675	0.625	0.687
Number of observations	38	38	38	38	21	21	21	21	26	26	26	26
F-statistic	8.52	30.93	7.07	25.66	4.72	11.78	4.92	10.65	8.54	9.66	6.94	8.83
Variance	0.736	0.502	0.760	0.519	0.519	1.353	0.463	1.308	0.617	1.877	0.650	1.809
Covariance	0.026		0.027		0.217		0.114		0.615		0.660	

Note: t-statistics are in parentheses.

Source: Author's calculations.

TABLE 4.7   U.S. Arm's-Length Exports and Sales by Affiliates in Three Manufacturing Industries: Pooled OLS Estimates

Model	(a) Without IPRs		(b) With IPRs		(c) With IPRs	
Equation	Arm's-length exports	Sales by affiliates	Arm's-length exports	Sales by affiliates	Arm's-length exports	Sales by affiliates
Chemicals and allied products	−0.853 (−0.50)	−14.045 (−5.72)	−1.305 (−0.67)	−15.957 (−5.74)	−1.205 (−0.60)	−15.774 (−5.62)
Nonelectrical machinery	−0.009 (−0.01)	−15.147 (−6.02)	−0.466 (−0.23)	−17.076 (−6.02)	−0.290 (−0.14)	−18.247 (−6.14)
Electric and electronic equipment	−0.584 (−0.34)	−15.315 (−6.14)	−1.031 (−0.53)	−17.203 (−6.14)	−1.124 (−0.56)	−17.545 (−6.18)
ln(GNP)	0.641 (7.38)	1.380 (11.01)	0.652 (7.23)	1.427 (11.09)	0.647 (6.98)	1.419 (10.88)
ln(GNP per capita)	−0.342 (−2.68)	−0.702 (−3.81)	−0.300 (−1.93)	−0.522 (−(2.35)	−0.295 (−1.84)	−0.474 (−2.10)
ln(Distance)	0.158 (0.64)	−0.755 (−2.11)	0.159 (0.64)	−0.754 (−2.12)	0.158 (0.62)	−0.674 (−1.88)
Tariff	−0.045 (−3.05)	−0.131 (−6.18)	−0.044 (−3.01)	−0.129 (−6.15)	−0.043 (−2.80)	−0.127 (−5.89)
Border	2.007 (3.86)	−0.100 (−0.13)	1.936 (3.57)	−0.397 (−0.51)	1.945 (3.50)	−0.242 (−0.31)
Language	0.611 (2.88)	1.056 (3.45)	0.618 (2.90)	1.089 (3.57)	0.620 (2.86)	1.061 (3.48)
IPRs			−0.075 (−0.49)	−0.319 (−1.44)		
IPRs* (chemicals and allied products)					−0.081 (−0.43)	−0.516 (−1.96)
IPRs* nonelectrical machinery)					−0.017 (−0.07)	−0.330 (−1.03)

(Continued)

TABLE 4.7   U.S. Arm's-Length Exports and Sales by Affiliates in Three Manufacturing Industries: Pooled OLS Estimates (Continued)

Model	(a) Without IPRs		(b) With IPRs		(c) With IPRs	
Equation	Arm's-length exports	Sales by affiliates	Arm's-length exports	Sales by affiliates	Arm's-length exports	Sales by affiliates
IPRs* (electric and electronic equipment)					−0.105 (−0.51)	−0.051 (−0.17)
Adjusted R-square	0.647	0.713	0.644	0.717	0.635	0.718
Number of observations	85	85	85	85	85	85
F-statistic	20.28	27.13	17.87	24.68	14.27	20.49
Variance	0.631	1.318	0.638	1.300	0.654	1.294
Covariance	0.297		0.292		0.302	

Note: t-statistics are in parentheses.
Source: Author's calculations.

distance for arm's-length exports have the expected signs and are statistically significant. The R-squares are comparable to the estimations of the individual industries; the positive estimated covariance suggests a complementary relationship between the two modes of delivery. The second specification includes the Park and Ginarte index across all industries. For arm's-length exports, the corresponding coefficient is close to zero and statistically not significant; for sales by affiliates, the coefficient is negative and significant at the 10 percent level. In the third model specification, the IPR index is allowed to differ for the three industries. The estimated IPR coefficients all show a negative sign but are not significant except for sales by affiliates in chemical and allied products, where the coefficient is significant at the 10 percent level.

In sum, the econometric evidence presented in this section suggests that stronger IPR regimes do not influence U.S. arm's-length exports or (for the total manufacturing aggregate) sales by overseas affiliates. A negative link between IPRs and sales by affiliates is found for chemicals and allied products, but only in the pooled regression. Estimation results for nonelectrical machinery and electric and electronic equipment have to be treated with caution because they are based on few observations.

V. IPRs and German Exports and FDI

This section evaluates the effect of IPR protection on German firms' export and FDI decisions. Data on the stocks of FDI for 1992 for four manufacturing industries (chemicals, nonelectrical machinery, electrical engineering, and transportation equipment) are from the Deutsche Bundesbank. Unfortunately, the Bundesbank does not publish data on sales by German overseas affiliates as the U.S. Department of Commerce does. Hence, one cannot compute the overall service of German firms abroad and estimate the effects of IPRs on total German international transactions. The only useful data available for manufacturing industries are the stock of FDI in a foreign country.[20] Although FDI stock is an imperfect measure of the service of German overseas affiliates, one would expect it to be closely correlated with sales by affiliates.

A further shortcoming is that data on German intrafirm trade flows are unavailable. It is thus impossible to compute trade flows at arm's length, and the estimation had to rely on total German exports. The empirical model and the explanatory variables used are the same as in the previous section for U.S. arm's-length exports and sales by affiliates. It is worth noting that the tariff rate for Germany's co–European Union members was set to zero. Appendix 4.A describes the sources of all dependent and independent variables and lists the countries included in the estimation.

Of the 30 countries for which FDI data were available, 5 had to be excluded because of data limitations in the explanatory variables. Because of the small number of observations for each industry aggregate, we decided to pool the four industries into one regression with industry-specific intercepts.[21] This methodology would give 100 observations. However, three observations that were disclosed and one that was equal to zero had to be dropped, such that the pooled regression is based on 96 observations.

Table 4.8 presents the estimation results. In the first model specification without the Park and Ginarte index, most gravity variables have the expected signs and are statistically significant; exceptions are the coefficients on the border dummy, which are statistically not significant. The R-squares lie in the upper 70th percentile for total exports and in the mid-50th percentile for FDI stock. The covariance takes a value close to zero, suggesting a nearly independent relationship between German total exports and FDI stocks. In the second specification, the Park and Ginarte index is included and forced to be the same across all industries; the estimated coefficient shows a significantly positive effect in the export

TABLE 4.8   German Total Exports and FDI Stocks in Four Manufacturing Industries: Pooled OLS Estimates

Model	(a) Without IPRs		(b) With IPRs		(c) With IPRs	
Equation	Total exports	FDI stock	Total exports	FDI stock	Total exports	FDI stock
Chemicals	-0.736	-9.667	2.212	-9.864	2.038	-9.797
	(-0.18)	(-4.44)	(1.50)	(-3.84)	(1.37)	(-3.77)
Nonelectrical machinery	0.226	-10.624	2.674	-10.820	2.773	-11.583
	(0.17)	(-4.89)	(1.81)	(-4.21)	(1.87)	(-4.48)
Electrical engineering	-0.354	-9.801	2.094	-9.997	2.462	-9.193
	(-0.27)	(-4.49)	(1.41)	(-3.88)	(1.64)	(-3.51)
Transportation equipment	-0.081	-10.18	2.365	-10.374	1.534	-9.318
	(-0.06)	(-4.63)	(1.59)	(-4.01)	(1.00)	(-3.48)
ln(GNP)	0.616	0.796	0.540	0.802	0.545	0.804
	(11.73)	(9.21)	(9.75)	(8.32)	(9.93)	(8.42)
ln(GNP per capita)	-0.198	-0.472	-0.353	-0.460	-0.351	-0.496
	(-1.70)	(-2.47)	(-2.92)	(-2.18)	(-2.92)	(-2.37)
ln(Distance)	-0.474	-0.390	-0.472	-0.390	-0.473	-0.388
	(-6.52)	(-3.26)	(-6.83)	(-3.25)	(-6.92)	(-3.26)
Tariff	-0.034	-0.050	-0.034	-0.050	-0.035	-0.052
	(-3.26)	(-2.95)	(-3.41)	(-2.93)	(-3.58)	(-3.06)
Border	0.102	-0.147	-0.070	-0.133	-0.074	-0.121
	(0.43)	(-0.37)	(-0.30)	(-0.33)	(-0.32)	(-0.30)
Language	0.607	0.876	0.477	0.886	0.481	0.887
	(1.83)	(1.60)	(1.50)	(1.60)	(1.53)	(1.62)
IPRs			0.324	-0.026		
			(3.16)	(-0.15)		
IPRs* (chemicals)					0.339	0.044
					(2.36)	(0.18)
IPRs* (nonelectrical machinery)					0.250	0.312
					(1.74)	(1.24)

TABLE 4.8 (Continued)

Model	(a) Without IPRs		(b) With IPRs		(c) With IPRs	
Equation	Total exports	FDI stock	Total exports	FDI stock	Total exports	FDI stock
IPRs* (electrical engineering)					0.164 (1.14)	-0.194 (-0.77)
IPRs* (transportation equipment)					0.539 (3.60)	-0.262 (-1.00)
Adjusted R-square	0.776	0.565	0.797	0.560	0.802	0.569
Number of observations	96	96	96	96	96	96
F-statistic	37.60	14.73	38.37	13.11	30.56	10.63
Variance	0.325	0.878	0.294	0.888	0.287	0.872
Covariance	0.068		0.072		0.084	

Note: t-statistics are in parentheses.
Source: Author's calculations.

equation but is close to zero and not significant in the FDI stock equation. Finally, the third model specification allows the coefficient on the IPR index to differ across the four industries. The resulting coefficients show a positive sign for all industries in the case of total exports; the coefficients are significant at the 5 percent level for chemicals, nonelectrical machinery, and transportation equipment. The corresponding coefficients in the FDI stock equation are all statistically not significant.

Overall, the German data confirm the positive link between IPRs and total exports identified in previous studies (see the second section of this chapter), but IPRs are found to have no influence on the direct investment stock of German firms in foreign countries.

VI. IPRs and German Receipts for Patents, Inventions, and Processes

This section presents empirical evidence on how the strength of countries' IPR systems affects German cross-border receipts from patents, inventions, and processes in six manufacturing industries. Although one could construct a case where stronger IPRs are negatively related to these receipts, there are strong reasons to believe that this link is positive. First, if a foreign country does not protect patent rights, the legal framework for licensing German technology on the basis of patented knowledge is fundamentally weakened. Second, if a German firm's patent is protected in the foreign country, the local licensee is likely to generate higher profits leading to higher royalties and license fees for the German patent holder.

Data on German receipts for patents, inventions, and processes for 1992 are drawn from the "technology balance of payments" compiled by the Deutsche Bundesbank. Unfortunately, the data are not divided into receipts from unaffiliated compared with affiliated foreign firms. Hence, the potential danger exists that receipts may be overvalued if some of the intrafirm receipts represent hidden profit repatriations caused by higher taxation abroad.[22] The Bundesbank reports data for five different manufacturing industries (chemicals and oil processing, metal production and processing, electronic and data processing equipment, precision and optical engineering, and food and kindred products) plus one residual industry aggregate. It is worth pointing out that chemicals and oil processing accounts for more than 50 percent of total receipts—consistent with the high R&D intensity and reliance on patents in that industry.

To explain German technology receipts in these six manufacturing categories, we used the same gravity variables as in the previous sections, except that tariff rates had to be dropped because of the different definitions of the industry aggregates. Appendix 4.A lists the 27 countries for which information on the dependent variable was available. Three of those countries had to be excluded because of limitations in the explanatory variables, which would leave 24 countries for each manufacturing industry. Because regressions on only 24 observations would not be reliable, the six industry aggregates were again pooled into one regression with industry-specific intercepts.[23]

Theoretically, the number of observations in this single regression would then be 144. However, 33 observations had to be excluded because either there were no receipts from a country (14 observations) or the value was disclosed (19 observations). Moreover, 22 observations were rounded to zero if the value of a receipt was below DM 500,000. To account for these 22 observations and to avoid a potential bias due to censoring, we adopted a Tobit model with a lower bound equal to DM 500,000.

The estimation results are presented in table 4.9. The first model specification estimates the gravity equation without the Park and Ginarte index. All coefficients have the expected signs and are statistically significant except the coefficient on geographic distance, which is not significant, and the coefficient on the border dummy, which is negative and not significant. This result suggests that technology

TABLE 4.9   German Receipts for Patents, Inventions, and Processes in Six Manufacturing Categories: Tobit Maximum Likelihood Estimates

Model	(a) Without IPRs	(b) With IPRs	(c) With IPRs
Chemicals and oil processing	−10.628 (−7.68)	−9.569 (−4.98)	−10.586 (−5.35)
Metal production and metal processing	−11.948 (−8.58)	−10.887 (−5.65)	−10.490 (−5.24)
Electronic and data processing equipment	−11.012 (−7.91)	−9.950 (−5.16)	−9.548 (−4.75)
Precision and optical engineering	−13.543 (−9.22)	−12.485 (−6.31)	−11.500 (−4.44)
Food and kindred products	−14.346 (−9.62)	−13.275 (−6.62)	−15.960 (−3.34)
Other manufacturing	−12.549 (−8.80)	−11.472 (−5.84)	−11.233 (−5.56)
ln(GNP)	0.898 (8.32)	0.846 (6.74)	0.848 (6.87)
ln(GNP per capita)	0.172 (1.36)	0.064 (0.34)	0.068 (0.39)
ln(Distance)	−0.087 (−0.65)	−0.079 (−0.59)	−0.086 (−0.65)
Border	−0.345 (−0.81)	−0.421 (−0.97)	−0.429 (−1.01)
Language	2.428 (5.28)	2.420 (5.29)	2.367 (5.25)
IPRs		0.196 (0.79)	
IPRs* (chemicals and oil processing)			0.505 (1.67)
IPRs* (metal production and metal processing)			0.053 (0.17)
IPRs* (electronic and data processing equipment)			0.049 (0.12)

(*Continued*)

TABLE 4.9 German Receipts for Patents, Inventions, and Processes in Six Manufacturing Categories: Tobit Maximum Likelihood Estimates (Continued)

Model	(a) Without IPRs	(b) With IPRs	(c) With IPRs
IPRs* (precision and optical engineering)			−0.090 (−0.12)
IPRs* (food and kindred products)			0.909 (0.77)
IPRs* (other manufacturing)			0.103 (0.28)
Number of observations	111	111	111
Variance	1.054	1.049	1.028
−2 ln λ (all coefficients)	127.21	127.82	131.74

Goodness of fit matrices for the Tobit analysis:

	Frequency of occurrence	
	Data are censored	Data are uncensored
Model (a) without IPRs		
Tobit predicts that data are censored	9	2
Tobit predicts that data are uncensored	13	87
Model (b) with IPRs		
Tobit predicts that data are censored	9	2
Tobit predicts that data are uncensored	13	87
Model (c) with IPRs		
Tobit predicts that data are censored	10	1
Tobit predicts that data are uncensored	12	88

Notes: t-statistics are in parentheses; −2 ln λ (*all coefficients*) is the likelihood ratio test statistic with the null hypothesis that all coefficients (except the intercepts) are equal to zero. This test statistic is asymptotically χ^2-distributed.

Source: Author's calculations.

flows can better be explained with cultural distance—as expressed by the positive and significant coefficient on the language dummy—than by geographic proximity. The likelihood ratio test suggests that all variables significantly contribute to the explanation of German technology outflows. The goodness of fit matrices suggest that the Tobit estimates correctly predict data censoring and noncensoring for more than 86 percent of the 111 observations.[24]

In the second specification, the Park and Ginarte index is included in the gravity equation, but its effect is forced to be the same across all industries. The resulting coefficient is positive but statistically not significant. The nonsignificance can be attributed to the colinearity between the level of economic development as represented by GNP per capita and the level of IPR protection (the Pearsonian correlation coefficient between the two variables is 0.86). In the estimate of this second specification of the model without GNP per capita (not shown), the coefficient on the Park and Ginarte index turns statistically significant. Finally, in the third model specification, the IPR index is allowed to differ across the six industry categories. Except for precision and optical engineering, the corresponding coefficients are always positive but statistically significant only for chemicals and oil processing. This result is in accordance with numerous studies that found the importance of patents to be most critical in the chemical and pharmaceutical industries (see Fink 2000). Similar to the second model specification, more IPR coefficients turn statistically significant when GNP per capita is excluded from the gravity equation.

These results suggest a weakly positive relationship between IPRs and German receipts for patents, inventions, and processes.[25] Especially the chemical and oil processing industries were found to rely heavily on a country's patent system for their licensing decisions. However, one should be careful in interpreting this result. Increased payments for German technology may not necessarily mean that German firms actually transfer more technology to other countries. Stronger protection may put German firms in a better position to negotiate higher license fees. A third possibility is that stronger IPRs facilitate the use of intrafirm licensing arrangements for profit repatriation purposes.

VII. Summary of Main Findings

This study has investigated empirically the link between IPRs and TNC activity. The basic findings can be summarized as follows. For the United States, IPRs do not seem to play an important role in influencing total international transactions of U.S. firms. Only in chemicals and allied products and in electric and electronic equipment could a negative relationship be identified, but this link was not robust across the different model specifications. These conclusions were largely confirmed when the effect of IPR protection was evaluated on the individual modes of delivery—arm's-length exports and sales by affiliates. In the case of chemicals and allied products, the negative relationship could be confirmed for sales of affiliates, but again this relationship was not robust across the different model specifications. Arm's-length exports were consistently found to be unaffected by the degree of IPR protection in U.S. partner countries.

In view of the theoretical considerations outlined in the second section of this chapter, the absence of a link between the degree of intellectual property protection and U.S. international transactions may be attributed to two factors. Either positive and negative effects offset each other, or IPRs are simply not important enough to have a measurable effect on the aggregate data analyzed in this study. The latter possibility is supported by the fact that not all international transactions by U.S. and German firms are in knowledge-intensive goods.

The estimation results obtained for total German exports suggested that the strength of IPR protection has a positive influence on total German exports. This result is in accordance with previous empirical evidence on the IPR-trade link from Fink and Primo Braga (see chapter 2) and Maskus and Penubarti (1995). However, IPRs were found to be irrelevant in explaining the direct investment stock of German firms in foreign countries.

Finally, German receipts for patents, inventions, and processes were found to be positively related to the degree of IPR protection, especially in the chemical and oil processing industries, where firms make extensive use of patents to protect new products and technologies. Whether this positive link is attributable to more technology being transferred at arm's length, to higher royalties and license fees, or to increased use of the IPR system to repatriate profits remained an open question, however.

Appendix 4.A: Data

United States International Transactions

Local sales of U.S. affiliates and intrafirm exports to affiliates, both for 1992, in thousands of U.S. dollars, are from U.S. Bureau of Economic Analysis (1994). For a few countries, the only information available was that figures are below US$500,000. For these cases, a figure of US$250,000 was assumed when computing total U.S. international transactions. It should be noted, however, that these figures were negligible compared with total U.S. exports.

Total U.S. exports, also for 1992, in thousands of U.S. dollars, were extracted from the UN Comtrade database. The data in the UN Comtrade database are classified in Standard International Trade Classification (SITC) codes; to match the

Standard Industrial Classification (SIC) codes of the U.S. Department of Commerce, an SITC-SIC equivalence was used.

Data on 1992 GNP, GNP per capita, and surface area were taken from the World Bank STARS database. Gross national product is computed in U.S. dollars according to the Atlas method. A country's surface area is measured in square kilometers.

Data on geographic distance and common language were taken from Fink and Primo Braga (chapter 2). The economies that share a common language with the United States (and that are included in this study) are Australia, Canada, Hong Kong (China), India, Ireland, Jamaica, New Zealand, Nigeria, the Philippines, Singapore, South Africa, Trinidad and Tobago, and the United Kingdom.

Data on most-favored-nation tariff rates were taken from the Trade Analysis and Information System (TRAINS) database published by the United Nations Conference on Trade and Development (UNCTAD). The tariff rates were averaged across the different industry groups according to the SITC categories used to derive the trade data.

From the 57 economies for which the U.S. Department of Commerce reports data, the Bahamas, Barbados, Bermuda, China, the Netherlands Antilles, Taiwan (China), and the United Arab Emirates had to be excluded because no IPR rankings were available. Costa Rica, the Dominican Republic, Guatemala, Jamaica, Panama, and Switzerland had to be dropped because no tariff data were available. Furthermore, Belgium and Luxembourg had to be excluded because trade data were only reported for these two countries together. Because Belgium and Luxembourg have different IPR regimes, it was not possible to consolidate the two countries. The remaining 42 economies are Argentina, Australia, Austria, Brazil, Canada, Chile, Colombia, Denmark, Ecuador, the Arab Republic of Egypt, Finland, France, Germany, Greece, Honduras, Hong Kong (China), India, Indonesia, Ireland, Israel, Italy, Japan, the Republic of Korea, Malaysia, Mexico, the Netherlands, New Zealand, Nigeria, Norway, Peru, Philippines, Portugal, Saudi Arabia, Singapore, South Africa, Spain, Sweden, Thailand, Trinidad and Tobago, Turkey, United Kingdom, and the República Bolivariana de Venezuela.

For the probit analysis, the following 101 economies were used in addition to the 42 listed above: Algeria, Antigua and Barbuda, Armenia, Azerbaijan, Bahrain, Bangladesh, Belarus, Belize, Benin, Bolivia, Botswana, Bulgaria, Burkina Faso, Burundi, Cameroon, Cape Verde, the Central African Republic, Chad, Comoros, the Republic of Congo, Côte d'Ivoire, Cyprus, the Czech Republic, Dominica, El Salvador, Equatorial Guinea, Estonia, Ethiopia, Fiji, Gabon, The Gambia, Georgia, Ghana, Grenada, Guinea, Guinea-Bissau, Guyana, Haiti, Hungary, Iceland, the Islamic Republic of Iran, Jordan, Kazakhstan, Kenya, Kiribati, Kuwait, the Kyrgyz Republic, the Lao People's Democratic Republic, Latvia, Lesotho, Lithuania,

Madagascar, Malawi, Maldives, Mali, Malta, Mauritania, Mauritius, Moldova, Morocco, Mozambique, Namibia, Nepal, Nicaragua, Niger, Oman, Pakistan, Papua New Guinea, Paraguay, Poland, Puerto Rico, Qatar, Romania, the Russian Federation, Rwanda, São Tomé and Principe, Senegal, the Seychelles, Sierra Leone, the Slovak Republic, Solomon Islands, Sri Lanka, St. Kitts and Nevis, St. Lucia, St. Vincent and the Grenadines, Sudan, Suriname, Swaziland, Tajikistan, Tanzania, Togo, Tonga, Tunisia, Turkmenistan, Uganda, Ukraine, Uruguay, Uzbekistan, Vanuatu, Zambia, and Zimbabwe.

German Total Export and FDI Stocks

Stocks of 1992 German FDI in millions of DM are from Deutsche Bundesbank (1996a).

Data on 1992 total German exports, GNP, GNP per capita, geographic distance, language, and most-favored-nation tariffs are from the same sources described above for the U.S. data. It is worth noting that the tariff rate for Germany's co–European Union members was set to zero. The two countries that share a common language with Germany (and that are included in this study) are Austria and Switzerland.

From the 30 economies for which information on FDI stock is available, Hungary had to be excluded because no IPR ranking was available. Switzerland had to be excluded because no tariff data were available. Trade data were unavailable for the Czech Republic. Belgium and Luxembourg had to be excluded because trade data were only reported for these two countries together (as for the United States). The remaining 25 economies included in the estimation were Argentina, Austria, Brazil, Canada, Denmark, Finland, France, Greece, Hong Kong (China), India, Ireland, Italy, Japan, Republic of Korea, Malaysia, Mexico, the Netherlands, Norway, Portugal, Singapore, Spain, Sweden, Turkey, the United Kingdom, and the United States.

German Receipts for Patents, Inventions, and Processes

Data on 1992 German receipts for patents, inventions, and processes in millions of DM are from Deutsche Bundesbank (1996b).

Data on GNP, GNP per capita, geographic distance, and language are from the same sources described above.

From the 27 economies for which information on German receipts for patents, inventions, and processes is available, China and Taiwan (China) had to be excluded because no IPR ranking was available. The aggregate Belgium-Luxembourg had to be excluded because the two countries have different IPR regimes. The remaining 24 economies used for the estimation were Argentina, Australia, Austria, Brazil, Canada, Denmark, Finland, France, Greece, India, Ireland, Italy, Japan, the Republic of Korea, Mexico, the Netherlands, Portugal, Spain, Sweden, Switzerland, Thailand, Turkey, the United Kingdom, and the United States.

Notes

1. The negative market power effect is implicitly also present in Fink (2000) but is always dominated by the positive market expansion effect.

2. The United Nations (1996) estimates that about one-third of worldwide trade is intrafirm. The share of trade in intermediate goods is likely to be higher, however, because intermediate goods are also traded at arm's length.

3. Mansfield's first findings are largely confirmed by a second study (Mansfield 1995), which extends the survey to German and Japanese firms. Frischtak (1993) quotes additional survey evidence that identifies IPRs as a relevant variable for FDI decisions but also points out that other variables are more important than IPRs.

4. Lee and Mansfield's analysis can be criticized on two grounds. First, the survey-based measure of IPRs implicitly includes firms' perceptions about other factors influencing foreign investment and the transfer of technology, such as the presence of potential imitators. Second, Lee and Mansfield's sample selection is biased toward countries that have at least some technological capabilities and in which international disputes over IPRs are common. Thus, their findings may overstate the influence on FDI that can be directly attributed to the protection of intellectual property.

5. This definition of total international transactions ignores sales by U.S. overseas arm's-length licensees because there are no data available on the economic performance of U.S. licensees abroad. However, the empirical significance of licensing as a self-standing international strategy is small compared with the significance of exports and FDI (see Caves 1996). In addition, arm's-length exports are likely to exceed exports in final goods because they include trade in intermediate goods between independent firms.

6. The use of average tariff rates as the only measure of trade restrictiveness ignores the existence of nontariff barriers to trade in the form of quotas, subsidies, or differences in national regulatory regimes. Unfortunately, no broader measure of trade restrictiveness that would account for nontariff trade barriers could be found for the set of countries used in this study's empirical investigation. Anderson (1998) compiles a more comprehensive Trade Restrictiveness Index (TRI) for a smaller sample of industrial and developing countries and finds that average (trade-weighted) tariffs underestimate trade restrictiveness as measured by the "uniform tariff equivalent" (the inverse of the TRI minus one).

7. Most gravity estimations use population instead of GNP per capita as the explanatory variable. The explanatory power of either approach is the same. The reason for using GNP per capita in the present model specification is that one can isolate the colinearity between GNP per capita and the degree of IPR protection.

8. It would have been ideal to have an index for 1992 and to test whether the estimation results would have been different. A few countries reformed their IPR regimes in the early 1990s. It is not clear, however, whether these reforms would have affected 1992 international transactions because it takes time to establish the reformed systems' credibility.

9. It is not possible to use countries for which the U.S. Department of Commerce does not report data by assuming a value of zero for these observations because most of the reported remainder aggregates (such as "Other Europe") are positive.

10. Specifically, one might expect the probability of data availability to increase with the magnitude of a (potential) international transaction. Such a relationship would lead to a positive correlation of the likelihood of data availability with the error term of the gravity equation, because included and excluded explanatory variables of the probability of data availability and the magnitude of an international transaction partly coincide.

11. The enlarged set of countries had to be excluded because of data limitations in the independent variables, because the process determining data availability in the dependent variable may be different from the process determining data availability in the independent variables. For more information on the extended data set, see appendix 4.A.

12. For average tariff rates, some observations were equal to zero. In the case of the Park and Ginarte index, a nonlogarithmic specification was preferred because the colinearity between the IPR index and GNP per capita was smaller in the nonlogarithmic case. Estimates with a logarithmic IPR index led, of course, to different estimates, but qualitatively to the same conclusions as the ones presented with the nonlogarithmic specification.

13. See, for example, Maddala (1996) for a general treatment of bivariate distributed probit regressions.

14. Note that in equation 4.4 the conditional density of v_i given u_i is $u_i(\rho/\sigma) + \varepsilon_i$, where ε_i is (univariate) normally distributed with mean zero and variance $1 - \rho^2$.

15. This predictive power can be compared with the "naive" model in which the probability of being assigned to the "available" and "unavailable" categories are 38/139 and 101/139, respectively—reflecting the revealed information on data availability. The naive model would correctly predict data availability and unavailability for $(38/139)^2 + (101/139)^2 \approx 60\%$ of the 139 observations.

16. For some industry aggregates, maximum likelihood estimates could be obtained when some explanatory variables were dropped. In all such cases, the estimated correlation coefficient between the disturbance terms was found to be not significant based on likelihood ratio tests.

17. It should be noted that F-tests could not reject the null hypothesis that the coefficients on the pooled variables are the same across the four industry groups. For a description of the methodology for testing a set of linear hypotheses, see, for example, Johnston (1984), pp. 182–85.

18. The exact numbers of zero observations that were dropped are 16 for nonelectrical machinery, 6 for electric and electronic equipment, and 23 for transportation equipment. For electric and electronic equipment, one observation was reported as being below US$500,000 (see appendix 4.A). In principle, this censoring could have been addressed by a limited dependent variable model; however, because there was only one such incidence of censoring, this observation was simply dropped.

19. It is worth pointing out that F-tests could not reject the null hypothesis that the coefficients on the pooled variables are the same across the three industry groups for arm's-length exports, but they rejected the same hypothesis for sales by foreign affiliates (at the 5 percent level of significance). Therefore, the results with regard to the pooled regression on sales by affiliates should be treated with caution.

20. The *stock of FDI* is defined as the sum of past FDI flows minus the depreciation of capital assets.

21. OLS-based F-tests could not reject the null hypothesis that the coefficients on the pooled variables are the same across the four industry groups for both total exports and FDI stocks.

22. The definition of an intrafirm licensing relationship is not clear cut. The majority of foreign equity holdings of TNCs are in joint ventures with local partners or other TNCs. However, the equity stake of a TNC is often a poor indicator of a firm's control over a foreign affiliate (even though it is used to separate direct investment from portfolio investment). Contractor (1985) argues that the share of licensing flows that have an arm's-length character is considerably larger than commonly assumed.

23. In an OLS framework, F-tests could not reject the null hypothesis that the coefficients on pooled variables are the same across the six industry groups.

24. This result can be compared with the naive model, in which the probabilities of being assigned to the censored and uncensored categories are 22/111 and 89/111, respectively—reflecting the revealed censoring information in the dependent variable. The naive model would correctly predict data censoring and noncensoring for $(22/111)^2 + (89/111)^2 \approx 68\%$ of the 111 observations.

25. The power of the obtained results depends on how strongly other development-related effects influence German technology receipts. A country's level of economic development may be a good indicator for a country's level of technological development. In this view, one would expect that countries with a higher level of economic development demand relatively more (expensive) technologies. It could also be argued, however, that licensing is a preferred mode of delivery in less developed countries because of the higher risk associated with a direct investment position in those countries (such as the risk of expropriation).

References

Anderson, James E. 1998. "Trade Restrictiveness Benchmarks." *Economic Journal* 108:1111–25.

Caves, Richard E. 1996. *Multinational Enterprise and Economic Analysis*. 2nd ed. Cambridge: Cambridge University Press.

Contractor, Faruk J. 1985. "Licensing versus Foreign Direct Investment in U.S. Corporate Strategy: An Analysis of Aggregate U.S. Data." In Nathan Rosenberg and Claudio R. Frischtak, eds., *International Technology Transfer: Concepts, Measures, and Comparisons*. New York: Praeger.

Deutsche Bundesbank. 1996a. "Kapitalverflechtung mit dem Ausland." Statistische Sonderveröffentlichung 10. Frankfurt am Main, Germany.

———. 1996b. "Technologische Dienstleistungen in der Zahlungsbilanz." Statistische Sonderveröffentlichung 12. Frankfurt am Main, Germany.

Dunning, John H. 1979. "Explaining Changing Patterns of International Production: In Defence of the Eclectic Theory." *Oxford Bulletin of Economics and Statistics* 41:269–95.

———. 1981. "Explaining the International Direct Investment Position of Countries: Towards a Dynamic or Developmental Approach." *Weltwirtschaftliches Archiv*. 117:30–64.

Ferrantino, Michael J. 1993. "The Effect of Intellectual Property Rights on International Trade and Investment." *Weltwirtschaftliches Archiv* 129(2):300–31.

Fink, Carsten. 2000. *Intellectual Property Rights, Market Structure, and Transnational Corporations in Developing Countries*. Berlin: Mensch und Buch Verlag.

Frischtak, Claudio R. 1993. "Harmonization versus Differentiation in Intellectual Property Rights Regimes." In Mitchel B. Wallerstein, Mary E. Mogee, and Roberta A. Schoen, eds., *Global Dimensions of Intellectual Property Rights in Science and Technology*. Washington, D.C.: National Academy Press.

Grossman, Gene M., and Elhanan Helpman. 1991. *Innovation and Growth in the Global Economy*. Cambridge, Mass.: MIT Press.

Johnston, Jack. 1984. *Econometric Methods*. 3rd ed. New York: McGraw-Hill.

Lee, Jeong-Yeon, and Edwin Mansfield. 1996. "Intellectual Property Protection and U.S. Foreign Direct Investment." *Review of Economics and Statistics* 78(2):181–86.

Maddala, G. S. 1996. "Limited-Dependent and Qualitative Variables in Econometrics." Econometric Society Monograph 3. Cambridge University Press, Cambridge, U.K.

Mansfield, Edwin. 1986. "Patents and Innovation: An Empirical Study." *Management Science* 32(2):173–81.

———. 1994. "Intellectual Property Protection, Foreign Direct Investment, and Technology Transfer." IFC Discussion Paper 19. International Finance Corporation, Washington, D.C.

———. 1995. "Intellectual Property Protection, Direct Investment, and Technology Transfer: Germany, Japan, and the United States." IFC Discussion Paper 27. International Finance Corporation, Washington, D.C.

Maskus, Keith E., and Mohan Penubarti. 1993. "How Trade-Related Are Intellectual Property Rights?" University of Colorado at Boulder. Processed.

———. 1995. "How Trade-Related Are Intellectual Property Rights?" *Journal of International Economics* 39:227–48.

OECD (Organisation for Economic Co-operation and Development). 1997. *Main Science and Technology Indicators*. Paris.

Park, Walter G., and Juan C. Ginarte. 1997. "Determinants of Patent Rights: A Cross-National Study." *Research Policy* 26:283–301.

Rapp, Richard, and Richard Rozek. 1990. "Benefits and Costs of Intellectual Property Protection in Developing Countries." Working Paper 3. National Economic Research Associates, Washington, D.C.

United Nations. 1996. *World Investment Report 1996*. Geneva.

U. S. Bureau of Economic Analysis. 1994. *U.S. Direct Investment Abroad, Preliminary 1992 Estimates*. Washington, D.C.: U.S. Department of Commerce.

World Bank. 1998. *World Development Report 1998: Knowledge for Development*. New York: Oxford University Press.

INTELLECTUAL PROPERTY RIGHTS AND LICENSING: AN ECONOMETRIC INVESTIGATION

Guifang (Lynn) Yang and Keith E. Maskus

I. Introduction

How international differences in intellectual property rights (IPRs) affect decisions to license technology is an important question that has attracted virtually no econometric study. Licensing is a crucial component of international technology transfers, but we have little systematic evidence about whether it is much influenced by the strength of local patent regimes. In pushing for the recent introduction of global minimum standards in IPRs through the World Trade Organization, governments in technology-exporting nations argued that stronger IPRs would encourage technology transfer and local adaptive innovation, allowing all regions of the world to benefit. However, some developing countries argued that tighter protection would only strengthen the monopoly power of potential licenser firms, which are largely based in industrial countries, to the detriment of technology-importing nations.

As we discuss later, the theoretical links between IPRs and technology trade are numerous and depend on varying circumstances. No unambiguous analytical

This chapter is adapted from a March 2001 article in *Weltwirtschaftliches Archiv*, 137(1):58–79. It is a substantial revision of a chapter of Yang's doctoral dissertation at the University of Colorado at Boulder. We are grateful to James R. Markusen, Robert McNown, Thomas Rutherford, Marie Thursby, and an anonymous referee from *Weltwirtschaftliches Archiv* for valuable suggestions.

prediction may be made, making the issue inherently empirical. On the one hand, stronger IPRs reduce imitation risk faced by the licenser, reduce licensing cost, and increase the licenser's rent share. These effects increase economic returns to the licenser and raise its incentives to innovate and license. On the other hand, the licenser has more monopoly power, thanks to tighter protection, and its incentive to innovate and license is correspondingly reduced.

Licensing has attracted little attention in the empirical literature. Much of it focused on operations of foreign subsidiaries of U.S. multinational enterprises (MNEs). Ferrantino (1993) found little effect from IPRs, as measured by membership in international conventions, on overseas affiliate sales of U.S. firms to their various trade partners in 1982. Similarly, Maskus and Konan (1994) could not find any relationship between an index of patent rights and the international distribution of foreign direct investment (FDI). In contrast, Lee and Mansfield (1996) examined the relationship between business perceptions of the strength of a country's system of IPRs and the volume and composition of U.S. FDI in that country. They found that countries in which the IPR regimes were perceived to be weak tended to attract lower FDI volumes.[1]

Regarding arm's-length licensing, three earlier studies are relevant. Survey evidence in Mansfield (1994) indicated that U.S. MNEs were less likely to transfer advanced technologies to unaffiliated firms in countries with weak patent rights. In terms of econometric work, Contractor (1980) examined a sample of 102 contracts for technology licenses and showed that total returns on licensing were higher in patented technologies than in others. Ferrantino (1993) used 1982 cross-country data to show that membership in the Paris Convention, which stipulates that patents will be awarded to foreign applicants without discrimination, stimulated flows of U.S. receipts of unaffiliated royalties and license fees from the host country. However, this effect pertained only if the host country's domestic IPR regime was sufficiently strong, as measured by patent duration.

Licensing to unaffiliated firms is a significant activity. For example, U.S. receipts of unaffiliated royalties and license fees were 21 percent of the country's total royalties and license fees received from all the countries in the world in 1995. In 1996, royalties and license fees from unaffiliated foreigners increased by 9 percent, reflecting an increase in both fees for the use of industrial processes and for the right to sell products under a particular trademark, brand name, or signature (U.S. Department of Commerce [1998]).

Our purpose here is to investigate the influence of international variations in patent regimes on global flows of technology, both within MNEs and at arm's length. In comparison with earlier studies, we use more recent data, assembled for several countries and over time, and a more accurate measure of IPRs to investigate the link between patents and licensing. Numerous industrial and developing countries substantially strengthened their patent regimes between 1986 and 1995. We exploit this fact by developing a panel data set for the years 1985, 1990, and 1995 in 23 recipient nations to examine the effects of patent strength on the flow of unaffiliated royalties and license fees by U.S. firms in both absolute and relative terms.

We begin in the next section by describing a theoretical model that analyzes the role of IPRs in encouraging licensing. The essential point is that licensing could rise or fall with the imposition of stronger IPRs. Given this ambiguity, we go on in the third section to specify an econometric model of technology contracting. Data are discussed in the fourth section, while the fifth section presents the empirical results on licensing. The key findings are as follows: First, stronger patent laws have positive and significant effects on both the absolute flows and the relative flows (relative to trade volume) of U.S. receipts of unaffiliated royalties and license fees when the initial degree of patent protection in the technology recipient country is higher than a critical value. Second, the results indicate that patent rights are more important in promoting arm's-length technology trade relative to licensing through FDI. Concluding remarks are provided in the final section.

II. Intellectual Property and Licensing

In principle, IPRs play an important role in technology trade. Patent protection is perhaps the most important means of safeguarding proprietary technology. Patent laws vary markedly across countries in terms of coverage, membership in international agreements, loss of protection, enforcement mechanisms, and duration (Primo Braga 1996). These differences in patent laws in host countries might influence licensing through several channels.

First, the degree of IPR protection could influence the decision to earn returns on a new technology by licensing it rather than exporting it through trade in products. Tighter patent protection should reduce imitation risk, uncertainty, and transaction costs involved in technology contracts, thereby encouraging licensing relative to commodity trade.

Second, the degree of IPR protection could influence the choice the firm makes between licensing and FDI (Horstmann and Markusen 1987). Strong IPRs could favor licensing by creating a legal framework for the enforcement of licensing and royalty contracts. In the presence of weak patents, problems of transacting information with licensing, such as the nonexcludability property of new knowledge, informational asymmetry, imitation risk, and transfer costs, could provide an internalization motive for FDI (Markusen 1995).[2] Among these problems in licensing, Rugman (1986), in particular, views imitation risk faced by the firm from licensees as a cornerstone of internalization theory. If IPRs are weak in the host country, the licensee could learn the technology quickly and imitate it to start a new domestic firm in competition with the MNE. In response, the MNE might exploit its firm-specific assets through internalization (Markusen 2001; Taylor 1994). Seen in this light, stronger patents reduce the imitation risk faced by the multinational firm and create a legal framework for the enforcement of licensing contracts, thereby encouraging licensing. Stronger patents also favor licensing because they reduce the legal costs associated with establishing and policing an arm's-length relationship.

Third, the strength of IPRs affects the sharing of rents between the licenser and licensee. Rent sharing is one of the salient features commonly observed in licensing contracts. Caves, Crookell, and Killing (1983) indicated that licensers earned, on average, 40 percent of the rents from innovation. One important strategic factor is that license rents are used by the licenser to deter imitation. Stronger patent protection makes it harder for the licensee to imitate, causing it to commit not to imitate at a lower rent share. But to preclude imitation, lax IPRs require higher rents for the licensee. Gallini and Wright (1990) showed that when imitation is possible and there is asymmetric information, the licenser sacrifices some rents though its share rises with imitation costs. Accordingly, the rent share accruing to the licenser rises with patent strength, raising the returns to licensing.

These effects suggest that unaffiliated licensing should rise as countries strengthen their patent regimes because of lower licensing cost and higher rent share. We call this possibility the *economic returns effect*. However, the ability to license depends on the pace at which new innovations are introduced by potential licensers. It is conceivable in theory that long-run innovation could slow down because the monopoly effect of stronger patents would reduce research and development (R&D) effort.[3] In turn, licensing could be reduced. We call this possibility the *monopoly power effect*.

These ideas have been formalized in a dynamic general equilibrium model with endogenous innovation and licensing to study the effects of stronger IPRs in the south on the incentives of firms in the north to innovate and to license advanced technologies (Yang and Maskus 2001). We present an overview of the model and its predictions here in order to motivate the current empirical work. This model was set up to capture the economic returns effect on licensing of stronger IPR protection.

In our model, innovation and licensing are random processes requiring resources. The northern innovative firm first chooses the intensity of effort it devotes to innovation. When the innovation is successful, it chooses whether to license. The advantage of licensing technology to the south is higher instantaneous profits caused by the lower wages there. However, licensing incurs costs, including those involved in negotiating contracts and in performing various activities to ensure the transfer of the necessary technology and know-how. Furthermore, the licenser has to give up some rents to the licensee in order to deter imitation. Therefore, the northern firm needs to strike a balance between saving labor costs, sacrificing rents, and incurring licensing-transfer costs.

The model results show that innovation and licensing decisions depend on labor endowments in both the north and the south, the cost of innovation in the north, the cost of licensing, and the rent share between the licenser and the licensee. Let n represent the extent of licensing, I the intensity of innovation, L_N the labor endowment in the technology-exporting country, L_S the labor endowment in the technology recipient country, and a_I the cost of innovation. The variable $a_L(\kappa,G)$ captures the cost of licensing, which depends negatively on κ, the strength of patent rights. It further depends on other factors, given by G, that determine the cost of licensing for a certain level of patent protection. The variable $\delta(\kappa,C)$ is the share of contract rents accruing to the licenser. This share depends positively on κ but is also a function of other factors, given by C, that determine the cost of imitation for a given level of patent rights. With this framework, we may express the innovation and licensing functions in steady-state equilibrium as follows:

(5.1) $$I = f(L_N,L_S,a_I,a_L(\kappa,G),\delta(\kappa,C))$$

(5.2) $$n = f(L_N,L_S,a_I,a_L(\kappa,G),\delta(\kappa,C))$$

As may be seen from equations 5.1 and 5.2, the degree of IPR protection determines not only the total economic returns from licensing but also their distribution between the two parties. We argue that stronger IPRs in the south both would reduce the imitation risk faced by innovative northern firms and would create an improved legal framework for the enforcement of licensing contracts. The risk reduction would permit the licenser to deter imitation by giving up a smaller share of the licensing rents to the licensee (larger δ). The legal certainty would lower the costs associated with establishing and policing arm's-length licensing relationships and, therefore, would increase the economic returns to licensing. In the model, both factors would combine to generate a higher rate of innovation in the north and a higher rate of technology licensing. Licensing would be encouraged in order to take advantage of lower labor costs in the south.

The effect of changes in the northern labor force on licensing is theoretically ambiguous. On one hand, a larger northern resource base would permit more resources to be deployed in R&D, generating higher rates of innovation and licensing. On the other hand, the additional resources could be allocated to production of goods in the innovator's home country, which could reduce transfer of production to the south. The effect of changes in the southern labor force on licensing is indeterminate also. With an expansion of the southern labor supply, the profit rate enjoyed by innovators would be higher because of the lower wage, generating more licensing. However, a larger labor force in the south permits greater learning by the south and a greater intensity of imitation, which would produce a lower rent share to the innovator and less licensing.

The extent of licensing would decline with increases in both the costs of innovation and the costs of licensing. However, licensing activity would go up with an increase in the licenser's rent share. Other factors in the cost vectors G and C are important as well. For example, given the level of IPR protection, the cost of licensing would depend negatively on the level of economic development and human capital abundance in technology-importing countries. However, the licenser's rent share would depend negatively on the efficiency of local imitation because a greater imitative threat would force the licenser to sacrifice higher profits.

III. An Empirical Model of Licensing

We now test our theoretical predictions about the effects of IPRs on licensing. In principle, a fully specified approach would use the structural forms of equations 5.1 and 5.2 to estimate the parameters.[4] However, it is difficult to find data on innovation cost and imitation cost. Thus, structural estimation is not feasible here.

Instead, on the basis of the theoretical predictions, we specify a reduced-form regression of equation 5.2 to study the effects of IPRs on the flow of licensing. We use various measures of the volume of licensing from the United States to its technology trade partners as dependent variables. It would be ideal to regress the flow of licensing from different technology-exporting countries to recipient countries on relevant characteristics of both the recipient and home countries, including an index of IPRs and endowments of both nations. However, figures on licensing to different destinations are not readily available for countries other than the United States. We do not regard this limitation to be serious because the United States is the world's largest supplier of technology licenses. Further, there is no a priori reason to believe that U.S. firms' overseas licensing practices are different from the typical worldwide pattern of technology suppliers. However, since the origin of technology licensing is the same in all cases, we must drop the origin country's characteristics in the regressions.

We use the volume of U.S. firms' receipts of royalties and license fees from unaffiliated foreigners to represent the flow of licensing in our primary specification. Any increase in these receipts could be caused by two factors. First, there could be more firms that license their technology, and second, given the number of licensing contracts, each firm could get a higher share of royalties and license fees. Unfortunately, we are unable to discriminate in the data between changes in rent share and changes in the number of contracts and must defer this question to future work.

For comparative purposes, we analyze two other licensing measures. First, we include the total volume of unaffiliated license fees for using industrial processes. It seems likely that industrial processes reflect transfers of proprietary technologies and should be captured by the features of our model. Second, we incorporate the volume of fees earned from affiliated enterprises. Because those transactions exist within MNEs, they should be less sensitive to variations in patent rights across nations. In addition, we include as a dependent variable the ratio of the volume of unaffiliated license fees to trade volume between the United States and the bilateral partner. This relative measure permits us to investigate the empirical tradeoff between technology trade and exports.

Regarding the independent variables in the regression, the legal strength of IPRs in the licensee country is our main focus. We use an index of patent strength developed by Ginarte and Park (1997), discussed further below. Because our theoretical model shows that the relationship between patent strength and licensing is nonlinear, we include the squared term of this index in the regressions. If the net effect of IPRs on licensing is positive, there is evidence that the economic returns effect dominates the monopoly power effect.

A human capital measure, defined as the ratio of skilled labor in the total labor force, is included to capture the efficiency of local imitation and the potential for the country to adopt and improve the new technology. The effect of this skilled-labor endowment on licensing is theoretically ambiguous. On one hand, a high human capital abundance means that local imitation is efficient and less costly. This imitation effect discourages licensing activity. On the other hand, a high human capital abundance indicates that local workers are more capable of adapting and improving the technology, thereby implying less training and licensing cost for the innovator. This cost effect encourages licensing activity. The net effect of human capital abundance on licensing depends on which effect is larger.

The total labor endowment in the licensee nation is another regressor. A larger labor force in the technology-importing country, other things equal, implies that the local relative wage is initially low and attracts licensing for production. Per capita real gross domestic product (GDP) in the recipient country is used to control both for local demand characteristics and for licensing costs of the recipient country beyond those captured by the skilled-labor endowment. It is reasonable to assume that the institutional and legal framework for licensing is more complete in a country with higher per capita income. Finally, we include an index of openness as another control variable because technology trade cannot readily be isolated from trade policies on goods and investment.

There are country-specific aspects of technology trade, such as persistent differences in institutions, culture, and tastes, which may not be captured by the included independent variables. Ignoring these country-specific effects in the regression would create omitted variables bias and inconsistent estimators. Thus, we use a panel data approach in this chapter, using country fixed effects and random effects in alternative specifications.

Collecting these ideas, the econometric model is specified as follows:

$$y_{it} = \alpha + \beta_1 IPRS_{it} + \beta_2 IPRSSQ_{it} + \beta_3 OPEN_{it} + \beta_4 TOTLAB_{it}$$

(5.3) $$+ \beta_5 GDP_{it} + \beta_6 SKILLR_{it} + u_{it}$$

(5.4) $$u_{it} = \mu_i + v_{it}$$

Here, y_{it} is the volume of U.S. licensing receipts from country i. We employ four separate measures of receipts—unaffiliated royalties and license fees, unaffiliated fees for using industrial processes, receipts of affiliated royalties and license fees, and the ratio of unaffiliated license fees to U.S. exports—depending on the specific regression. Unaffiliated fees for using industrial processes form the largest portion of total unaffiliated fees. Because the focus here is to investigate the link between the degree of patent protection and the flow of licensing in production of goods, unaffiliated fees for using industrial processes likely are the most relevant dependent variable.

The variable *IPRS* is the index of patent laws in the recipient country and *IPRSSQ* is this index squared. Therefore the marginal effect of intellectual property rights on licensing is

(5.5) $$\frac{\partial y_{it}}{\partial IPRS} = \beta_1 + 2\beta_2 IPRS$$

OPEN is the dummy variable indicating whether the licensee country is judged to be open to trade and investment. *TOTLAB* is the total labor endowment, *GDP* is real GDP per capita in 1990 U.S. dollars, and *SKILLR* is the ratio of skilled labor to total labor. The error component μ_i denotes the unobservable country-specific institutional and cultural factors that affect licensing. The component v_{it} reflects the remaining disturbance.

IV. Data Sources

The data were taken from various sources. The volumes of U.S. receipts of unaffiliated and affiliated royalties and license fees came from various monthly issues of *Survey of Current Business* published by the U.S. Department of Commerce in the years 1988, 1993, and 1998. Royalties and license fees consist of receipts for the use of patented techniques, processes, formulas, and other intangible property rights used in production of goods; for transactions involving copyrights, trademarks, broadcast rights, and other intangible rights; and for the rights to sell products under a particular trademark, brand name, or signature. Whereas affiliated royalties and license fees are from the multinational firm's foreign subsidiaries, unaffiliated royalties and license fees are from arm's-length licensing with unrelated foreigners.

A firm with a significant new product may engage in licensing agreements with foreigners that cover patents, trademarks, technical assistance, and other matters. Licensing agreements typically call for the licensee to pay a certain percentage of its sales to the licenser, plus a flat fee for technical help in some cases. Ownership of property rights is retained by the licenser. Licenses give permission to do something that would otherwise be an infringement of the property rights.

Affiliated royalties and license fees in the data were restricted to subsidiaries that were majority owned by direct investors. Thus, information on licensing transactions with minority-owned affiliates was unavailable. However, this factor is not restrictive because the data indicated that most U.S. firms had either no equity holding or at least a majority interest in licensed subsidiaries. Regarding unaffiliated fees, data for 1986 were the earliest available that were reliable and comparable to later figures. Because receipts of unaffiliated and affiliated royalties and license fees were reported in nominal U.S. dollars, we deflated them by the U.S. GDP deflator to get the real volumes of license fees in millions of 1990 U.S. dollars.

The index of patent strength in different countries in 1985 and 1990 came from Ginarte and Park (1997), and the 1995 index was provided separately by one of those authors.[5] Their index was constructed from information about the structure of national patent laws. It takes on values between zero and five, with higher numbers reflecting stronger levels of protection. The index consists of five categories: coverage of fields of technology, membership in international patent agreements, provisions of loss of protection, enforcement mechanisms, and duration. Each category takes on a value between zero and one. The sum of these five values gives the overall value of the patent index for each country.

Because this index incorporates broader categories of the patent system, particularly in the treatment of foreigners, it is more comprehensive and accurate than the dummy variable approach used by Ferrantino (1993). Moreover, the index exhibits greater variability across countries and is likely to support more precise estimation. However, the patent index remains subject to measurement error because there are surely gaps between the measured and actual levels of patent protection. Further, there is possible correlation between the patent index and broader country-specific effects, because each country's regime of intellectual property protection is inextricably bound up with its entire legal and social system and its attitude toward private property. We account for this possible correlation in our estimation. A final comment about the index is that the strength of patent laws across countries is highly correlated with the strength of trademark and copyright laws (Rapp and Rozek 1990). Accordingly, the patent index should be an acceptable measure of IPRs to include as a determinant of royalties and license fees, which include fees for using copyright and trademark rights in addition to patent rights.

The openness index was from Sachs and Warner (1995). They considered a country to have a closed trade policy if it had at least one of the following categories: First, nontariff barriers covered 40 percent or more of import categories. Second, average tariff rates were at least 40 percent. Third, the black-market exchange rate premium was 20 percent or more relative to the official exchange rate on average. Fourth, there was a socialist economic system. Fifth, a state monopoly existed on major exports. An *open economy* was defined as one in which none of the five conditions applied.

Per capita real GDP of recipient nations was taken from International Monetary Fund (1997). Annual real GDP figures in local-currency terms were converted into millions of U.S. dollars using 1990 exchange rates. Total labor force (measured in thousands) was from various issues of International Labour Organization, *Yearbook of Labor Statistics*. The same source provided figures on employment of skilled labor, defined as workers in managerial, scientific, and technical occupations. U.S. exports to different countries were compiled from various issues of the United Nations' *International Trade Statistics Yearbook*. They were converted to millions of 1990 U.S. dollars.

Using those definitions, a panel data set was constructed for 23 countries for 1985, 1990, and 1995. Table 5.1 presents summary statistics for the 23 countries and three years in the data.

In table 5.1, *UNFEE* is the volume of U.S. receipts of unaffiliated royalties and license fees, *PROCESS* is the volume of unaffiliated fees for using industrial processes, and *AFEE* is the volume of receipts of affiliated royalties and license fees. The index of *IPRS* is strongly and positively correlated with per capita real GDP.

V. Estimation Results

Results of the pooled ordinary least squares (OLS) regression are listed in the first four columns of table 5.2. As mentioned earlier, unaffiliated license fees and royalties (*UNFEE*), unaffiliated fees for using industrial processes (*PROCESS*), affiliated

TABLE 5.1   Summary Statistics and Correlation Coefficients (NT = 69)

Summary statistics	Mean	Standard deviation	Minimum	Maximum
UNFEE	117.94	262.67	2.34	1,686.09
PROCESS	85.04	219.01	1.52	1,350.43
AFEE	399.63	605.01	2.56	3,035.65
UNFEE/EXP	.0099	.0087	.0011	.0504
IPRS	3.18	0.90	0.33	4.24
OPEN	0.87	0.34	0.00	1.00
TOTLAB	18,236	20,555	1,235.0	79,663
GDP	13,330	9,431.8	476.10	34,039
SKILLR	18.72	10.19	3.78	48.56

Correlation coefficients	IPRS	OPEN	TOTLAB	GDP	SKILLR
IPRS	1.00	0.26	−0.35	0.63	0.36
OPEN		1.00	−0.06	0.36	0.09
TOTLAB			1.00	−0.27	−0.38
GDP				1.00	0.60
SKILLR					1.00

Note: The number of observations is 69.
Source: Authors' calculations.

license fees and royalties (*AFEE*), and unaffiliated license fees and royalties relative to trade volume (*UNFEE/EXPORTS*) are the dependent variables in the four regressions, respectively. The coefficient of IPRS is insignificantly negative, but its squared term (*IPRSSQ*) is significantly positive at the 10 percent level in all four regressions. The total labor endowment has a positively significant effect at the 1 percent level in all regressions, and the coefficient of per capita real GDP is significantly positive for both unaffiliated and affiliated license fees and royalties at the 10 percent level.

The next four columns provide estimation with fixed country effects. The row labeled $F_{(22,40)}$ reports tests of the hypothesis, maintained in the OLS regressions, that all constant terms are equal across countries. In all four regressions, the hypothesis that the country-specific fixed effects are the same is rejected at the 1 percent significance level. Therefore, the pooled OLS approach is inappropriate and the OLS estimates are inconsistent. We first assume that the individual country effects are fixed in nature, so that differences across units may be captured by

TABLE 5.2   Estimation of Determinants of Licensing Volumes

	Pooled				Fixed effects				Random effects			
	UNFEE	PROCESS	AFEE	UNFEE/EXPORTS	UNFEE	PROCESS	AFEE	UNFEE/EXPSORTS	UNFEE	PROCESS	AFEE	UNFEE/EXPORTS
CONS	−219.07 (−1.40)	−161.23 (−1.21)	−665.98*** (−1.84)	0.0003 (0.05)					−278.48*** (−1.92)	−189.46 (−1.57)	−825.21** (−2.07)	0.005 (0.88)
IPRS	−43.60 (−0.50)	−43.74 (−0.59)	−105.37 (−0.52)	−0.0009 (−0.30)	−157.05* (−2.78)	−119.85** (−2.55)	−345.49** (−1.95)	−0.0034 (−1.13)	−119.3** (−2.53)	−97.9** (−2.53)	−177.42 (−1.18)	−0.002 (−0.81)
IPRSSQ	28.64*** (1.77)	25.52** (1.85)	64.03*** (1.71)	0.001*** (1.89)	37.86* (1.96)	28.02*** (1.74)	67.47 (1.11)	0.0025** (2.40)	36.93* (2.49)	29.00** (2.36)	66.14 (1.56)	0.0016** (2.46)
OPEN	5.07 (0.07)	−2.33 (−0.04)	149.58 (0.83)	−0.003 (−1.22)	−21.74 (−0.47)	−21.10 (−0.55)	−12.18 (−0.08)	−0.004 (−1.57)	−16.09 (−0.39)	−18.54 (−0.55)	11.7 (0.09)	−0.003 (−1.60)
TOTLAB	0.007* (5.55)	0.006* (5.15)	0.015* (4.88)	0.00* (2.86)	0.02* (3.24)	0.014** (2.66)	0.06* (3.02)	0.000 (0.11)	0.01* (3.99)	0.008* (3.56)	0.02* (3.38)	0.000 (0.95)
GDP	0.007*** (1.73)	0.006 (1.58)	0.017*** (1.75)	0.000 (1.63)	0.02** (2.51)	0.019** (2.35)	0.09* (3.06)	0.000 (0.22)	0.02* (2.75)	0.014** (2.60)	0.05* (2.68)	0.000 (1.12)

SKILLR	-3.21	-3.32*	5.31	-0.0001	-1.32	-1.72	5.17	-0.0009*	-2.61	-2.59	1.98	-0.0005**
	(-1.03)	(-1.24)	0.73	(-0.76)	(-0.25)	(-0.39)	(0.31)	(-3.17)	(-0.63)	(-0.75)	(0.16)	(-2.61)
R-square F(22,40)	0.48	0.46	0.48	0.41	0.93 10.93	0.93 12.79	0.86 5.07	0.81 3.78	0.39	0.35	0.33	0.29
LM test									35.62	38.61	13.15	9.19
W test									4.98	3.06	11.07	5.93
Turning point					2.07	2.14	2.56	0.68	1.62	1.69	1.34	0.63
Elasticity					2.26	2.18	2.67	3.97	3.12	3.24	1.94	2.68

Note: Figures in parentheses are *t*-values. Significance levels are indicated by * (1 percent), ** (5 percent), and *** (10 percent) for two-tailed tests. Coefficient estimates for country dummies are not reported here because of limited space, but they are available upon request.

Source: Authors' calculations.

specific intercepts.[6] Thus, in equation 5.4 each μ is an unknown parameter to be estimated. The remaining error term v_{it} follows standard assumptions.

In the fixed-effects estimation, *IPRS* has a negatively significant effect at the 1 percent level, and its squared term has a positively significant effect at the 10 percent level on receipts of unaffiliated royalties and license fees. The net effect of the degree of patent protection on unaffiliated license fees depends on the initial level of patent protection. If we use equation 5.5, it is straightforward to compute that the net marginal effect becomes positive where the degree of patent protection achieves the critical level of 2.07, as shown in the penultimate row of table 5.2.

This result is intriguing and may be explained as follows. Consider a country where patent protection is initially weak. It is likely that this nation has a limited skilled-labor endowment and, therefore, represents only a slight risk of imitation. Tightening its patent law would reduce this risk somewhat and, in turn, incrementally lower licensing costs and raise the licenser's rent share. However, the stronger patent rights also would generate stronger monopoly power on the part of licensers. In this case, the monopoly power effect would dominate the economic returns effect. In consequence, the licenser would exploit more market power and would have less incentive to license new technology to the market in question. This outcome is consistent with the result in Smith (1999), in which the market power effect in international trade dominated for countries with low incomes and weak patent rights.[7] However, in countries where patent protection is already sufficiently strong, the economic returns effect would outweigh the monopoly power effect, and tighter patent protection would induce more licensing activity.

Note from appendix 5.A that the patent index was less than 2.07 for only a few countries in 1985 and 1990, and was greater than 2.07 in 1995 for all countries in our sample. This finding implies that the U.S. licensing volume to almost every country in our sample would increase in response to tighter patent protection. The implied elasticity of unaffiliated royalties and license fees to the change in the degree of IPR protection at the mean patent index is 2.26. Thus, U.S. real receipts of unaffiliated royalties and license fees would increase by 2.26 percent in response to a 1 percent rise in the recipient country's patent index.

Patent rights also positively affect fees for using industrial processes for almost all countries in our sample, with an elasticity of 2.18. Again, there is a quadratic relationship with a turning point in the patent index of 2.56. However, the marginal effect of *IPRS* on receipts of affiliated royalties and license fees is not straightforward, because the linear term has a negatively significant effect and its squared term has a positively insignificant effect. This result may suggest that, because imitation risk faced by affiliated licensing is lower than that for unaffiliated licensing, the monopoly power effect is more dominant in the former case. Thus, there is evidence that stronger IPRs favor unaffiliated licensing in relation to affiliated technology transfers by virtue of providing a legal system for enforcing licensing contracts.

Finally, the effect on the ratio of unaffiliated license fees and royalties to trade volume is strongly positive. In this case, the linear term is insignificant but the quadratic term is significant, suggesting that the substitution away from exports into licensing holds at all initial levels of protection. Indeed, the estimated turning point of the relationship is 0.68, well below the patent indexes in the sample. Moreover, the high estimated elasticity of 3.97 suggests that arm's-length licensing is quite responsive to stronger patents in relation to exports.

Real GDP per capita has a positively significant effect on unaffiliated license fees, fees for industrial process, and affiliated license fees. However, the effect on relative license fees is insignificant. Thus, licensing itself is attracted by higher levels of economic development, given that the institutional and legal framework for licensing is likely to be more complete. When we control for patent rights, however, increases in per capita income have balanced effects on licensing and trade. The coefficient on the dummy variable for openness has a negative sign but is not significant. The coefficient on total labor force is positively significant in all regressions except for the relative unaffiliated licensing receipts. A greater labor endowment means a higher supply of labor, suggesting that the initial wage rate would be lower and would thereby induce additional licensing for production. Furthermore, when licensing increases the demand for labor, follow-on wage increases are likely to be smaller with a larger labor supply. The positive coefficient on labor force may also reflect the influence of larger market size on licensing activity.

The coefficient on the ratio of skilled labor to total labor is negative but insignificant for unaffiliated licensing volumes (*UNFEE* and *PROCESS*), is negatively significant for relative unaffiliated licensing volumes, and is positive but insignificant for affiliated licensing (*AFEE*). As discussed in the third section, in principle there are offsetting effects of human capital abundance on technology trade. The imitation cost effect is negative, and the licensing cost effect is positive. It seems that the first effect dominates in unaffiliated licensing, particularly in relation to exports, because of the higher imitation risk under unaffiliated licensing. However, under FDI, the firm can exploit its firm-specific assets by internalization. Even if it faces imitation risk through having workers hired away, the imitation risk is smaller, and the second effect may dominate. Therefore, the signs on the coefficients of the skilled-labor ratio are reasonable, if imprecisely estimated.

We next consider a random-effects specification, in which the individual error terms are randomly distributed across cross-sectional units. In this case, in equation 5.4, μ_i is the random disturbance characterizing nation i and is constant over time. Assume that $E(\mu_i) = E(v_i) = 0$, $E(\mu_i^2) = \sigma_\mu^2$, $E(v_{it}^2) = \sigma_v^2$, $E(\mu_j v_{it}) = 0$ for all i, j, and t, $E(\mu_j \mu_i) = 0$ for $i \neq j$, and $E(v_{it} v_{js}) = 0$ for $i \neq j$ or $t \neq s$. Because σ_μ^2 and σ_v^2 are unknown, we first estimate the disturbance variances and then follow the feasible generalized least squares (GLS) procedure.

The random-effects estimation results are presented in the final four columns of table 5.2. Under this specification, the strength of patent laws continues to have positively significant effects on unaffiliated royalties, on unaffiliated industrial process fees, and on relative unaffiliated royalties at the 5 percent level. Its effect on affiliated royalties and license fees is insignificant. These results are similar to those from the fixed-effects model, but the elasticity of licensing royalties in response to patent protection is larger for the absolute unaffiliated royalties (3.12 for *UNFEE* and 3.24 for *PROCESS*) and lower for relative unaffiliated royalties (2.68). Per capita real GDP and total labor endowment continue to have positively significant effects on licensing, consistent with the results in the fixed-effects model.

We use the Lagrange multiplier (LM) test for the presence of random effects. Under the null hypothesis that no random effects exist, LM is distributed as chi squared with one degree of freedom. The LM ratios are presented at the bottom of table 5.2. The 1 percent critical value from the chi-squared distribution with one degree of freedom is 6.64. Therefore, we can reject the null hypothesis, and the evidence favors the presence of random effects.

In the model with random effects, the key assumption is that the country-specific effects are uncorrelated with the exogenous variables included in the model. If they are correlated, the random-effects estimator may suffer from inconsistency attributable to omitted variables. Such correlation is likely in the present case. For example, the index of IPRs is likely correlated with the individual effects caused by institutional and cultural factors. Therefore, we need to test for the orthogonality of the random effects and the regressors before we can rely on the estimation results. We use the specification test devised by Hausman (1978), under the hypothesis of no correlation. The test is based on the Wald criterion and is asymptotically distributed as chi squared with K degrees of freedom, where K is the number of regressors excluding the intercept. The calculated test statistics, labeled W, are presented in table 5.2. The 10 percent critical value is 12.59. Thus, we cannot reject the hypothesis that there is no correlation between the country-specific random effects and the included regressors. The GLS estimation with the random effects is permissible.

The issue to decide is which model, fixed effects or random effects, is more reliable in this case. The disadvantage of the random-effects model is that we must assume that there is no correlation between those effects and other regressors in order to avoid inconsistency. The fixed-effects specification does not suffer from this problem, but it does use up many degrees of freedom in estimating country-specific coefficients.

Although both approaches are permissible here, we argue that the specification of the fixed-effects model is better, given the sample and the problem we have at hand. First, the fixed-effects model is a reasonable approach when we can be confident that the differences between units may be viewed as parameter shifts of the regression function. Our sample of 23 economies covers the most important licensing partners of the United States, and therefore, it seems appropriate to specify that differences across units are captured in differences in the constant term. Second, even if we cannot reject the hypothesis that there is no correlation between the individual effects and other regressors in the random-effects model, the power of the Hausman test is often low.

Furthermore, from a practical point of view, if there is heteroskedasticity of unknown forms, estimation becomes more complicated in the random-effects model because it is difficult to know whether there is heteroskedasticity in the specific effects (μ_i), the remainder error term (ν_{it}), or both. Even if we could tell which error term has heteroskedasticity, we must find consistent estimators of each country's error variances to perform GLS. The conventional method is to divide the summation of OLS squared residuals across time periods for each country by ($T-1$) to get an estimator of the error variance. However, since we have a sample of only three periods, we doubt that this estimator would be accurate.

In the fixed-effects model, we may avoid this problem and still make appropriate inferences, without specifying the type of heteroskedasticity, by using the White estimator of the variance-covariance matrix of the coefficient estimators. The corrected t-ratios are presented in table 5.3 and suggest that the positive effect of *IPRS* is more precisely estimated. Note that the squared patent index now asserts a positively significant effect on affiliated royalties at the 10 percent level. The index for openness also becomes marginally significant in explaining the ratio of unaffiliated royalties to trade volume, which suggests that an open economy will attract relatively more exports from other countries and less licensing in the production of goods.

VI. Concluding Remarks

In this chapter, we undertook an initial investigation of how international variations in the strength of patent laws affect flows of international technology trade through licensing volumes, using data on U.S. receipts for intellectual property from foreign unaffiliated firms and U.S. affiliates overseas. The principal findings

TABLE 5.3.   Fixed-Effects Model with Heteroskedasticity-Consistent Standard Errors

	UNFEE	PROCESS	AFEE	UNFEE/EXPORTS
IPRS	−157.05**	−119.85**	−345.49**	−0.0034
	(−2.58)	(−2.42)	(−2.37)	(−1.24)
IPRSSQ	37.86**	28.02**	67.47***	0.0025**
	(2.53)	(2.19)	(1.68)	(2.44)
OPEN	−21.74	−21.10	−12.18	−0.004***
	(−1.24)	(−1.52)	(−0.20)	(−1.84)
TOTLAB	0.02*	0.014**	0.06*	0.000
	(2.77)	(2.29)	(2.94)	(0.11)
GDP	0.02*	0.019**	0.09*	0.000
	(2.72)	(2.58)	(3.34)	(0.22)
SKILLR	−1.32	−1.72	5.17	−0.0009**
	(−0.48)	(−0.75)	(0.63)	(−2.11)

Note: Figures in parentheses are *t*-values. Significance levels are indicated by * (1 percent),
** (5 percent), and *** (10 percent) for two-tailed tests.
Source: Authors' calculations.

are as follows: First, U.S. receipts of unaffiliated royalties and license fees rise with stronger IPRs in the technology recipient country when the degree of initial patent protection is higher than a critical value. Second, the ratio of U.S. receipts of unaffiliated royalties and license fees to U.S. exports is also higher with stronger IPR protection. The elasticity of this relative volume is higher than that for the absolute volume, indicating that patent rights are more important in promoting arm's-length technology trade. Third, IPRs have less significant effects on U.S. receipts of affiliated royalties and license fees, which is consistent with the internalization theory of MNEs. This finding is different from the results in Ferrantino (1993). Fourth, U.S. receipts of both affiliated and unaffiliated royalties and license fees are higher if the technology recipient country has a higher per capita GDP level and has a greater labor endowment. Finally, there is weak evidence that openness to trade encourages export trade in relation to licensing.

Although stronger patent rights induce greater dollar volumes of licensing, it is impossible on this evidence to claim that stronger patent rights encourage more licensing contracts and additional transfer of technological information. This problem arises because the increase in receipts for using intellectual property could be caused by either higher licenser rents per contract or a greater number of contracts. Thus, although our empirical results are suggestive, at best we cannot reject the hypothesis that stronger IPRs favor licensing through easing contract enforcement and raising imitation costs. Unfortunately, it is impossible to distinguish between price and quantity effects in the data as they currently exist. Nonetheless, making such a distinction is important in understanding the full implications of stronger patent rights for technology transfer and should be on the agenda for future research.

Appendix 5.A. Ginarte-Park Patent Index

The following table provides the values of the Ginarte-Park patent index for several countries in three different years. The index ranges in principle from 0 to5, with a value of 5 indicating the strongest possible level of patent protection. These figures were developed from a reading of the patent laws of individual nations.

Country	1985	1990	1995
Australia	3.23	3.32	3.86
Brazil	1.85	1.85	3.05
Canada	2.76	2.76	3.24
Germany	3.71	3.71	3.86
Hong Kong (China)	2.57	2.57	2.57
Indonesia	0.33	0.33	2.27
Israel	3.57	3.57	3.57
Italy	4.05	4.05	4.19
Japan	3.94	3.94	3.94
Korea, Rep. of	3.61	3.94	3.94
Malaysia	2.90	2.37	2.84
Mexico	1.40	1.63	2.52
Netherlands	4.24	4.24	4.24
New Zealand	3.32	3.32	3.86
Norway	3.29	3.29	3.91
Philippines	2.67	2.67	2.66
Singapore	2.57	2.57	3.91
South Africa	3.57	3.57	3.57
Spain	3.29	3.62	4.04
Sweden	3.47	3.90	4.24
Switzerland	3.80	3.80	3.80
United Kingdom	3.57	3.57	3.57
Venezuela, R.B. de	1.35	1.35	2.75

Notes

1. See also Maskus (1998) for evidence of a positive statistical relationship between patent rights and FDI.
2. See also Dunning (1983) and Ethier (1986) for discussions of internalization theory.
3. This possibility was first pointed out by Helpman (1993) in a theoretical model of imitation in a dynamic product cycle. Glass and Saggi (1995) refined that model, and Lai (1998) presented a dynamic FDI model in which IPRs could increase innovation.
4. The structural equations are in Yang and Maskus (2001) and are highly nonlinear.
5. We are grateful to Walter Park for these data. See appendix 5.A for a full listing of the patent data.
6. In all cases, the hypothesis that the time-specific fixed effects are the same over time cannot be rejected at the 10 percent significance level. Thus, use of the time dummy is not necessary.
7. See also Maskus (2000), who documented that patent rights display a similar quadratic relationship as incomes rise across economies.

References

Caves, Richard E., Harold Crookell, and J. Peter Killing. 1983. "The Imperfect Market for Technology Licenses." *Oxford Bulletin of Economics and Statistics* 45(3):249–67.

Contractor, Farok J. 1980. "The 'Profitability' of Technology Licensing by U.S. Multinationals: A Framework for Analysis and an Empirical Study." *Journal of International Business Studies* 11(2):40–63.

Dunning, John H. 1983. "Market Power of the Firm and International Transfer of Technology: A Historical Excursion." *International Journal of Industrial Organization* 1(4):333–51.

Ethier, Wilfred J. 1986. "The Multinational Firm." *Quarterly Journal of Economics* 101(4):805–33.

Ferrantino, Michael J. 1993. "The Effect of Intellectual Property Rights on International Trade and Investment." *Weltwirtschatliches Archiv* 129(2):300–31.

Gallini, Nancy T., and Brian D. Wright. 1990. "Technology Transfer under Asymmetric Information." *RAND Journal of Economics* 21(1):147–60.

Ginarte, Juan Carlos, and Walter G. Park. 1997. "Determinants of Patent Rights: A Cross-National Study." *Research Policy* 26(3):283–301.

Glass, Amy J., and Kamal Saggi. 1995. "Intellectual Property Rights, Foreign Direct Investment, and Innovation." Working paper. Ohio State University, Columbus. Processed.

Hausman, Jerry A. 1978. "Specification Tests in Econometrics." *Econometrica* 46(6):1251–71.

Helpman, Elhanan 1993. "Innovation, Imitation, and Intellectual Property Rights." *Econometrica* 61(6):1247–80.

Horstmann, Ignatius, and James R. Markusen. 1987. "Licensing versus Direct Investment: A Model of Internalization by the Multinational Enterprise." *Canadian Journal of Economics* 20(3):464–81.

International Labour Organization. Various years. *Labour Statistics Yearbook*. Geneva.

International Monetary Fund. 1997. *International Financial Statistics Yearbook*. Washington, D.C.

Lai, Edwin L.-C. 1998. "International Intellectual Property Rights Protection and the Rate of Product Innovation." *Journal of Development Economics* 55(1):133–53.

Lee, Jeong-Yeon, and Edwin Mansfield. 1996. "Intellectual Property Protection and U.S. Foreign Direct Investment." *Review of Economics and Statistics* 78(2):181–86.

Mansfield, Edwin 1994. "Intellectual Property Protection, Foreign Direct Investment, and Technology Transfer." IFC Discussion Paper 19. International Finance Corporation, Washington, D.C.

Markusen, James R. 1995. "The Boundaries of Multinational Enterprises and the Theory of International Trade." *Journal of Economic Perspectives* 9(2):169–89.

———. 2001. "Contracts, Intellectual Property Rights, and Multinational Investment in Developing Countries." *Journal of International Economics* 53(1):189–204.

Maskus, Keith E. 1998. "The International Regulation of Intellectual Property." *Weltwirtschaftliches Archiv* 134(2):186–208.

————.2000. *Intellectual Property Rights in the Global Economy*. Washington, D.C.: Institute for International Economics.

Maskus, Keith E., and Denise Eby Konan. 1994. "Trade-Related Intellectual Property Rights: Issues and Exploratory Results." In Alan V. Deardorff and Robert M. Stern, eds., *Analytical and Negotiation Issues in the Global Trading System*. Ann Arbor: University of Michigan Press.

Primo Braga, Carlos A. 1996. "Trade-Related Intellectual Property Issues: The Uruguay Round Agreement and Its Economic Implications." In Will J. Martin and L. Alan Winters, eds., *The Uruguay Round and the Developing Countries*. Cambridge: Cambridge University Press.

Rapp, Richard, and Richard Rozek. 1990. "Benefits and Costs of Intellectual Property Protection in Developing Countries." Working Paper 3. National Economic Research Associates, Washington D.C.

Rugman, Alan M. 1986. "New Theories of the Multinational Enterprise: An Assessment of Internalization Theory." *Bulletin of Economic Research* 38(2):101–18.

Sachs, Jeffrey D., and Andrew Warner. 1995. "Economic Reform and the Process of Global Integration." *Brookings Papers on Economic Activity: Macroeconomics* (1):1–118.

Smith, Pamela J. 1999. "Are Weak Patent Rights a Barrier to U.S. Exports?" *Journal of International Economics* 48(1):151–77.

Taylor, M. Scott 1994. "TRIPS, Trade, and Growth." *International Economic Review* 35(2):361–81.

United Nations. Various years. *International Trade Statistics Yearbook*. Geneva.

U.S. Department of Commerce. Monthly editions of various years. *Survey of Current Business*. Washington, D.C.: U.S. Department of Commerce.

Yang, Guifang, and Keith E. Maskus. 2001. "Intellectual Property Rights, Licensing, and Innovation in an Endogenous Product-Cycle Model." *Journal of International Economics* 53(1):169–87.

6

THE COMPOSITION OF FOREIGN DIRECT INVESTMENT AND PROTECTION OF INTELLECTUAL PROPERTY RIGHTS: EVIDENCE FROM TRANSITION ECONOMIES

Beata Smarzynska Javorcik

I. Introduction

Protection of intellectual property rights (IPRs) has been a prominent item on the international policy agenda. Despite the introduction of the Agreement on Trade-Related Aspects of Intellectual Property Rights (TRIPS), many developing economies are not eager to strengthen their IPR legislation and its enforcement, fearing that the losses resulting from this action would outweigh the benefits. This chapter contributes to a better understanding of potential gains from stronger

A version of this chapter was published in the *European Economic Review* in 2004 (48(1):39–62). The author wishes to thank Andy Bernard, François Bourguignon, Carsten Fink, Aart Kraay, Jenny Lanjouw, Phil Levy, Keith Maskus, Walter Park, Nadia Soboleva, T. N. Srinivasan, and two anonymous referees for their comments and Hans Peter Lankes for making the results of the European Bank for Reconstruction and Development survey available.

IPR protection by providing empirical evidence indicating that the extent of IPR protection in a host country affects the composition of the foreign direct investment (FDI) it receives. More specifically, this study finds that a weak IPR regime deters foreign investment in high-technology sectors, where intellectual property rights play an important role. Moreover, it tilts the focus of FDI projects from manufacturing to distribution.

The relationship between IPR protection and FDI is quite complex. On the one hand, a weak IPR regime increases the probability of imitation, which makes a host country a less attractive location for foreign investors. On the other hand, strong protection may shift the preference of multinational corporations from FDI toward licensing. As surveys of multinationals have shown, the importance of IPR protection varies between industries. The concern about the IPR regime also depends on the purpose of an investment project. Concern is highest in the case of research and development (R&D) facilities and lowest for projects focusing exclusively on sales and distribution (see Mansfield 1994, 1995).

This chapter investigates two hypotheses that emerge from the above studies. First, it tests whether foreign investors in IPR-sensitive sectors (as indicated by Mansfield 1995) are more affected by the extent of intellectual property protection in a host country than are investors in general. Second, it examines whether the IPR regime influences a foreign investor's choice between setting up production facilities and engaging in activities focused solely on distribution.

A unique firm-level data set used in this study allows for a more in-depth examination of this phenomenon than was possible in the earlier literature, which concentrated mostly on aggregate inflows and case studies. The data set was compiled from a worldwide survey of companies conducted by the European Bank for Reconstruction and Development (EBRD) in 1995. The survey recipients were asked whether they had undertaken FDI in 24 economies in Eastern Europe and the former Soviet Union and, if so, what types of projects they were engaged in. Those responses were supplemented with information on firm characteristics and variables specific to the host countries.

This study uses two measures of IPR protection. The first one is the index capturing the strength of patent rights developed by Ginarte and Park (1997) and extended by the author to include more transition economies. Although the Ginarte-Park measure is quite detailed, it focuses only on laws present on the books, not on their enforcement. Therefore, a second index, which was developed specifically for this study, is also used. The second index is cruder in nature but takes into account all IPR laws on the books as well as their enforcement.

The empirical analysis confirms the hypotheses, thus indicating that weak protection of IPRs has a significant effect on the composition of FDI inflows. First, it deters foreign investors in four technology-intensive sectors: drugs, cosmetics, and health care products; chemicals; machinery and equipment; and electrical equipment. Those are the sectors in which, according to survey studies, IPRs play a particularly prominent role. Second, weak protection encourages foreign investors to set up distribution facilities rather than to engage in local production. Interestingly, this effect is significant in the case of all investors, not just those in sensitive industries. Finally, the results suggest that investors respond to both laws on the books and their enforcement. These findings are robust to controls for privatization, transition progress, corruption level, and effectiveness of the legal system.

In addition to an intrinsic interest in transition, a focus on Eastern Europe and the former Soviet Union can offer insights into the broader question of the role of FDI in economic development throughout the world. Although investment in other developing regions has been studied extensively, one finding of that research has been the importance of previous investment experience as a determinant of current FDI flows (see Hallward-Driemeier 1996). Thus, the effect of current policy variables may be obscured and overcome by a long history of past policies, for which it is difficult to control. Transition economies offer almost a natural control since FDI in the region was negligible before 1989. Therefore, the results of this chapter suggest that the importance of IPR protection in developing countries may have been understated in past research.

This study is structured as follows: The next section briefly reviews the related literature and formulates the hypotheses to be tested. The following section describes the econometric specifications and the data set. Then, empirical results are presented. The last section concludes the study.

II. Related Literature and Hypotheses to Be Tested

The connection between technological capabilities of a firm and its decision to undertake FDI is highlighted in Dunning's (1993) OLI paradigm, which explains activities of multinational corporations in terms of ownership (O), localization (L), and internalization advantages (I).[1] When selling its products abroad, a firm is at least initially disadvantaged relative to local producers. Thus, to compete effectively with indigenous firms, a foreign producer must possess some *ownership advantages*. They can take the form of a superior production technology or improved organizational and marketing systems, innovatory capacity, trademarks, reputation, or other assets. Ownership advantages ensure a firm's ability to enter the host country's market, but they do not explain why the foreign presence should be established through production rather than exports. This issue is, in turn, addressed by *localization advantages* that arise because of differences in factor quality, costs and endowments, international transport and communication costs, host government policies, and ability to overcome trade restrictions. The last advantage, *internalization,* explains why a foreign firm prefers to retain full control over the production process instead of licensing its intangible assets to local firms. This decision may be attributable to high transaction costs involved in regulating and enforcing licensing contracts.

Weak IPR protection increases the probability of imitation, which erodes a firm's ownership advantages and decreases localization advantages of a host country. At the same time, a weak IPR system increases the benefits of internalization, because it is associated with a greater risk of the licensee's breaching the contract and acting in direct competition with the seller. An inadequate IPR regime, therefore, deters FDI and encourages exporting. A strong IPR system may also have a negative impact on FDI by making licensing a viable alternative to direct investment.[2] Thus, the overall relationship between the level of IPR protection and FDI is ambiguous.

The results of empirical studies exploring the effect of IPR protection on FDI lead to mixed conclusions. Ferrantino (1993) finds no statistically significant relationship between the extent of U.S. affiliate sales in a foreign country and that country's membership in an international patent or copyright convention. Similarly, Maskus and Konan (1994), who use the Rapp and Rozek (1990) index of IPR protection, as well as Primo Braga and Fink (2000), who use the Ginarte and Park (1997) index, do not obtain statistically significant results. Lee and Mansfield (1996), however, show that the strength of a country's IPR protection, as perceived by 100 U.S. firms surveyed, is positively correlated with the volume of U.S. FDI inflows into that country. Smith (2001) also finds a positive correlation between sales of U.S. affiliates and the strength of IPR protection in a host country. However, none of those studies looks at the effect of the IPR regime on the composition of FDI inflows.

Intellectual property rights do not play an equally important role in all sectors, or even in all technology-intensive industries. For instance, Mansfield (1995) mentions that IPR protection may be less crucial in sectors such as automobile production, in which firms frequently cannot use a competitor's technology without many complex and expensive inputs. However, the IPR regime is likely to be important for sectors such as drugs, cosmetics, and health care products; chemicals; machinery and equipment; and electrical equipment.[3]

Additionally, a survey of U.S. manufacturing firms conducted by Mansfield (1994) revealed that the importance of IPR regimes for investment decisions depends on the purpose of the investment project. For example, in the case of investment in sales and distribution outlets, only about 20 percent of survey respondents were concerned with IPR protection. In the case of investment in rudimentary production (that is, production involving basic technologies) and assembly facilities, 30 percent of respondents viewed IPR protection as important. This percentage increased to 50 to 60 percent for investments in manufacturing components and complete products and to 80 percent when R&D facilities were involved.

Case studies from transition economies echo the concerns of foreign investors about weak IPR protection and are consistent with the survey findings. For instance, Sharp and Barz (1997, p. 110) mention that ICI (a company producing synthetic organic chemicals) and Zeneca (a pharmaceutical company) "are wary of piracy and doubtful about transferring either product or process know-how to these countries [that is, transition economies]. Both companies, however, recognize that eventually Central and Eastern Europe and the FSU [former Soviet Union] will be important markets. That is why Zeneca is investing in developing its distribution links in high value-added areas such as medical supplies and equipment and healthcare systems." A similar picture emerges from the case study of Shell:

> Shell provides know-how to its Russian partners where necessary, but does not pass on anything it regards as commercially sensitive. A relevant example is Shell's contract with the Russian R&D Institute for Element-Organic Compounds (INEOS) to produce a new construction plastic, called Noril. Shell will supply the chemical intermediates for production, while the technology will be Russian. There is no question of the Russians either supplying the intermediates or obtaining access to the more up-to-date technology used by General Electric for the manufacture of Noril in the United States (Sharp and Barz, 1997, pp. 107–8).

Such examples are obviously not restricted to Eastern Europe and the former Soviet Union. Lan and Young (1996, p. 73, footnote 9) present a case from China: "Local staff [members] working in the laboratories of two foreign affiliates manufacturing detergents discovered the contents of production by repeatedly trying the combinations. They then moved out to set up their own firms. In only a few years, more than ten small local firms were manufacturing detergent."[4]

In light of the theoretical prediction presented above, as well as the conclusions emerging from interviews with foreign investors, the following testable hypotheses emerge. First, FDI in sectors relying heavily on protection of intellectual property is likely to be deterred by a weak IPR regime. It is not clear, however, that this same hypothesis should be true for FDI inflows in general. Second, in countries with weak protection of intellectual property, investors may be more inclined to engage solely in distribution activities rather than in local production. The two hypotheses are tested in this study.

III. Econometric Specification and Data

Econometric Specification

To test the first hypothesis, we estimate a probit model of the determinants of investment decision. The model is of the following form:

$$FDI_{ic} = 1 \text{ if } FDI_{ic}^* > 0$$
$$FDI_{ic} = 0 \text{ otherwise}$$
where
$$FDI_{ic}^* = d_i + X_c \beta_1 + d_{HT} X_c \beta_2 + u_{ic}$$

The dependent variable takes on the value of one if firm *i* has invested in country *c*, and zero if a firm has not undertaken FDI in country *c*. Thus, for each firm, the number of observations is equal to the number of possible destination countries in the sample. To control for unobserved firm characteristics, firm-specific dummy variables d_i are included. Additionally, country-specific explanatory variables X_c are included in the model. Because the effect of IPR protection and possibly other variables is expected to differ between sectors, the model allows for a separate coefficient for high-technology sectors in which IPRs play a more prominent role. It is achieved by interacting X_c with a dummy variable for those sectors. Following the survey findings of Mansfield (1995), the IPR-sensitive sectors include drugs, cosmetics, and health care products; chemicals; machinery and equipment; and electrical equipment. The errors are corrected for a correlation between observations for the same destination country.

One way of testing the second hypothesis would be to estimate a probit model with the dependent variable representing the choice between manufacturing projects and those focusing solely on distribution. This methodology, however, would imply that the decision to invest and the decision about the type of the investment project are made separately, which may not be the case. To overcome this limitation, we estimate a system consisting of two parts: (1) the decision whether or not to invest and (2) the decision regarding the purpose of the investment project, conditional on investment taking place. To learn more about investor characteristics that influence investors' choices, we use firm-specific variables rather than firm dummies in the regressions. Note that, anyway, it would not be possible to use firm fixed effects in the second part of the model because firms engaged in a single project or multiple projects of the same type would have to be dropped from the estimation.

As mentioned, the first part of the model describes the investor's decision to enter a particular host country *c*. As in the estimation above, we allow for a differing effect of host country characteristics on firms in IPR-sensitive sectors.

$$FDI_{ic} = 1 \text{ if } FDI_{ic}^* > 0$$

$$FDI_{ic} = 0 \text{ otherwise}$$

where

$$FDI_{ic}^* = X_i\theta + X_c\beta_3 + d_{HT}X_c\beta_4 + \varepsilon_{ic}$$

The second part describes the choice between setting up production facilities in country c (possibly accompanied by distribution networks) and engaging in a project focusing solely on distribution, conditional on FDI taking place. The dependent variable equals one in the case of manufacturing FDI. On the right-hand side, both firm-specific (X_i) and host country–specific (X_c) variables are included. The model allows for different effects of the intellectual property regime on IPR-sensitive sectors.

$$MANUFACTURING_{ic} = 1 \text{ if } MANUFACTURING_{ic}^* > 0 \text{ and } FDI_{ic}^* > 0$$

$$MANUFACTURING_{ic} = 0 \text{ if } MANUFACTURING_{ic}^* \leq 0 \text{ and } FDI_{ic}^* > 0$$

where

$$MANUFACTURING_{ic}^* = X_i\delta + X_c\beta + \pi d_{HT}IPR_c + \upsilon_{ic}$$

Assuming that (ε, v) are i.i.d. normal variables with zero means and a correlation coefficient of ρ, we estimate these equations (probit with sample selection) simultaneously by maximum likelihood. The errors are corrected for a correlation between observations for the same destination country. The number of observations in the FDI decision equation is equal to the number of firms in the sample, multiplied by the number of destination countries in the sample. In the second decision equation, the number of observations is equal to the total number of FDI projects in the sample. The latter number is smaller than the former because not all firms invest in all countries.

Data

The empirical analysis uses a unique firm-level data set based on the EBRD *Foreign Investment Survey.* In January 1995, a brief questionnaire was sent to all companies listed in Worldscope. Worldscope is a commercial database that provides detailed financial statements and business descriptions for about 10,000 public companies located in more than 50 countries. Sending the questionnaire to all of them ensured that all major public companies in the world would be included. Responses were obtained from 1,405 firms that answered questions regarding their undertaken and planned investments in Eastern Europe and the former Soviet Union. Additionally, information on the function of the projects (manufacturing, distribution, representative office) was collected.[5] The data set does not include any information on the time when each investment was undertaken. Because the magnitude of FDI inflows was marginal before 1989, the information collected pertains mostly to the period from 1989 to 1994.[6] Given the objective of this study to explore the effect of government policies on the magnitude and nature of FDI inflows, firms in the oil, gas, and coal sector, which are likely to be attracted to natural resource endowments, are excluded from the estimations.

Measures of IPR protection

The key variable in the regression is a proxy for the IPR regime. The indices of patent rights protection developed by Rapp and Rozek (1990) and Ginarte and Park (1997) are the two most popular measures used in the literature. The former index, though widely used, is inadequate for the purpose of this chapter because it covers only five countries from the data set and pertains to the pretransition period. The Ginarte-Park measure, however, covers 10 transition economies and includes information for 1995.[7] To test the hypotheses using the full data set, I have extended the Ginarte-Park index to cover nine more countries.[8]

The Ginarte-Park index takes into account five categories of patent laws: (1) extent of coverage, (2) membership in international patent agreements, (3) provisions for loss of protection, (4) enforcement mechanisms, and (5) duration of protection. Each of the categories is assigned a value between zero and one, and the unweighted sum of these values constitutes the patent rights index (see Ginarte and Park 1997 for a detailed description). Thus, the index ranges from zero to five, with the higher values indicating a stronger level of protection. The index refers to 1995 or the closest year for which the information was available. Table 6.1 lists the index values. The highest score in the group of countries under consideration was obtained by Hungary (3.75), while the lowest score (2.52) belongs to both Uzbekistan and former Yugoslav Republic of Macedonia. The average value of the index is 3.04. For comparison, the mean value of the index for 110 countries rated in 1995 was 2.67. A positive coefficient on the Ginarte-Park index will indicate that stronger patent laws are associated with a greater probability of FDI being undertaken. The advantages of the Ginarte-Park index are that it has a great level of detail and takes into account the treatment of foreigners. Its main disadvantage is that it focuses on the laws present on the books but does not capture their enforcement.

Because the issue of enforcement may have a crucial effect on foreign investors' decisions, this chapter also uses another index of IPR protection developed specifically for this study. This simple index captures both the legislative and the enforcement aspect of the IPR regime. It is based on the descriptions of IPR regimes

TABLE 6.1 Measures of IPR Protection

Country	Ginarte-Park patent rights index	IPR index based on IIPA Special 301 Watch List recommendations
Armenia		1
Azerbaijan		1
Belarus[a]	3.19	1
Bulgaria	2.57	2
Croatia[a]	3.71	
Czech Republic	3.19	3
Estonia[a]	2.86	2
FYR Macedonia[a]	2.52	
Georgia[a]	3.00	1
Hungary	3.75	3
Kazakhstan[a]	3.19	1
Kyrgyz Republic		1
Latvia[a]	2.88	2
Lithuania	2.57	1
Moldova[a]	3.00	2
Poland	3.23	3
Romania	2.71	1
Russia	3.04	2
Slovak Republic	3.19	3
Slovenia[a]	3.52	
Tajikistan		1
Turkmenistan		2
Ukraine	3.04	2
Uzbekistan[a]	2.52	1
Average	3.04	1.71

a. Index values calculated by the author.
Source: Ginarte-Park index provided by Walter Park, except for values marked as calculated by the author based on the methodology proposed by Ginarte and Park (1997). IPR index constructed by the author on the basis of the IIPA Special 301 Watch List recommendations as outlined in table 6.2.

provided by the International Intellectual Property Alliance (IIPA) in its recommendations for countries to be placed on the U.S. Special 301 Watch List. Those descriptions include the issue of enforcement and pay special attention to trademark and copyright laws. Note that the actual placements on the Special 301 Watch List have not been used in developing the index, because they depend not only on the extent of IPR violations in a specific country but also on the importance of the country to U.S. interests. Again, 1995 is used as a reference point in the rating. Table. 6.2 presents the rating criteria. A higher value of the index corresponds to stronger IPR

TABLE 6.2   IPR Index Based on IIPA Special 301 Watch List Recommendations

Points	Description
3	Close to adequate IPR legislation present by the end of 1995; some enforcement efforts undertaken
2	Close to adequate IPR legislation present by the end of 1995; no enforcement efforts undertaken
1	Lack of adequate IPR legislation at the end of 1995

Source: Author's calculations.

protection; thus, a positive coefficient on this variable is expected. Table 6.1 lists the values of the index. The correlation between the Ginarte-Park measure and this index is 0.57.

Other Control Variables

The IPR regime may be correlated with other host country characteristics, such as overall progress in reform, effectiveness of the legal system, corruption level, privatization policies, and openness to trade. Therefore, additional variables are included in the regression to control for those factors.

Multinational corporations are less likely to invest in risky and unstable countries, and the perceived risk of Eastern Europe and the former Soviet Union has often been cited as a factor discouraging foreign capital inflows (see, for example, Estrin, Hughes, and Todd 1997; Hunya 1997; World Bank 1996; Zloch-Christy 1995). Lankes and Venables (1996) find a negative association between EBRD transition indicators and country risk as perceived by the interviewed firms, with the rank correlation coefficient equal to −0.89. The transition indicators rate the progress of a country's reforms in the following areas: price liberalization and competition, trade and exchange system, large-scale privatization, small-scale privatization, enterprise restructuring, and banking reform. See EBRD (1994, p. 11) for a detailed description. Thus, in the empirical analysis, the average of the EBRD indicators is used as a proxy for risks associated with undertaking FDI in a given host country. Because the higher values of the transition index indicate greater progress in reform, one would expect to observe a positive coefficient on this variable.

Furthermore, the effectiveness of the legal system is controlled for by using another indicator produced by the EBRD (1995, p. 103). This indicator, ranging from 1 to 4[*], assesses the extent to which legal rules affecting investment are clear and accessible as well as adequately supported administratively and judicially. The value of 1 is assigned to countries where the legal rules are usually very unclear and often contradictory, the availability of independent legal advice is limited, and the administration of the law is substantially deficient. The highest value (4*) is assigned to countries with clear and readily ascertainable laws, sophisticated legal advice available, and well-functioning courts. Note that the maximum score achieved by the countries in the group is 4.

Moreover, a measure of the extent of corrupt practices in the country is added to the model. The measure is the 1999 Transparency International (TI) Corruption Perception Index, which pools information from 10 different surveys of business executives, risk analysts, and the general public. The original index ranges between 10 (highly clean) and 0 (highly corrupt). To facilitate interpretation of the results, the index was rescaled in the following way: rescaled TI index = 10 − original TI index. Thus, a higher index value corresponds to a higher level of corruption and a negative coefficient is expected.[9]

Because privatization policies may influence the inflows of FDI, the model also contains the share of gross domestic product (GDP) accounted for by the private sector. The figures pertain to 1995 and come from the EBRD (1995). Additionally, a measure of openness to trade (the sum of exports and imports as a percentage of GDP) is included in the model to control for tariff-jumping FDI. The data refer to 1993 and come from the EBRD.[10]

The existing literature finds the host country's market size to be an important determinant of FDI inflows (see Braunerhjelm and Svensson 1996; Caves 1996; Dunning 1993). Most studies show that a large market size encourages FDI inflows. Therefore, the model includes GDP per capita, which is a proxy for the purchasing power of local consumers, and the population size, which reflects the potential size of the market. Both variables come from EBRD (1994) and refer to 1993. They are entered in the logarithmic form. Finally, we control for the corporate income tax rate because higher taxation is likely to discourage investment. The figures (expressed as percentages) come from various reports by PricewaterhouseCoopers. If several rates apply, the highest one was used.[11]

As explained earlier, it is necessary to include firm-specific variables when testing the second hypothesis. Thus, standard variables found in most FDI studies are included in the model: firm size (measured by the firm's sales in U.S. dollars, entered as logarithm); R&D intensity (measured by R&D outlays as a percentage of net sales); advertising intensity (proxied by selling, general, and administrative expenses as a percentage of net sales);[12] and a proxy for production diversification (the number of four-digit Standard Industrial Classification, or SIC, codes describing a firm's activities). All information on firm characteristics was obtained from the Worldscope database and pertains to fiscal year 1993 (from April 1993 to March 1994). Additionally, we control for the investor's regional experience, proxied by a dummy variable indicating whether a firm had a trading relationship with the region before 1989. The last variable comes from the EBRD survey.

IV. Empirical Results

Effect of IPR Protection on Probability of FDI Taking Place

The empirical analysis confirms the first hypothesis of the study. The estimation results with the Ginarte-Park index are presented in table 6.3.[13] In five out of six regressions, the extent of intellectual property protection affects the probability of investment in those high-technology sectors that rely heavily on IPRs but not in other industries. The coefficients for the IPR-sensitive sectors bear, as expected, positive signs and are significant at least at the 5 percent level. In the last regression, both coefficients on the Ginarte-Park index are significant.

The other variables also have the anticipated signs. Population size is found to have a positive effect on FDI inflows in all industries. IPR-sensitive sectors do not appear to be affected differently by this variable. GDP per capita is positively related to FDI inflows, and in the majority of cases, it does not affect the high-technology sectors differently. As expected, progress in transition, greater effectiveness of the legal regulations governing investment, and more advanced privatization processes increase the probability of FDI in all sectors. Conversely, higher levels of corruption and higher corporate income tax rates deter foreign investors. The coefficients on the interactions of these variables with a dummy for IPR-sensitive sectors are not significant. The openness measure has a significant effect only on the IPR-sensitive sectors. A possible explanation is that firms in those sectors may be more reliant on imports because they tend to transfer only part of the production process (rather than the whole process) to the region for fear of losing their intangible assets.

Table 6.4 presents the estimation results with the second IPR measure. Unlike the Ginarte-Park index of patent rights protection, this index captures both the legal and the enforcement aspects of an IPR regime. It is also broader in scope because it pertains to IPRs in general rather than just to patents. As in table 6.3, we find that stronger IPR protection increases the probability that multinationals in the four sensitive sectors will undertake FDI. In five out of six cases, the coefficients are significant at the 5 percent or 1 percent level. Additionally, in four regressions, the strength of the IPR regime affects not only the sensitive sectors but also all investors. The signs and significance levels of other control variables are similar to those found in table 6.3.

The reason all firms, not just those in IPR-sensitive sectors, may be affected by the extent of intellectual property protection is that an IPR regime may also play a signaling role. As Lall (1997, p. 244) points out, "the 'signaling value' of the intellectual property regime has become extremely important in recent years. In general, countries that seek to attract technology-intensive foreign investment also offer strong protection to those investments." As the results in tables 6.3 and 6.4

TABLE 6.3 Probit Results with Ginarte-Park Index of Patent Rights Protection

Ginarte-Park index	0.30	0.25	−0.15	−0.25	0.32	0.37*
	(0.40)	(0.34)	(0.41)	(0.25)	(0.21)	(0.23)
IPR sensitive × Ginarte-Park index	0.40**	0.42***	0.43**	0.55***	0.56***	0.31*
	(0.18)	(0.16)	(0.18)	(0.15)	(0.21)	(0.18)
GDP per capita	0.00	−0.06	0.55***	0.44***	0.23***	0.15
	(0.17)	(0.14)	(0.19)	(0.15)	(0.07)	(0.09)
IPR sensitive × GDP per capita	0.12	0.10	0.05	0.01	0.01	0.35***
	(0.14)	(0.14)	(0.12)	(0.10)	(0.13)	(0.13)
Population	0.52***	0.56***	0.58***	0.61***	0.43***	0.40***
	(0.05)	(0.07)	(0.09)	(0.06)	(0.05)	(0.05)
IPR sensitive × population	0.00	0.01	0.00	0.02	0.00	0.12**
	(0.04)	(0.03)	(0.06)	(0.05)	(0.04)	(0.05)
Progress in reform	1.08***	1.21***				
	(0.17)	(0.15)				
IPR sensitive × progress in reform	−0.15	−0.10				
	(0.19)	(0.19)				
Corporate income tax rate		−0.02*				
		(0.01)				
IPR sensitive × corporate income tax rate		−0.01				
		(0.01)				

(Continued)

TABLE 6.3 Probit Results with Ginarte-Park Index of Patent Rights Protection (Continued)

Legal effectiveness	0.29* (0.15)			
IPR sensitive × legal effectiveness	–0.03 (0.09)			
Corruption		–0.40*** (0.08)		
IPR sensitive × corruption		–0.02 (0.05)		
Privatization			0.04*** (0.00)	0.04*** (0.00)
IPR sensitive × privatization			0.00 (0.01)	0.00 (0.00)
Openness				–0.17 (0.11)
IPR sensitive × openness				0.71*** (0.16)

Number of observations	6,707	6,707	6,707	6,354	6,707	6,707
Chi-squared	47.8	89.78	54.1	50.9	141.5	120.0
Probability > chi-squared	0.00	0.00	0.00	0.00	0.00	0.00
Pseudo R-squared	0.36	0.36	0.34	0.34	0.38	0.39
Log likelihood	–1,820	–1,801	–1,890	–1,828	–1,752	–1,746

Note: *** denotes significant at the 1 percent level, ** at the 5 percent level, * at the 10 percent level. Standard errors are in parentheses. Firm dummies have been included in all regressions. IPR sensitive denotes a dummy variable for IPR-sensitive sectors.

Source: Author's estimations.

TABLE 6.4 Probit Results with IPR Index

IPR index	0.25** (0.10)	0.27*** (0.06)	0.16 (0.16)	0.24** (0.10)	0.12 (0.08)	0.13* (0.07)
IPR sensitive × IPR index	0.29*** (0.10)	0.33*** (0.08)	0.33*** (0.09)	0.25** (0.10)	0.30*** (0.12)	0.03 (0.12)
GDP per capita	0.34*** (0.10)	0.28*** (0.11)	0.60*** (0.10)	0.46*** (0.11)	0.46*** (0.06)	0.43*** (0.09)
IPR sensitive × GDP per capita	0.03 (0.11)	0.01 (0.09)	0.01 (0.11)	−0.04 (0.11)	−0.01 (0.10)	0.48** (0.22)
Population	0.43*** (0.04)	0.45*** (0.04)	0.47*** (0.07)	0.48*** (0.06)	0.40*** (0.04)	0.40*** (0.04)
IPR sensitive × population	0.03 (0.04)	0.04 (0.04)	0.01 (0.05)	0.07 (0.07)	0.04 (0.04)	0.15*** (0.06)
Progress in reform	0.60*** (0.12)	0.66*** (0.14)				
IPR sensitive × progress in reform	−0.14 (0.13)	−0.14 (0.14)				
Corporate income tax rate		−0.02*** (0.01)				
IPR sensitive × corporate income tax rate		−0.02*** (0.01)				

Legal effectiveness			0.27** (0.12)		
IPR sensitive × legal effectiveness			−0.10 (0.07)		
Corruption				−0.31*** (0.08)	
IPR sensitive × corruption				−0.06 (0.10)	
Privatization					0.03*** (0.00)	0.03*** (0.00)
IPR sensitive × privatization					0.00 (0.01)	0.00 (0.01)
Openness						−0.05 (0.11)
IPR sensitive × openness						0.80*** (0.24)

(Continued)

TABLE 6.4 Probit Results with IPR Index (Continued)

Number of observations	7,329	6,631	7,329	6,631	7,329	7,329
Chi-squared	77.01	52.67	64.93	78.02	56.74	98.00
Probability > chi-squared	0.00	0.00	0.00	0.00	0.00	0.00
Pseudo R-squared	0.43	0.42	0.42	0.42	0.44	0.44
Log likelihood	–1,629.9	–1,595.5	–1,650.2	–1,603.4	–1,612.2	–1,606.7

Note: *** denotes significant at the 1 percent level, ** at the 5 percent level, * at the 10 percent level. Standard errors are in parentheses. Firm dummies have been included in all regressions. IPR sensitive denotes a dummy variable for IPR-sensitive sectors.

Source: Author's estimations.

suggest, signaling takes place only if the legislative changes are accompanied by enforcement efforts.

The following exercise was performed to further test the robustness of the findings. An ordinary least squares (OLS) regression was estimated with the dependent variables equal to the share of firms in the four sensitive sectors that undertook FDI in each of the countries in the sample.[14] The same explanatory variables as those in tables 6.3 and 6.4 were included. The results are presented in appendix table 6.A.1. They suggest that the earlier findings are quite robust. In 10 of 12 regressions, the IPR measure is significant and bears the expected sign. All regressions have a high explanatory power.

In summary, the empirical analysis indicates that the strength of patent laws and the overall level of IPR protection (both laws on the books and their enforcement) affect FDI inflows in several high-technology sectors where, as surveys show, IPRs play an important role. Moreover, there is some evidence that the overall strength of the IPR regime and its enforcement influences the investment decision of multinationals active in other sectors as well.

Effect of IPR Protection on the Choice of Project Function

Table 6.5 presents the empirical results from the test of the second hypothesis. As mentioned earlier, the hypothesis was tested by looking jointly at two decisions: (1) whether or not FDI is taking place and (2) conditional on an FDI project being undertaken, whether it involves setting up production facilities or focuses solely on building distribution networks. The results of the investment decision with respect to host country characteristics are consistent with those found in the earlier section. One interesting change is that the new model suggests that firms in IPR-sensitive sectors are more strongly deterred by corruption in a host country than firms in other industries. This finding may be associated with investor's fear that, in the case of legal disputes on, for instance, patent infringement, a higher level of corruption will lower the chances that the dispute will be adjudicated fairly.[15] The coefficients on firm characteristics also have the expected signs. Namely, the data suggest that larger firms and those with greater intangible assets, regional experience, and more diversified production are more likely to undertake investment in the region.

The hypothesis of interest is supported by the data. As table 6.5 indicates, foreign investors are more likely to engage in local production, rather than focus solely on setting up distribution networks, in countries with stronger IPR regimes. The relevant coefficient (Ginarte-Park index) is statistically significant in all regressions. Interestingly, this effect is significant for all sectors and does not appear to be stronger in the case of IPR-sensitive industries. These findings are

TABLE 6.5 Bivariate Probit with Sample Selection: Manufacturing versus Distribution Projects (Ginarte-Park Index)

Investment decision					
Ginarte-Park index	−0.26 (0.19)	−0.29 (0.19)	−0.29 (0.19)	0.21 (0.24)	0.08 (0.12)
IPR sensitive × Ginarte-Park index	0.22* (0.13)	0.33* (0.18)	0.33* (0.17)	−0.08 (0.16)	0.04 (0.19)
GDP per capita	0.28*** (0.07)	0.29*** (0.07)	0.29*** (0.07)	−0.04 (0.10)	0.02 (0.05)
IPR sensitive × GDP per capita	−0.01 (0.05)	−0.07 (0.08)	−0.07 (0.08)	0.05 (0.10)	0.16** (0.08)
Population	0.34*** (0.06)	0.35*** (0.07)	0.34*** (0.07)	0.37*** (0.04)	0.31*** (0.03)
IPR sensitive × population	0.11 (0.07)	0.11 (0.08)	0.11 (0.09)	−0.04 (0.04)	0.08 (0.06)
Corruption	−0.18** (0.07)	−0.17** (0.08)	−0.17* (0.09)		−0.08** (0.04)
IPR sensitive × corruption	−0.12*** (0.04)	−0.17*** (0.06)	−0.17*** (0.06)		−0.12*** (0.04)
Corporate income tax rate		−0.00 (0.01)	−0.00 (0.01)	−0.01 (0.01)	
IPR sensitive × corporate income tax rate		0.02 (0.01)	0.01 (0.01)	0.00 (0.00)	
Progress in reform				0.67*** (0.11)	
IPR sensitive × progress in reform				−0.06 (0.12)	
Privatization					0.03*** (0.00)
IPR sensitive × privatization					−0.01*** (0.00)
Openness					0.03 (0.08)

Investment decision					
IPR sensitive × openness					0.02 (0.12)
Firm size	0.17*** (0.02)	0.17*** (0.02)	0.17*** (0.02)	0.17*** (0.02)	0.17*** (0.02)
R&D intensity	0.03*** (0.01)	0.03*** (0.01)	0.03*** (0.01)	0.03*** (0.01)	0.03*** (0.01)
Advertising intensity	0.01*** (0.02)	0.01*** (0.00)	0.01*** (0.00)	0.01*** (0.00)	0.01*** (0.00)
Production diversification	0.04** (0.02)	0.04** (0.02)	0.04** (0.02)	0.04** (0.02)	0.04** (0.02)
Regional experience	0.95*** (0.04)	0.95*** (0.04)	0.95*** (0.04)	0.97*** (0.04)	0.98*** (0.04)
Constant	−5.37*** (0.71)	−5.32*** (0.69)	−5.33*** (0.75)	−7.65*** (0.61)	−6.74*** (0.50)
Decision regarding project type (manufacturing versus distribution)					
Ginarte-Park index	0.28* (0.16)	0.29* (0.17)	0.31** (0.16)	0.38** (0.18)	0.57*** (0.14)
IPR sensitive × Ginarte-Park index	−0.05 (0.03)	−0.05 (0.03)	−0.05 (0.03)	−0.01 (0.03)	−0.04 (0.04)
GDP per capita	−0.26** (0.12)	−0.25 (0.17)	−0.26 (0.22)	−0.16 (0.11)	−0.22* (0.13)
Population	−0.06 (0.12)	−0.04 (0.17)	−0.05 (0.21)	0.37*** (0.03)	0.19*** (0.03)
Corporate income tax rate			0.00 (0.01)		
Progress in reform				0.71*** (0.12)	
Privatization					0.02** (0.01)

(Continued)

TABLE 6.5 Bivariate Probit with Sample Selection: Manufacturing versus Distribution Projects (Ginarte-Park Index) (Continued)

Decision regarding project type (manufacturing versus distribution)					
Openness					−0.01 (0.14)
Firm size	−0.07 (0.07)	−0.06 (0.09)	−0.06 (0.11)	0.16*** (0.02)	0.08*** (0.02)
R&D intensity	−0.08*** (0.02)	−0.08*** (0.02)	−0.08*** (0.03)	−0.04*** (0.01)	−0.09*** (0.02)
Advertising intensity	−0.03*** (0.01)	−0.03*** (0.01)	−0.03*** (0.01)	−0.00 (0.00)	−0.03*** (0.00)
Production diversification	−0.06*** (0.02)	−0.06*** (0.02)	−0.06*** (0.02)	0.01 (0.02)	−0.05* (0.03)
Regional experience	−0.90*** (0.11)	−0.88*** (0.17)	−0.88*** (0.18)	0.60*** (0.12)	−0.36** (0.17)
Constant	4.93* (2.59)	4.57 (3.73)	4.69 (4.09)	−7.19*** (0.63)	−1.72 (2.01)
Rho	−0.84	−0.80	−0.82	0.98	0.01
Chi-squared (Wald test of rho = 0)	2.05	1.07	0.72	5.93	0.00
Probability > chi-squared	0.15	0.30	0.40	0.01	0.95
Number of observations	5,459	5,459	5,459	5,764	5,459
Number of observations (first equation)	4,959	4,959	4,959	5,260	4,959
Number of observations (second equation)	500	500	500	504	500

Note: *** denotes significant at the 1 percent level, ** at the 5 percent level, * at the 10 percent level. Standard errors are in parentheses.

Source: Author's estimations.

consistent with the survey evidence provided by Mansfield (1994) and the Zeneca case study previously cited.

The data also indicate that manufacturing FDI is more likely to take place in countries with a larger population, which may be explained by the economies of scale enjoyed in large markets. GDP per capita appears to be negatively correlated with the probability of local production. A possible explanation is that countries with higher GDP per capita tend to have higher labor costs, which make local production less attractive. The probability of manufacturing FDI is positively affected by the transition progress. Because setting up a production plant is more costly than setting up a distribution network alone, it is not surprising the foreign investors choose the former option in countries that appear to be more stable because of an advanced reform process. Manufacturing projects are also more likely to take place in economies where the privatization process is more advanced because privatization brings opportunities for acquiring domestic production facilities. Corporate taxation and openness to trade do not appear to have a statistically significant effect.

When we turn to investor characteristics, the findings indicate that firms possessing more intangible assets, as measured by R&D and advertising intensity, are less likely to undertake manufacturing projects. This finding may be because the potential for knowledge dissipation is greater when the production takes place in a host country than when the final products are imported. Firm size appears to be, albeit not very robustly, positively correlated with the probability of a manufacturing project. To the extent that larger firms have more resources for investment, this finding would indicate that the choice between the two types of activities is affected by financial constraints. Finally, we find that manufacturing projects are more likely to be undertaken by firms without previous regional experience.[16]

Table 6.6 presents the results obtained using the other IPR index. Although in this case the support for the hypothesis is much weaker, other results are broadly comparable with those in table 6.5.

As an additional robustness check, we estimated a multinomial logit model with the left-hand side variable reflecting three options available to a potential investor: (1) no investment at all; (2) investment solely in distribution networks; and (3) investment in production facilities, possibly accompanied by distribution networks. Appendix table 6.A.2 presents the results. Because the choice between manufacturing and nonmanufacturing projects is of interest, the results are presented relative to option 2—that is, investment in distribution networks. As the first part of the table indicates, in seven out of eight cases, the coefficient on IPR protection is positive and statistically significant, indicating that stronger IPR regimes increase the likelihood of FDI in production facilities relative to distribution-only projects. IPR protection, however, does not appear to have a statistically

TABLE 6.6 Bivariate Probit with Sample Selection: Manufacturing vs. Distribution Projects (IPR Index)

Investment decision					
IPR index	0.12* (0.07)	0.13** (0.06)	0.13 (0.08)	0.10 (0.10)	−0.06 (0.07)
IPR sensitive × IPR index	0.05 (0.06)	0.04 (0.05)	0.04 (0.05)	0.14* (0.07)	0.08 (0.08)
GDP per capita	0.30*** (0.05)	0.30*** (0.06)	0.30*** (0.06)	0.28*** (0.10)	0.35*** (0.08)
IPR sensitive × GDP per capita	0.04 (0.03)	0.04 (0.03)	0.04 (0.03)	−0.03 (0.05)	0.12*** (0.04)
Population	0.26*** (0.03)	0.26*** (0.04)	0.26*** (0.04)	0.29*** (0.04)	0.30*** (0.03)
IPR sensitive × population	0.13*** (0.03)	0.14*** (0.04)	0.14*** (0.04)	−0.01 (0.04)	0.14*** (0.03)
Corruption	−0.11*** (0.04)	−0.11** (0.04)	−0.10** (0.04)		−0.06** (0.03)
IPR sensitive × corruption	−0.11*** (0.02)	−0.13*** (0.05)	−0.13*** (0.04)		−0.15*** (0.03)
Corporate income tax rate		−0.00 (0.01)	−0.00 (0.01)	−0.01 (0.01)	
IPR sensitive × corporate income tax rate		0.01 (0.01)	0.01 (0.01)	0.00 (0.00)	
Progress in reform				0.29* (0.16)	
IPR sensitive × progress in reform				−0.07 (0.13)	
Privatization					0.02*** (0.00)
IPR sensitive × privatization					−0.01** (0.00)
Openness					0.25*** (0.08)

TABLE 6.6 Bivariate Probit with Sample Selection: Manufacturing vs. Distribution Projects (IPR Index) (Continued)

Investment decision					
IPR sensitive × openness					0.08 (0.06)
Firm size	0.17*** (0.02)	0.17*** (0.02)	0.17*** (0.02)	0.18*** (0.02)	0.17*** (0.02)
R&D intensity	0.03*** (0.01)	0.03*** (0.01)	0.03*** (0.01)	0.03*** (0.01)	0.03*** (0.01)
Advertising intensity	0.01*** (0.00)	0.01*** (0.00)	0.01*** (0.00)	0.01*** (0.00)	0.01*** (0.00)
Production diversification	0.04*** (0.01)	0.04*** (0.02)	0.04** (0.02)	0.04** (0.02)	0.04** (0.02)
Regional experience	0.95*** (0.04)	0.95*** (0.04)	0.95*** (0.04)	0.97*** (0.04)	0.96*** (0.04)
Constant	−6.84*** (0.36)	−6.80*** (0.48)	−6.80*** (0.44)	−8.29*** (0.54)	−8.41*** (0.72)
Decision regarding project type (manufacturing vs. distribution)					
IPR index	−0.04 (0.07)	−0.04 (0.06)	−0.04 (0.08)	0.19** (0.10)	0.11** (0.05)
IPR sensitive × IPR index	−0.03 (0.02)	−0.03 (0.02)	−0.03 (0.03)	−0.02 (0.04)	−0.03 (0.03)
GDP per capita	−0.42*** (0.08)	−0.41*** (0.07)	−0.41*** (0.08)	0.01 (0.12)	−0.48*** (0.09)
Population	0.13*** (0.02)	0.13*** (0.03)	0.13*** (0.03)	0.32*** (0.04)	0.16*** (0.03)
Corporate income tax rate			−0.00 (0.00)		
Progress in reform				0.41*** (0.13)	
Privatization					−0.01** (0.00)

(Continued)

TABLE 6.6 Bivariate Probit with Sample Selection: Manufacturing versus Distribution Projects (IPR Index) (Continued)

Decision regarding project type (manufacturing vs. distribution)					
Openness					-0.27*** (0.09)
Firm size	-0.12*** (0.02)	-0.12*** (0.02)	-0.12*** (0.02)	0.17*** (0.02)	-0.12*** (0.02)
R&D intensity	-0.06*** (0.01)	-0.06*** (0.00)	-0.06*** (0.01)	-0.05*** (0.01)	-0.06*** (0.01)
Advertising intensity	-0.02*** (0.00)	-0.02*** (0.00)	-0.02*** (0.00)	-0.01 (0.00)	-0.02*** (0.00)
Production diversification	-0.05*** (0.01)	-0.05*** (0.02)	-0.05*** (0.02)	0.01 (0.02)	-0.05*** (0.02)
Regional experience	-0.95*** (0.04)	-0.94*** (0.05)	-0.94*** (0.04)	0.53*** (0.12)	-0.93*** (0.05)
Constant	7.98*** (0.48)	7.94*** (0.37)	7.94*** (0.39)	-6.62*** (0.79)	8.73*** (0.81)
Rho	-1.00	-1.00	-1.00	0.95	-0.98
Chi-squared (Wald test 3.91 of rho = 0)	3.91	0.22	0.11	14.39	13.65
Probability > chi-squared	0.05	0.64	0.74	0.00	0.00
Number of observations	5,766	5,766	5,766	5,766	5,766
Number of observations (first equation)	5,292	5,292	5,292	5,292	5,292
Number of observations (second equation)	474	474	474	474	474

Note: *** denotes significant at the 1 percent level, ** at the 5 percent level, * at the 10 percent level. Standard errors are in parentheses.

Source: Author's estimations.

significant effect on the choice between investment in distribution networks and no investment at all.

In summary, the empirical results indicate that weaker protection of intellectual property discourages foreign investors from undertaking local production and tilts their preferences toward projects focusing on distribution alone. This result applies for all investors, not just those in IPR-sensitive sectors.

V. Conclusions

Governments all over the world compete fiercely to attract FDI, hoping that multinational corporations will bring new technologies, management skills, and marketing know-how. For a country to create an investment-friendly environment, it is important to understand the factors that influence FDI inflows as well as the determinants of the composition of such flows. This study sheds some light on this issue by examining the effect of IPR protection on the structure of FDI inflows.

Unlike the earlier literature, which focused on aggregate FDI flows, we use a unique firm-level data set describing investment projects in Eastern Europe and the former Soviet Union. Because that region was virtually closed to FDI before 1989, its sudden opening to foreign investment can be compared with a natural experiment. Therefore, the data set used in this study presents a unique opportunity to estimate the effect of IPR protection on FDI in the absence of investment history. It is possible that in earlier studies the lack of controls for past policy variables and investment history has obscured the effect of IPR protection on FDI.

Both hypotheses tested in the study find empirical support. First, the data indicate that investors in sectors relying heavily on protection of intellectual property are deterred by a weak IPR regime in a potential host country. There is also some evidence that weak IPR protection may discourage all investors, not just those in the sensitive sectors. Second, the lack of IPR protection deters investors from undertaking local production and encourages them to focus on distribution of imported products. Interestingly, this effect is present in all sectors, not only those relying heavily on IPR protection.

The results of this study suggest that more research is needed to improve our understanding of the implications of IPR regimes for the magnitude and composition of FDI inflows and their effect on developing countries. More specifically, it would be useful to study the characteristics of actual technologies transferred by multinationals to their subsidiaries to learn whether newer technologies are more likely to be transferred to host countries with stronger IPR protection while only older technologies are used in subsidiaries located in economies with weak intellectual property regimes.

Appendix 6.A. Robustness Tests

TABLE 6.A.1 Results of OLS Regressions

	(1)	(2)	(3)	(4)	(5)	(6)	(7)	(8)	(9)	(10)	(11)	(12)
Ginarte-Park index	0.07* (0.03)	0.08** (0.03)	0.03 (0.04)	0.04 (0.04)	0.07** (0.03)	0.07** (0.03)						
IPR index							0.05*** (0.02)	0.04*** (0.01)	0.04** (0.02)	0.05*** (0.02)	0.04** (0.02)	0.04** (0.02)
GDP per capita	−0.01 (0.02)	−0.02 (0.02)	0.04* (0.02)	0.02 (0.02)	0.01 (0.01)	0.01 (0.02)	0.00 (0.01)	0.00 (0.01)	0.02 (0.01)	0.01 (0.02)	0.01 (0.01)	0.01 (0.01)
Population	0.04*** (0.01)	0.05*** (0.01)	0.04*** (0.01)	0.05*** (0.01)	0.03*** (0.01)	0.03*** (0.01)	0.03*** (0.01)	0.04*** (0.01)	0.03*** (0.01)	0.03*** (0.01)	0.03*** (0.01)	0.03*** (0.01)
Progress in reform	0.08** (0.03)	0.10*** (0.02)					0.03** (0.01)	0.05** (0.02)				
Corporate income tax rate		−0.004** (0.00)						−0.004** (0.00)				
Legal effectiveness			0.01 (0.02)						0.01 (0.01)			
Corruption				−0.03** (0.01)						−0.02 (0.01)		
Privatization					0.003*** (0.00)	0.003*** (0.00)					0.001** (0.00)	0.001** (0.00)

Openness						0.00 (0.02)						0.00 (0.02)
Constant	−0.39*** (0.09)	−0.29*** (0.08)	−0.40*** (0.12)	−0.06 (0.19)	−0.41*** (0.07)	−0.42*** (0.10)	−0.20*** (0.06)	−0.10 (0.06)	−0.22*** (0.06)	0.00 (0.17)	−0.20*** (0.06)	−0.19*** (0.09)
Number of observations	19	19	19	18	19	19	21	19	21	19	21	21
F-statistic	12.86	18.11	7.31	9.85	19.87	14.81	22.05	26.27	16.46	16.49	21.87	16.42
Probability > F	0.00	0.00	0.00	0.00	0.00	0.00	0.00	0.00	0.00	0.00	0.00	0.00
R-squared	0.79	0.87	0.68	0.75	0.85	0.85	0.85	0.91	0.80	0.81	0.85	0.85
Adjusted R-squared	0.72	0.83	0.58	0.68	0.81	0.79	0.81	0.88	0.76	0.77	0.81	0.79

Note: *** denotes significant at the 1 percent level, ** at the 5 percent level, * at the 10 percent level. Standard errors are presented in parentheses.

Source: Author's estimations.

TABLE 6.A.2 Multinomial Logit Results: Manufacturing versus Distribution Projects versus No FDI

FDI in manufacturing facilities relative to FDI in distribution networks

Ginarte-Park index	0.83*** (0.30)	0.84*** (0.27)	0.63** (0.25)	0.97*** (0.20)				
IPR index					0.40** (0.18)	0.22 (0.22)	0.31** (0.14)	0.44*** (0.16)
GDP per capita	−0.64*** (0.24)	−0.73*** (0.23)	−0.74*** (0.20)	−0.57*** (0.20)	−0.41* (0.22)	−0.60** (0.25)	−0.79*** (0.22)	−0.62*** (0.24)
Population	0.32*** (0.07)	0.41*** (0.07)	0.41*** (0.05)	0.19*** (0.07)	0.27*** (0.09)	0.40*** (0.09)	0.40*** (0.07)	0.17** (0.08)
Progress in reform	0.96*** (0.26)	0.83*** (0.22)	0.99*** (0.20)		0.30 (0.24)	0.54** (0.25)	0.94*** (0.24)	
Corruption		−0.21** (0.09)	−0.15* (0.08)			−0.21 (0.16)	−0.03 (0.14)	
Corporate income tax			−0.02* (0.01)	0.04*** (0.01)			−0.04*** (0.01)	
Privatization								0.02* (0.01)
Openness				−0.27 (0.17)				−0.50** (0.20)

Firm size	0.01 (0.04)	0.01 (0.04)	0.01 (0.04)	0.02 (0.04)	0.02 (0.05)	0.01 (0.05)	0.01 (0.05)	0.02 (0.05)
R&D intensity	-0.13*** (0.03)	-0.13*** (0.03)	-0.13*** (0.03)	-0.13*** (0.03)	-0.15*** (0.04)	-0.14*** (0.04)	-0.14*** (0.04)	-0.15*** (0.04)
Advertising intensity	-0.03*** (0.01)	-0.03*** (0.01)	-0.03*** (0.01)	-0.03*** (0.01)	-0.03*** (0.01)	-0.03*** (0.01)	-0.03*** (0.01)	-0.03*** (0.01)
Production diversification	-0.01 (0.04)	-0.01 (0.04)	-0.01 (0.04)	-0.01 (0.04)	-0.01 (0.04)	0.00 (0.04)	0.00 (0.04)	-0.01 (0.04)
Regional experience	-0.69*** (0.14)	-0.70*** (0.14)	-0.70*** (0.14)	-0.68*** (0.14)	-0.68*** (0.14)	-0.70*** (0.14)	-0.69*** (0.14)	-0.69*** (0.14)
Constant	-0.57 (1.27)	1.81 (1.84)	2.30* (1.39)	-0.33 (1.44)	1.48 (1.27)	3.83 (2.33)	3.66* (2.02)	3.42** (1.69)
No FDI relative to FDI in distribution networks								
Ginarte-Park index	-0.08 (0.40)	0.14 (0.24)	0.18 (0.21)	0.01 (0.28)				
IPR index					-0.07 (0.22)	-0.10 (0.15)	-0.09 (0.15)	0.31** (0.13)
GDP per capita	-0.22 (0.17)	-0.15 (0.19)	-0.15 (0.18)	-0.49*** (0.12)	-0.65*** (0.23)	-0.64*** (0.17)	-0.66*** (0.17)	-1.14*** (0.20)

(Continued)

TABLE 6.A.2 Multinomial Logit Results:. Manufacturing versus Distribution Projects versus No FDI (Continued)

No FDI relative to FDI in distribution networks (continued)								
Population	-0.53*** (0.06)	-0.58*** (0.07)	-0.58*** (0.07)	-0.50*** (0.05)	-0.46*** (0.07)	-0.48*** (0.07)	-0.48*** (0.07)	-0.56*** (0.07)
Progress in reform	-0.80*** (0.19)	-0.65*** (0.24)	-0.70*** (0.25)		-0.52* (0.29)	-0.10 (0.26)	-0.03 (0.31)	
Corruption		0.25** (0.10)	0.22** (0.11)			0.24** (0.10)	0.28** (0.13)	
Corporate income tax rate			0.01 (0.01)				-0.01 (0.01)	
Privatization				-0.03*** (0.01)				-0.03*** (0.01)
Openness				-0.37** (0.16)				-0.88*** (0.21)
Firm size	-0.35*** (0.04)	-0.35*** (0.04)	-0.35*** (0.04)	-0.35*** (0.04)	-0.37*** (0.04)	-0.37*** (0.04)	-0.37*** (0.04)	-0.37*** (0.04)
R&D intensity	-0.08*** (0.01)	-0.09*** (0.01)	-0.09*** (0.01)	-0.08*** (0.01)	-0.08*** (0.01)	-0.08*** (0.01)	-0.08*** (0.01)	-0.04*** (0.00)
Advertising intensity	-0.04*** (0.00)	-0.04*** (0.00)	-0.04*** (0.00)	-0.04*** (0.00)	-0.04*** (0.00)	-0.04*** (0.00)	-0.04*** (0.00)	-0.04*** (0.00)

	(1)	(2)	(3)	(4)	(5)	(6)	(7)	(8)
Production diversification	-0.08**	-0.08***	-0.08**	-0.08**	-0.09**	-0.08**	-0.08**	-0.09**
	(0.03)	(0.03)	(0.03)	(0.03)	(0.04)	(0.04)	(0.04)	(0.04)
Regional experience	-2.25***	-2.26***	-2.27***	-2.26***	-2.25***	-2.25***	-2.25***	-2.25***
	(0.10)	(0.11)	(0.11)	(0.11)	(0.11)	(0.11)	(0.11)	(0.11)
Constant	15.80***	12.55***	12.58***	17.29***	18.11***	15.10***	14.97***	21.91***
	(0.97)	(1.38)	(1.42)	(0.78)	(1.30)	(1.10)	(1.05)	(1.69)
Number of observations.	5,795	5,490	5,490	5,795	6,405	5,795	5,795	6,405
Pseudo R-squared	0.26	0.27	0.27	0.27	0.30	0.29	0.29	0.31

Note: *** denotes significant at the 1 percent level, ** at the 5 percent level, * at the 10 percent level. Standard errors are presented in parentheses. Errors have been corrected for a correlation between observations for the same destination country.

Source: Author's estimations.

Notes

1. Other theories of FDI can be found in the surveys of Caves (1996), Dunning (1993), and Markusen (1995).

2. Indeed, Yang and Maskus (2001) find that licensing is more likely to take place in countries with strong IPR protection. Oxley (1999) also shows that U.S. companies tend to choose contract-based alliances rather than equity joint ventures when they partner with firms that are based in countries with strong intellectual property protection.

3. Baldwin (1996) also confirms that those sectors rely heavily on IPR protection.

4. Several western law firms active in Eastern Europe, when contacted by the author, confirmed that their clients, which were potential or actual foreign investors, expressed concerns about weak IPR protection in the region. Two firms represented foreign clients in patent infringement cases in transition economies.

5. Of the survey respondents, 117 were chosen for in-depth interviews, whose results are discussed in Lankes and Venables (1996).

6. Central and Eastern European countries and the former Soviet Union were virtually closed to foreign investment before 1989 (see Dunning and Rojec 1993; Hunya 1997; Meyer 1995). According to Dunning (1991), the number of joint ventures on January 1, 1989, in these countries was as follows: Hungary—270, Poland—55, Czechoslovakia—16, Bulgaria—25, Romania—5, and Soviet Union—291. The total was 662.

7. The author would like to thank Walter Park for kindly sharing the updated version of the index.

8. The sources used to extend the index include Garrison (various years), Baxter (various years), and Web sites of the State Intellectual Property Offices in Croatia and Latvia.

9. Although the mismatch in timing between the index and the data set is regrettable, it is not possible to use the ratings from earlier years, because they cover very few transition economies. Using an alternative measure of corruption, which is based on 1994 interviews with German exporters (see Ades and Di Tella 1997 for a description) leads to similar results not reported in this chapter.

10. The openness measure could potentially be endogenous, because FDI contributes to increased trade flows. Given, however, that the focus is on the beginning of the transition process, when the volume of FDI inflows was limited, the endogeneity problem is unlikely to affect results.

11. Because of data constraints, statutory tax rates are used, even though effective tax rates might be more appropriate. However, Wei's (1999) findings indicate that substituting the effective rates for statutory rates has a negligible effect on the results.

12. Note that this is a standard proxy in the literature and has been used, for instance, by Grubaugh (1987).

13. Note that the number of observations is equal to the number of firms in the sample times the number of possible destination countries. Because of firm-specific dummy variables, firms with no investment in the region drop out of the estimation. The sample is further reduced by the fact that the Ginarte-Park index covers only 19 countries.

14. In other words, the dependent variable is equal to the number of firms in IPR-sensitive sectors that invested in country c divided by the total number of firms in these sectors in the sample.

15. See Smarzynska and Wei (2000) for a discussion on the impact of corruption on the composition of FDI inflows.

16. Even though one would expect that less experienced firms would shy away from manufacturing projects, their investments may possibly take place through joint ventures, thus reducing the importance of previous regional experience because they can benefit from the knowledge of local partners (Smarzynska 2000).

References

Ades, Alberto, and Rafael Di Tella. 1997. "National Champions and Corruption: Some Unpleasant Interventionist Arithmetic." *Economic Journal* 107:1023–42.

Baldwin, John. 1996. "The Use of Intellectual Property Rights by Canadian Manufacturing Firms: Findings from the Innovation Survey." Statistics Canada, Ottawa. Processed.

Baxter, J. W., ed. Various years. *World Patent Law and Practice*. New York: M. Bender.

Braunerhjelm, Pontus, and Roger Svensson. 1996. "Host Country Characteristics and Agglomeration in Foreign Direct Investment." *Applied Economics* 28:833–40.

Caves, Richard E. 1996. *Multinational Enterprise and Economic Analysis*. 2nd ed. Cambridge: Cambridge University Press.

Dunning, John H. 1991. "The Prospects for Foreign Direct Investment in Eastern Europe." Discussion Paper in International Investment and Business Studies 155. University of Reading, U.K.

———. 1993. *Multinational Enterprises and the Global Economy*. Wokingham, U.K.: Addison-Wesley Publishing.

Dunning, John H., and Matija Rojec. 1993. *Foreign Privatization in Central and Eastern Europe*. Ljubljana, Sloenja: CEEPN.

EBRD (European Bank for Reconstruction and Development). Various years. *Transition Report*. London.

Estrin, Saul, Kirsty Hughes, and Sarah Todd. 1997. *Foreign Direct Investment in Central and Eastern Europe: Multinationals in Transition*. London and Washington, D.C.: Pinter/Royal Institute for International Affairs.

Ferrantino, Michael J. 1993. "The Effect of Intellectual Property Rights on International Trade and Investment." *Weltwirtschaftliches Archiv* 129(2):300–31.

Garrison, David, ed. Various years. *Intellectual Property: Eastern Europe and Commonwealth of Independent States*. New York: Oceana Publications.

Ginarte, Juan C., and Walter G. Park. 1997. "Determinants of Patent Rights: A Cross-National Study." *Research Policy* 26(3):283–301.

Grubaugh, Stephen G. 1987. "Determinants of Direct Foreign Investment". *Review of Economics and Statistics* 69:149–52.

Hallward-Driemeier, Mary. 1996. "Understanding Foreign Direct Investment by Firms: Market Pull, Cost Push, and Knowledge Accumulation." Massachusetts Institute of Technology, Cambridge, Mass. Processed.

Hunya, Gabor. 1997. "Large Privatisation, Restructuring, and Foreign Direct Investment." In Salvatore Zecchini, ed., *Lessons from the Economic Transition. Central and Eastern Europe in the 1990s*. Dordrecht, Boston, and London: Kluwer Academic Publishers.

IIPA(International Intellectual Property Alliance). Various years. *Special 301 Recommendations*. Available at http://www.iipa.com/.

Lall, Sanjaya. 1997. "Investment, Technology, and International Competitiveness." In John H. Dunning and Khalil A. Hamdani, eds., *The New Globalism and Developing Countries*. Tokyo, New York, and Paris: United Nations University Press.

Lan, Ping, and Stephen Young. 1996. "Foreign Direct Investment and Technology Transfer: A Case-Study of Foreign Direct Investment in North-East China." *Transnational Corporations* 5(1):57–83.

Lankes, Hans-Peter, and Anthony J. Venables. 1996. "Foreign Direct Investment in Economic Transition: The Changing Pattern of Investments." *Economics of Transition* 4(2):331–47.

Lee, Jeong-Yeon, and Edwin Mansfield. 1996. "Intellectual Property Protection and U.S. Foreign Direct Investment." *Review of Economics and Statistics* 78(2):181–86.

Mansfield, Edwin. 1994. "Intellectual Property Protection, Foreign Direct Investment, and Technology Transfer." IFC Discussion Paper 19. International Finance Corporation, Washington, D.C.

———. 1995. "Intellectual Property Protection, Direct Investment, and Technology Transfer." IFC Discussion Paper 27. International Finance Corporation, Washington, D.C.

Markusen, James R. 1995. "The Boundaries of Multinational Enterprises and the Theory of International Trade." *Journal of Economic Perspectives* 9(2):169–89.

Maskus, Keith, and Denise Eby Konan. 1994. "Trade-Related Intellectual Property Rights: Issues and Exploratory Results." In Alan V. Deardorff and Robert M. Stern, eds., *Analytical and Negotiating Issues in the Global Trading System*. Ann Arbor: University of Michigan Press.

Meyer, Klaus. 1995. "Direct Foreign Investment in Eastern Europe: The Role of Labor Costs." *Comparative Economic Studies* 37(3):69–88.

Oxley, Joanne E. 1999. "Institutional Environment and the Mechanisms of Governance: The Impact of Intellectual Property Protection on the Structure of Inter-Firm Alliances." *Journal of Economic Behavior and Organization* 38:283–309.

Primo Braga, Carlos, and Carsten Fink. 2000. "International Transactions in Intellectual Property and Developing Countries." *International Journal of Technology Management* 19:35–56.

Rapp, Richard T., and Richard P. Rozek. 1990. "Benefits and Costs of Intellectual Property Protection in Developing Countries." *Journal of World Trade* 24(5):75–102.

Sharp, Margaret, and Michael Barz. 1997. "Multinational Companies and the Transfer and Diffusion of New Technological Capabilities in Central and Eastern Europe and the Former Soviet Union." In David A. Dyker, ed., *The Technology of Transition. Science, and Technology Policies for Transition Countries*. Budapest: Central European University Press.

Smarzynska, Beata. 2000. "Technology Transfer and Foreign Investors' Choice of Entry Mode." Policy Research Working Paper 2314. World Bank, Washington, D.C.

Smarzynska, Beata, and Shang-Jin Wei. 2000. "Corruption and Composition of Foreign Direct Investment: Firm Level Evidence." NBER Working Paper 7969. National Bureau of Economic Research, Cambridge, Mass.

Smith, Pamela J. 2001. "How Do Foreign Patent Rights Affect U.S. Exports, Affiliate Sales, and Licenses?" *Journal of International Economics* 55:411–39.

Wei, Shang-Jin. 1999. "Does Corruption Relieve the Burden of Taxes and Capital Controls for International Investors?" Policy Research Working Paper 2209. World Bank, Washington, D.C.

World Bank. 1996. *World Development Report 1996: From Plan to Market*. New York: Oxford University Press.

Yang, Guifang, and Keith E. Maskus. 2001. "Intellectual Property Rights and Licensing: An Econometric Investigation." *Weltwirtschafliches Archiv* 137(1):58–79.

Zloch-Christy, Iliana. 1995. "Economic Transformation, External Imbalances, and Political Risk in Post-Communist Eastern Europe." In Iliana Zloch-Christy, ed., *Privatization and Foreign Investments in Eastern Europe*. Westport, Conn. and London: Praeger.

INTELLECTUAL PROPERTY EXHAUSTION AND PARALLEL TRADE

7

ENTERING THE JUNGLE OF INTELLECTUAL PROPERTY RIGHTS EXHAUSTION AND PARALLEL IMPORTATION

Carsten Fink

I. Introduction

The exhaustion doctrine related to the protection of intellectual property rights (IPRs) is one of the most complicated regulations of international business. It defines the territorial rights of intellectual property owners after the first sale of their protected products. Under a system of *national* exhaustion, a title holder can prevent parallel importation of his or her product from a foreign country, where it is sold either by the IPR owner or by an authorized dealer. In contrast, if rights exhaust *internationally,* the title holder loses his or her exclusive privilege after the first distribution of the product, thus allowing parallel imports from abroad. A hybrid between national and international exhaustion is *regional* exhaustion, whereby parallel trading is allowed within a particular group of countries, but parallel imports from countries outside the region are banned.

This chapter is adapted from a chapter published in Owen Lippert (ed.), *Competitive Strategies for Intellectual Property Protection*, (Vancouver, B.C., Canada: Fraser Institute, 2000). It was prepared for the two conferences on Competitive Strategies for Intellectual Property Protection, organized by the Fraser Institute and held in Santiago, Chile, on April 19, 1999 and in Buenos Aires, Argentina, on April 22, 1999. I gratefully acknowledge helpful comments by Octavio Espinosa and Jayashree Watal.

Parallel trade refers to trade in genuine products outside official channels of distribution; it should not be confused with trade in counterfeit goods, which refers to trade in products that infringe on an IPR. If unrestricted, parallel trading activities can generally take two forms. The most common form is *passive parallel imports*, whereby arbitrageurs buy goods in a foreign country and sell them in the domestic market. *Active parallel imports* occur when a foreign licensee (or distributor) of the IPR holder enters the domestic market to compete with the IPR holder or his or her official domestic licensee. Regardless of the form that parallel imports take, they are subject to the same border measures as regular imports are, including tariffs, quantitative restrictions, and technical standards.

The economic significance of the exhaustion doctrine is difficult to evaluate. The potential size of the market that could be subject to parallel trading activities, if unrestricted, is undoubtedly significant, because most tradable goods (besides commodities) and services are protected by at least one form of IPR (for example, trademarks).[1] Virtually no statistics are available on this so-called gray market segment of international trade. In addition, if intellectual property owners and their licensees respond to the threat of parallel imports by pricing more uniformly across national markets—thereby eroding international arbitrage opportunities—trade statistics would give an insufficient indication of the economic effect of parallel import policies.

The significance of the exhaustion doctrine depends also on the extent to which private contractual means can substitute for territorial rights exhaustion in restricting parallel imports. Territorial restraints in licensing agreements and restrictive purchasing contracts can limit active and passive parallel imports, respectively, even though IPRs may exhaust internationally. The extent to which such private contractual means can be used depends, in turn, on whether they are considered to be anticompetitive by prevailing competition laws.

Current exhaustion regimes differ widely among countries and across the different forms of IPRs. Although most industrial countries maintain significant restrictions on parallel imports, recent initiatives by policymakers in several Organisation for Economic Co-operation and Development (OECD) countries have been favorable to international exhaustion. It would be premature, however, to interpret these initiatives as a fundamental shift in the regulations that govern parallel imports. Parallel import policies have also received increasing attention in proposals for promoting differential pricing structures for pharmaceutical products; these structures may entail substantial price discounts of essential medicines in poor countries.[2] Finally, as intellectual property rules have become part of international trade agreements, future trade negotiations at the bilateral, regional, and multilateral levels may seek to develop obligations with regard to IPR exhaustion.

The effects of national or international exhaustion are complex and have been subject to extensive debate among economists, lawyers, lobbyists, and policymakers.

This chapter offers an introduction into this "jungle" of intellectual property exhaustion by focusing on the economic aspects of the debate. It starts by outlining the current state of national and international regulations that govern parallel imports. The subsequent two sections discuss the pros and cons of national versus international exhaustion and review the (limited) empirical evidence. The chapter concludes by pointing to some issues that may be relevant in the context of international trade negotiations covering exhaustion rules.

II. The Current Legal Framework

Unless bound by an international agreement, countries are free to adopt their preferred exhaustion regime for each form of IPR. So far, no international convention or multilateral agreement on IPRs has mandated a particular regime. The only provision in the various multilateral and plurilateral agreements of the World Trade Organization (WTO) that explicitly addresses the exhaustion issue is article 6 of the Agreement on Trade-Related Aspects of Intellectual Property Rights (TRIPS), which states:

> For the purposes of dispute settlement under this Agreement, subject to the provisions of Articles 3 and 4 above nothing in this Agreement shall be used to address the issue of the exhaustion of intellectual property rights.[3]

Article 6 of TRIPS is widely interpreted as an agreement to disagree, giving WTO members the freedom to opt for national, regional, or international exhaustion.[4] It reflects the negotiating history of TRIPS, in which, although the exhaustion issue was raised, member countries could not form consensus on a multilateral statute.

At the regional level, the European Union (EU) applies a system of regional exhaustion that denies parallel imports from outside the EU territories but does not restrict parallel trading within those territories. This system has emerged from jurisprudence by the European Court of Justice (ECJ). In the early 1970s, the ECJ ruled that national exhaustion would be inconsistent with the Treaty of Rome, which aims at "[uniting] national markets into a single market."[5] The regional exhaustion regime applies to all forms of intellectual property. However, in the past, the European Commission has considered the revision of the EU trademark directive, so as to free parallel imports from outside the EU (see NERA 1999).

Other regional trade agreements largely remain silent on the exhaustion issue. The North American Free Trade Agreement (NAFTA), for example, has no explicit provision on the exhaustion question, and the substantive provisions of NAFTA's chapter 17 on IPRs can be interpreted as giving member countries freedom to determine their preferred exhaustion regime. The Treaty of Asunción, which established the Southern Cone Common Market (Mercado Común del Sur, or MERCOSUR) between Argentina, Brazil, Paraguay, and Uruguay, also does not address the question of parallel imports.[6]

At the national level, the United States applies (with few exceptions) a system of national exhaustion for all forms of IPRs.[7] The exhaustion regimes of other OECD countries also lean toward national exhaustion, although there are important cases in which IPRs exhaust internationally. In Japan, for example, a recent decision by the Supreme Court confirmed the lawfulness of parallel imports of patented products unless restrictions are clearly displayed on the products.[8] In 1998, New Zealand became the first OECD country to adopt a system of international exhaustion with respect to copyright.[9] After the removal of parallel import restrictions on compact discs (CDs) in 1998, the Australian government considered expanding the international exhaustion rule in the area of copyright to books and computer software ("Australia Presses for Liberalization" 1999).

In non-OECD countries, regulations regarding parallel imports differ widely. According to a survey on parallel import protection in the area of copyright, for example, 25 non-OECD countries were classified as providing such protection and 21 non-OECD countries were classified as allowing parallel imports (the regime was unclear in 33 non-OECD countries).[10] Recent decisions by New Zealand and Australia to open their markets for parallel imports in copyright-protected products as well as the current initiative on reforming the EU trademark directive on this issue have brought increased attention to the parallel import question.[11]

Finally, exhaustion rules may be subject to future trade negotiations. For the foreseeable future, further negotiation is unlikely for TRIPS (although proposals for an exhaustion obligation were made before the launch of the Doha Round), but it may well happen in the context of bilateral or regional trade agreements. Indeed, the 2003 free trade agreement between the United States and Singapore has an implicit obligation to curtail parallel importation of pharmaceutical products.[12]

III. The Pros and Cons of National IPR Exhaustion Compared with International IPR Exhaustion

Before turning to the various arguments and counterarguments defending either exhaustion regime, it is useful to briefly recall the economic justification for granting IPRs.[13] One can broadly classify the various forms of IPRs into two categories: IPRs that stimulate inventive and creative activities (patents, utility models, industrial designs, copyright, plant breeders' rights, and layout designs for integrated circuits) and IPRs that resolve information asymmetries (trademarks and geographic indications).[14] IPRs in both categories seek to address certain failures of private markets to provide for an efficient allocation of resources.

IPRs in the first category can be seen as a solution to the problems created by the public good characteristic of knowledge and information. If creators of intellectual works cannot protect themselves against imitation and copying, they may not have an incentive to engage in inventive or creative activities because they may be unable to recoup any expenditures incurred in the process of creating new knowledge or information. Over history, societies have therefore granted exclusive commercial rights to intellectual works—most prominent, patents to foster industrial innovation and copyright to promote literary and artistic expression. Beginning in the late 1980s, these rights were extended to the development of biotechnology products, computer software and digital information.

IPRs in the second category resolve inefficiencies that result from asymmetries of information between buyers and sellers on certain attributes of goods and services. Thus, trademarks identify a product with its producer and his or her reputation for quality; trademarks assure consumers that they are purchasing what they intend to purchase.

There is an important difference between these two basic groups of intellectual property. IPRs that stimulate inventive and creative activities explicitly confer market power in the supply of the protected good to the titleholder, who can thereby reap monopolistic profits that finance knowledge and information–generating investments. From a welfare perspective, the market power entailed in patents and copyright poses a cost to society. This cost, however, is counterbalanced by the benefits that the creation of new knowledge and information brings to society. IPRs that resolve information asymmetrics, in contrast, are not designed to confer any direct market power. Trademarks do not restrict imitation or copying of protected goods as long as they are sold under a different brand name. This difference is reflected in the attribute that protection of IPRs in the first category is limited to a fixed time period (for example, 20 years for patents) to minimize the costs of a distorted market structure, whereas IPRs in the second category can endure virtually indefinitely provided they remain in use. At the same time, it should be noted that trademark owners typically differentiate their products (for example, through promotional activities) and thus are also able to create market power.

The remainder of this section will present and discuss six main arguments in favor or disfavor of a particular exhaustion regime. Although these arguments are not necessarily independent of one another, for analytical purposes, it is useful to consider them separately.

A. The Classic Free Trade Argument

The most general argument in favor of international exhaustion has been that a system of territorial market segmentation is at odds with the principle of free trade (Abbott 1998). For a long time, economists have argued the case for free trade. Through the international exchange of goods and services, countries can specialize in what they can do best, which leads to mutual gains for all trading partners. Dismantling trade barriers causes a reallocation of production based on comparative advantage, which expands countries' production possibility frontiers. As illustrated in the previous section, the free trade argument has been at the core of the EU's adoption of a regional exhaustion regime.

Undoubtedly, a system of national exhaustion poses a nontariff barrier to trade. However, can the classic free trade argument be applied in an ad hoc manner to parallel trade? In other words, do the assumptions on which economists base their case for free trade fit into the environment in which parallel trade takes place? The standard trade theory of comparative advantage—which has arguably provided the most significant intellectual thrust toward the worldwide liberalization of international trade—assumes that trade occurs under the conditions of free entry and perfect competition. In perfectly competitive markets, however, competition between different producers forces firms to set their prices equal to marginal costs in all free-trading countries, thereby eroding the basis for parallel imports. Parallel trading opportunities can arise only in an environment of imperfect competition, where firms have pricing power and, therefore, the ability to set different prices in different markets. Thus, parallel imports do not seem to fit into the standard framework in which economists make their case for free trade based on comparative advantage.[15] An ad hoc application of the classic free trade argument to parallel trade, therefore, seems problematic.

B. Abusive Price Discrimination or Welfare-Enhancing Price Differentiation?

A system of national exhaustion allows firms to charge different prices in different markets for the same goods and services. Some observers generally consider price discrimination to be the result of anticompetitive behavior (for example, taking the form of predatory pricing) and have stressed the policing function that parallel imports exercise in restraining abusive business practices (Abbott 1998). The potential for anticompetitive behavior in the presence of IPR ownership is well known, as firms may attempt to exploit their exclusive rights beyond the established limits.[16] The policing function of parallel imports may be especially important for small developing countries, where competition from substitute goods may be limited and competition policies are often absent or undeveloped (Hoekman and Holmes 1999).

However, although price discrimination can indeed be related to anticompetitive practices, it can also take a benign form. In these cases, it is labeled with the more neutral term *price differentiation*. Such welfare-enhancing price discrimination *may* occur when firms charge different prices to different consumer groups with heterogeneous demand structures—a practice known as *third-degree price discrimination.*[17] In the context of international price discrimination, this practice may be illustrated by the following example. Suppose there are two countries—one rich, one poor—and a firm would serve only the consumers in the rich country if parallel trade between the two countries were allowed and the firm could thus not price discriminate. In contrast, it would charge the same price to consumers in the rich country but also serve the consumers in the poor country at a lower price if parallel trade were prohibited. In the latter scenario, both the firm and consumers in the poor country would be better off, and consumers in the rich country would not be worse off.[18]

Malueg and Schwartz (1994) developed a formal partial equilibrium model and found that uniform pricing by a monopolist can yield lower global welfare than discriminatory pricing if the dispersion of demand across countries is sufficiently large. Moreover, Malueg and Schwartz showed that global welfare can be maximized if one places countries into designated groups and allows discriminatory pricing between those groups but allows uniform pricing within the groups.

Can this theoretical result give useful guidance for welfare-maximizing exhaustion regimes? It should first be pointed out that national regulations that maximize global welfare may not necessarily maximize national welfare. Consumers in countries that would have lower prices under international price discrimination than under uniform pricing would benefit from restrictions on parallel trade, whereas consumers in countries that would have higher prices under price discrimination would be worse off from such restrictions. Nevertheless, the high-price country would decide whether to curb parallel trade (ignoring voluntary restraints on parallel exports by low-price countries). This may partly explain why countries such as Australia and New Zealand, which are not significant producers of intellectual property, have begun to lift restrictions on parallel imports.

Second, IPR holders hardly operate as full monopolists. They typically compete with substitute goods in national and international markets and are thus limited in their pricing power and their ability to price discriminate. Third, it is difficult to generalize in which countries market demand is relatively more elastic for a given product and would thus imply a lower price. Although demand elasticities typically vary with per capita incomes, prices in developing countries are not always lower than in industrial countries. One example would be that suppliers target their products in poor countries to rich market segments, for which demand is less elastic than in the mass consumer market of industrial countries. Observed price differentials between countries may be a misleading indicator of differences in demand structures. Aside from transportation, distribution, and marketing costs, as well as duties and other taxes, price differentials are the result of differences in market structure or other supply characteristics.

The possibility of welfare-enhancing price discrimination is likely to be higher for goods covered by IPRs that stimulate inventive or creative activities compared with the other category of IPRs, because the exclusive rights of patents and copyrights put explicit limits on the degree to which a protected product may be substituted by competing products. Examples of goods for which the possibility of benign price discrimination has been indicated include pharmaceuticals and educational and scientific publications, which are often priced at substantial discounts in developing countries.

Assuming that there are cases in which price discrimination is indeed welfare enhancing, it would nonetheless be difficult to translate this potential benefit into explicit proposals for countries' exhaustion regimes. A system of territorial exhaustion would extend to all goods covered by a particular IPR, although price discrimination may be desirable only for a selected range of products. In addition, the concept of national exhaustion has its origin in the territorial character of IPRs in general. However, it seems unlikely that optimum exhaustion areas, as proposed by Malueg and Schwartz (1994), would coincide with national boundaries. The formation of regional exhaustion areas, in turn, would face many practical and political difficulties.[19] Notwithstanding these difficulties, the proposition that price discrimination may open otherwise unserved markets could be of importance with respect to certain developing (especially the least developed) countries.

C. National Exhaustion as a Reinforcement of IPRs

Restrictions on parallel trade give IPR holders the ability to fix a profit-maximizing price in each national market and therefore tend to raise their overall profitability. Consequently, firms may boost their investments in knowledge and information–generating activities, which may lead to an accelerated pace of industrial innovation and increased production of new literary and artistic works. Obviously, this argument applies only to IPRs that stimulate inventive and creative activities, not to trademarks and geographic indications. Simply stated, it means that a system of national exhaustion increases the strength of intellectual property protection.[20] This explains, for example, why the United States—as the world's largest producer of intellectual property—generally favors national exhaustion of patent rights and copyright both at home and abroad.

The optimal scope of IPR protection and the desirability of stronger IPRs have been subject to extensive debate, yet only a small body of empirical evidence has been collected. As such, it remains inherently difficult to evaluate the desirability of a national exhaustion regime in this context. It could be argued, however, that it would be better (if possible) to adjust the strength of IPR protection through other regulations—notably the length of protection—given the various other implications of parallel import protection.

D. The Special Case of Government Intervention

So far, prices have been assumed implicitly to be the outcome of competitive market forces. This is not always the case, however. In some industries, governments intervene in private markets by controlling prices or regulating companies' rates of return. Some observers have argued that parallel trade in goods covered by an IPR and subject to "artificially" low prices because of government intervention would represent unfair competition in intervention-free countries. This concern has been mentioned repeatedly in the pharmaceutical industry, in which government price controls are common in both industrial and developing countries. A system of national exhaustion would deny parallel imports from countries where the IPR holder or his or her licensee are subject to government intervention.

Obviously, this argument applies only to industries and countries in which governments intervene in private markets. In addition, it is relevant only for those government interventions that target domestic consumption and would thus lead to a different treatment of parallel exports compared with regular exports. In the particular case of pharmaceutical price controls—leaving aside their desirability and effectiveness—one could argue that parallel import restrictions are appropriate because the commonly stated goal of price controls is to make medicines affordable to domestic low-income consumers, and there would be little justification of extending such a national policy to foreign consumers.[21] At the same time, it could be reasoned that consumers in a particular country would benefit from low-priced parallel imports regardless of the cause of low prices.[22] However, if significant leakage from price-controlled countries leads to markedly lower worldwide profits for IPR holders, they may decide to stop serving price-controlled markets altogether.

E. National Exhaustion as an Extension of Vertical Control

Some observers have advocated national exhaustion on the grounds that such a system extends IPR holders' control over the international distribution of their goods and services. Several benefits of territorial market segmentation have been brought forward in this context. First, segmented distribution systems may protect investments in marketing as well as before- and after-sales services that may be associated with the sale of certain goods. Parallel imports from different sales territories that do not provide these services or, where such activities are substantially cheaper, would "free ride" on the investments made by official licensees and distributors. Territorial sales restraints are therefore in the interest of consumers, because the threat of parallel imports would lead firms to relinquish any marketing and sales support activities. At the same time, it should be mentioned that this argument is only valid insofar as sales support services (such as warranty or product maintenance) cannot be extended beyond national territories.

Second, parallel imports from different territories may exhibit a different quality than goods sold through official distribution channels; this may lead to the deception of consumers. In some cases, it has even been suggested that parallel imports may undermine the enforcement of technical, health, and safety standards in the importing country.[23] The potential magnitude of consumer deception is hard to generalize, however. Moreover, with the provision of adequate information, parallel imports of different quality can actually increase the choices of consumers and thus be beneficial. Third, IPR holders may be reluctant to license proprietary technology to a different market unless they are assured that the licensee will not compete with the IPR holder in his or her home market or a third market. This reluctance may slow the pace of technology diffusion and thus be harmful to follow-on innovation and productivity growth.[24]

Although vertical restraints can indeed be beneficial, there is no presumption that this is always the case. They also carry costs—most significantly, in the form of reduced intrabrand competition. In fact, there is no consensus among economists and competition lawyers about when vertical restrictions are pro-competitive and when they are detrimental. An IPR holder may even seek to encourage parallel trade between different territories to avoid collusive behavior among his or her various dealers. A general system of national exhaustion, therefore, seems an inapt regulation in reaping the potential benefits of vertical restraints. National exhaustion would apply to every good covered by a particular IPR and deny both passive and active parallel imports. Such a system would be inflexible because it may be desirable to have complete denial of parallel imports for some goods, restrictions on active but not passive parallel imports for others, and no limits on parallel trading for still others.

F. Statutory IPR Exhaustion or Private Contractual Arrangements?

One fundamental argument that has been brought against national exhaustion is that restrictions on parallel imports—if they are desirable—are better created through private contractual arrangements that can be scrutinized by competition laws (Gallini and Hollis 1996). This strategy seems appealing for several reasons. First, it allows a tailor-made approach that can directly address the specific environment of different sectors and products. Second, private restrictions on parallel imports may not necessarily be bound to national territories, which may be especially important for small countries. Third, governments would be able to address country-specific concerns in national competition laws.

Indeed, this approach is followed domestically in the United States and on a regional basis in the EU with regard to active parallel trading. With few exceptions, U.S. antitrust law and EU competition law permit territorial restraints in connection with the licensing of an IPR (Abbott 1998). Vertical restrictions in international licensing agreements are also common practice in many sectors.

Could private contractual means also be used to regulate passive parallel imports? In fact, this occurs under the common law approach to IPR exhaustion. In common law countries, exhaustion remains under the discretion of the IPR holder, who can deny parallel imports by including an appropriate notice of restriction in licensing and purchasing agreements (for example, by attaching a label on a product indicating "Not for sale in countries X, Y, and Z"). Whether such a system could work effectively on a worldwide level remains unclear. IPR holders would have to give proper notice—most likely in several languages —to all resellers involved (Heath 1997). This system's effectiveness would also depend on the degree to which restrictions on passive parallel imports are deemed desirable. Policymakers in both the United States and the EU deliberately decided to leave the internal market open to passive parallel trade. However, if restrictions on passive parallel imports are deemed to be welfare enhancing on a wider scale and uniformly across all goods covered by a particular type of IPR, a statutory regime of national or regional exhaustion may overall be less cumbersome.

Opponents of a system of private contractual arrangements contend that such a system is unrealistic in light of undeveloped competition policies and inadequate enforceability of private contracts in many developing countries. In addition, some observers have argued that such a system could not work effectively before a harmonization of national competition policies has taken place at the international level. It is unclear, however, how much harmonization is necessary and to what degree private restraints on parallel imports can be regulated effectively by national competition policies. Undoubtedly, the development of competition institutions in developing countries and increased international harmonization of competition policies would facilitate the functioning of private contractual regulations on parallel imports and thus ease the need for national exhaustion systems.

IV. The (Limited) Empirical Evidence

As mentioned in the introduction, virtually no statistics are available on the parallel segment of international trade. Available data on parallel trade come from a few business surveys in industrial countries and are confined mostly to goods for which producers are particularly sensitive to parallel trade, such as well-known consumer brands, CDs, or pharmaceuticals. Accordingly, it is difficult to develop a picture of the overall direction and magnitude of parallel trade flows. In addition, available evidence on the effect of parallel trade typically concentrates on prices in the importing countries and profits of intellectual property owners; no evidence exists with regard to the price effects in exporting countries. Notwithstanding these caveats, the fragmented evidence that is available gives some indication as to the causes and consequences of parallel trade.

Parallel imports became a cause of concern for U.S. policymakers in the mid-1980s, when they were estimated at 2 to 3 percent of total U.S. imports.[25] Parallel imports were concentrated in goods with well-known brands that typically involved heavy investments in marketing and promotion, suggesting the free-riding explanation of parallel trade discussed earlier. At the same time, parallel imports surged in line with the marked appreciation of the U.S. dollar up to the mid-1980s and fell sharply thereafter. This empirical pattern points to incomplete exchange rate pass-through as the cause of parallel trade (that is, firms adjusted prices in the United States or abroad by a smaller percentage than the dollar's relative appreciation).[26] Incomplete exchange rate pass-through could be caused by firms' behavior to adjust their prices to the new demand conditions created by the exchange rate movement (Dornbusch 1987). This would suggest a pattern of international price discrimination, although one cannot conclude that pricing to market was necessarily welfare enhancing. It is likely that U.S. parallel imports during the 1980s were caused by both free riding and price discrimination, and the relevance of these two factors is confirmed by several court cases during this time period (Gallini and Hollis 1996).

More recent empirical evidence on parallel imports comes from a study commissioned by the European Commission as part of its initiative to reform the EU trademark directive (NERA 1999). The study focuses on 10 different consumer goods sectors in which trademarks are important and the scope of parallel trade is significant.[27] Despite the absence of restrictions on parallel trade within the EU, substantial price differentials generally remain across EU member states. Some of the differentials may reflect factors such as transportation and distribution costs, transitory exchange rate movements, and tax differences, but it appears that parallel imports do not prevent trademark holders from price discriminating across national markets. The significance of parallel trade varies among the 10 sectors, from below 5 percent of sales for footwear and leather goods, domestic appliances, and alcoholic drinks to around 13 percent of sales for premium cosmetics and perfumes and up to 20 percent for some releases of musical recordings.

The study then considers the potential effect of opening the EU market to parallel imports from other countries, notably Japan and the United States. The scope of parallel trade in the 10 sectors seems large because there are significant differences between retail prices in the EU, Japan, and the United States. With some exceptions, it appears that retail prices in the United States are generally lower than in the EU, whereas retail prices are generally higher in Japan than in the EU. When estimating the effect of freeing parallel imports on EU retail prices and trademark holders' profits, the study finds only small or moderate decreases in prices (on average less than 5 percent) but marked falls in profits—by as much as 35 percent in the consumer electronics sector.

These estimates depend on various assumptions with regard to market structure and demand, and it is hard to evaluate how realistic the reported figures are. Anecdotal evidence from Australia, for example, is more optimistic about price reductions that resulted from the removal of parallel import restrictions on CDs in October 1998. Some retailers reduced the price of selected top-selling CDs by nearly one-third ("Australia Presses for Liberalization" 1999).

V. Conclusion

The question of whether businesses should be allowed to control parallel imports of goods and services from foreign countries on the basis of local IPR ownership has been subject to controversy. This chapter shows that the welfare implications of a particular exhaustion regime are theoretically ambiguous, are likely to differ among the various forms of IPRs, and involve various industry- and product-specific considerations. A better case can probably be made for international exhaustion of IPRs that resolve information asymmetries than of IPRs that stimulate inventive and creative activities. In the latter group of IPRs, imperfectly competitive market structures are inherently related to IPRs, and the possibilities of benign international price discrimination may thus be higher. At any rate, the empirical evidence on the causes and consequences of parallel imports is still too scattered to make a case for a particular exhaustion regime for one or more forms of IPRs.

A question fundamentally related to IPR exhaustion is whether it would be more desirable to regulate parallel imports through private contracts scrutinized by competition policy. Such an approach seems attractive because it would offer flexibility in addressing the specific environment of each industry and in accounting for country-specific concerns. It is not clear, however, whether such a system can be implemented practically on a global basis and to what degree it would presuppose harmonized competition policies.

Future trade negotiations may seek to negotiate binding obligations with regard to exhaustion rules. In principle, international negotiations on the exhaustion question may seem warranted because a country's choice of exhaustion regime imposes an externality on its trading partners in the form of either uniform or discriminatory international pricing strategies. Hence, the exchange of concessions on the exhaustion issue with concessions in other areas being negotiated could theoretically be a mutually beneficial affair. For many countries, it is far from obvious, however, whether a particular obligation on exhaustion would mean they would give or receive a concession.

The United States, as the world's single largest producer of intellectual property, has traditionally favored a statute of national exhaustion. The position of other industrial countries is less clear. Depending on the economic and political weight of intellectual property producers in these countries on the one hand and the potential benefits countries see in allowing parallel imports on the other, other industrial nations may be more or less open to a rule of international exhaustion. The stance of developing countries is also uncertain. When the exhaustion issue was raised during the Uruguay Round (1986–94), many developing countries supported a system of international exhaustion (Watal 1998). They were motivated by the expectation that parallel imports would lead to increased competition and could thus restrain monopolistic prices and potentially abusive behavior of IPR holders (especially against the background of stronger intellectual property standards as mandated by TRIPS). Many developing countries also saw the removal of parallel import restrictions as opening export opportunities. However, there is a potentially significant downside for developing countries of freeing parallel imports. If the threat of parallel imports leads IPR holders and their licensees to price their goods more uniformly across countries, prices in developing countries may well rise, and there may be only limited scope for parallel exports. Moreover, parallel exports are unlikely to be a reliable source of foreign exchange because they are highly sensitive to exchange rate movements.

As this chapter shows, however, various other considerations besides price discrimination are relevant in determining the desirability of restraints on parallel trade. Trade negotiators, like economists, may easily get lost in the exhaustion "jungle."

Notes

1. Arguably, the scope for parallel trade in services is smaller than for parallel trade in goods. The delivery of most services requires proximity between the supplier and the consumer, thus confining parallel trade to active parallel imports. In addition, differences in national standards or languages limit the substitutability of foreign and domestic services even though they may be supplied under the same service mark.

2. In May 2003, European governments adopted a regulation that promotes the cheap supply of medicines to combat HIV/AIDS, malaria, and tuberculosis to developing countries by providing the legal framework to ensure that drugs are not diverted back to the EU. See http://europa.eu.int/comm/trade/csc/med08_en.htm.

3. Articles 3 and 4 of TRIPS require national treatment and most-favored-nation treatment of intellectual property owners. Hence, exhaustion regimes that discriminate between foreign and national right holders or between foreign right holders can be challenged in WTO dispute settlement proceedings (Bronckers 1998). The full text of TRIPS is available on the WTO Web site: http://www.wto.org.

4. Notwithstanding article 6, some observers have argued that other provisions of TRIPS—notably article 28, which expounds the exclusive rights of patent owners (Barfield and Groombridge 1999)—or obligations under the 1994 General Agreement on Trade and Tariffs (Cottier 1998) mandate the adoption of a particular exhaustion regime. However, Bronckers (1998) convincingly argues that TRIPS, as *a lex specialis,* is the relevant WTO agreement that establishes multilateral disciplines on IPR protection (including IPR exhaustion). He argues that article 6 is the overriding provision of TRIPS that removes exhaustion from WTO dispute settlement. This view is supported by the fact that, to date, no case related to the exhaustion question has been brought to the WTO's dispute settlement system.

5. The quotation is from the ECJ's seminal ruling on the case of *Deutsche Grammophon v. Metro* of 1971, whereby Deutsche Grammophon invoked its copyright to block parallel imports. The regional exhaustion doctrine was subsequently applied by the ECJ to other forms of intellectual property (see Yusuf and von Hase 1992). In 1998, the ECJ underscored this doctrine by ruling that the EU trademark directive precludes individual member states from applying a rule of international exhaustion with respect to trademarks (*Silhouette International v. Hartlauer,* Case C-355/96 [July 16, 1998]).

6. In 1995, the MERCOSUR countries concluded the Protocol on the Harmonization of Provisions on Marks, Indications of Source, and Appellations of Origin (MERCOSUR/CMC/Decision No. 8/95). Article 13 of the protocol could be interpreted as sustaining a rule of international exhaustion. This protocol has not yet been ratified by the MERCOSUR member states, however.

7. One exception is the common control exception in the field of trademarks, which allows parallel imports if the domestic and foreign trademark holder are the same, are affiliated companies, or are otherwise subject to common ownership or control (see Gallini and Hollis 1996). In addition, a recent ruling by the U.S. Supreme Court found that a copyright holder cannot block parallel importation if the copyrighted work was lawfully manufactured under the U.S. copyright title and was subsequently exported abroad. See *Quality King Distributors v. L'anza Research International,* 96–470 (March 1998).

8. See *BBS v. Rasimex,* as discussed in Heath (1997).

9. New Zealand's move prompted severe protests from the United States Trade Representative, which feared that parallel imports could harm U.S. car, pharmaceutical, and compact disc manufactures. See "New Zealand Lifts Ban" (1998).

10. See International Intellectual Property Alliance (1998). It should be noted that the survey excluded Sub-Saharan African countries with the exception of South Africa.

11. An entirely different development that has raised new questions with regard to parallel trade has been the rapid growth of electronic commerce. If goods protected by an IPR are delivered through computer-mediated networks, it becomes close to impossible to enforce a system of national exhaustion because goods no longer cross borders in the traditional sense. In this regard, the two treaties concluded in 1996 to address copyright questions posed by the convergence of information and communication technologies—the World Intellectual Property Organization (WIPO) Copyright Treaty and the WIPO Performance and Phonograms Treaty—contain provisions similar to article 6 of TRIPS and giving member countries freedom on the exhaustion question.

12. Specifically, the agreement states that "each party shall provide a cause of action to prevent or redress the procurement of a pharmaceutical product, without the authorization of the patent owner, by a party who knows or has reason to know that such product is or has been distributed in breach of a contract between the right holder and licensee, regardless of whether such breach occurs inside or outside its territory." The text of the United States–Singapore Free Trade Agreement can be downloaded at http://www.ustr.gov.

13. For a more comprehensive review of the economic principles of intellectual property protection, see Primo Braga and Fink (1997) and Primo Braga, Fink, and Sepulveda (1999).

14. Trade secrets, which are also part of IPR systems, could be either classified as an IPR that stimulates inventive and creative activity or put in a separate category. They are not relevant to the present discussion, however, because they do not grant an exclusive right and are thus not subject to exhaustion.

15. It is worth noting that the so-called new trade theory introduces imperfectly competitive market structures into models of international trade (see, for example, Helpman and Krugman 1985). However, I am not aware of any formal general equilibrium trade model that has incorporated the possibility of price discrimination across national markets under free trade.

16. Article 40 of TRIPS recognizes "that some licensing practices or conditions pertaining to intellectual property rights which restrain competition may have adverse effects on trade and may impede the transfer and dissemination of technology." The agreement gives its signatories the freedom to adopt measures to prevent and control such abusive practices (Primo Braga, Fink, and Sepulveda 1999).

17. In the parlance of economics, there are three types of price discrimination. *First-degree price discrimination* refers to a situation in which a seller charges the highest price that buyers are willing and able to pay for each quantity of output sold. *Second-degree price discrimination* occurs when a seller charges different prices for different quantities of a good. *Third-degree price discrimination* occurs when a seller charges different prices to groups that are differentiated by an easily identifiable characteristic, such as location, age, or sex.

18. See Hausman and MacKie-Mason (1988) for a formal exposition of this example. They also show that price discrimination can have a further beneficial effect if it allows firms to achieve scale and learning economies.

19. The adoption of regional exhaustion systems based on existing regional trade agreements would be one conceivable possibility. Many regional trade agreements, however, are formed among countries at different stages of development. Malueg and Schwartz (1994) conjectured that the EU may not even constitute an optimum exhaustion area. Low-income countries, such as Greece, Ireland, or Portugal, may experience sharply curtailed sales because of uniform EU-wide pricing. It is interesting to note in this context that regional exhaustion does not violate the nondiscrimination requirement of TRIPS article 6, because nondiscrimination is required only with respect to the IPR holder, not with respect to the origin of parallel imports (Bronckers 1998).

20. Note, however, that the classic IPR tradeoff between innovation incentives and static welfare losses would not hold if price discrimination enhanced static welfare, for example, by opening new markets (see the discussion earlier). See also Hausman and MacKie-Mason (1988).

21. Parallel exports in this case may already violate certain regulations that apply in connection with the price control regime, for example, to avoid domestic shortages in the supply of drugs.

22. To the extent that price controls lead to lower profitability of IPR holders and thus weaken the innovation incentive, parallel exports further undermine IPRs by extending price controls to foreign consumers.

23. This argument does not appear convincing, however. As explained in the introduction, parallel imports are subject to the same border measures on technical standards as regular imports. For example, parallel imports of pharmaceutical products into Germany from other EU member states are packaged and sold according to German health and safety requirements.

24. A fourth argument sometimes made is that the absence of barriers to parallel imports may increase the occurrence of counterfeit imports. This has been evidenced in the musical recording industry, in which genuine and counterfeit CDs have been mixed in a single shipment. However, it generally does not seem appropriate to attack an illegal activity by curbing a legitimate activity.

25. The evidence presented on U.S. parallel imports is based on Malueg and Schwartz (1994).

26. At the same time, in 1984, the U.S. Supreme Court abolished the so-called authorized-use exception, which prevented trademark holders from blocking parallel imports of goods manufactured by (uncontrolled) foreign licensees (Yusuf and von Hase 1992). To what extent this decision may have contributed to the fall of parallel imports in the second half of the 1980s remains an open question.

27. The 10 sectors are footwear and leather goods, musical recordings, motorcars, consumer electronics, domestic appliances, cosmetics and perfumes, clothing, soft drinks, confectionery, and alcoholic drinks.

References

Abbott, Frederick M. 1998. "First Report (Final) to the Committee on International Trade Law of the International Law Association on the Subject of Parallel Importation." *Journal of International Economic Law* 1:607–36.

"Australia Presses for Liberalization of Parallel Imports." 1999. *Financial Times,* March 4.

Barfield, Claude E., and Mark A. Groombridge. 1999. "Parallel Trade in Pharmaceuticals: Implications for Innovation, Economic Development, and Health Policy." *Fordham Intellectual Property, Media, and Entertainment Law Journal* 10:185–249.

Bronckers, Marco C. E. J. 1998. "The Exhaustion of Patent Rights under World Trade Organization Law." *Journal of World Trade* 32(5):137–59.

Cottier, Thomas. 1998. "The WTO System and Exhaustion of Rights." Paper presented at the Conference on Exhaustion of Intellectual Property Rights and Parallel Importation in World Trade, organized by the Committee on International Trade Law of the International Law Association, Geneva, November 6–7.

Dornbusch, Rüdiger. 1987. "Exchange Rates and Prices." *American Economic Review* 77(1):93–106.

Gallini, Nancy T., and Aidan Hollis. 1996. "A Contractual Approach to the Gray Market." Working Paper UT-ECIPA-GALLINI-96-01. University of Toronto, Ontario, Canada.

Hausman, Jerry A., and Jeffrey MacKie-Mason. 1988. "Price Discrimination and Patent Policy." *RAND Journal of Economics* 19(2):253–65.

Heath, Christopher. 1997. "Parallel Imports and International Trade." *International Review of Industrial Property and Copyright Law* 28(5):623–32.

Helpman, Elhanan, and Paul R. Krugman. 1985. *Market Structure and Foreign Trade.* Cambridge, Mass: MIT Press.

Hoekman, Bernard, and Peter Holmes. 1999. "International Rules for Competition Policies?" World Bank, Washington, D.C., and University of Sussex, U.K. Processed.

International Intellectual Property Alliance. 1998. "Parallel Import Protection in 107 Selected Countries." Paper presented at the Conference on Exhaustion of Intellectual Property Rights and Parallel Importation in World Trade, organized by the Committee on International Trade Law of the International Law Association, Geneva, November 6–7.

Malueg, David A., and Marius Schwartz. 1994. "Parallel Imports, Demand Dispersion, and International Price Discrimination." *Journal of International Economics* 37:167–95.

NERA (National Economic Research Associates). 1999. *The Economic Consequences of the Choice of a Regime of Exhaustion in the Area of Trademarks.* Final report prepared for DGXV of the European Commission. London. Available at http://europa.eu.int/comm/internal_market/en/indprop/tm/report.pdf.

"New Zealand Lifts Ban on Parallel Imports—US Objects." 1998. *Financial Times,* May 20.

Primo Braga, Carlos A., and Carsten Fink. 1997. "The Economic Justification for the Grant of Intellectual Property Rights: Patterns of Convergence and Conflict." In Frederick M. Abbott and David J. Gerber, eds., *Public Policy and Global Technological Integration.* Dordrecht, Netherlands: Kluwer Academic Publishers.

Primo Braga, Carlos A., Carsten Fink, and Claudia P. Sepulveda. 1999. "Intellectual Property Rights and Economic Development," Discussion Paper 412, World Bank, Washington, D.C.

Watal, Jayashree. 1998. "The TRIPS Agreement and Developing Countries: Strong, Weak, or Balanced Protection?" *Journal of World Intellectual Property Protection* 1(2):281–307.

Yusuf, Abdulqawi A., and Andrés M. von Hase. 1992. "Intellectual Property Protection and International Trade: Exhaustion of Rights Revisited." *World Competition: Law and Economics Review.* 16(1):115–31.

8

PARALLEL IMPORTS IN A MODEL OF VERTICAL DISTRIBUTION: THEORY, EVIDENCE, AND POLICY

Keith E. Maskus and Yongmin Chen

I. Introduction

Parallel imports are products that, once placed into circulation in one country by the owner of a trademark, copyright, or patent, are sold in a second country without the authorization of the rights holder in the second market. For example, imagine that an authorized distributor of computer software in Thailand sells copies locally at a wholesale price below the retail price existing in Japan. If permitted to do so, a parallel trader could transport the copies to Japan and make a profit net of tariffs and shipping costs. Such goods are produced legitimately under trademark and are not unauthorized knockoffs or pirated products. Trade in such goods exists largely to profit from arbitraging against differential prices set by trademark owners in various markets, once control over their distribution escapes the original rights holder.

The legal treatment of parallel imports varies widely across countries and stems from each jurisdiction's choice of territorial exhaustion of intellectual property rights (IPRs). Under international exhaustion, rights to control distribution

This chapter is adapted from an article published in 2002 in *Pacific Economic Review* 7(2):319–34. It was prepared for the joint National Bureau of Economic Research–International Seminar on International Trade conference, held June 4–5, 1999. We wish to thank Jonathan Eaton and Damien Neven for insightful comments and Robin Koenigsberg for research assistance.

expire upon first sale anywhere, and parallel imports are permitted. Under national exhaustion, first sale within a nation exhausts internal distribution rights, but IPR holders may legally exclude parallel imports or exports. Finally, a policy of regional exhaustion permits parallel trade within a group of countries but not from outside the region.

Because IPRs are traditionally the province of national or territorial policy, policies on parallel imports have been the purview of each country. U.S. efforts to incorporate a global standard of precluding parallel trade into the Agreement on Trade-Related Aspects of Intellectual Property Rights (TRIPS) in the World Trade Organization (WTO) failed to reach consensus. As written, TRIPS (article 6) preserved the standard of national discretion, which was an outcome favored by numerous developing countries and several wealthy nations that tend to be net importers of intellectual property, such as Australia and New Zealand (Maskus 2000). More recently, U.S. negotiators have required countries to ban parallel imports when entering into a bilateral preferential trade agreement with the United States.

Most formal economic analysis of parallel imports treats them as a channel for overcoming third-degree price discrimination across countries (Malueg and Schwartz 1994). In Malueg and Schwartz's model, which focuses on price differences at the retail level and ignores distribution issues, countries differ in demand elasticities for homogeneous goods. Segmented markets permit discrimination, whereas parallel imports establish a uniform international price. Global welfare effects are ambiguous and depend on the balance of consumer surplus created and destroyed. Moreover, some high-elasticity (low-demand) nations might be eliminated as export markets under uniform pricing. Informal literature discusses the problems that exist when parallel importers free ride on the marketing and service investments of authorized wholesalers (Barfield and Groombridge 1998; Chard and Mellor 1989).

We argue that these two explanations for parallel imports ignore the main reason for their existence. Such trade arises endogenously in response to attempts by IPR holders to establish vertical price control by setting varying wholesale prices in unsegmented markets. The bulk of parallel trade exists by virtue of procuring goods at the wholesale distributor level. We study the incentives for parallel imports by comparing a regime of national exhaustion (segmented markets) with one of international exhaustion (integrated markets), considering price discrimination as a special case. The welfare effects of restricting parallel trade are ambiguous but informative for the debate about whether such a policy makes sense at the global, national, or regional level. Our results show that there is a significant link between declining trade costs and the gains from parallel imports, with such trade becoming more likely to improve welfare as trade barriers are reduced. Thus, permitting parallel imports may be most advantageous among countries in a regional trade agreement with declining trade costs, such as the Association of Southeast Asian Nations or Asia-Pacific Economic Cooperation.

In the next section, we present arguments in the policy debate over parallel imports and review some empirical evidence on its existence. In the third section, we describe the main results of a simple model of price setting within a vertical international distribution framework. This model establishes key welfare trade-offs among three features of parallel imports: pro-competitive trade between oligopolistic markets, resource cost of cross-hauling goods, and inefficient vertical pricing. The model establishes some distinguishing empirical predictions, which we examine econometrically in the fourth section. Those results confirm indirectly that our model is descriptive of actual behavior on international pricing. We conclude in the final section.

II. Policy Issues

There is active debate over the question of whether to establish a global ban on parallel imports or to maintain national policy discretion. Three arguments are made in favor of permitting parallel trade. One claim is that restrictions on such trade essentially act as nontariff barriers (NTBs) to goods that have escaped the control of IPR owners. Because these barriers partition markets, they both violate WTO proscriptions against NTBs and forgo consumer gains from market integration. As trade economists might put it, if international price differences exist because of manufacturers' attempts to set market-specific prices, the situation would be no different from price differences coming from other demand or supply characteristics.

A second argument is that parallel imports help prevent abusive price discrimination and collusive behavior based on private territorial restraints. In this sense, a policy of international exhaustion complements competition policy and limits the scope of IPRs (Abbott 1998). The claim that buttressing territorial restraints with restrictions against parallel imports could generate collusion is consistent with past evidence in the United States (Hilke 1988; Tarr 1985). A final objection is that government enforcement of territorial rights invites rent-seeking behavior.

Several arguments can be made in favor of prohibiting parallel imports. First, price discrimination can raise welfare under certain circumstances (Varian 1985). Banning parallel trade partitions markets and supports perfect discrimination (Malueg and Schwartz 1994). In contrast, parallel imports push the global economy toward uniform international pricing, subject to transport and marketing costs. Thus, consumers in economies with inelastic demand should face higher prices under price discrimination than under uniform pricing. If such countries are not significant developers of intellectual property, they are made worse off by price discrimination.

Countries with high demand elasticities should face lower prices under price discrimination. In the presence of parallel trade, such countries might not be supplied by foreign IPR owners because local demand might be insufficient under uniform pricing (Malueg and Schwartz 1994). In this view, international exhaustion could lower the well-being of developing economies through higher prices and lower product availability. Despite this possibility, most developing economies prefer not to restrict parallel trade (Abbott 1998). This position reflects concerns that banning parallel imports would invite abusive behavior in their markets on the part of foreign rights holders. Furthermore, many nations see opportunities for being parallel exporters. Indeed, foreign restrictions on parallel imports are sometimes seen as backdoor attempts by industrial countries to close markets through implicit NTBs.

A second complaint is that firms engaged in parallel imports free ride on the investment, marketing, and service costs of authorized distributors. These distributors incur the costs of building their territorial markets through advertising and postsale service activities. Thus, they require protection from parallel traders who procure the same goods without incurring similar costs. In this view, restrictions on parallel imports are a natural component of the right of IPR proprietors to control vertical markets. Such restrictions may be pro-competitive, both through increasing interbrand competition and through providing incentives to build markets and provide services.

Efficient international distribution could require a strong vertical control within an enterprise, and private contracts may be inadequate for this purpose. Exclusive distribution rights make it easier to monitor marketing efforts and enforce product quality. However, it may be difficult in foreign markets to enforce private contractual provisions that prohibit sales outside the authorized distribution chain. In this view, restrictions on parallel trade complement the existence of exclusive territories.[1]

From this discussion, it follows that whether regulating parallel imports is beneficial or harmful is an empirical issue that depends on circumstances regarding demand parameters, market structure, and innovation. Thus, it is not surprising that policies differ across countries. This situation may be seen in table 8.1, which lists protection regimes for goods subject to three primary forms of IPRs.

Parallel imports from outside the European Union (EU) are banned in all IPR fields, but the European Court of Justice (ECJ) has consistently upheld the right to resell legitimately procured goods within the area as a necessary safeguard for completing the internal market. Two important exceptions exist. First, countries

TABLE 8.1   Summary of Exhaustion Regimes

Country or region	Trademarks	Patents	Copyrights
Australia	International exhaustion	National exhaustion unless sold by patent owner without clear restrictions	National exhaustion except for compact discs and books
India	International exhaustion	International exhaustion	National exhaustion with exceptions
Japan	International exhaustion, unless agreed by contract or original sale to be price controlled	International exhaustion, unless agreed by contract or original sale to be price controlled	International exhaustion except for motion pictures
United States	National exhaustion limited by common control and no consumer confusion	National exhaustion	National exhaustion
European Union	Community exhaustion	Community exhaustion	Community exhaustion

Source: National Economic Research Association (1999) and International Intellectual Property Institute Web site (1998), http://www.iipi.org/.

are allowed to preclude parallel imports in pharmaceutical goods if they threaten to interfere with pricing regulations. It is noteworthy that Denmark, Germany, and the United Kingdom, where drug prices are least controlled and therefore highest, are open to parallel imports from other EU nations. Second, the ECJ affirmed that first showing of a theatrical movie or television broadcast abroad does not exhaust international distribution rights in light of the need to exploit copyright through repeated showings.

Within the national economy, the United States enforces a "first-sale doctrine," by which rights are exhausted when purchased outside the vertical distribution chain. Thus, U.S. firms cannot preclude purchasers from reselling products anywhere within the United States. This doctrine is seen as an important policing device for exclusive territories, which are permissible subject to a rule-of-reason inquiry. Regarding parallel imports in trademarked goods, the United States follows a "common-control exception," affirmed by the U.S. Supreme Court.[2] The principle allows trademark owners to block parallel imports except when both the U.S. and foreign trademarks are owned by the same entity or when the U.S. and foreign trademark owners are in a parent-subsidiary relationship (Palia and Keown 1991). Furthermore, the ability to block such imports rests on a showing that they are not identical in quality to original products and could cause consumer confusion. Owners of U.S. patents may bar parallel imports under a right of importation. Copyrighted goods may not be parallel imported under the terms of the Copyright Act of 1976. Recent attempts by producers of trademarked goods to extend this protection by claiming copyright protection for labels have been denied by the U.S. Supreme Court.[3]

Japan permits parallel imports of trademarked and patented goods unless they are contractually barred or their original sale was subject to foreign price regulations. Copyrighted goods may be imported by parallel traders, except for motion pictures. Japanese case law has affirmed that Japan is substantially more open to parallel imports than is the United States (Abbott 1998). Australia generally allows parallel imports in trademarked goods, but patent owners may restrict them. Australia eliminated protection for copyrighted compact discs in 1998, following on its earlier deregulation of book imports. In a similar vein, New Zealand is open to parallel imports of copyrighted goods. As these cases suggest, high-income economies with relatively little stake in developing intellectual property (at least in the past), such as Australia, Japan, and New Zealand, take a liberal view of parallel imports.

India follows a regime of international exhaustion in trademarked and patented goods. Its protection against parallel imports of copyrighted goods is stronger, in keeping with its traditional protective stance in copyrights. In general, few developing countries restrict parallel imports in any field of protection.

III. A Model of Vertical Distribution and Parallel Imports

In this section, we summarize the results of a simple model of parallel imports arising from pricing behavior within a vertical distribution chain.[4] Consider a manufacturer selling a product in two countries, A and B. The manufacturer sells directly to consumers in country A, its country of location, but sells in country B through a franchised distributor. Demand curves in the two markets are linear and vary only by an intercept term, which permits either country to have a higher retail price. The manufacturer has constant marginal costs of supplying its distributor, and both firms have constant retailing costs. The manufacturer cannot prevent its distributor from selling the product back to country A as parallel imports, although if the distributor does so, it incurs a constant marginal trade cost, reflecting either or both the shipping costs and tariff. The distributor and the manufacturer are Cournot competitors in country A in the event of parallel imports.

The manufacturer offers the distributor a two-part contract, involving both a wholesale price and a franchise fee. Efficient vertical pricing requires that the wholesale price equal the marginal cost of supplying the distributor, but this efficiency will be upset by the possibility of parallel trade. The equilibrium to the game consists of optimal quantities sold in country A by the manufacturer and the distributor for any contract offered, along with profit-maximizing choices of sales by the distributor in country B and the contract itself. In equilibrium, the contract permits the manufacturer to extract all surplus from the distributor. Thus, the manufacturer ultimately bears the cost of transporting parallel imports.

Given reasonable restrictions on extreme parameter values, there is a unique solution to the model. This solution provides a series of propositions, which we discuss in turn.

The first proposition is that the equilibrium value of the wholesale price rises as transport costs increase from zero to a certain level and then falls as transport costs increase beyond that level. The retail price in country A rises as this transport cost increases to a certain level and then remains constant at its monopoly level for further increases in trade costs. The retail price in country B rises as transport costs increase to the same certain level and then decline for higher trade costs. Finally, the volume of parallel imports declines as trade costs increase to that critical level and then are zero for higher levels of transport costs.

The first part of this proposition provides a fundamental result. There is a nonlinear relationship between the profit-maximizing wholesale price and the cost of parallel trading. As shown in figure 8.1, in which we assume that the demand intercept in both markets is the same, at low levels of trade costs the wholesale price (w) rises as trade costs go up. In this range, as the last result indicates, there

FIGURE 8.1 Wholesale Price and Parallel Imports

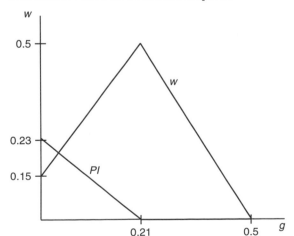

Note: g = trade costs, Pl = parallel imports, w = wholesale price.
Source: Derived by the authors from the theoretical model in Maskus and Chen (2004).

is parallel trade in equilibrium, which declines as trade costs increase and reaches zero at a particular level of trade costs. The wholesale price is set to strike a profit-maximizing balance between reducing parallel imports (*PI*) and achieving an inefficient retail price in the distributor market. Thus, parallel imports are reduced both by rising trade costs and by a higher wholesale price. At the critical value of trade costs, parallel trade ceases in equilibrium, but the possibility that it could exist remains a threat to the pricing decisions of the manufacturer. As trade costs increase further, the manufacturer is able to reduce its wholesale price without suffering parallel imports. At the highest level of trade costs, parallel trade is deterred by those costs, and the manufacturer can set the efficient wholesale price, which equals its marginal distribution cost, assumed here to be zero.

In the model, parallel imports arise because of a difference in the wholesale price at the distributor level in country *B* and the retail price in country *A*. In this context, the interesting possibility emerges that parallel trade could exist even when the retail price in country *B* exceeds the retail price in country *A*—a phenomenon that has not been explained in the literature before now. In particular, the second proposition is that there are parallel imports from country *B* to country *A* if and only if trade costs are below the critical level in the first proposition. However, in this case, the retail price is higher in country *A* than in country *B* if demand in the former country is sufficiently larger than in the latter, whereas the opposite is true if demand in country *B* is sufficiently larger than in country *A*.

This proposition demonstrates that parallel imports can flow from a high-price area to a low-price area if demand in the latter is relatively low.[5] The key to this unusual result is that the cost of acquiring products to a parallel trader might not be the market retail price but could be the wholesale price charged to a distributor.

We now turn to a result on joint profits of the manufacturer and distributor. Thus, our third proposition is that the combined industry profit decreases as trade cost goes up to a particular level (different from the earlier critical level) and then increases as higher trade costs help segment the two markets.

This proposition points out that industry profit is nonmonotonic with respect to trade costs, as shown in figure 8.2. Parallel imports reduce the profits (π^*) of the manufacturer (joint industry profits) not only because they establish competition in the country receiving them but also because they incur additional transportation costs. Parallel imports also prevent the manufacturer from achieving efficient vertical pricing. Again, at the highest level of trade costs, parallel imports are deterred, and the manufacturer can achieve profit-maximizing prices.

A final question relates to combined social surplus in the two countries—our measure of social welfare. As the discussion of the model suggests, there are three effects on welfare from parallel imports. First, parallel trade achieves a pro-competitive

FIGURE 8.2 Profits and Trade Costs

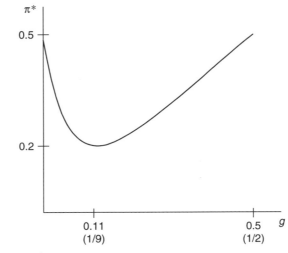

Note: π^* = profits, g = trade costs.
Source: Derived by the authors from the theoretical model in Maskus and Chen (2004).

gain through Cournot competition because it destroys market segmentation. Second, parallel trade incurs welfare-reducing transport costs, or cross-hauling costs. Third, the existence or threat of parallel imports prevents the achievement of efficient vertical pricing within the distribution network. Our model generates a final proposition, which is that global (two-country) welfare decreases as trade cost rises below the first critical level and then increases as the trade costs go up beyond that level.

Thus, there is a U-shaped welfare curve with respect to the cost of parallel trading, as shown in figure 8.3. This finding is related to that of Brander and Krugman (1983); they found reciprocal dumping of homogeneous goods with symmetric duopolists. Their model presents a tradeoff between pro-competitive pricing and cross-hauling resource waste. However, they do not consider vertical distribution relationships. Note that in our model, welfare depends on trade costs in a similar fashion but within a very different context. Our approach incorporates Brander and Krugman's two effects but adds a further tradeoff between efficient vertical pricing and parallel imports. Without parallel trade, the wholesale price would equal marginal supply costs to the wholesaler. But parallel imports induce the manufacturer to raise the wholesale price above marginal cost, thereby creating a pricing distortion. This additional cost must be compared with the net effects of consumer gains from competition and cross-hauling losses.

To understand how global surplus can rise in trade costs, consider that when that cost exceeds the critical value, the manufacturer sets the wholesale price in

FIGURE 8.3 Social Surplus

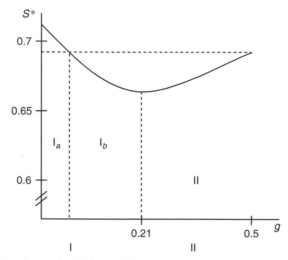

Note: I = region of trade costs in which parallel imports exist in equilibrium; I_a = portion of region I in which global welfare is higher under permitting parallel imports than banning them; I_b = portion of region I in which reducing trade costs raises welfare; II = region of trade costs in which parallel imports do not exist; g = trade costs; S^* = combined two-country welfare.

Source: Derived by the authors from the theoretical model in Maskus and Chen (2004).

country B sufficiently high that the distributor will not ship goods back to country A. A higher trade cost permits the manufacturer to set a lower wholesale price to achieve this objective, which in turn reduces the price distortion in the country B market and raises social surplus.

Our result is that if trade costs were sufficiently low that there is parallel trade in equilibrium, a reduction in those costs would increase social welfare through the pro-competitive effect. However, if parallel imports were deterred by the man-ufacturer through a high wholesale price, an increase in the cost of trade would raise social welfare. Thus, to the degree that the costs of parallel imports are affected by government regulations and trade policies, our results bear a policy implication. In particular, an appropriate policy is one that either reduces trade cost as much as possible or raises it as much as possible but does not leave it at some intermediate value.[6]

One obvious policy would be simply to ban parallel imports. Our model sup-ports two conclusions from inspecting this possibility. First, such a restriction would raise price in the country receiving parallel imports and would reduce price in the country from which parallel imports originate. Second, banning parallel trade could either raise or lower combined social surplus.

In this regard, our analysis is informative for the question of whether banning parallel trade should be adopted as a global policy. Our findings indicate that neither a policy that always precludes parallel imports nor one that always permits it is justified on the grounds of economic efficiency. Instead, because the effects vary according to market conditions, the legal position of parallel imports (and, in consequence, of vertical restraints) might be subject to a rule of reason. The analysis further suggests that policy decisions are interrelated with trade policy. If it were desirable to permit parallel imports, it would be desirable also to eliminate trade barriers that increase trading costs. Our model also suggests that parallel imports are likely to be most beneficial among countries with limited trade costs, such as members of a regional free trade agreement.[7]

IV. Empirical Evidence

There appear to be multiple causes of parallel trade, including pricing to market (arbitrage against price discrimination under circumstances of limited pass-through of exchange rate changes) and free riding on high-end consumer goods (Maskus and Chen 2004). Our interest is in discovering whether our model of vertical distribution is consistent with international behavior. Unfortunately, we cannot do so with data on the quantity of parallel trade because no such data are collected.

However, our analysis posited two unique predictions that would not arise in other explanations of parallel trade and that may be examined indirectly with price data. First, it is possible that parallel trade flows from countries with high retail prices to countries with low retail prices. A 1999 survey by National Economic Research Associates indicated that parallel trade within the EU accounts for shares of sales in 10 sectors, ranging from below 5 percent to up to 15 percent. More appropriate for our purposes is that survey respondents claimed that the adoption of international exhaustion would result in increases in parallel imports from outside the EU. Some of the likely sources for rising parallel imports included countries with evidently higher retail prices than those in the EU. For example, the average 1993 retail price in Japan for specific passenger vehicles exceeded that in the EU by 23 percent, according to retail transaction prices. Respondents to the National Economic Research Associates survey also claimed that wholesale price differences across markets were a major factor in driving parallel trade within the EU. Furthermore, a survey of U.S. exporters to Asia in 1989 found that some distributors faced competition from U.S. suppliers, which sold products in the United States at higher retail prices than in Asia (Palia and Keown 1991).

A second key proposition is that there is an inverted U-shaped relationship between trade costs and wholesale prices, as depicted in figure 8.1. Thus, we can use regression analysis of international wholesale prices to test this implication indirectly. The tariff rate in the home nation of the manufacturer is a useful measure of this cost because the manufacturer is concerned with foreign wholesalers reexporting goods back to the source country.

A related point comes from an extension of our model. If the manufacturer sold its product through several independent wholesalers in a foreign country, then competition among those wholesalers would enable the manufacturer to raise its wholesale price without worsening the vertical price distortion. The manufacturer would set a higher wholesale price in competitive wholesale markets, which would reduce parallel imports with a smaller distortion in vertical pricing. We test this supplemental proposition by regressing wholesale prices on a measure of concentration in wholesale trade in each export market, expecting to find a negative coefficient.

The empirical arena in which we test our model involves a single manufacturer setting different wholesale prices in various export markets. We use U.S. export prices for 1993 in 26 highly disaggregated (10-digit Harmonized System classification) products that some observers claim are parallel traded to some degree. We equate wholesale prices in each export market with U.S. export unit values to each country, adjusted for estimates of ad valorem transport costs and tariffs in the importing country. These prices reflect marginal costs as seen by local distributors. International trade prices should reflect wholesale prices because substantial amounts of trade occur through distributors. In 1994, for example, 46 percent of U.S. intrafirm exports over all industries were shipped to foreign wholesalers.[8]

To control for price outliers and product heterogeneity, which exist even at the 10-digit level, we first exclude any importer for which the U.S. export price is greater than 2.5 times the median price or less than 40 percent of the median price. Second, we include in the regression the number of product subcategories in each of our 10-digit categories. This variable provides a control for product heterogeneity within each product class. The 26 categories we use and the number of countries per category are listed in table 8.2.

The regression equation we use is as follows:

$$w_{ij} = b_0 + b_1 GDPPC_j + b_2 HET_i + b_3 HERF_{ij} + b_4 TARUS_i + b_5 (TARUS_i)^2 + \Sigma b_r D_r$$

The dependent variable w is the wholesaler marginal cost for product i in importing country j. This marginal cost is defined as $w_{ij} = e_{ij}(1 + t_{ij})(1 + c_{ij})$, where e is the U.S. export price at the border, t is the product-specific tariff rate in the importer, and c is an estimate of percentage transport costs from the United States to the importer. Thus, we attempt to explain statistically the structure of wholesaler marginal costs across countries. Percentage transport costs are estimated from differences in the bilateral values of U.S. imports from each market, measured with and without charges for cost, insurance, and freight (CIF). The variable $GDPPC$ is per capita income in the importing country, which we expect to have a positive coefficient if it reflects demand size. The variable HET is our measure of product heterogeneity and should have a positive sign if prices rise with product differentiation.

TABLE 8.2   Product Categories

Harmonized System number	Product	Number of countries	U.S. tariff rate (percent)
2208306020	Bourbon whiskies	43	3.0
2208309020	Whiskies except bourbon	32	3.0
4901910020	Dictionaries	23	3.0
4901990075	Rack-size paperbacks	48	0.0
4902902040	Business periodicals	38	0.0
8414400000	Air compressors 1	32	3.4
8414801018	Air compressors 2	24	3.4
8414801042	Air compressors 3	35	3.4
8414801067	Air compressors 4	36	3.4
8414801075	Air compressors 5	27	3.4
8414801080	Air compressors 6	29	3.4
8415100040	Air conditioners 1	50	2.2
8415100060	Air conditioners 2	54	2.2
8415100080	Air conditioners 3	50	2.2
8415810010	Air conditioners 4	41	2.2
8415810030	Air conditioners 5	39	2.2
8415820005	Air conditioners 6	35	2.2
8415820010	Air conditioners 7	33	2.2
8415820015	Air conditioners 8	35	2.2
8524904040	Laser disk sound recordings	49	5.3
8528104000	Video recorders	37	3.9
8528108005	Color televisions	31	5.0
8703240050	4-cylinder automobiles	31	2.5
8703240060	6-cylinder automobiles	53	2.5
8711500000	Motorcycles	40	3.7
9006530000	Professional photo cameras	27	3.0

Source: Compiled by authors from Feenstra (1997).

Concentration in the wholesale market is captured by the variable *HERF*, which is the Herfindahl index for wholesale trade in each importing country, disaggregated by corresponding Standard Industrial Code category. We expect this variable to have a negative coefficient. The variable *TARUS* is the U.S. ad valorem tariff rate, a proxy for the cost of shipping the good back to the United States. According to our model, there should be a positive sign on the linear term and a negative sign on the quadratic term.

We further incorporate regional dummy variables *D*, defining regions as the EU, other Europe, Canada, Mexico and Central America, South America, East

Asia, and other developing countries. We exclude the dummy variable for the EU, making it the reference case. There are two reasons for including regional effects. First, they control for idiosyncratic pricing decisions associated with regions. Second, our model posits that the U.S. exporting manufacturer would set a higher price in countries or regions that permit parallel trade because such trade could find its way back to the United States. In our sample, parallel trade is prohibited by the EU, other Europe, Canada, and Mexico. It is permitted by most countries of East Asia, including Japan, and by most developing countries in other regions.

The export unit-value data and CIF rates for 1993 were taken from data provided in Feenstra (1996, 1997). The number of product subcategories within each 10-digit Harmonized System category was taken from the U.S. National Trade Data Bank.[9] Tariff rates by Harmonized System product category were provided by the World Bank. Herfindahl indexes were calculated from firm-specific sales in each country (covering both domestic and foreign-owned distributors) and are available from infoUSA, a private data service.[10] Herfindahl indexes could not be constructed because of missing data in a number of product-country pairs, primarily in developing countries. Thus, we have two data samples, one including Herfindahl indexes (522 observations) and one excluding Herfindahl indexes (972 observations).

Table 8.3 presents the regression results performed with ordinary least squares but with standard errors adjusted to be heteroskedastic consistent. The first equation includes the Herfindahl index in wholesale distribution; the second one excludes it. Thus, the second equation embodies a larger sample, adding data primarily from developing countries. Our first result is that gross domestic product (GDP) per capita exerts a negative influence on wholesale price. This finding comes as a surprise because we would expect higher prices in markets with stronger demand. Perhaps a better measure of demand would be aggregate market size. One explanation for this result may be seen from the coefficient on the Herfindahl index. As our theory predicts, more concentrated distribution markets experience lower wholesale prices because U.S. manufacturers have additional power to control vertical pricing decisions and to deter parallel imports. The data show a strong negative correlation between GDP per capita and market concentration. However, when the Herfindahl index is excluded, the coefficient on GDP per capita falls by half and becomes less significant. Thus, without controlling for market power of distributors, the marginal cost of purchasing U.S. manufactures seems little affected by per capita income. The control for product heterogeneity has a positive coefficient, as anticipated.

A key finding is that the U.S. tariff rate, a measurable component of the costs of parallel shipping goods back from foreign distributor markets to the United States, operates as predicted. There is an inverted quadratic relationship between wholesale marginal costs and the U.S. tariff rate by product category. Thus, for

TABLE 8.3   Estimation of Vertical Pricing Model

Variable	Wholesaler marginal cost	Wholesaler marginal cost
Constant	–339.5 (–0.19)	–3,411 (–2.49)
GDP per capita	–0.249 (–2.60)	–0.130 (–1.64)
Heterogeneity	4,244 (9.28)	3,814 (10.67)
Herfindahl	–4,104 (–3.70)	
U.S. tariff	354,161 (7.11)	381,567 (12.29)
U.S. tariff squared	–0.56e + 7 (–7.32)	–0.59e + 7 (–12.19)
Europe other	–476.4 (–0.52)	–1,396 (–1.64)
Canada	–279.1 (–0.22)	13.1 (0.01)
Mexico and Central America	–953.3 (–0.54)	–2,418 (–2.08)
South America	–72.6 (–0.04)	–1,387 (–1.25)
East Asia	3,676 (3.41)	1,920 (2.25)
Other developing countries	–1,610 (–0.94)	–1,924 (–1.45)
Sample size	522	972
Adjusted R^2	0.29	0.26
F	20.3	35.7

Note: Figures in parentheses are t-statistics. Standard errors are heteroskedastic consistent.
Source: Authors' calculations.

products with low tariff rates, U.S. exporters set foreign marginal costs that rise with those rates to reduce parallel imports. But for products with high tariff rates, U.S. exporters set wholesale prices that fall as tariffs increase. On the basis of the coefficient estimates from the first column, the slope of this relationship changes from positive to negative at a tariff rate of 3.15 percent (3.23 percent in the second column). As may be seen in table 8.2, several categories have tariff rates that exceed this value, suggesting that the critical tariff rate lies within our sample.

It is difficult to cite a reason outside our model for the systematic dependence of export prices to foreign destinations on domestic tariff rates in this inverted U fashion. We consider this finding to be strong indirect confirmation of our claim that parallel trade at the wholesaler level affects vertical pricing decisions.

Most of the regional dummy variables are insignificant, suggesting that there is little variation in prices relative to those set on exports to the EU. The main exception is that wholesaler costs in East Asia are significantly higher than those in other regions. Except for Japan, these countries have lower average incomes than countries in the EU, so this difference is not likely the result of demand elasticity. Within the context of our model, this result is consistent with the incentive for U.S. manufacturers to set high wholesale distribution prices in East Asian economies to limit or preclude parallel exporting back to the United States. These countries generally permit such exports and are often the subject of complaints from U.S. manufacturers about shipping parallel goods.

V. Concluding Remarks

We set out a model of parallel imports that arise because of differences between wholesale prices in the distributor market and retail prices in the home market of an original manufacturer. This model provides a consistent explanation for two empirical facts that could not be readily answered within prevailing theories of parallel imports. First, parallel imports are procured in considerable proportion at the wholesale level, with distributors in one country shipping the goods in bulk to another country for resale at the retail level. Second, examples exist of products being shipped in parallel fashion from countries with high retail prices to countries with low retail prices. Econometric analysis of the pattern of export prices set by U.S. manufacturers at the wholesale level supports key predictions of the model. In particular, there is an inverted quadratic relationship between the distribution of export prices and U.S. tariff rates. This relationship is highly significant and finds explanation in our theory.

If vertical price control is an important determinant of parallel imports, as our model and empirical work suggest, an important policy implication emerges. Between countries where transport costs are high, attempts to deter parallel trade through setting a wholesale price are socially inefficient. Thus, it seems advisable to preclude parallel imports in such cases. However, between countries where transport costs are low, a policy of permitting parallel trade would be beneficial. This finding suggests that a policy of regional exhaustion among free trade areas whose members are in close proximity is sensible. This policy already exists in the EU but might be extended to agreements such as the North American Free Trade Agreement and any potential trade agreements within the Asia-Pacific area. We caution that this policy conclusion is specific to our model.

Notes

1. Three other arguments against permitting parallel trade are less relevant for our purposes: (a) international price discrimination may be an efficient means of allocating research and development costs across markets, (b) parallel imports could interfere with national price controls established to regulate pharmaceutical markets, and (c) permission of parallel imports could make it difficult to exclude counterfeit goods.

2. *K-Mart Corporation v. Cartier,* 486 US 281 (1987).

3. *Quality King Distributors v. L'anza Research International,* 96-470 (1998).

4. The full model is developed in Maskus and Chen (2004), which was available as a working paper at the time this article was written.

5. In the case depicted in figures 8.1 through 8.3, this possibility does not arise.

6. Two caveats must be raised. First, this formulation does not take into account the tariff revenues collected on parallel imports. Second, it is conceivable that another policy, such as competition enforcement against the manufacturer, could be optimal relative to changing trade costs.

7. Malueg and Schwartz (1994) developed a similar policy conclusion, although in the context of retail price discrimination without transport costs.

8. Compiled by the authors from U.S. Department of Commerce (February 1997).

9. The U.S. National Trade Data Bank is made available by the U.S. Department of Commerce and may be found at http://www.stat-usa.gov.

10. This company may be contacted at http://www.infousa.com.

References

Abbott, Frederick M. 1998. "First Report (Final) to the Committee on International Trade Law of the International Law Association on the Subject of Parallel Importation." *Journal of International Economic Law* 1:607–36.

Barfield, Claude E., and Mark A. Groombridge. 1998. "The Economic Case for Copyright Owner Control over Parallel Imports." *Journal of World Intellectual Property* 1:903–39.

Brander, James A., and Paul R. Krugman. 1983. "A Reciprocal Dumping Model of International Trade." *Journal of International Economics* 15:313–21.

Chard, J. S., and C. J. Mellor. 1989. "Intellectual Property Rights and Parallel Imports." *World Economy* 12:69–83.

Feenstra, Robert C. 1996. "U.S. Imports, 1972–1994: Data and Concordances," NBER Working Paper 5515. National Bureau of Economic Research, Cambridge, Mass.

———. 1997. "U.S. Exports, 1972–1994: With State Exports and Other U.S. Data," NBER Working Paper 5990. National Bureau of Economic Research, Cambridge, Mass.

Hilke, John C. 1988. "Free Trading or Free Riding: An Examination of the Theories and Available Evidence on Gray Market Imports." *World Competition* 32:75–92.

Malueg, David A., and Marius Schwartz. 1994. "Parallel Imports, Demand Dispersion, and International Price Discrimination." *Journal of International Economics* 37:167–95.

Maskus, Keith E. 2000. "Intellectual Property Issues for the New Round." In Jeffrey J. Schott, ed., *Preparing for the Seattle Ministerial*. Washington, D.C.: Institute for International Economics.

Maskus, Keith E., and Yongmin Chen. 2004. "Vertical Price Control and Parallel Imports: Theory and Evidence." *Review of International Economics* 12:551–70.

National Economic Research Associates. 1999. *The Economic Consequences of the Choice of Regime in the Area of Trademarks*. London: National Economic Research Associates.

Palia, Aspy P., and Charles F. Keown. 1991. "Combating Parallel Importing: Views of Exporters to the Asian-Pacific Region." *International Marketing Review* 8:47–56.

Tarr, David G. 1985. "An Economic Analysis of Gray Market Imports." U.S. Federal Trade Commission, Washington, D.C. Processed.

U.S. Department of Commerce. February 1997. *Survey of Current Business*. Washington, D.C.: U.S. Department of Commerce.

Varian, Hal R. 1985. "Price Discrimination and Social Welfare." *American Economic Review* 75:870–5.

9

DEVELOPING AND DISTRIBUTING ESSENTIAL MEDICINES TO POOR COUNTRIES: THE DEFEND PROPOSAL

Mattias Ganslandt, Keith E. Maskus,
and Eina V. Wong

I. Introduction

Perhaps the most critical task currently facing the global economy is devising mechanisms that encourage research aimed at finding treatments for diseases that are common in impoverished nations and that achieve widespread international distribution of those treatments at sufficiently low costs to be effective and affordable. This issue has achieved prominence by virtue of the severe epidemic of HIV, which almost inevitably leads to the onset of AIDS, in Sub-Saharan Africa and, increasingly, in South Asia and Southeast Asia.

HIV/AIDS is not the only disease that plagues poor nations; malaria, tuberculosis (TB), and other maladies are equally lethal and debilitating. Indeed, HIV/AIDS is unusual in that strong incentives for pharmaceutical companies to develop treatments for sufferers in high-income economies have resulted in medicines that effectively permit patients to function well for many years before onset of the disease. In that regard, the current debate is about how best to transfer these medicines to poor countries. In contrast, virtually no research and development

---

This chapter is adapted from an article published in *The World Economy: The Americas* 24(6): 779–95.

(R&D) efforts are aimed at producing new treatments for malaria or TB. This situation arises largely because those who suffer are overwhelmingly poor and cannot afford medicines in sufficient quantities to cover R&D costs. The problem is accentuated by weak patent protection in potential markets, further reducing the willingness of pharmaceutical enterprises to develop new drugs and vaccines.

In economic terms, under the current system, the incentives to achieve efficient dynamic and static provision of medicines are grossly inadequate in the face of massive poverty. Two programs have been advanced in recent years to address the problem; these programs are considerably at odds with each other. On the one hand, the Agreement on Trade-Related Aspects of Intellectual Property Rights (TRIPS) within the World Trade Organization (WTO) requires member countries to grant and enforce patents for new pharmaceutical products (Maskus 2000a; Gorlin 1999). More precisely, developers of new drugs have enjoyed exclusive marketing rights (EMRs) to all WTO members since January, 1995. Although product patents are not required until 2005 in the least developed countries, EMRs provide similar protection. Various economic studies suggest that this new regime could raise prices of new drugs markedly in developing countries (Fink 2000; Lanjouw 1998; Subramanian 1995; Watal 1999), though substantial uncertainty remains on this point.[1] Thus, some possibility exists that patents will raise incentives for R&D in these neglected diseases (Lanjouw 1998). However, this policy shift does nothing directly to increase the incomes of patients, who would, if anything, become less able to afford new medicines.[2]

Conversely, considerable pressure has mounted on pharmaceutical companies to provide their drugs at marginal production cost (or less) to poor countries. Several firms have responded, such as Merck & Co., Bristol-Myers Squibb Co., GlaxoSmithKline PLC, and Abbott Laboratories. For example, Merck & Co. recently announced it would reduce the prices of two AIDS-controlling drugs in Africa by 40 to 55 percent, adding to sharp price cuts announced in 2000 (*Wall Street Journal* 2001a). Abbott announced that it would sell its two AIDS drugs, Norvir and Kaletra, at a price that would earn the company no profit (*Wall Street Journal* 2001b). To some degree, these actions are a competitive response to offers by two Indian producers of generic AIDS drugs, Cipla Ltd. and Hetero Drugs Ltd., to provide medicines at even lower prices. As we note in the next section, however, even at these prices, the drugs may be beyond the reach of most patients.

The research-intensive pharmaceutical firms that invented these drugs have three concerns about a low-cost distribution program. First, provision at marginal cost or lower adds nothing to firms' ability to cover the fixed costs of R&D. Second, although they may be willing to circulate their medicines cheaply, the firms are anxious to retain the exclusive distribution rights inherent in patents and EMRs. Indeed, this preference to forestall generic competition was the root of the recent lawsuit raised by 39 drug makers in South Africa aimed at striking down that country's 1997 Medicines and Related Substances Control Act (*Wall Street Journal* 2001c).

Third, and perhaps most significantly, original drug developers worry that the availability of far cheaper treatments in poor countries could erode their price-setting power in rich countries. This erosion could happen directly through unauthorized parallel trade in drugs or indirectly through political pressure mounted by patients and insurance companies on health authorities to require significant price reductions. Because the vast bulk of returns to R&D are realized in the European Union (EU), the United States, and other industrial nations, pharmaceutical companies argue that such price spillovers would significantly hamper their incentives to develop new treatments.[3]

Control over patent rights in AIDS treatments is now before the WTO in a dispute raised by the United States against Brazil in February 2001. Under article 71 of Brazil's 1997 Patent Act, foreign firms must manufacture patented drugs within Brazil before three years have elapsed from patent grant. Failure to meet these working requirements could result in an order by the Brazilian Health Ministry to local firms to manufacture generic substitutes, a threat that currently faces makers of the AIDS drugs efavirenz (Merck & Co.) and nelfinavir (Roche) (*New York Times* 2001b). TRIPS appears to restrict considerably Brazil's ability to enforce working requirements. Thus, this case could set an important precedent concerning the ability of countries to limit private rights to exploit patents.

Putting these elements together, we see that drug development and distribution involve tradeoffs that implicate important principles underlying protection of intellectual property rights (IPRs). There is a strong global public interest in providing sufficient incentives for the continual development of new medical treatments for diseases that afflict the poor. Within the intellectual property system, these incentives stem largely from exclusive production and distribution rights provided by EMRs and patents. However, such rights may be inadequate for meeting the needs of extremely poor patients, who do not have enough income to purchase new medical treatments, even at low prices.

Furthermore, such rights are national or territorial in scope, meaning that governments may choose their own regimes concerning whether rights holders can prevent parallel trade.[4] Indeed, TRIPS affirms that countries have the authority to decide whether exclusive rights are exhausted at national borders. The threat that products may be shipped from lower-priced countries to higher-priced countries reduces the enthusiasm of rights holders to supply them at low cost.

The current system generates numerous undesirable outcomes. First, there are not enough incentives to develop new treatments for endemic diseases in impoverished markets. The resulting high rates of infection and contagion impose external costs on others both within and across borders, in part because of lower productivity. Surely, the industrial economies suffer some costs from slower growth in the afflicted countries. In this sense, development and provision of effective drugs is a global public good.

Second, demands that drugs be provided at marginal cost in some countries force patients in higher-priced countries to accept a disproportionate share of the burden of financing R&D cost recovery. Put another way, patients in lower-priced nations effectively free ride on the pricing systems of the United States and other industrial nations. In fact, the free riding has at least two dimensions. In addition to the low prices in poor countries, price controls in Canada, Europe, and elsewhere mean that patients in those nations provide limited contributions to recovering fixed R&D costs.[5] In that context, U.S. patients and insurance companies bear the brunt of paying for R&D and any losses associated with distribution programs abroad. Thus, neither pharmaceutical companies nor their patients may be expected to embrace the costs of distribution and development.

Third, pharmaceutical firms chronically undersupply the medicinal needs of poor countries, partly because of limited exclusivity in rights, including the need to restrain parallel trade.

These problems point squarely to the need for further public involvement in encouraging new drugs and in procuring and distributing medicines. In this chapter, we set out a proposal for addressing the fundamental problems in a manner that is least disruptive to the international system of IPRs. First, it increases public assistance or public health budgets in the rich countries to fund purchases by a body such as the World Health Organization (WHO) of exclusive licenses to distribute selected medicines in poor countries. The license fees should be sufficient to cover all or a substantial portion of fixed R&D costs, thereby establishing a strong incentive for pharmaceutical and vaccine firms to produce new treatments. In terms of distributing these products in poor markets, the WHO would be free to do so at a per unit price less than its marginal private costs in recognition of the external benefits from improved health status. Finally, each country or region that avails itself of this program would be required to assert strong controls on parallel exports to safeguard prices in markets of high-income economies.

The procurement portion of our proposal is similar to the idea for a vaccine-purchase fund put forward by Sachs, Kremer, and Hamoudi (2002).[6] However, their proposal involves a guaranteed price per dosage without contemplating difficulties in effecting distribution or in segmenting markets. It also bears similarity to current proposals for ensuring tiered pricing of existing HIV/AIDS drugs (Barton 2001; Subramanian 2001), but these programs make no provisions for managing dynamic R&D incentives. Thus, we offer our proposal as complementary to both these ideas.

In the next section, we provide basic evidence on the extent of the R&D, distribution, and pricing problems in the current system. In the third section, we discuss the economics of optimal provision in recognition of the significant externalities involved. In the fourth section, we set out the proposal explicitly and discuss ideas for its implementation. We conclude in the final section.

II. Scope of the Problem

The incidence and costs of endemic diseases in poor countries are staggering. These maladies not only afflict high rates of mortality but also significantly reduce the health status and productivity of the affected population. Table 9.1 provides estimates by the WHO of deaths and productive time lost (measured in disability-adjusted life years or DALYs) to three major diseases in 1999 for Africa, the Americas, and Southeast Asia. HIV/AIDS is thought to have killed 2.7 million people globally in 1999, with 2.2 million of these in Africa. It claimed 81,000 victims in the Americas and 360,000 victims in Southeast Asia, where the problem is rising rapidly. The disease was also responsible for 89.8 million DALYs lost to morbidity and mortality. Again, this loss was concentrated in Africa, where 74.4 million DALYs were lost.

The victims of TB are spread more evenly throughout the developing world. TB killed 1.7 million people in 1999, with 357,000 in Africa, 59,000 in the Americas, and 723,000 in Southeast Asia. TB is frequently contracted by HIV/AIDS sufferers, and surveys suggest that up to 70 percent of TB patients are infected with HIV (UNAIDS and WHO 2001). Such joint cases are concentrated in Sub-Saharan Africa. Malaria is also concentrated in Africa, killing 953,000 people in 1999 and sacrificing 36.8 million DALYs. According to the WHO, the direct and indirect costs of malaria in Sub-Saharan Africa exceed US$2 billion per year (WHO n.d.). Malaria is not at this time a large problem in the Americas.

TABLE 9.1   Deaths and DALYs Caused by HIV/AIDS, TB, and Malaria, 1999 (thousands)

Disease	World		Africa		Americas		Southeast Asia	
	Deaths	DALYs	Deaths	DALYs	Deaths	DALYs	Deaths	DALYs
HIV/AIDS	2,673	89,819	2,154	74,449	81	2,815	360	8,866
TB	1,669	33,287	357	8,721	59	1,114	723	14,101
Malaria	1,086	44,998	953	36,838	2	76	69	3,071

DALYs = Disability-Adjusted Life Years.
Source: WHO (2000).

Additional figures illustrate the scope of HIV/AIDS in Africa. There are now 25.3 million Africans living with HIV or AIDS.[7] In eight countries, at least 15 percent of adults are infected. Infection rates in African women in their early 20s are three times higher than in men of the same age group. In Botswana, 36 percent of adults are now infected with HIV, whereas in South Africa, the figure is 20 percent. South Africa has 4.2 million infected people, the largest number in the world. These figures are rising at alarming rates.[8] Among the 1.4 million children under the age of 15 living with HIV/AIDS at the end of 2000, 1.1 million resided in Sub-Saharan Africa. Approximately 12.1 million children have been orphaned by the disease in that region.

Economic studies suggest that the South African gross domestic product (GDP) will be 17 percent lower in 2010 than it would be without AIDS, removing US$22 billion in output from the economy. In Botswana, there could be a 13 to 15 percent reduction in the income of the poorest households. The fiscal cost of the disease is also debilitating. It has been estimated that in 7 of 16 African countries surveyed, public health spending for AIDS alone exceeded 2 percent of GDP in 1997 compared with total spending for health care of 3 to 5 percent of GDP (WHO 2000).

These three diseases display different characteristics in terms of treatment costs and R&D incentives. TB is curable with a single drug treatment that costs as little as US$10 to US$15 per patient (UNAIDS and WHO 2001). Unfortunately, TB is an airborne virus, and in crowded environments with large numbers of sufferers, it is difficult and expensive to achieve eradication. The effective approach to TB is procurement programs to purchase and distribute these treatments widely to eradicate its presence, a task that lies beyond the economic reach of many health ministries in poor countries. Note also that there is little research into new treatments for TB. The WHO (1996) estimated that of the US$56 billion spent globally on medical R&D in 1994, less than 0.2 percent was spent on TB, diarrheal maladies, and pneumonia together. Virtually all of the latter research was performed by public agencies and military authorities.

Malaria can be prevented partially through sanitation programs and prophylaxis, and it can be treated with available drugs. Again, these drugs may be out of the reach of poor patients. Moreover, because the disease tends to build resistance to drugs over time, there is a continuous need for research into new medicines. The most effective long-term solution, in addition to vector control strategies, is to develop malaria vaccines that can be administered to children (Sachs, Kremer, and Hamoudi 2002). However, there is insufficient R&D in antimalarial vaccines or drugs. Sachs, Kremer, and Hamoudi (2002) cite a Wellcome Trust study that found public and nonprofit malaria research amounted to US$84 million in 1993, with vaccine research amounting to a small portion of that spending. Private

TABLE 9.2   International Price Comparison for a Selection of HIV/AIDS Drugs: Prices in South Africa, Sweden, and the United States, March 2001 (in US$)

Product (U.S. brand name)	South Africa (original manufacturer price)	South Africa (price of generic substitute)	Sweden (original manufacturer price)	U.S. (original manufacturer price)
Epivir	232	98–190	1,709	3,271
Zerit	252	47–70	3,078	3,589
Viramune	483	202–340	2,565	3,508
Stocrin	500	1,179	3,231	4,730
Combivir	730	293–635	4,535	7,093
Crixivan	600	2,300	3,339	6,016

Note: Prices are for yearly treatment of a single adult patient with regular dosage.
Sources: Wall Street Journal (2001b), FASS database (http://www.fass.se).

sector spending was lower still. We should note that more research into vaccines and antimalarial drugs is under way under the auspices of the Multilateral Initiative on Malaria, involving the United Nations Development Programme, the World Bank, and the WHO, as well as the Medicines for Malaria Venture, a public-private sector cooperative initiative. However, funding for the former comes to approximately US$3 million per year and the latter group is soliciting support from foundations in the hopes of achieving US$30 million per year. This amount seems inadequate for the job, given the underlying costs of developing and testing new drugs. It also fails to exploit private incentives within the intellectual property system.

As a final observation on the current problem, note that even though many pharmaceutical firms have slashed their prices for HIV/AIDS treatments in poor African countries, the prices still do not reduce per patient cost burdens relative to those in rich nations. Table 9.2 shows the current average prices in U.S. dollars of six AIDS drugs for an annual treatment for a single patient in South Africa, Sweden, and the United States. For South Africa, we show both the prices offered by pharmaceutical companies that own patents on these drugs in the United States and prices offered by Indian generic producers. For example, in 2001 U.S. dollars, the drug Viramune costs US$3,508 in the United States, US$2,565 in Sweden, and is now offered at US$483 (original version) and US$340 (generic version) in South Africa. In that context, the prices are far lower in South Africa than in the United States.[9]

However, as shown in table 9.3, when these prices are divided by the U.S. dollar value of per capita GDP in 1998, the burden of these drugs in income units is essentially the same in all three markets. Indeed, the price as a proportion of per

**TABLE 9.3   International Price Comparison for a Selection
of HIV/AIDS Drugs: Prices as a Share of GDP Per
Capita (percent)**

Product (U.S. brand name)	South Africa (original manufacturer price)	South Africa (price of generic substitute)	Sweden (original manufacturer price)	U.S. (original manufacturer price)
3TC	7.2	3.0–5.9	6.3	10.1
Zerit	7.8	1.5–2.2	11.4	11.1
Viramune	15.0	6.3–10.6	9.5	10.8
Stocrin	15.5	36.6	11.9	14.6
Combivir	22.6	9.1–19.7	16.8	21.9
Crixivan	18.6	71.4	12.3	18.6

Notes: GDP per capita, 1998. The average exchange rates in 1998 were US$1 = 5.54 ZAR and US$1 =
7.95 SEK and in 2001 (until 25 March 2001) were US$1 = 7.81 ZAR and US$1 = 9.69 SEK.
Sources: World Bank (2000), *OECD* (2000).

capita GDP is lower in South Africa than in the United States in two drugs only
and is higher in three.[10] The range of prices of available generic substitutes generally lies below the original manufacturer's price in South Africa, but not in all cases.

III. The Economics of Developing and Distributing Drugs

A key health policy objective of most countries is to give patients access to existing pharmaceutical drugs at a reasonable cost. From a welfare point of view, effective medicines have a value both to the individual and to society as a whole. First
and foremost, pharmaceutical drugs have value to the individual, in some cases as
a treatment of symptoms, in other cases as a cure. In addition, they have additional value to society as a method to limit the risk for healthy individuals to be
harmed by infectious diseases. Total welfare is maximized in the short run if
existing drugs are provided at a price equal to, or in some cases below, the marginal cost of production.

The problem, however, is that developing new drugs typically involves substantial investments in R&D. The average cost to develop a new pharmaceutical drug
is approximately US$300 million; in some cases, it is substantially higher.[11] These
costs are mainly fixed and sunk once the drug is developed.

If prices were set equal to, or even below, the marginal cost of production, the
pharmaceutical companies would not be able to recoup their investments and the
economic incentives for R&D would disappear. The result of marginal cost pricing

is, therefore, that too little investment in R&D takes place and too few drugs are developed in the long run. To correct for this market imperfection, patents exist to reduce competition and allow pharmaceutical companies to exercise some market power to recover their investments in R&D.

The welfare optimization problem in a closed economy, thus, involves a trade-off between giving patients access to existing drugs at reasonable costs versus providing profits for pharmaceutical companies, which are incentives for researching and developing new drugs in the future. Unfortunately, monopoly pricing of existing drugs causes static problems of insufficient market access for patients. Such problems can be solved, at least in theory, if the short-run and long-run objectives are separated. The first-best solution from a welfare perspective is to reward innovations with a fixed, lump-sum transfer to the innovating firm and to distribute existing drugs at competitive, or even below competitive, prices.

Although a policy to separate fixed and variable costs of pharmaceutical drug production might be impractical or even impossible to implement in most cases, it can be useful in particular situations. More precisely, cost-based pricing and lump-sum payments for innovations could be the only way to achieve both the current and future health objectives in the poorest countries of the world.

So far, we have discussed the problem of static distortions and dynamic efficiency in general terms. It is, however, important to recognize the international dimension of this issue. First of all, the tradeoff between different objectives is not identical in all countries, and, consequently, the optimal policy differs across nations. Moreover, in a global economy with trade in pharmaceutical products, health care policy in one country has important implications for policy in other countries.

Starting with the issue of different objectives in industrial and developing countries, we must note that the weights put on short-run and long-run objectives depend on several factors, and the optimum is likely to vary across countries with different levels of income. Countries with high average income are likely to put more weight on new and improved drugs relative to countries with medium or low average income. As long as future drugs are normal goods, rich countries can be expected to have a higher willingness to pay for R&D. Lower rates of time preference in industrial countries also could affect the tradeoff in the same direction. Governments in industrial countries are therefore more willing to accept high profits in the pharmaceutical industry to promote future innovations and improved drugs, whereas governments in developing countries, to a larger degree, prefer to give patients access to existing drugs at low costs.

Restricting our attention to the pricing problem of pharmaceutical companies, we find that the optimal prices in local markets typically depend on the price elasticity of demand as well as the potential for arbitrage between markets. If the average income differs across two segmented markets, optimal prices for a monopolist are likely to be different in the two locations. Giving rebates to consumers with low income is often profitable for the monopolist as long as the rebated price is above the marginal cost of production and the scope for resale to high-income consumers is limited. When discounts for a homogeneous good are the same for all consumers within a specific market but vary across different markets, the pricing strategy corresponds to third-degree price discrimination.

Arbitrage between markets—often referred to as *parallel imports*—limits the scope for third-degree price discrimination. If both markets are served by the monopolist, the price in the low-income country is likely to rise as a result of parallel trade, whereas the price in the high-income country is likely to fall. The pharmaceutical company receives less revenue from both the low-income market and the high-income market when parallel imports result in equalized prices. With large differences in average income across markets, as is the case with developing and industrial countries, it is quite possible that parallel trade makes it unprofitable to serve low-income markets. Under such circumstances, it is beneficial for all parties—more precisely a Pareto improvement—to restrict parallel imports and to increase the degree of price discrimination.[12]

The trade regime affects not only the scope for monopoly price discrimination but also, and more generally, the range of differences in health policies in different countries. More precisely, parallel trade undermines the independence of health authorities in both industrial and developing countries. In practice, most industrial countries maintain a policy that allows the pharmaceutical companies to recover their investment in R&D through monopoly markups on existing drugs primarily in the European, Japanese, and U.S. markets. In this context, it is clear that marginal cost-based pricing in developing countries could have significant effects on the incentives to introduce drugs in the poorest countries unless the price spillover to industrial countries is limited.

A necessary, but not sufficient, condition for an effective solution to the access development problem for pharmaceutical products in developing countries is, therefore, to limit parallel exports from the developing countries as well as parallel imports into the industrial countries.

IV. A Proposal for a Developing Economies' Fund for Essential New Drugs

In this section, we set out a new proposal that would help resolve the incentive problems plaguing development and dissemination of drugs under the current system. We term our initiative the DEFEND proposal, which stands for Developing Economies' Fund for Essential New Drugs.

A. Criteria

The magnitude of the problem with HIV/AIDS, TB, and malaria in developing countries, particularly in Sub-Saharan Africa, suggests that any proposal to solve the problem must meet several criteria.

First and foremost, giving the poorest countries access to existing therapies and drugs would require prices equal to, or in most cases below, marginal cost. The magnitude of the epidemic and the low level of income in the poorest countries make low prices a necessity. This point can easily be illustrated with a hypothetical experiment. Assuming that all HIV-positive individuals in Sub-Saharan Africa were treated with a typical AIDS cocktail therapy (Crixivan, AZT, and Epivir) bought at U.S. prices, the total expenditure for these drugs would be more than the total GDP of the Sub-Saharan countries put together.[13]

Moreover, for countries with very low median income, even a small or moderate monopoly markup can be expected to generate a substantial allocative inefficiency and deadweight loss. This is a fundamental reason to separate the incentives for the development of new drugs from the distribution of existing drugs. The distribution of existing drugs in the poorest countries should, therefore, be founded on cost-based pricing, whereas the incentives for development of new drugs have to be achieved by other means. We will turn to this latter problem next.

The second criterion for good policy is that it include incentives to encourage innovation and development of new therapies and drugs. The problem is not that it is too profitable to innovate for poor countries, but rather that it is too unprofitable. For the world's three most deadly infectious diseases—AIDS, TB, and malaria—effective vaccines have yet to be invented. Moreover, most of the existing treatments for HIV/AIDS have serious and sometimes lethal side effects. In other words, more research on new drugs as well as improvements of existing drugs for the poorest countries is needed in the future.

The typical incentive for R&D for new pharmaceutical products is the prospect of future profits. However, we have argued previously that it would be inexpedient and unrealistic to generate sufficient incentives for R&D through monopoly markups in the world's poorest countries. Relying on future monopoly profits is not a desirable incentive scheme for three reasons: the monopoly markup is distortionary, the potential rents are too small, and the political risks involved are too large for the pharmaceutical companies (for example, the risk of compulsory licensing or generic substitution). The solution to these problems is to design a scheme with fixed lump-sum payments for new innovations, partly subsidized by the industrial countries with a long-term guarantee to the pharmaceutical companies that they will receive some reasonable return on their investment in new and effective drugs.

The third criterion any realistic proposal must meet is that it must be developed within the limits of international law and treaties and must be supported by established international organizations. The most important examples are the rules of the WTO and the offices of the WHO. In particular, TRIPS requires all parties to give patent protection to new innovations, including pharmaceutical products. However, it also leaves the question of the legality of parallel imports to national governments.

As we previously stressed, the problem of access to existing and new drugs in developing countries not only is a question of trade, patents, and pricing but also requires financial aid from industrial countries. This latter task is best carried out as a coordinated program by the WHO. The main functions of the WHO are to give worldwide health guidance; to set global health standards; to cooperate with governments to strengthen national health programs; and, finally, to develop and transfer appropriate health technology, information, and standards.

The fourth and final criterion is to limit coverage of inexpensive distribution to well-defined and restricted geographical areas. The health policies of most industrial countries must be taken as given and must be isolated from the strategy for access to pharmaceutical drugs in developing countries. To avoid spillovers to the high-income, high-priced Organisation for Economic Co-operation and Development (OECD) markets, the policy should include official restrictions on parallel imports of the program drugs into the industrial nations. Moreover, developing countries need to impose restrictions on parallel exports from their own markets to deter slippage into countries not designated as recipients. Put briefly, we envision a regime of regional exhaustion within the WHO-designated program areas but tight controls to prevent the low-cost drugs from escaping those areas.

B. Outline of the Proposal

In the previous section, we stressed that a successful strategy to give people in developing countries access to effective medicines involves four components. First, the cost of giving patients access to existing drugs must be separated from the incentives for pharmaceutical companies to improve and develop new drugs. Second, the financial incentives to invent new drugs for the world's developing countries must be subsidized by the industrial countries. Third, a coordinated strategy should be jointly financed by the industrial countries and implemented by an established international organization within the limits of international treaties. Fourth, the strategy should be focused on the developing countries, and price spillovers should be limited by restrictions on parallel exports. A fund for essential new drugs could potentially help solve this problem.

The principal structure of the strategy would be an international fund managed by the United Nations Programme on AIDS (UNAIDS) or WHO. With contributions from the industrial—and possibly some middle-income developing countries—the fund would buy licenses to produce and sell patented essential drugs in those developing nations that choose to be part of the program. Contributions to the fund should be in the form of cash to finance current expenditure. Equally important would be binding commitments to pay for future drugs, in particular vaccines for HIV, TB, and malaria.

The program should be open to least-developed countries and all other low-income countries in Sub-Saharan Africa.[14] Any government, international organization, or nongovernmental organization should be allowed to use the license in the participating countries under three conditions: the original patent is respected in nonparticipating markets, the distribution is restricted to patients in the participating countries, and parallel trade to other markets is prohibited.[15] The portfolio of licenses managed by the international fund should be limited to the most essential drugs. A board representing donors would regularly review the portfolio of current and future licenses.

Payments to patent holders should be in the form of a fixed, yearly, lump-sum transfer that features three characteristics. First, it should guarantee successful drug and vaccine developers a net present value over the life of the program that should equal expected R&D costs. Second, it should be positively related to the social value (associated with reduced mortality, morbidity, and spillovers) of the drug in the licensed areas to tie R&D incentives to underlying needs. Third, given that there may be broader markets for the new drugs and vaccines, it should be positively related to the global share of patients in the licensed areas.

In addition to paying patent holders for licenses, the fund could provide subsidies to purchase and distribute essential drugs in countries where a large fraction of the population is infected or the production cost of the drug is too high in relation to the average income. For available life-extending treatments—such as the existing AIDS therapies—a possible policy would be to subsidize purchases so that a specific treatment would not cost more than a predefined share (such as 40 percent) of the average gross national product per capita in a particular country (the remainder would have to be financed by the local government, nongovernmental organizations, donors, or the patients as a form of copayment). For vaccines, these purchases could be subsidized to a larger degree (up to 100 percent) because widespread access to vaccines has positive externalities in both the local community and the global community.

C. Implementation of the Proposal

The implementation of the proposal could be gradual. Starting with HIV/AIDS treatment, the fund could buy a portfolio of five or six licenses for the most important HIV/AIDS drugs.[16] For Sub-Saharan Africa, a reasonable payment for these licenses could be in the range of US$500 million to US$1 billion per year.[17] Adding a subsidy for distribution of the drugs, which would guarantee that the treatment does not cost more than 40 percent of GDP per capita in a specific country, would require additional funds. On the basis of prices of generic substitutes, a cocktail of three HIV/AIDS drugs may be expected to cost between US$400 and US$600 per patient per year. Thus, the subsidy from the fund would sum up to a maximum total cost of US$4.7 billion to US$8.1 billion per year for all HIV-infected individuals in Sub-Saharan Africa. This funding, however, would not be a substitute for the US$3 billion WHO and UNAIDS estimate needed for basic care and prevention efforts. The total cost for an international strategy is, therefore, in the range of US$8.2 billion to US$12.1 billion annually. According to the OECD, total levels of official development assistance from bilateral donors and multilateral agencies amounted to US$84.9 billion in 1999, 2 percent of which was devoted to basic health needs.[18] Thus, this commitment would represent a substantial portion of the current aid funding. However, it would correspond to only 0.03 to 0.05 percent of total GDP in the OECD countries in 1998. To add further perspective, we note that if this amount were fully paid by the EU, Japan, and the United States, it would come to only US$13.50 per person in those countries per year. In another view, US$12.1 billion may be compared with the anticipated loss in South African GDP of US$22 billion in the year 2010.

V. Concluding Remarks

The poorest nations of the world suffer from extreme disease burdens, which go largely untreated because weak incomes and the prevailing system of IPRs fail to provide sufficient incentives to develop new treatments and distribute them at low cost. Recent price reductions for HIV/AIDS drugs are encouraging but offer only a limited solution.

In this chapter, we analyzed the economic tradeoffs involved in supporting drug and vaccine research through exclusive rights and distributing the fruits of that research to poor countries. Such research is expensive and would not be undertaken by private firms without some prospect for recovering expected R&D costs. However, even if they were developed, private property rights to the distribution of these drugs, in the form of patents and EMRs, could support inefficiently high prices and generate large deadweight welfare losses compared with the social optimum in poor countries. This system fails to account for the strong external benefits of providing additional treatments and vaccines in poor countries. These benefits accrue also to the rich countries, both for reasons of humanity and because lower economic activity in developing countries is costly in trade terms.

We offer a proposal to overcome those incentive problems. Our DEFEND proposal would work within the existing international legal structure but significantly raise the returns to R&D in critical medicines and expand distribution program. A public international organization would purchase the license rights for designated areas and distribute the drugs at low cost with a required copayment from local governments. Furthermore, governments would restrict parallel trade to support desirable price discrimination. Costs would be funded largely by increased foreign assistance from the industrial nations, but these costs would be low in relation to current aid budgets. We believe a strong program could be mounted for US$8 billion to US$12 billion per year and would be an extremely effective use of foreign aid.

Notes

1. See Rozek and Berkowitz (1998) for a dissenting view.

2. See Abbott (2000) for a legal analysis of the pharmaceutical aspects of TRIPS claiming that the agreement raises difficult contradictions between the trading system and needs for protecting public health.

3. *New York Times* (2001a).

4. Maskus (2000b) provides an overview of the economics of parallel trade.

5. The general nature of this problem is reflected in recent legislative proposals in the United States to deregulate restrictions partially on parallel imports of prescription pharmaceuticals to permit U.S. patients to gain access to cheaper foreign sources of supply.

6. An earlier version of this working paper was available at the time the present article was published.

7. These figures are from "Fact Sheet: HIV/AIDS in Africa," available at http://www.unaids.org/EN/other/functionalities/Search.asp. There are also 5.8 million living with HIV/AIDS in South Asia and Southeast Asia; see "AIDS Epidemic in Asia" available at the same website.

8. At the same time, successful prevention programs in a few African countries, such as Uganda, have reduced national infection rates.

9. Note that Bristol-Myers Squibb Co. offered Zerit to South Africa for US$54 per patient per year, making that price much less than indicated. See *Wall Street Journal* (2001c).

10. We use 1998 GDP per capita for this purpose because it is the latest year available. Note that the South African rand depreciated by 29 percent (and the Swedish krona by 18 percent) relative to the U.S. dollar from 1998 to 2001, making the rand-denominated burdens yet higher to the extent that nominal depreciation reflects GDP changes.

11. Sachs, Kremer, and Hamoudi (2002) estimate the average cost for a new drug to be US$300 million and predict that developing vaccines for HIV, TB, and malaria would "potentially cost several times as much given the scientific challenges involved."

12. As noted in Varian (1988), this result is quite robust. If price discrimination results in a new market being opened up, then it is typically a Pareto-improving welfare enhancement. Hausman and MacKie-Mason (1988) study this problem in the context of new patents.

13. The total GDP in Sub-Saharan Africa is approximately US$285 billion, according to the most recent figures from the World Bank (*World Economic Indicators 2000*). A therapy with Crixivan, AZT, and 3TC is US$11,800 per patient per year at U.S. prices, and the total for the Sub-Saharan countries would be US$299 billion per year, if all 25.4 million HIV-infected individuals were treated.

14. The United Nations defines low-income economies as countries with a 1999 gross national product per capita of US$755 or less. In the most recent classification (as of the year 2000), there were 64 countries in this category. More information may be found at http://www.unctad.org/Templates/Page.asp?intItemID=1676&lang=1.

15. Production and distribution under these licenses should not be allowed for companies that produce generic substitutes that compete with the patented product in nonparticipating markets. The main reason for this restraint is to avoid strategic spillovers caused by cost efficiencies in the production of the licensed product. If, for example, a firm in country A were certified to produce a drug under a publicly procured license, with sales intended for designated recipient countries, its expanded output could provide it with a competitive advantage in nonparticipating countries by virtue of increasing returns to scale.

16. Examples of drugs for an initial portfolio include 3TC, Zerit, Viramune, Stocrin, Combivir (AZT plus 3TC), and Crixivan.

17. The lower bound of these license payments would be US$442 million per year and is based on the assumption of a portfolio with 10 patents, an average R&D cost of US$360 million per drug (Danzon 1997), a patent length of 20 years with approval coming 8 years after the patent was filed, a 5 percent discount rate, and a 75 percent contribution to development costs from the fund (with the remainder being covered by profits from high-income markets). The upper bound would be US$1.165 billion per year and is based on the same assumptions with the discount rate changed to 10 percent and the fund's contribution to development costs raised to 100 percent.

18. See http://www.oecd.org/department/0,2688,en_2649_34447_1_1_1_1_1,00.html

References

Abbott, Frederick M. 2000. "The TRIPS-Legality of Measures Taken to Address Public Health Crises: Responding to USTR-State-Industry Positions That Undermine the WTO." Florida State University, Tallahassee. Processed.

Barton, John. 2001. "Draft on Tiered Pricing for WG-4." Stanford University Law School, Palo Alto, Calif. Processed.

Danzon, Patricia M. 1997. *Pharmaceutical Price Regulation: National Policies versus Global Interests.* Washington, D.C.: American Enterprise Institute.

Fink, Carsten. 2000. "Patent Protection, Transnational Corporations, and Market Structure: A Simulation Study of the Indian Pharmaceutical Industry." World Bank, Washington, D.C. Processed.

Gorlin, Jacques J. 1999. *An Analysis of the Pharmaceutical-Related Provisions of the WTO TRIPS (Intellectual Property) Agreement.* London: Intellectual Property Institute.

Hausman, Jerry, and Jeff MacKie-Mason. 1988. "Price Discrimination and Patent Policy." *RAND Journal of Economics* 19:253–65.

Lanjouw, Jean O. 1998. "The Introduction of Pharmaceutical Patents in India: Heartless Exploitation of the Poor and Suffering?" NBER Working Paper 6366. National Bureau of Economic Research, Cambridge, Mass.

Maskus, Keith E. 2000a. *Intellectual Property Rights in the Global Economy.* Washington, D.C.: Institute for International Economics.

———. 2000b. "Parallel Imports." *World Economy* 23(9):1269–84.

New York Times. 2001a. "Group Says Discount AIDS Drugs Endanger Research." February 13, 2001.

———. 2001b. "Brazil May Defy U.S. and Make More AIDS Drugs." February 14, 2001.

OECD (Organisation for Economic Cooperation and Development). 2000. *Main Economic Indicators: May 2000.* Paris.

Rozek, Richard P., and Ruth Berkowitz. 1998. "The Effects of Patent Protection on the Prices of Pharmaceutical Products: Is Intellectual Property Protection Raising the Drug Bill in Developing Countries?" *Journal of World Intellectual Property* 1:179–243.

Sachs, Jeffrey, Michael Kremer, and Amar Hamoudi. 2000. "The Case for a Vaccine Fund." CID Policy Paper No. J, Center for International Development, Harvard University, Cambridge, Mass.

Subramanian, Arvind. 1995. "Putting Some Numbers on the TRIPS Pharmaceutical Debate." *International Journal of Technology Management* 10:252–68.

———. 2001. "The AIDS Crisis, Differential Pricing of Drugs, and the TRIPS Agreement: Some Notes." International Monetary Fund, Washington DC. Processed.

UNAIDS (United Nations Programme on AIDS) and WHO (World Health Organization). 2001. "World TB Day 2001: Access to TB Cure a Human Rights Imperative." Joint press release. Available at http://www.who.int/inf-pr-2001/en/pr2001-14.html.

Varian, H. 1988. "Price Discrimination." In R. Schmalensee and R. Willig, eds., *Handbook of Industrial Organization.* Amsterdam: North-Holland.

Wall Street Journal. 2001a. "Price War Breaks Out over AIDS Drugs in Africa as Generics Present Challenge." March 7, 2001.

———. 2001b. "Abbott to Cut Prices on AIDS Drugs Distributed in Sub-Saharan Africa." March 27, 2001.

———. 2001c. "Big Drug Firms Defend Right to Patents on AIDS Drugs in South African Court." March 6, 2001.

———. 2001d. "Bristol-Myers Squibb Offers to Sell AIDS Drugs in Africa at Below Cost" (March 15, 2001).

Watal, J. 1999 "Introducing Product Patents in the Indian Pharmaceutical Sector: Implications for Prices and Welfare." *World Competition* 20:5–21.

World Bank. 2000. *World Development Indicators 2000.* Washington DC.

WHO (World Health Organization). n.d. "Malaria." Fact sheet 94. Available at http://www.who.int/mediacentre/factsheets/fs094/en/.

———. 1996. *Investing in Health Research and Development: Report of the Ad Hoc Committee on Health Research Relating to Future Intervention Options.* Geneva.

———. 2000. *World Health Report 2000.* Geneva.

INTELLECTUAL PROPERTY, MARKET STRUCTURE, AND INNOVATION

10

PATENT PROTECTION, TRANSNATIONAL CORPORATIONS, AND MARKET STRUCTURE: A SIMULATION STUDY OF THE INDIAN PHARMACEUTICAL INDUSTRY

Carsten Fink

I. Introduction

The protection of patent rights is considered to be a critical precondition for private investment in pharmaceutical research and in the development of new drugs. The importance of patent protection in this industry can be attributed to the ease with which new chemical entities can be imitated in comparison with the large research and development (R&D) outlays and long product cycles associated with research-based drugs. In economic terms, new chemical entities—unless legally protected by patents—are weakly appropriable from the viewpoint of the innovating firm.

The origins of the pharmaceutical industry go back to the commercialization of the first research-based drugs, Prontosil and penicillin, in the 1930s. Since the 1960s, the development and production of pharmaceuticals has been dominated

This chapter is adapted from an article published in 2001 in the *Journal of Industry, Competition, and Trade* 1(1):101–21. Helpful comments by Clive Bell, Tony Venables, Jayashree Watal, and seminar participants at the World Trade Organization and World Bank are gratefully acknowledged. Any remaining errors are the author's own responsibility.

by a limited number of transnational corporations (TNCs) from industrial countries (mostly from France, Germany, Japan, Switzerland, the United Kingdom, and the United States). Despite the escalating costs of R&D, the declining rate of new drug development, the expiry of patents on many blockbuster drugs in the late 1980s, and the squeezing of public health budgets, the composition of the global pharmaceutical industry remained largely the same up to the early 1990s (Tarabusi 1993).[1] Pharmaceutical companies have extensive international production systems. U.S. pharmaceutical TNCs, for example, have, on average, 33.8 foreign affiliates per parent firm—a larger number than in any other U.S. manufacturing industry (Maskus 1998). This pattern fits well into the ownership-location-internalization framework (OLI) of international production: TNCs are firms with significant knowledge-based assets—patents, trademarks, and marketing expertise in the case of the pharmaceutical industry—which are internationally often most profitably exploited by taking a direct investment position in a foreign country (Dunning 1979, 1981).

This chapter examines the effect of patent protection on the behavior of pharmaceutical TNCs and market structure in India, which has traditionally been a fierce opponent of stronger intellectual property rights (IPRs). The Indian Patents Act of 1970 specifically excludes patent coverage for pharmaceutical products. To meet its obligations under the Agreement on Trade-Related Aspects of Intellectual Property Rights (TRIPS)—one of the outcomes of the Uruguay Round (1986–94)—India will have to amend its patent laws to allow for pharmaceutical product patents by 2005. The signing of TRIPS by the Indian government has been accompanied by forceful publicity predicting that stronger patent rights will lead to soaring prices for pharmaceuticals and to a dominance of TNCs as they "wipe out" Indian firms. This study is intended to shed some light on these issues and may also serve as a reference point for other developing countries that are introducing pharmaceutical product patents in a post-TRIPS world.

The method of analysis is the calibration of a theoretical model to actual data from the Indian pharmaceutical market and a simulation exercise to answer the hypothetical question of what the market structure would be if India allowed patents for pharmaceutical products. This technique is in the same spirit as the studies by Baldwin and Krugman (1988) on the Japanese and U.S. semiconductor industries and by Dixit (1988) on the Japanese and U.S. automobile industries, studies that focus on the simulation of alternative trade policy regimes.

The model developed for the simulation analysis explicitly accounts for the complex demand structure for pharmaceutical goods that results from the presence of therapeutic substitute drugs and from drug manufacturers' practice of differentiating their products through the use of trademarks and advertising. Consumer demand is represented by a three-level utility function, whereby preferences for different chemical entities and brands are characterized by constant-elasticity-of-substitution (CES) functions. In the absence of patent protection, firms are assumed to maximize profits, taking as constant the sales of other market participants. If patents are protected, the patent holder has a monopoly for the chemical entity but still competes with producers of therapeutic substitutes.

This model is calibrated for two therapeutic groups—quinolones and synthetic hypotensives—using 1992 brand-level data for each chemical entity sold in the two therapeutic groups that would have received patent protection in Europe (referred to as on-patent chemical entities throughout this chapter), as well as brand-level data for all off-patent chemical entities in these two groups. The simulations reveal to what extent price increases, profits, and static consumer welfare losses depend on the values of the model's parameters. They provide valuable insights with regard to the role of competition among therapeutic substances. It is important to stress that the simulation exercise presented in this chapter is hypothetical, in the sense that the drugs that are analyzed will never receive patent protection in India. The introduction of patents as spelled out in TRIPS does not extend to drugs that are already on the market; that is, there is no obligation for "pipeline" protection of pharmaceutical products.

The chapter is organized as follows. The next section describes the development of India's pharmaceutical industry and outlines the industry's main features. Accounting for these features, the following section develops a partial equilibrium model of the Indian pharmaceutical market by specifying the demand and supply behavior of consumers and producers of drugs. The brand-level data used for the empirical investigation is then described, followed by an explanation of how the partial equilibrium model is calibrated to these data. Then the simulation procedure is illustrated and the simulation results are discussed. Finally, the paper's main findings are summarized and put into perspective.

II. Industry Structure

One of the stated objectives of the Indian Patents Act of 1970 was the development of an independent Indian pharmaceutical industry. The abolition of pharmaceutical product patent protection from the inherited British colonial law was seen as the key element in advancing this objective. If we look at the pure numbers, the Indian Patents Act was a success. The number of supplying firms increased from 2,237 licensed drug manufacturers in 1969–70 to an estimated 16,000 producers in 1992–93 (OPPI 1994a). The production of drug formulations grew at an average annual rate of 14.4 percent between 1980–81 and 1992–93; the negative balance of trade in bulk drugs and drug formulation that prevailed throughout the 1970s and 1980s turned into a trade surplus by 1990.[2]

The period 1970–93 also saw a declining market share of TNCs in India. In 1970, Indian-owned firms held only 10 to 20 percent of the total pharmaceutical market, TNCs accounted for the remaining 80 to 90 percent. By 1980, Indian firms and TNCs had equal shares of about 50 percent; by 1993, Indian firms had raised their share to 61 percent.[3] Redwood (1994) argues that the relative decline of TNCs in the Indian pharmaceutical market has been against the international trend: most other countries have seen the relative share of TNCs rise at the expense of locally owned firms.[4]

It is, of course, difficult to attribute the falling market share of TNCs directly to the abolition of product patent protection through the Indian Patents Act. Other factors may also have contributed to this trend. Investment and ownership restrictions under the Foreign Exchange Regulation Act may have discouraged many TNCs from investing in India. Severe price controls on segments of the pharmaceutical markets may have reduced the prospects of profitability. Moreover, it is possible that low Indian prices could have leaked to other markets, either in the form of parallel imports or through price controls in foreign markets tied to reference indices of prices in other markets (such as India). These factors may have caused some TNCs to shun the Indian market. However, given the critical role of product patent protection for the development of research-based pharmaceuticals, it seems reasonable to attribute the relative decline of TNCs at least in part to the Indian Patents Act.

This proposition is supported by the fact that the imitation and production of drugs protected by patents in other countries has indeed been a widespread activity among Indian-owned firms. Redwood (1994) estimates that 20 percent of the brands marketed by the 15 leading Indian firms in 1993 were based on chemical entities that were covered by pharmaceutical product patents in Europe, and a further 37 percent were based on chemical entities for which the patent had expired somewhere between 1972 and 1993. It is worth noting that Indian firms required no formal technical assistance from abroad to produce foreign patented drugs. The published patent titles have provided sufficient information to imitate the newly developed chemical entities. This ability has been attributed to a well-developed chemical infrastructure and the process skills of the local Indian pharmaceutical industry.

Copied brands of drugs patented in foreign countries have typically been introduced in the Indian market soon after the world introduction of these drugs (Lanjouw 1997). TNCs thus have not enjoyed a substantial first-mover advantage in selling a newly developed drug on the Indian market. This fact has most likely contributed to the trend of many TNCs choosing not to supply the Indian market in the first place. Indeed, in 1993, of the world's 30 largest pharmaceutical TNCs, only 16 had a direct investment position in India (Redwood 1994).

Expenditure on R&D by pharmaceutical companies in India has been modest. In 1992–93, the industry spent an estimated 1.4 percent of sales on R&D—as compared with 1 percent of sales by Indian industry in general (OPPI 1994a) and more than 15 percent of sales by the parent groups of TNC subsidiaries (Redwood 1994). Most R&D activity by Indian-owned firms has concentrated on imitating and adapting pharmaceutical products developed in foreign countries. Only very little R&D by Indian firms has been geared toward the development of new drugs.[5] There has been no marked difference in R&D spending between Indian-owned firms and the subsidiaries of TNCs. Foreign-owned companies have relied heavily on product and process technologies supplied by their parent groups and have conducted little original R&D.

Profitability in the Indian pharmaceutical industry has continuously declined from an estimated 15.5 percent of sales (before taxes) in 1969–70 to 1 percent in 1991–92 (OPPI 1994a). Redwood (1994) reports evidence from a sample of Indian- and foreign-owned companies that suggests that profitability has been higher for pharmaceutical exports, but he confirms that in the early 1990s, home sales of pharmaceutical companies in India were doing little better than breaking even. Moreover, Redwood finds no marked difference between the profitability of Indian firms and foreign-owned companies.

The absence of patent protection for pharmaceutical products, the large number of supplying units, the low degree of profitability, and the very low drug prices in India—by international standards—could be taken as an indication of a highly competitive market. Although this seems a plausible scenario, one should be careful in drawing premature conclusions based solely on these descriptive indicators. There are many well-known problems related to the comparison of prices from different countries that are quoted in different currencies.[6] In addition, not all market participants compete directly with each other. The market for antibiotics, for example, can be considered as being independent of the market for, say, cardiovascular drugs. Competition is limited to a group of drugs that are therapeutic substitutes for each other. Finally, pharmaceutical companies in India, as in industrial countries, differentiate their products through trademarks and promote their brands through advertising, thus generating market power even though a large number of other brands of the same drug may be available (Lanjouw 1997). The model developed in the next section accounts for these special features of the pharmaceutical industry.

III. The Model Setup

Several studies simulate the effect of patent protection on prices and welfare in developing countries' pharmaceutical industries (Maskus and Konan 1994;

Nogués 1993; Subramanian 1995). These studies rely on aggregate data on the patent-protected segment of the pharmaceutical market and simulate the transition toward a patent-induced monopoly by making various assumptions about the pre-patent market structure and market demand.[7] However, they can give only rough estimates of the effect of patent protection, because they do not take into account the independence of different therapeutic groups and the different market structures that may exist in these therapeutic groups.

Watal (1998) improves upon these studies by using brand-level data for all on-patent chemical entities in the Indian pharmaceutical market and simulating the transition toward a patent-induced monopoly for each on-patent chemical entity. Brands of the same entity are assumed to be perfect substitutes, and, in the absence of patent protection, market participants are assumed to engage in Cournot-Nash competition. Watal's study considers both a linear and a constant-elasticity demand function and links the assumed demand elasticity to the level of therapeutic competition expressed by the market share of the chemical entity in the overall therapeutic group.

Watal's simulated price increases and welfare losses are, to date, the most detailed figures available for the Indian market. However, the study's methodology can be criticized on two grounds. First, the assumption that brands of the same chemical entity are perfect substitutes seems at odds with the observed pattern of product differentiation through trademarks and advertising described in the previous section.[8] Second, the market share of a chemical entity in the overall therapeutic group may not be a good indicator of the level of therapeutic competition faced by this entity. The degree to which one drug can be substituted for another is likely to depend on the therapeutic properties of the drugs rather than on the revealed market share.

The partial equilibrium model developed in this section addresses those issues. It seeks to capture the specific features of the Indian pharmaceutical industry as described in the previous section. Market demand is modeled by a three-level utility function that accounts for therapeutic substitution and product differentiation. In the absence of patent protection, firms are assumed to maximize profits, taking as constant the sales of other market participants. If patents are protected, the patent holder has a monopoly for the chemical entity but still competes with producers of therapeutic substitutes.

Demand for Drugs

Modeling the demand for pharmaceutical goods is quite a complex task. Standard economic theory assumes that the decision to purchase a good, to make the payment, and then to consume the good are undertaken by one person. For pharmaceuticals, however, this is hardly ever the case. Indeed, this decision may involve as many as four different persons: the doctor, who chooses and prescribes the drug; the pharmacist, who may choose among branded or generic substitutes; the insurer, who may pay in full or for a portion of the drug; and the patient, who consumes the drug and may also influence the choice of drug and make partial or full payment. The details of this decisionmaking process vary from country to country and depend on various institutional and economic circumstances, such as the freedom of the doctor to prescribe the drug most suitable for the patient, policies that may encourage generic substitution, the availability and design of health insurance plans, and the patient's income.

We model the decision to purchase a pharmaceutical good as a two-stage process. First, a decision has to be made on a particular chemical entity to fight the patient's disease. The choice usually rests with the doctor who prescribes the chemical entity. Although no two different chemical entities have exactly the same effect, there are therapeutic substitutes that fight the same disease. Unless the doctor chooses a particular drug on a purely medical basis, the prices of different substitutes may influence the doctor's choice of which chemical entity to prescribe. In this decision, the doctor is influenced by the patient's means. Once a particular chemical entity has been prescribed, a second decision has to be made about the particular brand.[9] This decision is made by the doctor, the pharmacist, or the patient, or by more than one of these individuals.[10] It is primarily influenced by the patient's budget and brand loyalty induced by marketing and advertising, as well as by past experience.

Formally, this two-stage decisionmaking process is modeled by a three-level utility function. Upper-tier preferences of a representative patient are represented by a quasi-linear utility function:

$$(10.1) \qquad u(X,Y) = aX^{(\varepsilon-1)/\varepsilon} + bY, \quad a,b > 0$$

where X corresponds to a subutility level derived from all the chemical entities that are available to fight a particular disease, Y is a bundle of other goods and services, and a and b are functional parameters. The subutility X is determined by a CES function of chemical entities in the therapeutic group:

$$(10.2) \qquad X = \left[\sum_{i=1}^{n} v_i X_i^{\rho} \right]^{1/\rho}, \quad \sum_{i=1}^{n} v_i = 1, \quad \rho < 1,$$

where X_i corresponds to a "sub-subutility" level derived from all the brands supplying chemical entity i, n is the number of chemical entities available in the therapeutic group, v_i are distribution parameters that permit the relative importance of chemical entities to vary, and ρ is the substitution parameter. As is well known for CES functions, the elasticity of substitution σ between any pair of chemical entities is given by $\sigma = 1/(1-\rho)$. The third level of the utility function relates the sub-subutility X_i to all brands supplying chemical entity i—again using a CES function:

$$(10.3) \qquad X_i = \left[\sum_{j=0}^{m_i} w_{ij} X_{ij}^{\delta_i} \right]^{1/\delta_i}, \qquad \sum_{i=0}^{m_i} w_{ij} = 1, \quad \delta < 1$$

where X_{ij} is the output of brand j for chemical entity i, $m_i + 1$ is the number of brands supplying chemical entity i, w_{ij} are distribution parameters that permit the relative importance of brands to vary, and δ_i is the substitution parameter.[11] The substitution elasticity ϕ_i between any pair of brands is given by $\phi_i = 1/(1-\delta_i)$. We would expect that $\phi_i > \sigma$, because brands of the same chemical entity are better substitutes for each other than chemical entities of a given therapeutic group.

This three-level utility function captures the fact that not only are different chemical entities imperfect substitutes for one another, but also brands of the same chemical entity are imperfect substitutes because of experience, trademarks, and promotional activities. The model imposes four restrictions on drug preferences. First, marginal rates of substitution between any two chemical entities are independent of the quantity consumed of other goods and services. In other words, the consumer's upper-tier preferences are separable from the preferences for chemical entities once a choice on the therapeutic group has been made. Second, marginal rates of substitution between any two brands of the same chemical entity are independent of the quantity consumed of brands of different chemical entities (separability of middle-tier preferences). Third, elasticities of substitution between any two brands of the same chemical entity are the same and are constant. Fourth, the elasticity of substitution between any two chemical entities is the same and is constant. These restrictions seem mild in relation to the complexity of the overall demand structure.

Because preferences at each level are separable, we can solve the consumer's problem of maximizing the utility function implied by equations 10.1 to 10.3, subject to the usual budget constraint in stages. At the therapeutic group level, the quasi-linear utility function in equation 10.1 implies an overall demand function with constant elasticity:

$$(10.4) \qquad D = kP^{-\varepsilon}, \qquad k = \left(\frac{b\varepsilon}{a(\varepsilon - 1)} \right)^{-\varepsilon} P_Y^{\varepsilon}$$

where P is a price index for the therapeutic group and P_Y is a price index of other goods and services. For the subutility function (equation 10.2) and the sub-subutility function (equation 10.3), maximization yields the following demand functions for a chemical entity, D_i, and for a brand, D_{ij}:[12]

$$(10.5) \qquad D_i = v_i^\sigma D \left(\frac{P_i}{P} \right)^{-\sigma}$$

$$(10.6) \qquad D_{ij} = w_{ij}^{\phi_i} D_i \left(\frac{P_{ij}}{P_i} \right)^{-\phi_i}$$

where P_i is a price index for chemical entity i, and P_{ij} is the product price for brand j of chemical entity i. Substituting equations 10.4 and 10.5 into equation 10.6 gives

$$(10.7) \qquad D_{ij} = w_{ij}^{\phi_i} v_i^\sigma k P^{\sigma-\varepsilon} P_i^{\phi_i-\sigma} P_{ij}^{-\phi_i}$$

which represents the demand function perceived by a firm that supplies brand j of chemical entity i.

Supply of Drugs

The production of a drug formulation typically consists of transforming an intermediate input in the form of one or more bulk drugs into tablet or liquid form, then packaging and labeling it. Bulk drugs are produced in-house, purchased locally from an Indian firm, or imported from another country. There do not seem to be significant economies of scale related to the production of drug formulations (Caves, Whinston, and Hurwitz 1991). Hence, it is assumed that drug-producing firms face constant marginal costs. This assumption is convenient because one can ignore firms' export decisions.

Consider the market for chemical entity i in a given therapeutic group and assume initially that there is no patent protection for pharmaceutical products in India. There are then two types of firms that contemplate entering the market for i. The TNC that invented the chemical entity supplies brand 0, while Indian imitators supply m_i competing brands. In line with actual ownership patterns (see discussion in the next section), we allow for the possibility that firms supply more than one brand of chemical entity i or brands of other chemical entities in the therapeutic group. Regarding market behavior, we assume that firms maximize profits, taking as constant the sales of other market participants. Appendix 10.A shows that this leads to the first-order conditions

$$(10.8) \quad P_{ij}\left(1 - \frac{1 - \left(s_{ij} + \sum_k s_{ik}\right)}{\phi_i} - \frac{\left(s_{ij} + \sum_k s_{ik}\right)(1 - t_i) - \sum_l s_l t_l}{\sigma} - \frac{\left(s_{ij} + \sum_k s_{ik}\right)t_i + \sum_l s_l t_l}{\varepsilon}\right) \leq c_i$$

for $j = 0, 1, \ldots, m_i$ and $i = 1, \ldots, n$, where

$$s_{ij} = \frac{P_{ij}D_{ij}}{\sum_{i=0}^{m_i} P_{il}D_{il}}$$

and

$$t_i = \frac{P_i D_i}{\sum_{l=1}^{n} P_l D_l}$$

are brand j's and drug i's market shares, respectively, and c_{ij} is the marginal cost of producing brand j. The index k includes all other brands of chemical entity i that are supplied by the firm that supplies brand j. Similarly, the index l includes all other chemical entities for which the firm that supplies brand j of chemical entity i produces a brand, and the market share s_i relates to exactly this brand.

Intuitively, the second term in the bracket in equation 10.8 captures the recognition of firms that they can induce consumers to switch to their brands from other brands, the third term captures the influence of therapeutic substitution on firms' sales decisions, and the final term captures the effect of overall market demand on these decisions.

Note that equation 10.8 holds with equality only if the output of firm j is positive. In particular, it may be that the patent owner of i is not active in the Indian market in the absence of patent protection—indeed, this is the case for the drugs analyzed in this chapter. In that case, the model assumes that the market is served entirely by local firms and that output in equilibrium is thus determined by competition among Indian firms only. This, in turn, assumes that the absence of the patent owner in the Indian market does not pose an obstacle to imitating a chemical entity. As explained in the preceding section, this scenario seems to be a realistic description of the observed pattern: the patent title published abroad provides sufficient information for Indian firms to imitate a newly developed chemical entity. If an on-patent drug is not introduced in India, it is only because of low market demand and can, for the purposes of this model, be ignored.[13]

We assume that the TNC faces fixed costs F_{i0} to enter the Indian market for chemical entity i and all Indian firms face fixed entry costs F_{ij}. With otherwise unrestricted entry into the industry, the number of Indian firms is endogenously determined by the structure of fixed and marginal costs in the imitating industry. As was pointed out earlier, actual profitability in the Indian industry is small. This fact is consistent with the present model if firms' operating surpluses are largely absorbed by their fixed costs. A later section calibrates this model to the firm-level data from the Indian pharmaceutical market.

Following that calibration, we simulate the effect of patent protection by assuming that the patent holders' brands will take over the markets for all on-patent chemical entities. Setting $s_{i0} = 1$, the second term in the bracket in equation 10.8 drops out, and it is apparent that the TNC's sales decision depends only on the degree of therapeutic competition and on overall market demand. Stated differently, if patent rights are protected, the TNC has a monopoly at the level of the chemical entity but still competes with substitute chemical entities. In contrast to the calibrated equilibrium, we will take the number of Indian firms in the off-patent market segment as exogenously given and base our simulation on the same brands and ownership patterns observed in the calibrated equilibrium.[14] Of course, it would have been more realistic to allow for the possibility of entry or exit in the off-patent market segment, but this was ruled out by the lack of data on the fixed cost structure among Indian firms.

IV. The Data

The data used for the calibration of the model developed in the previous section come from the Operations Research Group (ORG) pharmacy audit of December 1992 (ORG 1993).[15] The ORG audit does not cover the very small company sector or sales to hospitals and the public sector (for example, sales to the military). Watal (1996) conjectures that the unaudited share of the total pharmaceutical market is likely to be lower in India than in the United States, where it is estimated to be 11 percent. Although the basis for this conjecture is not clear, it seems reasonable to assume that the share of the pharmaceutical market not audited by ORG is small (in any case, brand-level data for the small company sector and sales to hospitals and to the public sector were not available). Moreover, in terms of the model used in this study, the exclusion of the hospital market and government procurement may actually be an advantage, because these market segments may exhibit a different demand behavior than the one assumed in the last section.

Redwood (1994) identifies 24 chemical entities from 13 different therapeutic groups that were among the top 500 pharmaceutical products on the Indian pharmaceutical market in 1993 and were under active patent protection in

Europe.[16] Using the ORG classification, the *Indian Pharmaceutical Guide* (1997), the *Drug Index* (1997), and the *Current Index of Medical Specialities* (1998), one could identify all brands and firms for each on-patent chemical entity, all off-patent therapeutic substitutes in the respective therapeutic groups, and all brands for each off-patent chemical entity. I then chose two of the 13 therapeutic groups—quinolones and synthetic hypotensives—for the calibration and simulation exercises.[17] The choice of these two groups was guided by two factors. First, all chemical entities under investigation had to be free of price controls.[18] For example, this requirement led to an exclusion of antipeptic ulcerants (with three on-patent chemical entities) because the prices of ranitidine, one of the best-selling drugs on the Indian pharmaceutical market in 1992, were controlled (see Redwood 1994). Second, for these two therapeutic groups, a large number of (imitating) brands supplied each on-patent chemical entity, and there was an ample number of chemical entities. Hence, the effects of patent-induced monopolies and the role of therapeutic substitution are likely to be important in these two therapeutic groups.

Using the *Merck Index* (Budavari 1989), I identified the patent owners for each on-patent chemical entity in the two therapeutic groups. In all cases, the patent owner did not supply the Indian market. The absence of the patent owner may have been due to one of two factors: either the title holder did indeed decide to abstain from the Indian market or the title holder was active through a licensee. Since no information could be obtained on licensing relationships, it was assumed that the patent owner decided to abstain from the Indian market.[19] This assumption, of course, could lead to a potential bias if licensing had been a widely used method of serving the Indian market for the six on-patent chemical entities. At the same time, it could be argued that potential royalties and license fees may have been small precisely because product patent protection was not available.

For each brand name, the ORG data list the total sales revenue and the quantity sold, from which the brand's average market price could be computed. In two instances, it was found that one Indian firm supplied two brands of the same chemical entity.[20] In addition, there were numerous cases in which one firm supplied two or more brands of different chemical entities in the same therapeutic group. As in similar studies, only the tablet form and only the most popular dosage form for each chemical entity were used (Caves, Whinston, and Hurwitz 1991; Watal 1998). However, different package sizes (with the same dosage) were aggregated to compute a single price, and the variables were expressed in single dosage units (instead of packages). Finally, figures were transformed in terms of their monthly average because, for selected cases, firms entered the market during 1992. This averaging was possible because the month of entry was listed in the ORG data. Although one ignores possible seasonal

TABLE 10.1   Quinolunes: Overview

Chemical entity	Patent owner	Year of patent expiry	Number of brands in India	Total sales (Rs)	Weighted average price (Rs)	Weighted standard deviation of prices
Ciprofloxacin	Bayer AG	2001	37	555,515,000	17.63	1.23
Norfloxacin	Kyorin and Roger Bellon/ Dainippon	1998	24	467,238,000	4.43	0.63
Pefloxacin	Roger Bellon/ Dainippon	1998	8	125,370,000	8.92	0.68
Ofloxacin	Daiichi Seiyaku Co.	2001	2	48,778,000	20.01	0.35
Nalidixic acid	Off-patent	Off-patent	4	69,260,000	0.93	0.08

Note: The patent owners were inactive in the Indian market for all five on-patent chemical entities. Figures are for 1992.
Source: Redwood (1994), ORG (1993), and Budavari (1989).

fluctuations by this procedure, it was preferred over simply excluding these market entrants.

Table 10.1 lists the five different quinolone entities, the patent owners, the years of patent expiry in Europe, the numbers of brands supplying the chemical entities, total annual sales, the weighted average prices, and the weighted standard deviations of prices. As can be seen, four on-patent chemical entities competed with one off-patent chemical entity. The four on-patent chemical entities accounted for approximately 53 percent of the total sales value of all 24 on-patent chemical entities identified in Redwood's study. Table 10.2 presents the same information for the group of synthetic hypotensives. In this group, two on-patent chemical entities competed with nine off-patent drugs. The two on-patent chemical entities accounted for 4 percent in sales of the 24 on-patent drugs identified by Redwood. Note that five off-patent entities were supplied by monopolists.

As one can see by comparing tables 10.1 and 10.2, the two therapeutic groups chosen represent two alternative pre-patent market structures. In the case of quinolones, the on-patent drugs dominated the market and competed with only one off-patent drug. The reverse holds for synthetic hypotensives—the on-patent drugs had a minority market share and competed with a large number of off-patent drugs.

TABLE 10.2 Hypotensives: Overview

Chemical entity	Patent owner	Year of patent expiry	Number of brands in India	Total sales (Rs)	Weighted average price (Rs)	Weighted standard deviation of prices
Enalapril maleate	Merck & Co.	1999	14	67,639,000	1.19	0.12
Captopril	Squibb	1997	5	36,591,000	2.18	0.10
Nifedipine/ atenolol	Off-patent	Off-patent	12	66,064,000	1.70	0.22
Methyldopa	Off-patent	Off-patent	8	56,920,000	1.59	0.21
Lisinopril	Off-patent	Off-patent	9	10,260,000	2.46	0.21
Clonidine	Off-patent	Off-patent	2	8,518,000	0.36	0.06
Indapamide	Off-patent	Off-patent	1	7,609,000	2.52	n.a.
Prazosin	Off-patent	Off-patent	1	3,130,000	0.92	n.a.
Perindopril	Off-patent	Off-patent	1	1,156,000	16.22	n.a.
Hydralazine	Off-patent	Off-patent	1	765,000	0.07	n.a.
Reserpine	Off-patent	Off-patent	1	237,000	0.13	n.a.

n.a = not applicable.
Note: The patent owners were inactive in the Indian market for both on-patent chemical entities. Figures are for 1992.
Source: Redwood (1994), ORG (1993), and Budavari (1989).

V. Model Calibration

To calibrate and simulate the model developed earlier, we need to have values for the elasticities ϕ_i, σ, and ε. Unfortunately, no outside estimate for any of these three elasticities was available. In principle, one could have tried to estimate values of substitution and demand elasticities econometrically, but this possibility was ruled out by the lack of availability of time-series data on prices and quantities. Moreover, one would face the standard identification problem, because data on prices and quantities are determined by supply and demand simultaneously, and it would be difficult to think of effective "supply-shifting" instruments.

The only additional information available is an estimate of firms' average profit margins. On the basis of pharmaceutical companies' annual reports, Redwood (1994) estimates that variable costs of firms averaged 65 percent of sales, with operating profit margins of 35 percent of sales. We therefore assume two alternative values for each of the three elasticities and evaluate whether different combinations of these values are realistic by comparing the implied average operating margin with the 35 percent benchmark. Obviously, this approach is far from perfect, but the different assumptions for ϕ_i, σ, and ε give a reasonable indication of how sensitive the simulation results are to these parameters and of the overall magnitude of the effect of patent protection in the two therapeutic groups.

Because we expect two brands of the same chemical entity to be good substitutes for each other, we take relatively high values for the substitution elasticity among brands ($\phi_i = 3.5$ and $\phi_i = 5.5$). Note that the two alternative assumptions on ϕ_i apply to all firms in the therapeutic group. The substitution elasticity among chemical entities is assumed to be comparatively smaller ($\sigma = 1.1$ and $\sigma = 2.0$). Finally, for the overall elasticity of demand in the therapeutic group, we use a low price-sensitivity assumption ($\varepsilon = 1.5$) and high price-sensitivity assumption ($\varepsilon = 2.5$).[21]

With values for ϕ_i, σ, and ε, and the actual data on prices and market shares, we can use equation 10.8 to directly calculate firms' marginal cost of production, c_{ij}. Next, we can compute the weight parameters w_{ij} of the CES function in equation 10.3. From equation 10.6, it follows that

$$D_{ij}w_{ij}^{-\phi_i}P_{ij}^{\phi_i} = D_{iz}w_{iz}^{-\phi_i}P_{iz}^{\phi_i}, \qquad \text{for all } j, z \ (j \neq z),$$

which can be solved for w_{iz}. With $\sum_{z=0}^{m_i} w_{iz} = 1$, this leads to

$$(10.9) \qquad w_{ij} = \left[1 + D_{ij}^{-1/\phi_i}P_{ij}^{-1} \sum_{z \neq j} D_{iz}^{1/\phi_i}P_{iz} \right]^{-1}.$$

A problem is that the patent holders are not active in the calibrated equilibrium ($D_{i0} = 0$). This situation would lead to weights w_{i0} equal to zero—because consumers do not consider consuming the TNC's product if it is not available. For the purpose of this analysis, however, preferences have to be broader and include the patent holder's product in consumer choice. Specifically, consumers must know that the patent holder's product exists and possibly choose to buy it, if it were available.[22] The calibration therefore assumes that the patent holder's brand is, on average, valued like any other brand. In computing the weight parameters w_{ij}, we therefore set P_{i0} equal to the weighted average price of a chemical entity and D_{i0} equal to the average firm output.[23] This approach is somewhat unsatisfactory, but there does not seem to be a good alternative.

With the values obtained for w_{ij} and equation 10.3, we can compute figures for the sub-subutility levels X_i. Price indices for chemical entities are given by[24]

$$(10.10) \qquad P_i = \left[\sum_{j=0}^{m_i} w_{ij}^{\phi_i} P_{ij}^{1-\phi_i} \right]^{1/(1-\phi_i)}.$$

Next, we calibrate the model at the level of chemical entities by taking steps parallel to the ones taken at brand level. First, the weight parameters v_i can be computed through

$$(10.11) \qquad v_i = \left[1 + D_i^{-1/\sigma} P_i^{-1} \sum_{z \neq i} D_z^{1/\sigma} P_z \right]^{-1}.$$

This equation allows us to calculate the subutility of the therapeutic group X using equation 10.2. The price index of the therapeutic group is given by

$$(10.12) \qquad P = \left[\sum_{i=1}^{n} v_i^{\sigma} P_i^{1-\sigma} \right]^{1/(1-\sigma)}.$$

Finally, with these values for the subutility level, the overall price index, and the assumption for ε, we can solve for the parameter k in the overall demand function in equation 10.4.

Table 10.3 (for quinolones) and table 10.4 (for hypotensives) present the calibrated weight parameters v_i for each chemical entity and for the alternative assumptions for ϕ_i and σ (v_i is independent of ε). It is worth pointing out that, in both therapeutic groups, there are only small differences in the values of the weight parameters for the two assumptions for the substitution elasticity among

TABLE 10.3 Quinolones—Calibrated Weight Parameters

Chemical entity	$\phi_i = 3.5$		$\phi_i = 5.5$	
	v_i ($\sigma = 1.1$)	v_i ($\sigma = 2.0$)	v_i ($\sigma = 1.1$)	v_i ($\sigma = 2.0$)
Ciprofloxacin	0.463	0.587	0.464	0.592
Norfloxacin	0.332	0.213	0.333	0.216
Pefloxacin	0.118	0.117	0.118	0.114
Ofloxacin	0.042	0.067	0.042	0.062
Nalidixic acid	0.044	0.017	0.044	0.017

Note: Variables are explained in the text. Weights may not sum to one because of rounding errors.
Source: Author's calculations.

TABLE 10.4   Hypotensives—Calibrated Weight Parameters

Chemical entity	$\phi_i = 3.5$		$\phi_i = 5.5$	
	v_i $(\sigma = 1.1)$	v_i $(\sigma = 2.0)$	v_i $(\sigma = 1.1)$	v_i $(\sigma = 2.0)$
Enalapril maleate	0.259	0.232	0.259	0.232
Captopril	0.142	0.146	0.142	0.145
Nifedipine/Atenolol	0.256	0.247	0.256	0.248
Methyldopa	0.207	0.157	0.208	0.163
Lisinopril	0.052	0.110	0.052	0.110
Clonidine	0.030	0.019	0.029	0.018
Indapamide	0.030	0.035	0.030	0.033
Prazosin	0.012	0.014	0.012	0.013
Perindopril	0.007	0.036	0.007	0.034
Hydralazine	0.002	0.002	0.003	0.002
Reserpine	0.001	0.001	0.001	0.001

Note: Variables are explained in the text. Weights may not sum to one because of rounding errors.
Source: Author's calculations.

brands, ϕ_i; the weight parameters are more sensitive to the assumed elasticity of substitution among chemical entities, σ.

To allow us to evaluate the plausibility of the assumed elasticities, tables 10.5 and 10.6 present the simple average and sales-weighted average profit margins in the two therapeutic groups for each combination of the three elasticities. In the case of quinolones, this profit margin is quite sensitive to the assumed elasticity of substitution among brands ϕ_i but insensitive to the other two elasticities. For this chemical entity, the assumption $\phi_i = 5.5$ leads to average profit margins that lie always below the 35 percent benchmark (on both an unweighted and a sales-weighted basis).

TABLE 10.5   Quinolones—Average Profit Margins (percent)

	$\varepsilon = 1.5$		$\varepsilon = 2.5$	
	$\sigma = 1.1$	$\sigma = 2.0$	$\sigma = 1.1$	$\sigma = 2.0$
$\phi_i = 3.5$	32.1	30.6	31.3	29.7
	(40.3)	(35.4)	(37.2)	(32.4)
$\phi_i = 5.5$	22.5	20.9	21.6	20.1
	(32.3)	(27.5)	(29.2)	(24.4)

Note: Sales-weighted averages are in parentheses.
Source: Author's calculations.

TABLE 10.6 Hypotensives—Average Profit Margins (percent)

	$\varepsilon = 1.5$		$\varepsilon = 2.5$	
	$\sigma = 1.1$	$\sigma = 2.0$	$\sigma = 1.1$	$\sigma = 2.0$
$\phi_i = 3.5$	40.3	33.4	39.5	32.6
	(54.7)	(39.7)	(52.4)	(37.4)
$\phi_i = 5.5$	32.0	25.0	31.2	24.2
	(49.0)	(34.0)	(46.7)	(31.7)

Note: Sales-weighted averages are in parentheses.
Source: Author's calculations.

Hence, the assumption $\phi_i = 3.5$ appears to be more realistic. In the case of hypotensives, a more mixed picture emerges, although average profit margins are consistently lower for $\phi_i = 5.5$ than for $\phi_i = 3.5$. Again, with reference to the 35 percent benchmark, the combination of $\phi_i = 3.5$ and $\sigma = 2.0$ seems to be the most realistic for this chemical entity.

VI. Model Simulation

To simulate the effect of "overnight" patent protection on the two therapeutic groups analyzed, we need to have a value for the TNC's marginal cost of production c_{i0}. Because the patent holder is inactive in the calibrated equilibrium, we again face the problem of requiring data about something that does not exist. We therefore assume that the TNC faces the same marginal cost as any other Indian firm. Specifically, c_{i0} is taken to be the output-weighted average marginal cost of all Indian firms active in the calibrated equilibrium for the given chemical entity. In addition, the simulation assumes that the TNC will become active after pharmaceutical patent protection is introduced.[25]

As mentioned earlier, we simulate the case whereby the TNC gains a monopoly for its patented chemical entity ($s_{i0} = 1$ for all on-patent chemical entities). Equilibrium values for all endogenous variables can be computed using the first-order conditions in equation 10.8, the demand function (equation 10.7), the formulas for the subutility (equation 10.2) and sub-subutilities (equation 10.3), and the price indices (equations 10.10 and 10.12). This nonlinear system of equations has no analytical solution and, therefore, must be solved with a numerical procedure.

It is also desirable to evaluate the effect of patent protection on welfare. We concentrate on consumer welfare here because potential changes in producer surplus are hard to evaluate without any information on Indian firms' fixed costs. In addition, although we assume a fixed number of firms are supplying off-patent chemical entities in the simulation, it is more likely that changes in market condition result in the entry or exit of firms. This claim is supported by the low actual profitability observed in the industry.

As for consumer welfare, the quasi-linear utility function in equation 10.1 implies the following indirect utility function:

$$(10.13) \qquad V(P,P_Y,I) = \frac{b}{P_Y}\left[\frac{AP^{1-\varepsilon}}{\varepsilon-1} + I\right],$$

where I denotes the overall income of patients who require medical treatment with a drug of the therapeutic group. We can compute compensating variations—that is, the additional income needed to make consumers as well off after patent introduction as before patent protection—by using the two different values for the price index P from the calibrated and simulated equilibria and computing the change in the term $AP^{1-\varepsilon}/(\varepsilon-1)$.

VII. Simulation Results

The simulation results for the alternative assumptions for the three elasticities are presented in table 10.7 for the four on-patent quinolones and in table 10.8 for the two on-patent hypotensives. The tables present percentage price increases and the TNC's operating profits that would result from overnight patent protection. Price increases are computed relative to the weighted average prices listed in tables 10.1 and 10.2. Figures for TNC profits are on a monthly basis.[26]

As can be seen in the tables, price increases and TNC profits vary widely depending on the assumptions of demand and substitution elasticities. Several general observations can be made, however. To begin with, a larger value for the substitution elasticity among brands, ϕ_i, implies larger price movements. This is caused by the more competitive pre-patent market structure that prevails if brands are better substitutes for one another. The main determinant of price changes, however, is the elasticity of substitution between chemical entities, σ. For all on-patent chemical entities, the percentage price increases for $\sigma = 1.1$. exceed several times the percentage increases for $\sigma = 2.0$. This result supports the frequent claim that effective competition from therapeutic substitutes limits excessive prices of on-patent drugs.

For the group of quinolones, a somewhat surprising result is that, for $\sigma = 1.1$, the percentage price increases of on-patent chemical entities that have a smaller number of imitating brands in the pre-patent market structure exceed those that have a larger number of brands. The explanation for this result is that the drugs that have the larger number of pre-patent brands also have a larger share of the therapeutic group's market. By inspection of the pricing formula (equation 10.8),

TABLE 10.7 Quinolones—Simulation

	ε = 1.5				ε = 2.5			
	σ = 1.1		σ = 2.0		σ = 1.1		σ = 2.0	
	Price increase (percent)	TNC profit (Rs thousand)	Price increase (percent)	TNC profit (Rs thousand)	Price increase (percent)	TNC profit (Rs thousand)	Price increase (percent)	TNC profit (Rs thousand)
$\phi_1 = 3.5$								
Ciprofloxacin	233.5	11,185	45.8	8,171	119.1	1,474	30.8	2,075
Norfloxacin	251.5	9,643	43.2	8,269	140.9	1,303	29.5	2,081
Pefloxacin	353.0	3,400	35.6	4,210	267.6	493	27.3	1,094
Ofloxacin	318.6	1,189	20.6	2,603	308.5	173	21.0	652
$\phi_1 = 5.5$								
Ciprofloxacin	276.7	13,845	68.4	11,646	145.7	2,773	45.8	4,155
Norfloxacin	297.9	11,855	63.6	10,968	170.9	2,437	44.4	3,879
Pefloxacin	416.5	4,100	50.6	4,664	319.5	905	41.9	1,694
Ofloxacin	370.5	1,401	30.0	2,312	357.2	311	31.5	811

Note: The price increase refers to the difference between the TNC's price under patent protection and the weighted average price of all suppliers in the absence of patent protection. The figures for TNC profits are on a monthly basis.

Source: Author's calculations.

TABLE 10.8 Hypotensives—Simulation

| | ε = 1.5 | | | | ε = 2.5 | | | |
| | σ = 1.1 | | σ = 2.0 | | σ = 1.1 | | σ = 2.0 | |
	Price increase (percent)	TNC profit (Rs thousand)	Price increase (percent)	TNC profit (Rs thousand)	Price increase (percent)	TNC profit (Rs thousand)	Price increase (percent)	TNC profit (Rs thousand)
$\phi_i = 3.5$								
Enalapril maleate	285.4	2,807	32.5	909	179.7	1,396	30.0	645
Captopril	142.3	1,676	12.4	860	105.6	849	12.5	600
$\phi_i = 5.5$								
Enalapril maleate	333.0	3,027	49.6	1,260	211.3	1,680	43.7	955
Captopril	166.4	1,780	19.3	1,051	123.9	1,009	18.0	783

Note: The price increase refers to the difference between the TNC's price under patent protection and the weighted average price of all suppliers in the absence of patent protection. The figures for TNC profits are on a monthly basis.

Source: Author's calculations.

we find that the patent holder's sales decision puts a relatively greater emphasis on the overall demand elasticity, ε, in the therapeutic group. If $\sigma < \varepsilon$, this has a *relative* offsetting effect on the patent holder's operating profit margin relative to chemical entities that have a smaller market share in the therapeutic group. It turns out that for $\sigma = 1.1$, this offsetting effect is large enough to lead to a smaller percentage increase in price, even though there is a larger number of imitating brands in the pre-patent market equilibrium.

Does stronger therapeutic competition, as reflected by a larger value of σ, lower the profits of the patent holders? Not necessarily. Consider, for example, the case of ofloxacin in table 10.7. For all combinations of ϕ_i and ε, profits are higher under more intense therapeutic competition ($\sigma = 1.1$). Although patent protection raises ofloxacin's price, under strong therapeutic competition ofloxacin experiences increased demand as prices for other on-patent chemical entities also rise. This demand shift is due to the particular properties of the CES subutility function in equation 10.2, combined with the fact that ofloxacin was calibrated as relatively unimportant in consumer preferences, as reflected by its low values for v_i in table 10.3.

But another mechanism is at work. Consider the case of ciprofloxacin in table 10.7. For a demand elasticity of $\varepsilon = 2.5$, profits are higher under more intense therapeutic competition. In this case, this result cannot be due to a demand shift, because ciprofloxacin was calibrated as relatively important in consumer preferences, as reflected by its high values for v_i in table 10.3. Instead, lower profits are due to the "mistakes" patent holders commit by taking other firms' sales decisions as given. In the specific case of ciprofloxacin and the assumed elasticities, the cost of such mistakes can outweigh the benefit of lower therapeutic competition.

In sum, a variety of forces is at work with regard to TNC profits. By comparing the simulation results for the on-patent quinolones with the results for the on-patent hypotensives, however, one can still draw a useful conclusion. If the number and weight of off-patent chemical entities is significant—as is the case for hypotensives—a higher degree of therapeutic competition is likely to lead to lower TNC profits, as demand unambiguously shifts from on-patent to off-patent chemical entities. In addition, overall profit levels depend significantly on the elasticity of demand ε. If the therapeutic group is highly sensitive to price movements ($\varepsilon = 2.5$), profits are lower than if demand is inelastic ($\varepsilon = 1.5$)—as expected.

It is interesting to use the simulation results to ask the hypothetical question: Would product patent protection in India lead to accelerated R&D by TNCs and consequently to a greater rate of drug discovery (particular for the type of diseases most prevalent in low-income countries such as India)? Consider again the case of ciprofloxacin and assume the more realistic $\phi_i = 3.5$. Under the most favorable circumstances, the patent owner realizes operating profits equal to Rs 134.2 million or about US$5.2 million (on an annual basis).[27] In the worst-case scenario, the TNC makes profits of only Rs 17.7 million or US$700,000. Note that the TNC's fixed costs of doing business in India still need to be subtracted from these figures, so revenue available for R&D is likely to be much smaller.

One estimate puts the direct and indirect cost over a 10-year period of developing a new drug at US$231 million (OPPI 1994b). Annual profits of US$5.2 million would seem quite significant in this context, especially for a low-income country such as India and if one allows for the possibility that R&D could be performed less expensively in India. However, the amount of money available for R&D is likely to be smaller than US$5.2 million annually. In addition, ciprofloxacin was one of the best-selling drugs on the Indian market in 1992. Hypothetical profits are therefore likely to be much smaller for other on-patent chemical entities than in the case of ciprofloxacin. Notwithstanding, one cannot dismiss the possibility that, in the long term, patent protection in India could affect private R&D decisions and contribute to new drug discoveries—especially against diseases particular to developing countries.[28]

Finally, tables 10.9 and 10.10 present the simulated static consumer welfare losses for the two therapeutic groups, which are expressed as compensating variations. As one would expect, welfare losses are smaller the more price elastic overall demand is in the therapeutic group and the higher the degree of substitutability is among chemical entities. The latter effect is relatively more pronounced in the case of hypotensives because the presence of a larger off-patent market segment makes therapeutic competition more effective.

The figures shown seem very high relative to TNCs' profits.[29] For example, in the case of quinolones, welfare losses on an annual basis range from Rs 744.2 million (US$28.7 million) to Rs 1,810.4 million (US$69.9 million)—again assuming the

TABLE 10.9 Quinolones—Simulated Consumer Welfare Losses (Rs thousands)

	$\varepsilon = 1.5$		$\varepsilon = 2.5$	
	($\sigma = 1.1$)	($\sigma = 2.0$)	($\sigma = 1.1$)	($\sigma = 2.0$)
$\phi = 3.5$	150,867	107,167	68,921	62,015
$\phi = 5.5$	135,993	88,185	66,025	55,020

Note: Figures shown are compensating variations; that is, the additional income consumers would need in order to be as well off after patent introduction as before patent introduction. Figures are on a monthly basis.

Source: Author's calculations.

TABLE 10.10   Hypotensives—Simulated Consumer Welfare Losses (Rs thousands)

	$\varepsilon = 1.5$		$\varepsilon = 2.5$	
	($\sigma = 1.1$)	($\sigma = 2.0$)	($\sigma = 1.1$)	($\sigma = 2.0$)
$\phi = 3.5$	14,203	6,413	9,398	5,359
$\phi = 5.5$	12,632	5,232	8,486	4,449

Note: Figures shown are compensating variations; that is, the additional income consumers would need in order to be as well off after patent introduction as before patent introduction. Figures are on a monthly basis.

Source: Author's calculations.

more realistic $\phi_i = 3.5$. These large figures are due to the properties of the CES sub-subutility function in equation 10.3. Specifically, the compensating variations capture not only the traditional deadweight loss owing to higher prices, but also the loss in product variety, insofar as consumers cannot choose anymore among different brands for on-patent chemical entities once patents are introduced.

VIII. Summary of Main Findings

This study has simulated the effects of the introduction of product patent protection on two therapeutic drug groups in the Indian pharmaceutical market. Such an analysis is of interest because India will have to amend its current patent regime in this regard by 2005.

The usefulness of a simulation of overnight patent protection is limited for several reasons. First, as already pointed out, the introduction of patent protection for pharmaceutical products as spelled out in TRIPS does not extend to drugs that are already on the market. This exclusion implies that the six on-patent drugs examined in this chapter indeed will never receive patent protection in India. It is worth emphasizing that the introduction of patent protection for pharmaceutical products as required by TRIPS will lead neither to actual price increases nor to the direct displacement of Indian imitators. For any newly developed chemical entity, however, protection applies from the first day on the market.

Second, it was necessary to make strong assumptions about the weight of the TNC's product in the demand function and the TNC's marginal costs of production. The simulation suffered from inadequate data with regard to demand and substitution elasticities.[30] Moreover, the neglect of potential licensing activity may have biased the calibrated and simulated equilibria. Third, it was assumed that all other market conditions remain equal. This assumption is clearly a simplification. For example, stronger patent protection may induce the Indian government to impose price controls or grant compulsory licenses. From this view, the simulation results can be seen as a worst-case scenario that would occur in the absence of any policy response.

These reservations notwithstanding, the simulation highlights some relevant variables that are likely to determine the effect of pharmaceutical patent protection in India on prices, TNC profits, and welfare. Specifically, it clearly demonstrates the relevance of therapeutic competition. The availability of close, off-patent therapeutic substitutes can restrain prices and limit potential welfare losses. Stated differently, if future drug discoveries are mainly new varieties of existing therapeutic treatments, the effect is likely to be relatively small. If newly discovered drugs are medicinal breakthroughs, however, prices may be significantly above competitive levels, and static welfare losses may be relatively large.

From the viewpoint of TNCs, potential profits depended crucially on the overall price elasticity in the therapeutic group. If demand is highly price elastic, as one may expect in a low-income country where insurance coverage is limited, TNC profits are likely to be small. However, if one takes into account the possibility that future changes in the Indian health care system—such as the opening of medical insurance provision to private competition (Lanjouw 1997)—may reduce the price sensitivity of demand, patent holders' profits could increase substantially.

The lack of reliable estimates for structural model parameters and the wide variations in simulated profit levels precluded an assessment of whether the introduction of patent protection in India will boost the R&D activity of TNCs and lead to an acceleration in the rate of new drug discovery. In the long run, it is possible that TNCs will do more research on, for example, tropical diseases, given that most developing countries will move toward stronger patent rights in a post-TRIPS world. Given its favorable cost structure, well-educated scientists, and English-speaking doctors who can supervise drug trials, India may well emerge as an attractive location for the conduct of R&D. Anecdotal evidence points indeed to an increasing number of alliances between TNCs and Indian pharmaceutical companies. Such a development would lead to additional long-term gains from strengthened patent protection.

From the viewpoint of Indian consumers, the simulated welfare losses in this study were quite large—in part owing to a loss in brand variety implied by the CES sub-subutility function. However, it needs to be emphasized that, as of 1993, the patented market segment in India accounted for only 10.9 percent of the total sales values of the top-500 pharmaceutical products in India. Moreover, as already emphasized, the Indian government will have some flexibility in restraining high prices through the granting of compulsory licenses and price controls.

Appendix 10.A
Derivation of First-Order Condition

This appendix derives the first-order condition (equation 10.8) that results from firms' profit-maximizing behavior. From equations 10.4, 10.5, and 10.7, we obtain the following implicit demand functions:

$$(10.A.1) \qquad P = k^{\frac{1}{\varepsilon}} D^{-\frac{1}{\varepsilon}}$$

$$(10.A.2) \qquad P_i = v_i k^{\frac{1}{\sigma}} P^{\frac{\sigma-\varepsilon}{\sigma}} D_i^{-\frac{1}{\sigma}}$$

$$(10.A.3) \qquad P_{ij} = v_i^{\frac{\sigma}{\phi_i}} w_{ij} k^{\frac{1}{\phi_i}} P^{\frac{\sigma-\varepsilon}{\phi_i}} P_i^{\frac{\phi_i-\sigma}{\phi_i}} D_{ij}^{-\frac{1}{\phi_i}}.$$

Differentiating equation 10.A.1 with respect to D, equation 10.A.2 with respect to D_i, and equation 10.A.3 with respect to D_{ij} yields

$$(10.A.4) \qquad \frac{\partial P}{\partial D} = -\frac{1}{\varepsilon} \frac{P}{D}$$

$$(10.A.5) \qquad \frac{\partial P_i}{\partial D_i} = -\frac{1}{\sigma} \frac{P_i}{D_i} + \frac{\sigma-\varepsilon}{\sigma} \frac{P_i}{P} \frac{\partial P}{\partial D} \frac{\partial D}{\partial D_i}$$

$$(10.A.6) \qquad \frac{\partial P_{ij}}{\partial D_{ij}} = -\frac{1}{\phi_i} \frac{P_{ij}}{D_{ij}} + \left[\frac{\phi_i-\sigma}{\phi_i} \frac{P_{ij}}{P_i} \frac{\partial P_i}{\partial D_i} + \frac{\sigma-\varepsilon}{\phi_i} \frac{P_{ij}}{P} \frac{\partial P}{\partial D} \frac{\partial D}{\partial D_i} \right] \frac{\partial D_i}{\partial D_{ij}}.$$

The changes in the subutility level and sub-subutility levels can be computed directly from equations 10.2 and 10.3:

$$(10.A.7) \qquad \frac{\partial D}{\partial D_i} = \frac{v_i D_i^{\frac{\sigma-1}{\sigma}}}{\sum\limits_{z=0}^{n} v_z D_z^{\frac{\sigma-1}{\sigma}}} \frac{D}{D_i} = t_i \frac{D}{D_i}$$

$$(10.A.8) \qquad \frac{\partial D_i}{\partial D_{ij}} = \frac{w_{ij} D_{ij}^{\frac{\phi_i-1}{\phi_i}}}{\sum\limits_{z=0}^{m_i} w_{iz} D_{iz}^{\frac{\phi_i-1}{\phi_i}}} \frac{D_i}{D_{ij}} = s_{ij} \frac{D_i}{D_{ij}}$$

Using these two partial derivatives and substituting equations 10.A.4 and 10.A.5 into 10.A.6, we can compute the inverse demand elasticity perceived by the firm supplying brand j:

$$(10.A.9) \qquad \frac{\partial P_{ij}}{\partial D_{ij}} \frac{D_{ij}}{P_{ij}} = -\frac{1-s_{ij}}{\phi_i} - \frac{s_{ij}(1-t_i)}{\sigma} - \frac{s_{ij}t_i}{\varepsilon}.$$

Next, we consider brand k of chemical entity i, which is supplied by the same firm that supplies brand j. Differentiating k's demand function

$$(10.A.10) \qquad P_{ik} = v_i^{\frac{\sigma}{\phi_i}} w_{ik} k^{\frac{1}{\phi_i}} P^{\frac{\sigma-\varepsilon}{\phi_i}} P_i^{\frac{\phi_i-\sigma}{\phi_i}} D_{ik}^{-\frac{1}{\phi_i}}$$

with respect to D_{ij} yields

$$(10.A.11) \qquad \frac{\partial P_{ik}}{\partial D_{ij}} = \left[\frac{\phi_i-\sigma}{\phi_i} \frac{P_{ik}}{P_i} \frac{\partial P_i}{\partial D_i} + \frac{\sigma-\varepsilon}{\phi_i} \frac{P_{ik}}{P} \frac{\partial P}{\partial D} \frac{\partial D}{\partial D_i}\right]\frac{\partial D_i}{\partial D_{ij}}.$$

Using these partial derivatives, we can compute the inverse cross-demand elasticity:

$$(10.A.12) \qquad \frac{\partial P_{ik}}{\partial D_{ij}} \frac{D_{ij}}{P_{ik}} = \left[\frac{1}{\phi_i} - \frac{1-t_i}{\sigma} - \frac{t_i}{\varepsilon}\right]s_{ij}.$$

Finally, we consider the brand of chemical entity l that is produced by the same firm that supplies brand j of chemical entity i. Differentiating the demand function

$$(10.A.13) \qquad P_{l.} = v_l^{\frac{\sigma}{\phi_l}} w_{l.} k^{\frac{1}{\phi_l}} P^{\frac{\sigma-\varepsilon}{\phi_l}} P_l^{\frac{\phi_l-\sigma}{\phi_l}} D_{l.}^{-\frac{1}{\phi_l}}$$

with respect to D_{ij} yields

$$(10.A.14) \qquad \frac{\partial P_{l.}}{\partial D_{ij}} = \left[\frac{\phi_l-\sigma}{\phi_l} \frac{\sigma-\varepsilon}{\sigma} + \frac{\sigma-\varepsilon}{\phi_l}\right]\frac{P_{l.}}{P} \frac{\partial P}{\partial D} \frac{\partial D}{\partial D_i} \frac{\partial D_i}{\partial D_{ij}},$$

which leads to the following inverse cross-demand elasticity:

$$(10.A.15) \qquad \frac{\partial P_{l.}}{\partial D_{ij}} \frac{D_{ij}}{P_{l.}} = s_{ij}t_i\left[\frac{\varepsilon-\sigma}{\sigma\varepsilon}\right].$$

Now consider the profits π_{ij} of the firm that supplies brand j of chemical entity i. These profits are given by

$$(10.A.16) \qquad \pi_{ij} = D_{ij}(P_{ij}-c_{ij}) + \sum_k D_{ik}(P_{ik}-c_{ik}) + \sum_l D_{l.}(P_{l.}-c_{l.}).$$

Cournot behavior with respect to brand j of chemical entity i leads to the following first-order condition:

$$(10.A.17) \qquad P_{ij} + D_{ij}\frac{\partial P_{ij}}{\partial D_{ij}} + \sum_k D_{ik}\frac{\partial P_{ik}}{\partial D_{ij}} + \sum_l D_{l\cdot}\frac{\partial P_{l\cdot}}{\partial D_{ij}} = c_{ij}$$

Using the demand elasticities in equations 10.A.9, 10.A.12, and 10.A.15 and the fact that $\sum_z D_{iz}P_{iz} = D_i P_i$, equation 10.A.17 can be transformed into condition 10.8, as stated in the text. It is left to the reader to show that Bertrand behavior leads to the same first-order condition.

Notes

1. Starting in the late 1980s, the new research tools unleashed by the science of molecular genetics fundamentally altered the pharmaceutical R&D process and have provoked a large number of mergers and buyouts, thus changing the traditional picture of the industry.

2. In 1992–93, the production of drug formulations was valued at about US$2.13 billion, exports were about US$544 million, and imports were approximately US$482 million (OPPI 1994a).

3. These numbers are taken from Redwood (1994) and are based on data from the Operations Research Group—the same source of data underlying this chapter's investigation. As will be further explained later, the figures do not include the unaudited Indian small company sector and the Indian government sector, including hospital and military markets. This exclusion causes a downward bias in the market shares of local firms. Redwood (1994) conjectures that, in 1993, the true market share of Indian firms was probably 70 percent. It is also worth pointing out that in 1971, only two Indian-owned firms were among the top-10 companies in the Indian market (in terms of sales value), whereas in 1992, six Indian-owned firms ranked among the top-10 companies. See Lanjouw (1997) and Redwood (1994).

4. It is worth pointing out, however, that in Argentina, which introduced pharmaceutical product patents only in the 1990s, the market share of locally owned companies increased from 45 percent in 1975 to 58 percent in 1988 (Fundación de Investigaciones Económicas Latinoamericanas 1990).

5. Lanjouw (1997) reports that during 1975–95, only 65 of approximately 100,000 U.S. patents related to drug and health innovations were granted to Indian inventors.

6. One popular and often-cited comparison of drug prices is between India and Pakistan. Keayla (1994), for example, finds substantially higher prices in Pakistan (converted into Indian rupees using a market exchange rate) than in India and attributes this difference to the absence of patent protection for pharmaceutical products in India. The causality is unlikely to hold in this case, however, because Pakistan also did not accept product patents during the period of comparison (Watal 1998).

7. Nogués (1993) assumes a perfectly competitive pre-patent market structure. Maskus and Konan (1994) assume that in the absence of patents a dominant, foreign-owned firm competes with a domestic fringe industry. Subramanian (1995) uses an upper-bound scenario (perfect competition) and a lower-bound scenario (duopoly) as alternative pre-patent market structures.

8. In fact, an earlier version of this chapter tried to simulate the effect of patent protection using a model that also treated brands of the same chemical entity as perfect substitutes and assumed Cournot-Nash behavior. This approach was abandoned because this model could be brought into consistency with the data only if one assumed unrealistically low demand elasticities.

9. Note that the term *branded drug* differs in the Indian context from branded drugs in industrial country markets. In industrial countries, a branded drug often refers to the patented product first introduced in the market. *Generic drugs* typically refer to copies of products for which the patent has expired. This terminology is sometimes confusing, because generic drugs may have a brand name protected by a trademark. Because India does not protect product patents, there are only generic drugs on the market, but generic drug producers generally prefer to differentiate their products with brand names.

10. Lanjouw (1997) reports evidence that Indian patients exhibit a strong influence on the choice of drugs and that it is generally easy to obtain prescription-only drugs without prescriptions.

11. As will become clear when I model the supply side, it is convenient to introduce $m_i + 1$ brands to facilitate the distinction between the patent holder's brand (brand 0) and the brands of m_i Indian imitators.

12. For a derivation of these demand functions, see Armington (1969).

13. By definition, there is no patent holder for off-patent chemical entities. In this case, the market is served by Indian firms only. If a patent on a chemical entity has expired and the former patent-holding TNC is active in the Indian market, this TNC can, for the purpose of this model, be treated as an Indian firm.

14. Note that ownership patterns remain unchanged only as far as off-patent chemical entities are concerned. Indian firms lose, of course, ownership of brands of on-patent chemical entities in the simulated equilibrium.

15. I would like to thank Jayashree Watal for granting me access to the ORG data.

16. According to Redwood (1994), the top-500 pharmaceutical products represented 67.7 percent by value of the total pharmaceutical market audited by ORG. Brands based on the 24 on-patent chemical entities accounted for sales of Rs 3.28 billion, or 10.9 percent of the total sales value of the top 500 products in 1993.

17. In deciding which set of chemical entities constitutes a therapeutic group, I used the ORG classification.

18. The Indian government has made wide use of Drug Price Control Orders to keep prices for medicines low. Fixed price ceilings would lead to different market behavior by drug producers than that assumed here. Fink (2000), for example, demonstrates that price ceilings do not lead to a unique Nash equilibrium if the TNCs' and the imitators' goods are perfect substitutes and firms engage in Cournot competition.

19. In the case of quinolones, Japanese TNCs owned three of the four patents. Several analysts have pointed out that Japanese firms decided to drop the Indian market because of weak patent protection. See Redwood (1994).

20. The exact strategy behind supplying two brands of the same chemical entity remains a bit unclear. One possible explanation is that the two firms previously experienced mergers or acquisitions and preferred to keep existing brands in order to maintain customer loyalty.

21. In India, only a small minority of the population is covered by health insurance. In 1990, 78 percent of all Indian health care spending was paid for privately (World Bank 1993). With undeveloped private health insurance plans, this figure implies that about three-quarters of drug expenditures are paid directly by the patients (Redwood 1994). One would therefore expect demand for drugs in India to be much more sensitive to price changes compared with demand in industrial countries with comprehensive health insurance coverage.

22. Since preferences described by a CES function value variety, consumers actually suffer a utility loss through the unavailability of the patent holder's brand (see later discussion).

23. Note that this procedure does not change the importance of any two existing Indian brands relative to each other. The ratios of any two weight parameters w_{ij} and w_{iz} are independent of the inclusion of the patent holder's product in the preference structure.

24. For a derivation of the price index formula, see Armington (1969).

25. Theoretically, it is possible that the patent holder's monopoly profits are not sufficient to cover its fixed costs F_{io} of doing business in India.

26. Simulation results for the off-patent chemical entities as well as figures for changes in subutility levels and price indices are suppressed, as they would add little information.

27. To convert rupees into U.S. dollars the average 1992 exchange rate from the International Monetary Fund's International Financial Statistics database was used: Rs 25.918 per US$1.00.

28. Currently, only a very small portion of worldwide R&D is spent on diseases prevalent in developing countries, and most of it is conducted by publicly funded organizations or by the military in the industrial world (see Lanjouw 1997).

29. The figures are also much higher than estimated welfare losses in Watal (1998).

30. Editors' note: Since the conclusion of this study, Chaudhuri, Goldberg, and Jia (2003) have estimated price elasticities and supply-side parameters for the quinolones segment of the Indian pharmaceutical market.

References

Armington, Paul S. 1969. "A Theory of Demand for Products Distinguished by Place of Production." *IMF Staff Papers* 16:159–78.

Baldwin, Richard E., and Paul R. Krugman. 1988. "Market Access and International Competition: A Simulation Study of 16K Random Access Memories." In Robert Feenstra, ed., *Empirical Methods for International Trade.* Cambridge, Mass.: MIT Press.

Budavari, Susan, ed. 1989. *Merck Index.* Rahway, N.J.: Merck & Co.

Caves, Richard, E., Michael D. Whinston, and Mark A. Hurwitz. 1991. "Patent Expiration, Entry, and Competition in the U.S. Pharmaceutical Industry." In Martin N. Baily and Clifford Winston, eds., *Brookings Papers on Economic Activity: Micro Economics.* Washington, D.C.: Brookings Institution.

Chaudhuri, Shubham, Pinelopi K. Goldberg, and Panle Jia. 2003. "Estimating the Effects of Global Patent Protection in Pharmaceuticals: A Case Study of Quinolones in India." Yale University, New Haven, Conn. Processed.

Current Index of Medical Specialities. 1998 (January–March). Vol. 21, No. 1. Bangalore: Bio-Gard Private Limited.

Dixit, Avinash. 1988. "Optimal Trade and Industrial Policies for the U.S. Automobile Industry." In R. Feenstra, ed., *Empirical Methods for International Trade.* Cambridge, Mass.: MIT Press.

Drug Index. 1997 (October–December). New Delhi: Sarvesh Passi.

Dunning, John H. 1979. "Explaining Changing Patterns of International Production: In Defence of the Eclectic Theory." *Oxford Bulletin of Economics and Statistics* 41:269–95.

———. 1981. "Explaining the International Direct Investment Position of Countries: Towards a Dynamic or Developmental Approach." *Weltwirtschaftliches Archiv* 117:30–64.

Fink, Carsten. 2000. *Intellectual Property Rights, Market Structure, and Transnational Corporations in Developing Countries.* Berlin: Mensch und Buch Verlag.

Fundación de Investigaciones Económicas Latinoamericanas. 1990. *Protection of Intellectual Property Rights: The Case of the Pharmaceutical Industry in Argentina.* Buenos Aires.

Indian Pharmaceutical Guide. 1997. New Delhi: Pamposh Publications.

Keayla, B. K. 1994. "Patent Protection and the Pharmaceutical Industry." In K. R. G. Nair and Ashok Kumar, eds., *Intellectual Property Rights.* New Delhi: Allied Publishers.

Lanjouw, Jean O. 1997. "The Introduction of Pharmaceutical Product Patents in India: 'Heartless Exploitation of the Poor and Suffering'?" NBER Working Paper 6366. National Bureau of Economic Research, Cambridge, Mass.

Maskus, Keith E. 1998. "The Role of Intellectual Property Rights in Encouraging Foreign Direct Investment and Technology Transfer." *Duke Journal of Comparative and International Law* 109:109–61.

Maskus, Keith E., and Denise Eby Konan. 1994. "Trade-Related Intellectual Property Rights: Issues and Exploratory Results." In Alan V. Deardorff and Robert M. Stern, eds., *Analytical and Negotiating Issues in the Global Trading System.* Ann Arbor: University of Michigan Press.

Nogués, Julio J. 1993. "Social Costs and Benefits of Introducing Patent Protection for Pharmaceutical Drugs in Developing Countries." *Developing Economies* 31(1):24–53.

OPPI (Organization of Pharmaceutical Producers of India). 1994a. "Pharmaceutical Industry in India—Key Facts and Statistics." Bombay (Mumbai).

———. 1994b. "Trade-Related Intellectual Property Rights (TRIPS)—A Background Note." Bombay (Mumbai).

ORG (Operations Research Group). 1993. "Retail Market for Pharmaceutical Formulations in India—December 1992." Baroda, India.

Redwood, Heinz. 1994. *New Horizons in India: The Consequences of Pharmaceutical Patent Protection*. Felixstowe, U.K.: Oldwicks Press.

Subramanian, Arvind. 1995. "Putting Some Numbers on the TRIPS Pharamceutical Debate." *International Journal of Technology Management* 10(2–3):252–68.

Tarabusi, Claudio C. 1993. "Globalisation in the Pharamceutical Industry: Technological Change and Competition in a Triad Perspective." *STI Review* 13:123–61.

Watal, Jayashree. 1996. "Introducing Product Patents in the Indian Pharmaceutical Sector: Implications for Prices and Welfare." *World Competition: Law and Economics Review* 20(2):5–21.

———. 1998. " Product Patents, Pharmaceutical Prices, and Welfare Losses: The Indian Numbers Revisited." Photocopied.

World Bank. 1993. *World Development Report 1993: Investing in Health*. New York: Oxford University Press.

11

STRENGTHENING INTELLECTUAL PROPERTY RIGHTS IN LEBANON

Keith E. Maskus

I. Introduction

An issue of great concern to decisionmakers in many developing countries is the effect of strengthening the protection of intellectual property rights (IPRs). In this chapter, simple partial equilibrium models are used to analyze and discuss the likely economic effects of introducing stronger IPR protection in Lebanon. Such strengthening will be required by virtue of Lebanon's future accession to the World Trade Organization (WTO) and the consequent requirement that it adhere to the Agreement on Trade-Related Aspects of Intellectual Property Rights (TRIPS).[1]

The chapter is structured as follows. It begins with a brief description of the IPR system in Lebanon as of 1996. This discussion is followed by a summary of a survey of Lebanese manufacturing and service firms in key sectors that provided information on industrial structure and the use of IPRs, along with anticipated effects of a new intellectual property regime. I then discuss the economic effects that could emerge in a small economy such as Lebanon in response to strengthened IPRs. In the next section, illustrative calculations are undertaken of the possible static effects of stronger IPRs on key sectors. The final section concludes.

This chapter is adapted from a chapter published in B. Hoekman and J. Zarrouk, eds., *Catching Up with the Competition: Trade Opportunities and Challenges for Arab Countries*, Studies in International Economics (Ann Arbor: University of Michigan Press, 2000).

II. The Existing IPR System in Lebanon

Legislation in Lebanon covers patents, industrial designs, trademarks, copyrights, unfair competition, and penalties for infringement. The provisions of the law stem directly from related French intellectual property law developed in the 19th century. The law rests on two foundations. First, Lebanese IPR officials undertake no substantive examinations of applications for industrial property protection (patents, designs, trademarks) for novelty but rather inspect applications solely for their satisfaction of formal requirements. Opportunities are provided for private opposition to grants. Second, enforcement of IPRs is left largely to private actions, in which firms assemble evidence of infringement and use the police and courts to achieve its elimination or deterrence. Those principles are commonly followed in developing countries. Lebanon is unusual primarily in having an enforcement system that provides effective disciplinary action against infringement in some circumstances. As in many developing countries, in a variety of respects existing IPR protection is inconsistent with requirements under TRIPS. Although Lebanon is not a WTO member, these inconsistencies will have to be removed if the government decides to seek accession.

As an illustration, patents are awarded in Lebanon without substantive examination for novelty relative to prior art in the field; the applicant need fulfill only certain formalities in the application. Any interested party can file an opposition claim in the courts (not with the Intellectual Property Office), arguing that the invention is not sufficiently novel, that the claim is misleading, or that the technical specifications in the application are inadequate to reveal the nature of the invention to skilled practitioners. Patents are awarded for 15 years from the filing date. Patents are not awarded for pharmaceutical compositions (drug products), an exclusion that is standard in developing countries but would have to be removed under TRIPS. Approximately 10 to 15 percent of patent applications are denied by patent officials during initial review, largely because the technical specifications are inadequate. Patentees have exclusive rights to exploit their inventions through production, importation, and licensing, subject to revocation for not working the patent, which means failing to produce the good in Lebanon.

Industrial designs and models are protected upon filing, subject to a requirement of novelty and originality, again enforced through potential opposition claims in the courts. Protection implies the exclusive right to sell or otherwise work the design or model. The initial period of protection is 25 years, with an automatic renewal upon application of a further 25 years. This duration far exceeds standard international practice. An industrial design patent lapses if the applicant does not publicize the design or actively request maintenance of its protection within 5 years.

Trademarks are protected upon filing, subject to certain formalities and basic exclusions relating to government symbols and public morality. There is no protection for geographical indications and no explicit protection of well-known marks that are not registered in Lebanon. Filings are subject to opposition within 5 years in the courts if other firms have written proof of first use. Trademarks provide exclusive rights to market products using the names and marks and to prevent use of confusingly similar names and marks. Protection of registered marks lasts 15 years and is indefinitely renewable. Approximately 20 percent of trademark applications are denied on the basis of inadequate satisfaction of formalities or because of prior registry of marks.

The Lebanese copyright law protects all types of literary, artistic, and musical creation without explicit exclusions. Copyrights are provided for the life of the author plus 50 years and for 50 years in the case of corporate copyrights. Those periods are fully consistent with international norms under TRIPS. Copyrights provide exclusive rights to produce and sell copies of literary and artistic creation and are fully transferable by creators.

As in most developing economies, Lebanon's Intellectual Property Office is woefully understaffed, and the officials are not specifically trained in intellectual property issues. A small reorganization is contemplated currently, with a slight increase in staff and a split of the office into branches for industrial property and for literary and artistic property. This change will help the technical situation only marginally. The limited resources and expertise of the intellectual property officials will continue to act as a drag on the exploitation of IPRs in Lebanon for the foreseeable future.

III. The Relevance of IPRs for Industries

The simulation analysis that follows is based on a survey of 117 Lebanese manufacturing and service firms that have some potentially important relation to IPRs, using a questionnaire developed by the author and administered by a consulting firm in Beirut in July 1996. The industries are basic chemicals and metals; clothing and textiles; cosmetics; food products; furniture; leather products; films, publishing, and broadcasting; pharmaceuticals; plastics, paper, and glass; and software. Selected firms in each category provided information on sales, employment, trade patterns, and cost structures.

The use of IPRs in Lebanese business is limited. In several industries (basic metals, clothing, furniture, leather products, and plastics, paper, and glass), IPRs were seen as relatively unimportant in setting business strategies. Patents are infrequently applied for (and the number is falling, according to private intellectual property experts); they are typically requested for minor improvements in inventions; and the disclosure requirements provide little effective technology transfer. Firms rarely try to enforce their patents or designs against infringement, both because of the limited penalties available (suggesting a small deterrent effect) and because court procedures in patent cases can be quite lengthy and costly. Indeed, deficiencies in technical expertise relating to patents within the administrative and judicial systems is probably a strong factor contributing to the limited use of patents. In the absence of effective patent protection, Lebanon suffers from limited indigenous technological development and technology transfer.

Trademarks are more heavily registered and used than patents and designs. Several consumer goods firms have developed distinctive trademarks or work to protect their rights relative to foreign trademarks for which they have a licensing agreement and that they register in Lebanon. In part, this greater use of trademarks may be attributed to Lebanon's reasonably effective (according to trademark lawyers) private enforcement mechanism, which is backed up by powers of police seizure, customs measures at the border, and judicial relief. These procedures are already largely consistent with TRIPS standards. However, numerous industrialists complain about trademark piracy in nearby countries. Complaints also arise about the high cost of legal enforcement of trademarks in Lebanon and neighboring countries, a cost that is viewed as a disincentive to product development.

Counterfeiting should be of special concern to a country such as Lebanon, in which consumer products firms, service firms, and others bear great potential to build recognizable brand loyalty in the region and even in European markets. To date, such firms have had limited incentives to invest in such market building in the Middle East, which points to the need for pursuing effective trademark protection in the region as well.

Firms tend to focus their research and development (R&D) functions on local market research. The larger firms tend to believe that they will benefit from stronger IPRs as the smaller firms, which are more prone to undertake infringing activity, come under greater pressure to reduce trademark piracy. Enhanced trademark protection could well generate additional product and design development by these firms for sale in Lebanon and the region.

Lebanese pharmaceutical firms primarily produce drug formulations for sale under their own brand names. Pharmaceutical products are not currently patentable in most developing countries, so that active chemical ingredients, which might be patentable in some regions, are widely available. Generic substitutes are also commonly available. Thus, competition is based primarily on price and reputation, protected by trademarks. Several Lebanese brands are well known in the Middle East and Africa.

There is some licensed production in Lebanon of products on patent abroad, and these drugs have a market in Lebanon and neighboring countries owing to brand appeal. However, the core of the production market lies in wide access to competitive ingredients in the global marketplace. The core business of Lebanese drug firms (as in most developing countries) is product differentiation in drugs and cosmetics based on slight variations of chemical formulations. This is perfectly legal. However, the extension of patents to drug products in Lebanon, if they were registered by foreign firms and their local agents, would remove access to generic copies of patented ingredients and could markedly raise input costs. Process patents would also become harder to invent around if Lebanon accepts the international standard of reversal of the burden of proof in such cases. Many Lebanese drug firms would need to pursue technology-licensing agreements with the major international pharmaceutical firms in order to convince those firms to place production facilities in the country. It is unlikely that Lebanese drug firms, on their own, could afford to engage in the massive R&D programs required to develop patentable active ingredients in order to support their own products.

The cosmetics and food products industries are sensitive to patents and trademarks. Both rely to some extent on inputs that could be patented under the new law and are, therefore, vulnerable to associated increases in cost or reductions in availability. At the same time, both sectors have a noteworthy history of product and brand-name development, with the larger food products makers owning recognizable names in Lebanon and regional markets. Both groups currently suffer from significant trademark infringement and will benefit from stronger enforcement of their rights.

In the entertainment and media sectors (films, music, publishing, and broadcasting), copyright protection is a key component of incentives for creation. Despite limited copyright enforcement, Lebanon has established a clear competitive advantage within the Middle East as a producer and distributor of literary and creative works, including films, television, advertising, music, and books and periodicals. The ultimate source of this advantage is the relatively large pool of creative talent in Lebanon.

Unauthorized copying of videotapes and music recordings is common, and book publishers complain that their texts are frequently copied and sold, both in Lebanon and in neighboring nations. The firms interviewed already pay full charges to foreign copyright owners for their sales rights and do not anticipate a rise in these fees with stronger Lebanese copyrights. Rather, they expect sharply rising sales and prices as local copiers are closed down. Interestingly, even though Lebanese film and television program producers do not claim to suffer pirated copying of their products, they intend to produce more films for regional distribution in the event of stronger copyrights.

The software industry is heavily dependent on copyright protection. Unauthorized copying is widespread in Lebanon, with as much as 95 percent of the programs in use being obtained this way. Such copying is largely confined to well-known international programs, such as Windows, AutoCAD, Lotus, Excel, and FoxPro. The Lebanese industry is characterized by considerable inventiveness and fluidity on the part of local programmers, who develop applications programs for particular uses, such as banking, finance, and transportation. They also perform custom installation of software systems, service, and networking. Several firms are affiliated with foreign software companies and either pay license fees or buy platform software at full price, including charges for use rights. Other firms routinely load pirated software into the hardware packages they sell. If Lebanon strongly enforced copyrights, hundreds of small software-copying houses would close down, as software firms would be unable to incorporate unlicensed copies into systems installations. Software would be more expensive in Lebanon, though of higher quality. Applications designers would likely benefit from the changes owing to business expansion and improvement in Lebanon's reputation for software development.

IV. The Economics of IPRs in a Small Developing Economy

For the purposes of discussion, the effects of strengthening intellectual property protection in a small developing economy can be categorized as (1) short-run (static) effects through pricing, output, and trade for a given market structure and (2) long-run (dynamic) effects through foreign direct investment (FDI), technology transfers, and innovation within and for the Lebanese market.

Short-Run (Static) Economic Effects

Lebanon is largely a net importer of technological information and innovative products and services. At present, there is relatively little basis for technology and product development. One anticipated outcome of stronger protection would be a rise in royalty payments to foreign rights holders. Firms (including domestic exclusive agents) that are in an exclusive position to sell their goods that are protected by IPRs might be expected to raise the prices charged to consumers and industrial users. Particularly sensitive goods such as pharmaceuticals, software, and agricultural chemicals raise the greatest fears in terms of price increases. However, if stronger IPRs expand the use of, and access to, leading foreign technologies, the result could be a reduction in production costs and transaction costs on the input side. Also, IPRs do not necessarily create strong monopoly positions that generate high prices and limited access. Rather, like a right to tangible property, they define the conditions under which a rights owner competes with potential rivals. A rights holder is rarely placed in a strong monopoly position by a patent, trademark, or copyright. Rather, there is typically competition from other products and technologies.

The likelihood and extent of such monopolization depends on how competitive markets are otherwise. To some degree, this measure is a function of the scope of the protected claim (subject matter in patents, reverse-engineering possibilities in software, fair use in textbooks, and so on). For example, a patent grant carries a disclosure requirement in which the technical aspects of patented materials are made available for inspection, allowing others to use the information to develop follow-on inventions. The narrower the claim, the easier it is to invent around a patent. Thus, IPRs may help spur dynamic competition even if, at times, they may limit competition among existing products and technologies. This incremental nature of innovation is a crucial characteristic of most technical progress, especially in developing economies.

Stronger IPRs will, other things being equal, encourage rights owners to engage in additional price discrimination across markets, with prices dependent on demand elasticities. The more inelastic demand is in a particular country, the higher will be the price, though again the precise effect depends on the scope of the property right, including enforcement, and alternative regulatory mechanisms. Thus, it is important to understand the basic determinants of demand elasticity.

One determinant is the extent of product and technology differentiation available. Countries that have stronger incentives for such differentiation may experience lower markups on IPR-protected goods. Product differentiation is most in evidence in wealthy countries and in middle-income economies that have growing consumption possibilities and expanding technical sophistication in production. Countries that erect limits on domestic competition tend to experience stronger price effects of IPRs.

A second determinant is the degree of market segmentation across countries, because segmented markets are key for supporting differential pricing strategies. Stronger IPRs themselves are means of expanding such segmentation, particularly if patents, trademarks, and copyrights are protected in conjunction with rigorous controls on parallel imports. A similar conclusion holds for trade barriers and investment restrictions. Thus, the potential effect of stronger IPRs on a small developing economy, such as Lebanon, depends greatly on the country's approach to international competition, including its treatment of parallel imports and exhaustion in the definition of exclusive rights.

A third determinant of demand elasticity is the set of regulations on prices or quantities in key areas, such as drugs. Such regulations need to be firmly grounded in economic and social objectives and designed to minimize interference with effective competition.

Finally, and quite importantly, demand elasticity for each firm's product depends critically on the structure of market competition, even if products are not much differentiated. Market structure is a function of market size (the number of firms a market can support); regulations covering entry and exit (for example, exclusive agent contracts or trade restrictions and limits on establishment rights); the number of potential external supply sources (exporting nations); and the scope of intellectual property protection, among many other things.

Thus, for understanding the static price effects of stronger IPRs, it is convenient to think of domestic and foreign firms as contesting the local market before and after the change in policy (see, for example, Maskus 1990, Maskus and Konan 1994, Subramanian 1991). Such a framework illustrates the crucial importance of information on the prevailing market structure and changes therein. If it is believed that the effect of introducing pharmaceutical product patents is to convert a perfectly competitive market into a monopolized market, the resulting price increase could be very high (Maskus and Eby Konan 1994). Much more likely, however, is a situation in which domestic firms produce and sell both pirated drugs and legitimate competing drugs (generics or similar products). In this case, the effect will be limited, especially if it is recognized that the aggregate price impact of drug patents will be attenuated by foreign competition.

In assessing such effects, it must be remembered that Lebanon is a small, open economy and prices are, therefore, intimately linked to prices established in international markets. In most cases, one would not expect the introduction of stronger IPRs in Lebanon perceptibly to alter the pricing strategy of foreign firms in Lebanon, because the market is so small. However, this conclusion needs qualification to the extent that such firms might view Lebanon as an entree into the larger Middle East market. Moreover, if Lebanon were to adopt a policy banning parallel imports of IPR-protected goods, the resulting segmentation of its market from world markets could support higher prices.

It is likely that the more tangible effect of strengthened IPRs will be to reduce competition from infringement of patented and trademarked goods and from unauthorized copying of copyrighted goods. In this context, domestic prices may be expected to rise for key products, services, and technologies, though the degree of such price increases will depend on the remaining extent of legitimate competition. There could be an important welfare gain from higher product quality for consumers and industrial users as protected goods supplant infringing goods, and this gain could have an important dimension of dynamic spillover in terms of feeding better technologies into Lebanese production.

On the supply side, one of the initial effects from enforcing stronger IPRs is a reduction in the output and employment of firms that had been producing counterfeit copyrighted and trademarked products or using patented inputs. Whether this reduction promises net economic costs or benefits depends on the particular circumstances. Direct losses in employment, wages, and output themselves depend on market structure, including the extent of copying. However, as indicated above, such output could be replaced by higher-quality goods and technologies, albeit at (perhaps) higher prices. Furthermore, the resources displaced should find their way into other forms of economic activity. Many of the sectors that would be negatively affected by stronger IPRs (software copying; book, music, and video copying; clothing and perfume knockoffs; and the like) are highly fluid in terms of resource use and have low barriers to entry and exit. Moreover, with stronger copyrights and trademarks, foreign rights holders could choose to license such production to new or existing domestic firms. There is evidence from some nations that have reformed their IPR policies that counterfeiting firms can readily shift to legitimate production under the new regime. It is even conceivable that net effects on wages and employment could be positive, with a lag, though again much depends on where the output is to be sold and the relevant demand characteristics. If labor must be transferred out of such activities, the country's ability to do so is a positive function of its growth rate, its skill basis, and the depth of the economy's industrial structure.

Long-Run (Dynamic) Economic Effects

Dynamic effects of stronger IPRs include effects on FDI and technology transfers. Firms become multinational enterprises because FDI helps them exploit some combination of ownership, location, or internalization advantages (Dunning 1980; Markusen 1995). Ownership advantages refer to some characteristic of products or technologies that are proprietary to the firm and provide a marketing or cost advantage. Obvious examples include new products, processes, computer programs, and trade names. Thus, a direct role for IPRs, especially patents and trademarks, arises in raising the returns to such advantages through FDI. IPRs can also be relevant in protecting internalization advantages, which pertain to the ability of firms to save on transaction, contracting, and monitoring costs by undertaking certain activities within the firm. For example, if firms license their technology or product to an unrelated foreign firm, it may be hard to prevent that firm from revealing the technology or diminishing the product quality (thereby damaging the original owner's reputation). To the extent that stronger IPRs in a country improve confidentiality, contract maintenance, and monitoring capabilities, one would anticipate additional inward technology flows. FDI could fall, however, since arm's-length contracting costs would also fall. It seems likely that the balance of the positive ownership effects and the negative internalization effects would be a net increase in incentives to invest as IPRs are strengthened.

The empirical evidence favors the notion that stronger IPRs attract investment (Mansfield 1994). In a simultaneous econometric framework in which U.S. firms can choose four ways to exploit their proprietary goods or technologies (exporting them, taking out patents, selling from subsidiaries, and making a new FDI), Maskus (1998) found that the strength of patent laws in developing countries has a strongly positive effect on both local sales and FDI: other things being equal, nations that have stronger IPRs attract more investment interest from U.S. multinationals.

V. Estimates of Static Output and Employment Effects of Stronger IPRs

For several reasons, is impossible to provide accurate predictions about the expected effects of stronger IPRs on sales, employment, prices, and trade in domestic industries. The ultimate effects depend critically on changes in the market structure that will emerge after the policy change, including various elasticities of demand and supply, competition among firms, trade flows and the number of foreign trading partners, and FDI. Changes in many of these variables are difficult to predict. Attempts to quantify some of the potential effects of stronger IPRs can, therefore, be only illustrative and should be interpreted with great caution. Nonetheless, it is useful to undertake simulations such as those presented here because they help to identify the likely gainers and losers from reform.

It is useful to organize industries into groups that rely on different forms of IPRs: copyrights, patents, and trademarks. Copyright industries include software and publishing and entertainment. Industries that rely on patents and trademarks include chemicals and pharmaceuticals, cosmetics, and food products. In what follows, the results of numerical simulations made using partial equilibrium models of the pharmaceuticals, software, and publishing and entertainment industries are reported. The models are linked across segments of each sector, including a domestic set of small manufacturing firms, large manufacturing firms, import distribution firms, and importing firms that infringe IPRs, as appropriate.

The framework of the partial equilibrium models used is laid out in appendix 11.A, which includes key equations. Important parameters include demand and supply elasticities; substitution elasticities in demand among market segments, which produce differentiated goods; the share of input costs spent on goods subject to royalty charges for the use of IPRs; markups over the marginal cost of importer-distributors; the extent of piracy; and market shares of producing segments. The models are capable of estimating relative changes in prices, quantities, revenues, value added, and employment, subject to data or assumptions about key parameters. They are static models only, however, and do not account for endogenous dynamic effects of IPRs.

Patent and Trademark Sectors: Pharmaceuticals

One of the industries most affected by IPRs is pharmaceuticals. There are three types of pharmaceutical firms in Lebanon. First, there are approximately eight medium-size to large manufacturing firms, producing mainly generic drugs, suppositories, and unpatented treatments. Average sales in these firms are about US$1 million, and average employment is 55 workers. According to the *Report on Industrial Census* (Lebanese Republic 1995), the ratio of value added to output in chemicals is 0.47, which I take as the initial ratio for the simulations. The same source provides data on the employment and salaries of full-time and part-time workers. Combining these figures with the employment reports in our survey reveals an average wage in these firms of some US$4,100. This figure compares with the implicit ratio of value added to labor of US$8,545. Some 10 percent of revenues are spent on patented intermediate inputs, such as active ingredients for particular formulations, while another 5 percent might be spent on implicit trademark charges. These figures are summarized in the first panel of table 11.1.

Survey respondents also indicate that there are three sizable import distributor firms in pharmaceuticals; for one of these firms, drugs are one of many distributor lines. Average sales revenues for these three firms are US$16 million from their pharmaceuticals operations, with employment of 200 per firm. The average wage of US$3,700 is lower because of these firms' higher use of part-time workers. Using the value added ratio for manufacturers would be inappropriate here because value added basically consists of the markup over import costs, used to pay for local distribution costs. If we assume a 50 percent markup (mentioned as reasonable in the survey), the revenue figure is calibrated to be consistent with distributors having 75 percent of the market initially, which also accords with interview responses. This procedure generates per firm revenues of US$16 million and per firm value added of US$5.3 million. Value added per worker then becomes US$26,500, reflecting the large markup in distribution. I assume that IPR cost shares are double those of the large manufacturers, because distributors deal directly with foreign firms that own intellectual property.

Some 30 small manufacturing firms also exist, with average revenues of perhaps US$50,000 and employment of 5 workers. I apply the 0.47 ratio to generate value added per firm and then value added per worker of US$4,700, in comparison with an average wage of US$3,800. I assume these manufacturers have the same IPR cost shares as the larger ones but that a small share (10 percent) of revenues in the small fringe firms is garnered by falsifying trademarks.

TABLE 11.1 Static Effects of Stronger Patent and Trademark Protection on Pharmaceuticals Firms

	Small	Large	Distributors	Infringing Imports	Net
	(1)	(2)	(3)	(4)	
1. Basic data (segment number)					
Number of firms	30	8	3	200	
Average revenue (US$)	50,000	1,000,000	16,000,000	32,000	
Average value added (US$)	23,500	470,000	5,300,000	15,000	
Average employment	5	55	200	4	
Value added/employment (US$)	4,700	8,545	26,500	3,750	
Average wage (US$)	3,800	4,100	3,700	2,800	
Total revenue (US$)	1,500,000	8,000,000	48,000,000	6,400,000	
Trademark piracy (US$)	150,000	—	—	5,440,000	
Patent piracy (US$)	—	—	—	960,000	
Total value added (US$)	705,000	3,760,000	16,000,000	3,008,000	
Cost share, patents (percent)	0.1	0.1	0.2	0	
Cost share, trademarks (percent)	0.05	0.05	0.1	0	
2. Patent cost effects (50 percent of rise in patent charges and removal of infringing imports) Parameters: $e_{D1} = e_{D2} = e_{D3} = e_{D4} = -3.0$; $e_{S1} = e_{S2} = 2.0$					
Number of firms	26	7	2	192	
Average revenue (US$)	55,452	1,099,000	20,000,000	30,000	
Average value added (US$)	23,772	470,901	5,600,000	14,983	
Average employment	5.1	55.1	211.3	4.0	
Total revenue (US$)	1,442,000	7,689,000	40,000,000	5,760,000	
Trademark piracy	144,175	—	—	5,760,000	
Patent piracy (US$)	—	—	—	0	
Total value added (US$)	618,058	3,296,000	11,200,000	2,877,000	
Cost share, patents (percent)	0.15	0.15	0.3	0	

Changes

Number of firms	–4	–1	–1	–8
Employment	–18	–54	–177	–33
Total revenue	–58,253	–310,680	–8,000,000	–640,000
Total value added	–86,942	–463,689	–4,800,000	–131,200
Price (percent)	+1.9	+1.9	+8.3	+5.0

3. Trademark cost effects (50 percent reduction in piracy; 20 percent rise in trademark charges)

Parameters: $e_{D1} = e_{D2} = e_{D3} = e_{D4} = -3.0$; $e_{S1} = e_{S2} = 2.0$

Number of firms	25	7	2	160
Average revenue (US$)	55,289	1,090,000	19,273,000	24,000
Average value added (US$)	23,805	458,667	5,258,000	14,990
Average employment	5.1	53.7	198.4	4.0
Total revenue (US$)	1,382,000	7,628,000	38,545,000	3,840,000
Trademark piracy (US$)	138,200	—	—	3,840,000
Total value added (US$)	595,127	3,211,000	10,516,000	2,398,000
Cost share, trademarks (percent)	0.06	0.06	0.12	0.0

Changes

Number of firms	–1	0	0	–32
Employment	–5	–10	–26	–128
Total revenue (US$)	–59,523	–61,148	–1,455,000	–1,920,000
Total value added (US$)	–22,931	–85,639	–683,636	–478,401
Price (percent)	+2.1	+0.4	+1.8	+16.7

TABLE 11.1 Static Effects of Stronger Patent and Trademark Protection on Pharmaceuticals Firms (Continued)

	Small	Large	Distributor	Infringing Imports	Net
4. Demand substitution effects					
Parameters: $e_D = -0.5$; $e_{D1} = e_{D2} = e_{D3} = e_{D4} = -3.0$; $e_{S1} = e_{S2} = 2.0$; $e_{S4} = 3.0$; $e_{C1} = e_{C2} = 2.0$; $e_{C3} = 1.0$; $e_{C4} = 2.45$					
Number of firms	27	7	2	125	
Average revenue (US$)	54,726	1,183,000	19,279,000	24,025	
Average value added (US$)	23,563	498,123	5,260,000	15,006	
Average employment	5.0	58.3	198.5	4.0	
Total revenue (US$)	1,478,000	8,284,000	38,557,000	3,003,000	
Trademark piracy (US$)	147,800	—	—	3,003,000	
Total value added (US$)	636,193	3,487,000	10,520,000	1,876,000	
Changes					
Number of firms	+2	0	0	−35	
Employment	+9	+32	0	−139	
Total revenue (US$)	+95,378	+656,189	+11,954	−836,859	
Total value added (US$)	+41,066	+276,188	+3,261	−522,688	
Price (percent)	+2.3	+2.9	0	−5.4	
5. Joint changes of all policies and responses					
Number of firms	−3	−1	−1	−75	−80
Employment	−15	−32	−203	−300	−550
Total revenue (US$)	−22,397	+284,362	−9,443,000	−3,400,000	−12,600,000
Total value added (US$)	−68,807	−273,141	−5,480,000	−1,130,000	−6,960,000
Price (percent)	+6.3	+5.2	+10.2	+16.2	+10.0

— = not calculated.

Source: Author's calculations.

There are frequent complaints about the prevalence of pirated drugs imported from neighboring nations. Speculative evidence on the extent of this activity suggests it is about 10 percent of the market. Imports are calibrated at this level, assuming that all of them violate trademarks. An assumption of 200 such small firms, with 4 workers on average and a similar ratio of value added to sales, generates the remaining data. I also assume that these firms make no attempt to pay for authorized trademarks and patents; thus, IPR cost shares are zero.

The static effects of stronger patents and trademarks are calculated using the model in appendix 11.A. To determine changes in employment and the number of firms (I assume free entry and exit, which may be inappropriate in the distribution sector), I maintain a fixed ratio of value added per firm and of value added per worker, as given in the top panel of the table. Import distributors are assumed to maintain a fixed 50 percent markup throughout the policy changes, which implies a demand elasticity for their goods of –3.0. Next, stronger patents are captured by assuming a 50 percent rise in explicit and implicit charges for their use on the existing volume of patented inputs, in addition to a reduction in infringing imports as discussed later. Finally, stronger trademarks are captured by assuming both that the volume of trademark piracy is reduced by 50 percent and that there is a 20 percent rise in charges for legitimate trademark use.

Because foreign and domestic firms would take some advantage of a stronger patent law, they would be expected both to register more patents and to charge higher fees for the use of patented chemicals that are inputs into pharmaceuticals production. Recent experiences in Brazil and Italy suggest that as much as a doubling of prices of key patented ingredients could occur. Because Lebanon is a small and competitive market, it seems unlikely that such strong increases could emerge; thus, I simulate the effects of a 50 percent rise in fees for patent use and prices of patented chemicals. Also, some unknown percentage of imported pharmaceuticals from countries that lack stronger patent regimes will be judged illegal in the future as Lebanon enforces the patent law. I capture this possibility by assuming that 15 percent of current pharmaceutical imports from infringing firms would violate potential patents and are, therefore, removed from commerce. I also assume that domestic firms do not produce such infringing goods in appreciable quantities. The changes envisioned here would emerge only after a phase-in period of Lebanon's choosing, such as 10 years under terms of TRIPS.

The second panel of table 11.1 provides the results of the simulations, which depend on assumed elasticities. First, enforcement against import infringement is assumed to eliminate patent violations. The removal of the infringing 15 percent of imports raises prices in that segment by 5.0 percent, given the demand elasticity of –3.0, and reduces revenues by US$640,000. Value added falls by US$131,200, causing eight firms to leave the sector and employment to fall by 33 workers.

Both the small manufacturers and the large manufacturers are directly affected by the higher patent fees, raising their patent cost shares from 0.1 to 0.15. This cost increase translates into a price rise of 1.9 percent, which is calculated from the original cost shares and the elasticities of demand and supply. That is, the 50 percent rise in patent fees generates a 5 percent rise in costs, given the patent cost share, of which 1.9 percent is passed on in higher prices. It may be that this "pass-through elasticity" is unreasonably low, though it could also be argued that Lebanon's product prices are largely fixed through both import competition effects and government regulation. In any case, this result points out that even large increases in patent charges on the Lebanese market need not translate into significant price hikes. Because demand is assumed to be elastic in each segment, revenues fall for both groups of firms. Furthermore, value added is squeezed on the cost side by more than the price increases, causing value added to fall by about US$87,000 across the small firms and about US$464,000 across the large firms. This effect results in four small firms and one large firm leaving production, with joint employment falling by 72 workers.

I assume that the importer-distributors maintain a markup of 50 percent over import costs, which is equivalent to assuming a fixed demand elasticity of −3.0. I also assume that these distributors are capable of purchasing as much pharmaceuticals as they wish at the prices set by foreign patent-owning firms. Suppose that initially such firms charge a 20 percent patent markup and that stronger Lebanese patents induce a 50 percent increase in this markup, to 30 percent. Then the implicit rise in import price to distributors is 8.3 percent $[(1.3/1.2) − 1 = 0.083]$. Distributors pass this increase directly on to users, which induces a reduction in quantity demanded of 25 percent along a fixed demand curve. Under these circumstances, distributors experience a decline in revenues of US$8 million and in value added of US$4.8 million. In response, one such firm leaves the market and employment falls by 177 workers. Of course, these results may be too strong. If, for example, distributors had a fixed markup of 100 percent (assuming a demand elasticity of −2.0), then employment would fall by only 128 workers. Similarly, the effects would be weaker if the underlying cost share accorded to patents or the increase in patent charges were lower.

Overall, stronger patents and their enforcement are simulated to reduce static employment over the phase-in period by 282 workers, or 14 percent of the initial employment industrywide. Revenue and value added decline sharply in the import-distribution sector.

I attempt to capture the effects of a stronger and better-enforced trademark law by assuming that it generates both a 50 percent reduction in trademark piracy and a 20 percent increase in trademark licenses and embodied prices. The former change is consistent with recent experiences in other developing countries that are attempting to clean up trademark counterfeiting. It is possible to remove a significant portion of counterfeiting but nearly impossible to eliminate it entirely. The assumption that the trademark-induced price increase of 20 percent is lower than its counterpart for patents comes both from the fact that pharmaceutical firms in Lebanon largely operate under their own trademarks and would face little increase in such costs from abroad and from the fact that trademarks tend to embody lower license fees and implicit prices than patents.

Stronger trademarks hit the infringing import sector hardest. By assumption, all its revenue after the patent change stems from piracy. The cut of 50 percent (by volume) enforced by the Lebanese customs authorities generates a price increase of 16.7 percent on remaining pirated goods, given the demand elasticity of –3.0. Accordingly, revenues fall by a third, while value added falls somewhat less because the loss in import volume is offset by the price gain. The number of firms is simulated to fall by 32, with an employment loss of 128 workers.

In this case, there is a difference between small and large manufacturers, because the former are assumed to include some trademark infringers in Lebanon. In particular, assume that 10 percent of revenues of small firms derive from counterfeiting pharmaceutical trademarks, which may well be an underestimate. Such piracy is assumed also to be cut by 50 percent in volume, generating a 1.67 percent price hike. However, this industry segment also pays trademark fees, which are assumed to rise from 5 percent of costs to 6 percent (a 20 percent increase). This cost increase generates an additional, partially passed-through price increase, so that the full price increase is 2.1 percent. One more small firm closes down, causing an additional loss of five jobs, although net effects on revenues and value added are small in relation to industry size. In contrast, large manufacturing firms are assumed not to be engaged in trademark piracy. They are affected only by the relatively minor cost increase from stronger trademarks. Although no additional firms shut down, another 10 workers are laid off because of marginally lower value added in the segment.

Distributors find their trademark cost shares rising from 0.1 to 0.12. The implicit price increase from foreign trademark owners is 1.8 percent, which distributors pass on fully at a fixed markup. Revenues again fall because of elastic demand, generating a follow-on loss in value added of about US$684,000 and in employment of 26 jobs. Overall, trademark cost effects would reduce employment by 169 jobs beyond the patent cost effects, or 8.5 percent of industry employment. In this case, however, job losses are concentrated among the counterfeiting import firms.

Finally, it must be recognized that, because the products marketed by various market segments are imperfect substitutes, as prices change there will be demand shifts among the industry groups. Appendix 11.A provides a methodology for sorting those shifts out relative to aggregate price and quantity indexes. In brief, segments in which price increases are higher (lower) than the industry's weighted-average price hike will find demand for their products declining (expanding). Weights are given by segment shares in initial industry revenues. In the fourth panel of table 11.1, I maintain the same own-demand and supply elasticities (adding a high supply elasticity for segment four, given its role as a residual importer) but incorporate values for cross-elasticities of demand. I assume that the cross-elasticities are fairly high (2.0) for the manufacturing groups but lower for the import distributors, which reflects the idea that consumers may have fairly low substitution between recognized imported drugs and locally produced substitutes. The cross-elasticity for the infringing import sector is calibrated to balance the market with the change in the aggregate quantity index. Thus, I assume separability in demand between pharmaceuticals and other goods, which may be too strong an assumption but prevents the need for a general equilibrium specification of demand. This calibration results in a cross-elasticity of 2.45.

With these parameters, the model simulates that demand will rise noticeably in the two manufacturing groups but not appreciably in the distribution sector.[2] As a result, price rises by 2.3 percent and 2.9 percent in the manufacturing groups, with the large firms enjoying a revenue gain of perhaps US$656,000 and a gain in employment of 32 workers. However, demand shifts sharply away from the infringing import segment, which is a point worth noting explicitly. In particular, as an economy clamps down on counterfeit activity, the price of remaining pirated goods tends to rise, causing demand to be diverted into other sources of supply, a phenomenon that has been noted in other developing countries. This fall in demand reduces prices by 5.4 percent and value added by nearly US$523,000, with a fall in employment of another 139 workers.

The fifth panel of the table calculates the joint effects of these changes, although no allowance is made for interaction effects among them. Overall, in static terms the economy is simulated to lose 80 firms, most of them in the infringing import sector. Employment is simulated to fall by 550 workers, or 27.6 percent of initial industry employment.[3] These job losses are concentrated in import distribution and in the pirating import firms. Overall revenues are predicted to decline by about US$12.6 million, and it is interesting to note that the large manufacturing firms actually register a revenue expansion, though a decline in value added. The weighted-average price increase is 10.0 percent.[4] Again, these static effects would be experienced over a period of years as the new industrial property law was implemented and enforced or as Lebanon joined TRIPS.

Caveats

These calculations rely exclusively on comparative static partial equilibrium models of the pharmaceuticals sector. Readers should not infer any welfare implications from these results, because they cannot be used to compute changes in consumer well-being or social utility. Rather, they are presented solely as illustrative calculations of important potential market responses to changes in IPR regulations. In that sense, they provide a useful characterization of prospective price and output effects within the pharmaceutical sector alone. Policymakers may wish to consider such effects in assessing wider regulatory positions. For example, although a 10 percent price increase for drugs over some transition period may not seem significant, the possibility of higher prices for medicines should alert the Ministry of Health to budgetary costs and issues of consumer access to treatments. The ministry already has an extensive system of price controls in place for pharmaceutical formulations, covering both imports and domestic production and sales. Such regulation is acceptable under the terms of TRIPS, as long as it does not unduly prejudice the interests of patent holders through compulsory licensing and punitive price limits. Like other countries, Lebanon will need to establish a balance between ensuring access at reasonable prices and discouraging imports and production through excessive regulation.

Because Lebanon is a net importer of pharmaceutical products and technologies and because it has relatively little inventive capability in the sector currently, static effects of stronger patents are likely to be negative, as the calculations indicate. There is no evidence available to support calculations of dynamic effects, and I do not attempt to make such calculations. However, there are some important dynamic effects that could emerge over time and that are worth mentioning here. First, demand for pharmaceuticals is income elastic, meaning that as the Lebanese economy grows, there should be rising relative demands in the sector. Whether this demand is concentrated on imports or on domestic production depends importantly on competitive actions taken over the near term by Lebanese pharmaceutical firms. Second, although it is quite unlikely that any Lebanese drug firm would undertake the massive amounts of R&D required to develop new and patentable medicines and ingredients, stronger trademark protection should provide additional incentives for brand-name development, marketing, and product differentiation of legitimate medical formulations. Third, as Lebanon cleans up trademark counterfeiting and recognizes patentable formulations, it will become a relatively more attractive location for foreign firms to invest in local production and even minor R&D facilities, as opposed to distribution facilities alone. The Lebanese pharmaceutical industry is currently characterized by a remarkable absence of technology-sharing agreements and FDI in comparison with the country's income levels. Lebanese pharmaceutical firms will find it increasingly important to link with major international firms in order to ensure access to technologies and production rights as patent coverage is tightened. Successful links of this sort should imply growing demand for Lebanese production that could easily outweigh the negative static effects on output and employment noted above. However, this process is likely more dependent on political stability and regional marketing prospects than on the provision of stronger patents.

Copyright Sectors: Software

A somewhat different modeling approach is adopted in the computer sector to account for the effects of important joint products: computer programs (software) and computers themselves (hardware). According to respondents to the survey, there are 70 to 100 "recognized" software development firms, 7 of which are also manufacturers, and another 400 or so small firms. I take the latter group to be the fringe firms, which sell pirated software in two forms: direct copies and copies embodied in hardware purchases. The minimum sales reported in the survey for a recognized firm were US$70,000. I assume that average sales of the fringe firms are US$50,000. Employment in the former group averages about 10 workers per firm, although there is a wide range, while employment in the latter group might average 5 workers per firm. Assuming that 3 of these workers are full time, earning an annual salary of US$4,000, and 2 are part time, earning an annual salary of US$1,000, salary costs per fringe firm amount to US$14,000. Of the recognized firms, two are also distributors of software imports under license to companies such as Microsoft, Sun, and Novell. These firms are larger, averaging 50 employees.

The fringe firms sell two products: personal computers (PCs) and pirated software off the shelf. PCs are sold with the pirated software loaded. Distributors sell legitimate copies of software programs, whereas applications firms sell both their own programs and PCs with the licensed software loaded. Approximately 15,000 PCs per year are sold in Lebanon, with average prices of perhaps US$1,500 (fringe) or US$2,000 (legitimate). Moreover, it is estimated that 95 percent of software sold by volume in Lebanon is pirated. Putting these data together, I construct the basic data in panel 1 of table 11.2. Calibrating sales volumes to reported average revenues per firm and to firm sizes yields the figures indicated.

A simpler model is used for software copyrights than is used for patents. The software industry is better captured by three segments (infringers, distributors, and developers) than by the four-segment breakdown. Moreover, in buying foreign software platforms and legitimate copies, Lebanese developers and distributors already are paying prices that embody international protection of copyrights. It is unlikely that stronger copyrights in Lebanon would induce higher costs for those inputs, so I ignore the possibilities of higher copyright charges. Thus, the effect of stronger copyrights would raise only the costs of avoiding detection on the part of infringing firms, causing a reduction in the supply of pirated program copies and a hike in their price. Accordingly, rather than calibrate demand substitution effects to an

TABLE 11.2   Simulated Effects of Stronger Copyrights on Software

	Fringe	Distributors	Developers	Net
1. Basic data (Segment number)	(1)	(2)	(3)	
Number of firms	400	2	90	
Average revenue (US$)	50,000	850,000	295,000	
Average employment	5	50	10	
Revenue/ employment (US$)	10,000	17,000	29,500	
Average wage (US$)	2,800	3,800	3,500	
Total PCs sold	8,000	0	7,000	
PC price (US$)	1,500	—	2,000	
Total software sold (units)	408,000	2,500	19,500	
With PCs	8,000	—	7,000	
Pirated shelf	400,000	0	0	
Price (US$)	20	—	—	
Legitimate shelf	0	2,500	12,550	
Price (US$)	—	680	1,000	
Revenues (US$)	20,000,000	1,700,000	26,500,000	
2. Copyright enforcement effects (50 percent reduction in piracy) **Parameters: $e_{D1}^{PC} = -2.0$; $e_{D1}^{SW} -1.5$**				
Number of firms	257	2	90	
Average revenue (US$)	49,935	850,000	295,000	
Average employment	5.0	50	10	
Total PCs sold	4,000	0	7,000	
PC Price (US$)	1,875	—	2,000	
Total software sold (units)	204,000	2,500	19,500	
With PCs	4,000	—	7,000	
Pirated shelf	200,000	0	0	
Price (US$)	26.67	—	—	
Legitimate shelf	0	2,500	12,500	
Price (US$)	—	680	1,000	
Revenues (US$)	12,833,000	1,700,000	26,500,000	
Changes				
Number of firms	−143	0	0	
Employment	−717	0	0	
Revenues (US$)	−7,167,000	0	0	

(*Continued*)

**TABLE 11.2   Simulated Effects of Stronger Copyrights
on Software (Continued)**

	Fringe	Distributors	Developers	Net
Price, PCs (percent)	+25.0	n.a.	0	
Price, software (percent)	+33.0	0	0	
3. Substitution effects (Parameters: $e_{D3}^{PC} = -1.5$; $e_{S3}^{PC} = 2.0$; $e_{C3}^{PC} = 2.0$; $e_{D3}^{SW} = -1.5$; $e_{S3}^{SW} = 2.0$; $e_{C2}^{SW} = 2.5$; $e_{C3}^{SW} = 1.5$)				
Number of firms	257	4	124	
Average revenue (US$)	49,935	779,167	295,809	
Average employment	5.0	45.8	10.0	
Total PCs sold	4,000	0	8,647	
PC price (US$)	1,875	—	2,235	
Total software	204,000	4,583	24,150	
sold (units)				
With PCs	4,000	—	8,647	
Pirated shelf	200,000	0	0	
Price (US$)	26.67	—	—	
Legitimate shelf	0	4,583	15,503	
Price (US$)	—	680	1,117	
Revenues (US$)	12,833,000	3,117,000	36,656,000	
Changes				
Number of firms	0	+2	+34	
Employment	0	+83	+343	
Revenues (US$)	0	+1,417,000	+10,106,000	
Price, PCs (percent)	0	n.a.	+11.7	
Price, software (percent)	0	0	+11.7	
4. Joint changes				
Number of firms	−143	+2	+34	−107
Employment	−717	+83	+343	−291
Revenues (US$)	−7,200,000	+1,400,000	+10,100,000	+4,400,000
Price, PCs (percent)	+25.0	n.a.	+11.7	+17.8
Price, software (percent)	+33.0	0	+11.7	+18.5

— = not calculated; n.a. = not available.

Source: Author's calculations.

average price increase in the segment, I simply use cross-elasticities of demand between infringing software and legitimate software. Note that prices for legitimate copies and domestically produced programs will rise by virtue of removing much of the supply of illegitimate copies from the marketplace.

Suppose that Lebanon clarifies that software is copyrightable and undertakes an enforcement program that is 50 percent effective in reducing sales of pirated programs, both through PCs and off the shelf. In the partial equilibrium model, I assume first that PCs are imperfect substitutes because the cost of software programs and the service contracts provided by legitimate firms differ from those offered by infringing firms. Second, software programs sold by fringe firms, distributors, and applications firms are imperfect substitutes. The cross-elasticity with respect to applications programs is surely smaller than that with respect to the distributors' programs, which are legitimate versions of the pirated copies. Hence, the former elasticity is assumed to be 1.5 and the latter 2.5. Third, distributors maintain a fixed (50 percent) markup on software programs, and their foreign suppliers do not raise their license fees with stronger copyrights. Demand elasticity for their distributed software is −3.0 and is held constant as the market adjusts. Fourth, for the developers, software supply elasticity is 2.0 and demand elasticity is −1.5, while both elasticities are held constant. Fifth, fringe firms buy single legitimate copies of several platforms and spread these fixed costs over copies for PCs and other sales. Sixth, revenues per firm are held the same after the introduction of copyrights and after there is free entry into each segment of the market. Revenue per employee is held constant in each segment. The first five assumptions are designed to reflect responses indicated by managers interviewed in extensive meetings but may well not be accurate.

Applying stronger copyrights to the infringing firms generates the copyright enforcement effects in the second panel. Copyrights are assumed to cut in half the pirated sales of software through PCs and over the counter. There is an exit of firms out of pirating, but by less than half the number of original firms because of price increases per unit of output. With the assumed demand elasticities, the cost of pirating software (and its unit price) rises by 33 percent because of additional efforts to avoid detection. PC prices also rise by 25 percent. Declining sales volumes cause employment to fall by 717 workers in the fringe segment, or 36 percent of that segment's initial work force. Revenues fall by more than US$7 million. Clearly, there is substantial uncertainty about these figures.

Panel 3 contains results of the substitution in demand away from infringing PCs and software programs to products of developers and distributors, assuming no subsequent demand shifts back toward fringe firms. Two firms are simulated to enter the distributor market (the change in per firm revenue is required to achieve an integer figure for firms) and 34 firms to enter the applications development market.

More distributors emerge as foreign software providers find it advantageous to establish additional contacts with agents in Lebanon. Distributors sell more legitimate copies of foreign software programs at a constant price (reflecting my assumptions of a constant markup and no rise in foreign charges), generating US$1.4 million more in revenues and expanding employment by 83 workers. The entry of firms into applications could reflect, in part, decisions by some fringe firms to shift into legitimate production. Applications firms sell more PCs at an 11.7 percent higher price and a markedly higher amount of own-developed programs. Revenue rises sharply for these firms overall, by more than US$10 million, with employment expanding by 343 workers.

Overall, there is a net reduction in firms of 107 and of employment in the software industry of 291 workers (9.7 percent of total initial employment). There is a gain in revenues of US$4.4 million. The weighted-average price increase in PCs is 17.8 percent and in software is 18.5 percent. Again, the essential reason that legitimate firms experience positive static effects in software, as opposed to the effects in pharmaceuticals, cosmetics, and food products, is that such firms already pay global market prices for basic software platforms, which prices embody returns to copyrights.[5] It is unlikely that the acquisition costs of these programs would rise in the event of stronger Lebanese copyrights, so there is no direct cost increase. At the same time, these firms currently find their sales prospects in Lebanon and the surrounding nations to be seriously curtailed because of endemic software piracy by the small fringe concerns. Accordingly, it is sensible to expect stronger demand shifts toward programs sold by local developers and distributor firms as copyrights take hold.

Again, these calculations must be treated with great caution because they reflect only a guess about the relevant elasticities, informed by limited market-based data. However, they do illustrate some useful points. First, output and employment declines in the fringe firms will be offset to a significant degree by increases in the legitimate firms. If this program were phased in over five years, the per year change in employment would be quite small in relation to Lebanon's economy, although it is possible that the fringe firms would close down more rapidly than the expanding firms would take up the available workers, suggesting a temporary adjustment problem. Second, intersegment price relationships can be fairly subtle, depending on cross-elasticities and cost-generated supply shifts. In most cases, the elasticities assumed here are understated because software products are probably highly substitutable in practice. Using higher estimates would tend to magnify the intersegment shift of resources. Third, some of these changes would be significantly blunted if no entry were possible into the distributor segment and if existing distributors reacted to the stronger copyrights by raising their markups. For example, an increase in the markup to 75 percent, associated with a reduction in demand elasticity from −3.0 to −2.33, could be expected to cut software program sales through distributors to about 2,800 units and raise basic software program prices by perhaps 38 percent. In turn, this would result in higher software program costs for the applications firms. I should note that, in interviews, distributors indicated a clear intention to expand sales in the event of stronger copyrights.

This rough analysis is strictly static in nature. There is no evidence available to support calculations of dynamic changes. Some potential qualitative effects are worth pointing out, however. First, as the presence of pirated software diminishes in Lebanon, the demand for legal copies will likely rise in order to improve the interoperability of computer systems and to raise the quality of computing operations. The demand for the services of legitimate software firms for applications and service contracts should also increase. Indeed, several of these firms are quite enthusiastic about their business prospects under strong copyrights, predicting sales increases of anywhere from 100 percent to 1,000 percent over five years. Second, whereas I have assumed fixed revenues per firm, it is likely that many applications firms will expand and use additional revenues to fund further program development, with potentially important technological benefits for software-using sectors, such as banks, hotels, and insurance firms. Third, larger markets for software should increase the incentives for Lebanese firms to reverse-engineer platform programs and applications programs. This process is important for ensuring effective technology acquisition from software purchases and should be allowed under Lebanese law as long as it does not result simply in unauthorized copying. In this context, it is important to reiterate the need for Lebanon to update its copyright law to incorporate provisions for information technologies. Finally, it is evident that Lebanon has a strong and entrepreneurial set of programmers with businesses that are well positioned to export to Middle Eastern markets. This fact is likely to attract additional technology-sharing agreements and joint ventures with foreign software firms, particularly if additional regional integration and harmonization of copyright law and enforcement take place.

Printing and Publishing, Music, and Film

Printing, editing, and publishing; music recording and video distribution; and the creation of theatrical film and television programs are all significant industries in Lebanon. Some are considerably more subject to piracy than others. Film videos and recorded music are widely copied in Lebanon and surrounding countries. Unauthorized copies of textbooks are also frequently marketed and appear to be easily available at university bookstores. Arabic literature, which represents the main business activity of several publishers, induces some illegitimate copying, but it occurs in smaller volumes because literary books and poetry encounter

TABLE 11.3 Effects of Stronger Copyrights on Printing and Publishing

	Printers				Publishers			
	Fringe	Small	Large	Net	Fringe	Small	Large	Net
1. Basic data (segment number)	(1)	(2)	(3)		(4)	(5)	(6)	
Number of firms	300	100	20		250	75	15	
Average revenue (US$)	20,000	42,000	1,200,000		30,000	40,000	2,000,000	
Average employment	4	6	30		4	5	40	
Revenue/employment (US$)	5,000	7,000	40,000		7,500	8,000	50,000	
Average wage (US$)	2,800	3,200	3,800		3,800	2,800	3,800	
Revenues (US$)	6,000,000	4,200,000	24,000,000		7,500,000	3,000,000	30,000,000	
Pirated (US$ million)	6,000,000	—	—		7,500,000	—	—	
Copyright, cost share	—	—	—		0	0.1	0.1	
2. Copyright and demand substitution effects (50 percent decline in piracy and 50 percent rise in copyright fees) (Parameters: $e_{D1} = e_{D2} = e_{D4} = e_{D5} = -2.0$; $e_{D3} = e_{D6} = -1.5$; $e_{S2} = e_{S3} = e_{S5} = e_{S6} = 2.0$; $e_{C2} = 2.0$; $e_{C3} = 1.0$; $e_{C4} = 2.18$; $e_{C5} = 2.5$; $e_{C6} = 1.5$)								
Number of firms	225	130	24		164	75	15	
Average revenue (US$)	20,000	42,000	1,194,000		30,073	40,059	1,972,000	
Average employment	4.0	6.0	29.8		4.0	5.0	39.9	
Revenues (US$)	4,500,000	5,460,000	28,645,000		4,932,000	3,004,000	29,900,000	
Pirated (US$)	4,500,000	—	—		4,932,000	—	—	
Copyright, cost share	—	—	—		0	0.15	0.15	

3. Changes by segment

Number of firms	−75	+30	+4	−41	−86	0	0	−86
Employment	−300	+180	+116	−4	−342	+1	−2	−343
Revenues (US$)	−1,500,000	+1,260,000	+4,645,000	+4,405,000	−2,568,000	+4,000	−83,000	−2,647,000
Price (percent)	+25.0	+10.0	+6.5	+13.2	+37.3	−0.3	+0.5	+7.3

4. Net changes (industrywide)

Number of firms	−127
Employment	−347
Revenues (US$)	+1,758,000

— = not calculated.

Source: Author's calculations.

smaller niche markets. Lebanon has a new and vibrant industry making Arabic-language films and television programs, which experience virtually no copying.

An analysis similar to that for software can be applied to those sectors. Assume stronger copyrights in the publishing sector result in a 50 percent cut in sales volume of unauthorized books and a 50 percent rise in the cost share by publishers for copyright charges, reflecting higher royalty payments. Assume further that the initial cost share is 10 percent and that printers do not directly pay those charges.[6] Any price increases in the printing sector affect costs in the publishing sector as well, so the model in appendix 11.A is used to calculate demand substitution effects.

When we combine these circumstances, revenues for the legitimate firms in the fringe printing segment fall, as does the share of pirated printing. Revenues of small and large legitimate printers rise. Applying the fixed coefficients for revenues per firm and per employee to these changes, the number of pirating (fringe) firms falls by 25 percent. Entry by new firms would take up production and virtually offset the employment loss (table 11.3).

In the publishing sector, there is a decline of pirating firms, with an associated job loss, reflecting copyright enforcement and demand shifts away from higher-priced illegitimate books. For legitimate publishers, the cost increase from higher copyright charges essentially balances the demand increases deriving from the substitution effect, causing virtually no effect on net production or employment.

In the case of music and video, stronger copyright enforcement would increase prices significantly and reduce employment in fringe firms that are engaged in pirating activities (table 11.4). Net revenues increase as the turnover of large domestic producers exceeds the losses incurred by pirating firms.

In films, television, and broadcasting, the industry gains unambiguously. In contrast to video copying, the production of cinematic films, television programs, recorded advertising, and broadcasting is costly. Accordingly, the industry is not directly affected by piracy. Lebanese films and programs are not copied, both for technical reasons and because there is little economic gain to be had in doing so. Moreover, the sector pays little in copyright fees because it develops its own creative programming. Lebanon has a young and strong film, advertising, and television sector. Stronger copyright enforcement could have a small indirect effect on this industry segment by shifting demand from pirated videos to Lebanese-produced filmed entertainment. Thus, assuming a cross-elasticity of demand between video piracy and Lebanese films of 0.5, demand for the latter would rise by 8.4 percent. Revenues would rise, perhaps inducing entry of an additional firm and more employment.

The net reduction in firms and employment in table 11.4 reflects the closure of small firms that currently infringe on protectable copyrights that would be better enforced. Such firms tend to be small and to have assets that could be relatively

TABLE 11.4   Effects of Stronger Copyrights on Music and Video, and Film Industries

	Music and video		Film	
	Fringe	Large	Net	Large
1. Basic data (segment number)	(1)	(2)	(3)	
Number of firms	500	23		8
Average revenue (US$)	15,000	1,000,000		4,000,000
Average employment	3	20		100
Revenue/ employment (US$)	5,000	50,000		40,000
Average wage	2,800	3,800		4,000
Revenues (US$)	7,500,000	23,000,000		32,000,000
Pirated (US$)	7,500,000	—		—
Copyright, cost share	0	0.1		0
2. Copyright enforcement and demand–substitution effects (50 percent reduction in piracy and 50 percent rise in copyright fees) (Parameters: $e_{D1} = -3.0$, $e_{D2} = -2.0$, $e_{D3} = -1.5$; $e_{S2} = e_{S3} = 3.0$; $e_{C2} = 1.5$, $e_{C3} = 0.5$)				
Number of firms	333	26		9
Average revenue (US$)	15,015	1,007,000		3,801,000
Average employment	3.0	20.1		95.0
Revenues (US$)	5,000,000	26,200,000		34,200,000
Pirated (US$)	5,000,000	—		—
Copyright, cost share	0	0.15		0
3. Changes by segment				
Number of firms	−167	+3	+1	−164
Employment	−500	+64	+55	−436
Revenues (US$)	−2,500,000	+3,179,000	+2,207,000	+679,000
Price (percent)	+16.7	+8.0	+2.3	+10.1

— = not applicable.
Source: Author's calculations.

easily transferred to other activities. Displaced workers are likely to be relatively unskilled. Some will find their way into employment in the expanding firms, probably at a higher average wage.

Because piracy in Lebanon is aimed primarily at copying foreign textbooks, movies, and music, stronger copyright enforcement is unlikely to induce a creative response by Lebanese firms in terms of literature, music, and films, because they do not face much direct copying. However, some dynamic gains could be induced by stronger and more harmonized copyright protection in the Middle East. Lebanon is well positioned as a regional net exporter of television programming and broadcasts, cinematic films, and music.

VI. Concluding Remarks

The calculations performed in the foregoing subsections should be approached with great caution. They are based on highly simplified partial equilibrium models within each industry and calibrated to data that provide only rough approximations of true economic activity. The simulations performed are sensitive to the elasticities assumed. They are strictly static, allowing only for effects of cost increases from stronger enforcement, foreign reactions in raising charges for IPRs, and demand shifts across imperfectly substitutable product segments. Indeed, it is likely that the computations are excessively static, in that in multiple-segment industries (pharmaceuticals, cosmetics, food products, and publishing), the potential effects of demand expansion are constrained by calculating demand shifts relative to an aggregate price increase. However, the computations do not allow for the possibility that stronger IPRs would enhance the market power of local agents. It is uncertain how important this effect would be in practice; much depends on the particular industry, its market structure, and its demand characteristics.

The most important limitation of static calculations is that they necessarily imply a reduction in activity in those firms that had been engaging in unauthorized use of intellectual property and now must pay for it or lose access to it altogether, without recognizing potential dynamic gains that could emerge over the long term. It is worth briefly reiterating them.

First, Lebanon may reasonably expect some increase in FDI after phasing in stronger IPRs. The new regulatory environment, if well enforced, would raise the returns to FDI—particularly in sensitive sectors such as pharmaceuticals and local biological research, though there could be additional interest also in trademark-sensitive consumer products. The responsiveness of FDI to improved IPRs is not well understood in the literature, though evidence suggests it is positive in large developing countries (Mansfield 1994). However, IPRs are only one of a set of factors that influence FDI, factors that include local treatment of investment, market size and dynamism, human capital availability, and macroeconomic stability. For example, FDI will be little changed in Lebanon if stronger IPRs are not accompanied by appropriate deregulation of restrictions on foreign investment. Similarly, FDI is likely to be more sensitive to regional economic integration and policy harmonization that could expand market size and enhance business certainty.

Second, Lebanon could experience increases in product development by local firms, which are currently suffering the largest injuries from inadequate IPRs. Although it is unlikely that Lebanese firms would generate significant technical advances that could be protected and marketed globally, numerous opportunities exist for developing additional consumer products and business services for the Lebanese and regional markets. Lebanese sectors that seem particularly well positioned for this purpose include cosmetics, food products, software applications, publishing, and film production and advertising. It is likely that this will be the strongest dynamic gain forthcoming from the new policy regime.

Third, Lebanese firms should find it easier to enter into joint ventures and technology-sharing or product-licensing agreements with foreign firms as a result of stronger IPRs. Thus, while stronger IPRs will make it harder for local firms to imitate foreign technologies, products, and designs, they should assist legitimate firms in providing greater access to authorized information. Provided that this enhanced technology transfer is used in a competitive fashion in Lebanon, the economy should reap some dynamic benefits.

Fourth, to the extent that there is additional technology transfer to Lebanon and further local product development, the average quality of products and services on the market should rise. Although the associated price effects would be problematic for low-income consumers, there should be dynamic gains from greater efficiency of inputs over time, while consumers will benefit from additional certainty about the signaling value of trademarks.

Appendix 11.A
General Equations for Partial-Equilibrium Models

Effects of Cost Increases Caused by Higher Fees for IPRs or Input Prices

Firms that use inputs for which royalties are charged or whose prices incorporate charges for using patents, trademarks, or copyrights would expect to see a rise in those costs with the advent of stronger IPRs. The rise in costs would reduce value added unless firms can pass the costs on to consumers in higher prices. Assume that a final good j uses n intermediate inputs but that only the first input is subject to IPR-related price changes. Other input prices are invariant to IPRs. Also, assume that physical input coefficients (a_{ij}) are fixed. Then, value added is

$$VA_j = Q_j(P_j - P_1 a_{1j} - \Sigma P_i a_{ij})$$

where the summation covers non-IPR inputs. The term in parentheses is known as a *value added price* in the trade literature. Taking the total derivative of this expression yields

$$dVA_j = Q_j(dP_j - a_{1j}dP_1) + (P_j - P_1a_{1j} - \Sigma P_ia_{ij})dQ_j$$

With further manipulation this expression may be converted to

$$dVA_j = Q_jP_j(dP_j/P_j) - Q_ja_{1j}P_1(dP_1/P_1) + VA_j(dQ_j/Q_j)$$

We can write this expression in discrete terms as

$$VA_j^1 - VA_j^0 = Q_j^0\,P_j^0\{(P_j^1/P_j^0) - 1\} - Q_j^0a_{ij}P_1^0\{(P_1^1/P_1^0) - 1\} + VA_j^0\{(Q_j^1/Q_j^0) - 1\}$$

These components are observable. Initial value added is computed as a share of gross output, with data taken from the *Report on Industrial Census* (Lebanese Republic 1995). The term $Q_j^0P_j^0$ is initial sales revenue. The term $Q_j^0a_{ij}P_1^0$ indicates the costs of IPR goods, which may be calculated if we know the IPR cost share of total revenues. The survey results provided some information on those shares. The terms in parentheses are percentage changes in prices and quantities, which may be computed from assumed elasticities. Notice that value added can rise or fall as a result of stronger IPRs on inputs, whereas the effect of this cost increase is proportional to the share of IPRs in costs. A rise in the cost of input 1 shifts the supply curve up proportionally. It is straightforward to show that this shift is captured by

$$P_j^2/P_j^0 = 1 + (1/P_j^0Q_j^0)\{Q_j^0a_{1j}P_1^0[(P_1^1/P_1^0) - 1]\}$$

Again, each of these terms is observable if we know the proportional increase in per unit charges for use of IPRs. Although this is the upward shift in the supply curve, the actual effect on market price depends on market demand and supply elasticities:

$$P_j^1/P_j^0 = \{1 - (e_{Dj}/e_{Sj})\}/\{(P_j^0/P_j^2) - (e_{Dj}/e_{Sj})\}$$

where the demand elasticity is negative and the supply elasticity is positive. Having calculated the proportional price change, the quantity change is

$$Q_j^1/Q_j^0 = 1 + e_{Dj}\{(P_j^1/P_j^0) - 1\}$$

An Importer-Distributor with a Fixed Markup

Some of the equations above would not hold for imperfectly competitive firms. I assume that all firms are competitive except importers that have an exclusive agency relationship with one or more foreign exporters. There may be several such distributors, but the agency relationship constitutes an effective entry barrier. In general, markups are endogenous and depend on demand elasticity, but to simplify the analysis, I assume that each distributor charges a fixed markup θ.

Thus, $P = MC(1 + \theta)$. For this firm, marginal cost is the price charged by its foreign suppliers, including any implicit or explicit royalty charges. Assume that Lebanon is a small country in the sense that the basic foreign price is fixed but that foreign suppliers could react to observing stronger IPRs by changing their royalty charges. Then $P_f^0 = P_N(1 + \tau^0)$ and $P_f^1 = P_N(1 + \tau^1)$ give marginal costs to the importer, where τ indicates exogenous royalty charges. If we ignore sectoral subscripts, with a fixed markup the ratio of home market prices charged by the distributors in Lebanon before and after the increase in IPR price is simply:

$$P^1/P^0 = (1 + \tau^1)/(1 + \tau^0)$$

and the distributor's import sales change according to demand elasticity:

$$M^1/M^0 = 1 + e_D(P^1/P^0 - 1)$$

The formulas developed earlier for changes in value added hold in this case as well.

Substitution Effects among Market Segments

As prices change within each market segment, demand will shift among the segments under the assumption that they produce differentiated goods. This issue is quite difficult to handle in a partial equilibrium framework and requires some simplifying assumptions. Assume first that price and expenditure changes in an industry group are separable from other products and services. Second, because the existence of multiple market segments makes it complicated to handle all possible relative price shifts, define an aggregate price index that is a weighted average of segment price indexes:

$$dP/P = \Sigma\omega_i^0(dP_j/P_j)$$

where the weights are each segment's share of initial industry total revenues. The price changes calculated here are those after accounting for the cost effects of stronger IPRs. Assume that an industry group demand function exists with price elasticity e_D. It captures the economy's overall demand for, say, pharmaceuticals, within which consumers allocate expenditures according to price and quality. I choose initial market shares as weights and hold them fixed here (a Laspeyre index) for convenience because of lack of data. A better approach would be to construct weights based explicitly on specified preferences in some aggregate utility function.

Having calculated the aggregate price change and knowing the aggregate elasticity, we may calculate the aggregate quantity change in demand, dQ/Q. The key issue is how to allocate this shift among segment quantity changes. For this purpose, consider the following system of equations:

$$dQ_j/Q_j = e_{Cj}(dP/P - dP_j/P_j)$$
$$\Sigma \omega_j dQ_j/Q_j = dQ/Q$$
$$e_{Cj} > 0$$

Here, the e_{Cj} terms are cross–demand elasticities for each segment with respect to the average price increase within the group. I assume that all goods are substitutes, so the elasticities are positive. I impose the constraint that the weighted average of resulting demand changes must exhaust the aggregate demand change. The first two equations really are $(n + 1)$ equations in $2n$ unknowns: the output changes and the elasticities. Thus, the analyst needs to find data for (or assume values for) $n - 1$ of the elasticities and use these to calibrate the final elasticity and calculate the output changes. This is the procedure adopted in the text.

The implied demand shifts are incomplete because they do not allow for iterative changes in demand, as could be accomplished in a more complicated model. However, these second-order effects are usually small, and they are ignored here. Within each market segment, as demand rises (for those sectors with below-average price increases) or falls (for those with above-average price increases), there will be subsequent effects on quantity and price. These demand shifts have effects analogous to those of the supply shifts above. Let Q_j^2/Q_j^0 indicate the relative demand shift calculated in the last set of equations. In competitive markets, the actual relative quantity and price changes would be

$$Q_j^1/Q_j^0 = (Q_j^1/Q_j^2)(Q_j^2/Q_j^0), \text{ where}$$
$$Q_j^1/Q_j^2 = \{1 - (e_{Sj}/e_{Dj})\}/\{(Q_j^2/Q_j^0) - (e_{Sj}/e_{Dj})\}$$
$$P_j^1/P_j^0 = 1 + (1/e_{Sj})\{(Q_j^1/Q_j^0) - 1\}$$

Finally, note that, under the assumption that Lebanon is small, the higher IPR-inclusive price charged to import distributors is unchanged as a result of these demand shifts. Accordingly, with a fixed markup, these firms experience only a relative quantity change.

Notes

1. When this article was edited in 2003 for inclusion in this book, Lebanon was negotiating its agreements to accede to the WTO. Demands that Lebanon improve its intellectual property laws and enforcement featured prominently in the negotiations.

2. The small effect in distribution reflects its large initial weight in industry revenues, so that the price increase here is nearly identical to the aggregate price increase.

3. Readers should not take literally the claim that initial employment is 1,990 workers. This is just an estimate based on the survey and likely misses a substantial portion of actual employment. However, the processes illustrated here would suggest a decline in employment of a similar percentage of whatever actual employment is.

4. The weights are based on each industry segment's share of initial industry revenues.

5. Results for cosmetics and food products may be found in Maskus (1997).

6. According to interviewees, copyright fees are currently 7 to 10 percent of publishing sales. A 50 percent rise in average license fees (likely an overestimate) would then increase costs by a maximum of 5 percent.

References

Dunning, John. 1980. "Toward an Eclectic Theory of International Production: Some Empirical Tests." *Journal of International Business Studies* 11(1): 9–31.

Lebanese Republic. 1995. *Report on Industrial Census: Final Results*. Ministry of Industry and Petroleum, Directorate of Industry.

Mansfield, Edwin. 1994. "Intellectual Property Protection, Foreign Direct Investment, and Technology Transfer." Discussion Paper 19. World Bank and International Finance Corporation, Washington, D.C.

Markusen, James R. 1995. "The Boundaries of Multinational Enterprises and the Theory of International Trade." *Journal of Economic Perspectives* 9: 169–90.

Maskus, Keith E. 1990. "Normative Concerns in the International Protection of Intellectual Property Rights." *World Economy* 13: 387–409.

———. 1997. "Intellectual Property Rights in Lebanon." International Trade Division, World Bank, Washington, D.C. Processed.

———. 1998. "The International Regulation of Intellectual Property." *Weltwirtschaftliches Archiv* 134: 196–208.

Maskus, Keith E., and Denise Eby Konan. 1994. "Trade-Related Intellectual Property Rights: Issues and Exploratory Results." In Alan V. Deardorff and Robert M. Stern, eds., *Analytical and Negotiating Issues in the Global Trading System*. Ann Arbor: University of Michigan Press.

Subramanian, Arvind. 1991. "The International Economics of Intellectual Property Right Protection: A Welfare-Theoretic Trade Policy Analysis." *World Development* 19: 945–56.

12

INTELLECTUAL PROPERTY RIGHTS AND ECONOMIC DEVELOPMENT IN CHINA

Keith E. Maskus, Sean M. Dougherty, and Andrew Mertha

I. Introduction

After a long period of rapid economic growth and significant structural change, the Chinese economy increasingly makes use of advanced production technologies, as demand shifts toward higher-quality goods and services. Furthermore, Chinese enterprises place growing emphasis on developing brand-name recognition, a reputation for quality, and product innovation. In such an environment, the provision and enforcement of intellectual property rights (IPRs) take on considerable importance as framework conditions for promoting further economic development. Failing to support an adequate IPR regime could act as a drag on future growth. In an era of substantial and ongoing structural reform in Chinese enterprises, it is important to establish incentives for the development and expansion of businesses in high-growth sectors, such as information technology, entertainment, plant genetics, and biotechnology, and to support innovation in

This chapter is adapted from a longer version that was prepared for the Southwest China Regional Conference on Intellectual Property Rights and Economic Development, held in Chongqing, September 15–18, 1998. This paper was written while Dougherty was doing fieldwork in China for the MIT Science and Technology Initiative. He is now with the Organisation for Economic Co-operation and Development.

consumer products, such as processed foods, clothing, and household goods. Properly structured, IPRs help achieve these goals.

At the highest levels, the Chinese government recognizes the need for a workable IPR system. This recognition is spreading among modern Chinese enterprises, which likely suffer the largest losses from trademark and copyright infringement in the economy. Chinese enterprises also are aware that their access to frontier foreign technologies depends to a growing extent on IPRs. Thus, significant economic interests are emerging in favor of a stronger system.

In response both to this change and to considerable external pressure, China is undertaking a dramatic reform of its intellectual property laws. Since 1990, China has revised and updated its laws covering copyrights, trademarks, patents, and trade secrets ("anti–unfair competition" laws) and has adopted protection for integrated circuits. China has also enacted protective systems for plant varieties and pharmaceutical marketing rights. However, China has yet to establish protection for geographical indications, which specify particular locations at which a product such as wine is made. Beijing has joined nearly all major international IPR conventions, including the Paris Convention in 1984, the Madrid Protocol and the Washington Treaty in 1989, the Berne Convention and the Universal Copyright Convention in 1992, the Geneva Phonograms Convention in 1993, and the Patent Cooperation Treaty in 1994. It also is a member of international agreements on the classification of patents and trademarks and the deposit of microorganisms (see La Croix and Konan 1998 for further details).

China must make further revisions in order to conform to the requirements of the Agreement on Trade-Related Aspects of Intellectual Property Rights (TRIPS) in the World Trade Organization (WTO). However, it has signaled its intention to do so, and corresponding reforms are under consideration. When the reforms are completed, China will have a modern legislative structure for IPRs on a par with many industrial economies.

Beijing also established education and training programs in IPRs and upgraded its administrative and legal systems for enforcing these rights. For example, China recently set up special IPR courts in eight cities. Furthermore, in 1997, a Software Title Verification Office was established as a joint Sino-U.S. initiative to examine the legitimacy of software purchases by Chinese factories and offices. However, significant problems remain in the administration and enforcement area. Victims of infringement complain loudly about weak monetary and civil penalties, frustrating delays in administrative and court procedures, and local protectionism that makes enforcement actions difficult to sustain in regional jurisdictions.

The evolving system of IPRs presents both opportunities and challenges for the Chinese economy. As will be discussed in detail in later sections, the opportunities stem from establishing an improved environment for technical innovation, product development, and inward technology and investment flows. The challenges include moving resources out of infringing activities into legitimate businesses, coping with higher costs of imitating products and technologies, and absorbing the costs of administering a stronger system.

Stated differently, stronger IPRs will shift economic incentives away from encouraging static competition through copying toward promoting dynamic competition through innovation, technology absorption, and product design. The latter policy environment is appropriate for an economy, such as China, that has aspirations to be a leader in technology development. However, such an environment will place competitive pressures on lagging sectors and will raise concerns about the distribution of costs and benefits among individuals and enterprises.

In this context, the ultimate objective of a stronger system is to maximize the competitive gains from additional innovation and technology acquisition over time, with particular emphasis on raising innovative activity by domestic entrepreneurs and enterprises. Upgrading protection for IPRs alone is a necessary but not sufficient condition for this purpose. Rather, the system needs to be strengthened within a comprehensive and coherent set of policy initiatives that optimize the effectiveness of IPRs. Among such initiatives are further structural reform of enterprises, trade and investment liberalization, promotion of financial and innovation systems to commercialize new technologies, expansion of educational opportunities to build human capital for absorbing and developing technology, and specification of rules for maintaining effective competition in Chinese markets. Developing these inititiatives is the overriding challenge facing Chinese policymakers in the IPR realm.

The chapter proceeds as follows. In the next section, we discuss the intricate relationships between IPRs and economic development, reviewing available evidence on that subject. We analyze recent trends in the use of IPRs in China in the following section, considering both data and information learned from a series of interviews with enterprise managers, Chinese administrative bureau personnel, scholars, and local enforcement agents. Furthermore, we develop some crude indications of how Chinese economic development could be affected by stronger IPRs. In the final section, we provide conclusions and recommendations.

II. IPRs and Economic Development

The relationship between IPRs and economic development is extremely complex and can only be summarized here.[1] The evidence is sometimes difficult to interpret because many of the concepts involved are not well measured. However, there is a growing consensus that stronger IPRs increase economic growth and improve development processes if they are properly structured.

How Economic Development Affects IPR Systems

To date, most economists have focused on one direction of causation, from economic development to strengthening of standards for intellectual property protection. For example, in one recent article, an index of strength of patent laws in 1984 across countries was developed (Maskus and Penubarti 1995). There is a strong positive relationship between patent strength and real per capita gross national product (GNP):

$$\text{Patent} = -0.51 + 0.49 \times \text{GNP} \quad R^2 = 0.37$$

The regression points out that national policies depend on growth in income levels, among other factors. It is easy to understand the political economy of this process (see Evenson and Westphal 1997; La Croix 1992; Sherwood 1990; Siebeck 1990). The poorest countries allocate virtually no resources to invention or innovation and have little intellectual property to protect. As incomes and technical capabilities grow to moderate levels, some inventive capacity emerges, particularly of the adaptive kind, but competition remains based on imitation, and the majority of economic and political interests prefer weak protection. As an economy develops, additional inventive capacity and demands for high-quality products emerge, and more firms lobby for effective protection, a process that is abetted by foreign firms interested in servicing growing markets. Finally, protection shifts up sharply at the highest levels of income.

There is a strong correlation between the strengths of patents, trademarks, and copyrights, although many developing economies have enacted reasonably strong trademark and copyright laws (see Rapp and Rozek 1990; Ryan 1998). The strength of enforcement efforts also differs with economic development levels. On the part of poor countries, this reflects both an unwillingness to pay the costly administrative expenses and an inability to manage complicated technical and judicial issues associated with IPRs.

Note from this analysis that if a country has widely varying income levels and technological capabilities in different regions, there will be strong differences in interest in IPRs. China currently seems to be in this position, with far higher incomes in the coastal and urban regions, as we show in a later section. In turn, firms from those regions tend to be much more active in using IPRs and in wishing to see them protected, leading potentially to interregional disputes over intellectual property infringement and enforcement.

How IPRs Stimulate Economic Development

The evidence presented above may argue for simply waiting until economies become sufficiently developed to adopt stronger regimes themselves. There is certainly cause for concern that an expansion of legal rights without significant interest in its behalf is unlikely to be well enforced or effective.

However, economists now recognize that there are stimulative effects of IPR protection on economic development and growth. We discuss several general channels of influence, all of which are related to one another.

Stimulation of Invention and Innovation   *Invention* refers to the creation of new knowledge, and *innovation* (or *commercialization*) refers to the development of marketable products from that knowledge. An inadequate set of IPRs can stifle both these processes even at low levels of economic development. For example, most invention is specific to local market circumstances; it is not necessary to invent frontier-level international technologies to benefit from local patent or utility model protection. In the vast majority of cases, invention is a mundane process involving minor adaptations of existing technologies, with cumulatively powerful effects on growth. It is as important for firms to adapt new management and organizational systems and new product and quality control mechanisms as it is to find new technologies. Those investments can be quite costly and will be undertaken only when the risk of their loss to unfair competition and trademark infringement is minimized. In an environment of weak protection, it is difficult also to foster attitudes of creativity, invention, and risk taking. Rather, the economy stagnates in a mode favoring copying and counterfeiting.

It is equally important to adapt available foreign or domestic technologies to specific uses in agriculture, industry, and services. Technology itself may be readily transferable, but mastering the tacit knowledge or know-how implicit in it requires costly effort and investment. Investments are required in process control, product quality maintenance, product mix, and other factors. Such investments have high economic and social returns in that they are fundamentally necessary to raise productivity toward international levels. Although they rarely result in inventions that meet international or domestic patentability requirements, they do generate small improvements in processes and product designs.

Effective systems of utility models, which involve low levels of novelty and limited periods of protection, can be critical in spurring this process in technology-follower countries. For example, one study of the farm machinery industry in Brazil demonstrated that utility models were instrumental in allowing Brazilian producers to win a dominant market share from foreign producers by adapting their technologies to Brazilian conditions (Dahab 1986). Another study demonstrated that utility models in the Philippines stimulated successful adaptive invention of rice threshers (Mikkelsen 1984). The original threshing technologies were provided by the International Rice Research Institute, a public entity that was willing to operate in the presence of weak patents when private firms would not do so. Yet another study demonstrated econometrically that Japan's system of utility models contributed positively and significantly to its postwar rise in productivity (Maskus and McDaniel 1999).

Trademarks also provide strong incentives for the entry of new firms and the development of new products with quality guarantees, even in poor nations.[2] The introduction of new firms and products based on local foods, cultural advantages, and indigenous crafts responds elastically to trademark protection, and such firms find it easier to move up the value added chain as they grow larger and their trademarks are better recognized. This process has two positive effects on industrial development. First, it stimulates the entry of small and medium-size enterprises into market niches. Second, it encourages the more successful enterprises to grow and take advantages of scale economies through interregional production and marketing. As such enterprises grow, they establish specialized departments for marketing, strategy, and research and development (R&D), which then become sources of important technical change. Some may even become significant exporters as they stabilize their quality levels.

Seen in this light, an absence of effective trademark protection acts as a significant drag on industrial development prospects. It deters the entry of new firms, which would not undertake the significant costs of investing in quality maintenance and reputation without such protection. It diminishes the prospects for exploiting scale economies, particularly to the extent that protection varies across regional markets. It prevents the entry into export markets of reputation products. Instead, weak protection favors the production of low-quality goods in small production runs and imitative activities. Although this strategy may yield short-run profits, it becomes a significant restriction on growth over time. Moreover, weak protection forces legitimate firms to produce relatively low-quality products to be competitive with infringers.

Similar comments apply to copyrights. Sectors that are dependent on copyrights, such as publishing, entertainment, and software, will not find much entry by local firms in the absence of copyrights, even if there is considerable activity in copying markets. Creation of new films, music, and software is expensive and little worth the investment by local entrepreneurs if their products will be copied. Accordingly, lower-quality copies may be widely and cheaply available, but society's long-run cultural and economic development is stunted.

There is evidence that strengthened IPRs stimulate innovation in developing countries. For example, in a survey of 377 Brazilian firms by the Brazilian Ministry of Industrial Development and Commerce and the American Chamber of Commerce, it was found that 80 percent of those firms would invest more in internal R&D and labor training if better legal protection were available (Sherwood 1990).

Market Deepening   Innovation is not only about developing new products. It is equally about establishing marketing and distribution networks that support expansion and scale economies. It is difficult to do this in an environment of weak IPR protection because rights holders cannot readily prevent their marketing channels from debasing the quality of their products. Put differently, IPRs provide improved certainty of contracts, which allows better monitoring and enforcement of activities at all levels of the supply network. In turn, both innovative firms and their distributors are willing to invest in marketing and brand-name recognition.

Quality Assurance   As firms build reputations for quality through trademarks, incentives grow to deter the false use of those marks. Fake products sold under a misappropriated trademark quickly ruin reputations, particularly for new firms, and it can be more costly to overcome such damage than to enter the market in the first place. Therefore, effective trademark enforcement increases the average quality of products over time, meaning that consumers may be less wary of knockoffs. This is particularly important in cases of beverages, foodstuffs, and medicines, where fake products can be dangerous to health and nutrition.

Domestic and International Diffusion of Knowledge   As mentioned above, patents play a positive role in disseminating knowledge to other users. Patent claims are published, disclosing technical information to rivals. They cannot directly copy the original claim but may use the knowledge to develop further inventions that may then be protected. Survey evidence in the United States indicates that patented technology becomes incorporated into further technical change within 10 to 12 months on average (Mansfield 1985). This cumulative process of invention, which depends critically on the breadth of patent claims, is a key source of technical change (Scotchmer 1991). Moreover, patents provide a legal basis for trading and licensing technologies, thereby improving information flows through formal markets. Trademarks and trade secrets protection also facilitates information exchange by ensuring that licensees do not cheat on their contracts.

There is considerable evidence that international flows of technology depend on the strength of IPRs, among many other factors. For example, international trade in manufactures is positively affected by the strength of patent regimes in large developing countries (Maskus and Penubarti 1995; Smith 1998). Such trade often embodies considerable technical knowledge that may be learned in recipient countries (Coe, Helpman, and Hoffmaister 1997). In turn, this knowledge may stimulate the development of local technological capabilities.

More significant international conduits of technology are foreign direct investment (FDI) and technology contracts. Joint venture agreements typically involve the transfer of technology to local partners, who may supply land, labor, or other inputs. FDI in subsidiaries may be designed to keep technology proprietary within the firm, but such investments also train local employees and managers and transfer knowledge to local suppliers and purchasers. Licensing contracts directly embody technical information in return for royalty payments.

Unquestionably, the strength of IPRs (and of contracts and enforcement more generally) affects decisions by multinational firms on where to invest, how much to invest and in what forms, and whether to transfer advanced technologies. Studies of the relationship between American FDI and patent strength find clear evidence that firms limit their investments in countries with weak patents (Lee and Mansfield 1996; Maskus 1998a). Moreover, survey evidence indicates strongly that the level of technology transferred depends on the ability to maintain control over the technology through the defense of intellectual property. For example, firms in nearly all industries express reluctance to build R&D facilities in countries that have weak patent protection, and frontier technologies are rarely transferred to production sites in such countries (Contractor 1980; Mansfield 1995; Yang and Maskus 1998). Licensing also tends to rise with stronger IPRs because of reduced contracting costs and greater legal certainty. And international firms are more willing to build vertically integrated relationships with suppliers and marketers.

There are several practical lessons from such findings. First, countries that have weak IPRs find themselves isolated from modern technologies; they have high *technological distances* in economic terminology.[3] In turn, they must attempt to develop technological knowledge largely through their own investments, which is a highly costly way to duplicate available technologies and therefore a growth-limiting factor. Second, such countries experience fewer spillover benefits and demonstration effects of new technologies and production techniques in their economies. Third, available technologies tend to be outmoded. Although this approach makes some sense in standardized manufactures, such as textiles and apparel, it limits exposure to new information in high-technology industries. Fourth, countries that have weak IPRs suffer from both inadequate stimulus to domestic innovation and limited inward technology flows that would also stimulate domestic technical change.

Composition of Global Research and Development   As IPRs are strengthened in particular markets, more R&D expenditures are aimed at meeting the specific needs of those markets. Thus, with stronger IPRs there should be more international invention and innovation aimed at Chinese demands in medicine and production technology.

How IPRs Limit Economic Development

A balanced treatment of IPRs must recognize that they also bear a potential for imposing economic damages. There may even be net losses in the short run after a stronger regime is introduced, because the dynamic benefits sketched above may take longer to appear. This aspect of costs and benefits imparts a bias against serious and effective reform in poor countries, because it is difficult to mobilize future beneficiaries into a current political force. It also explains why external pressure is a catalyst for change. We discuss these potential costs of IPRs here.

Administrative Costs   The costs of administering and enforcing a modern IPR system are high. For China, they easily will amount to annual sums in excess of US$10 million.[4] They include the costs of training examiners, judges, lawyers, and enforcement officers, along with the costs of running various offices. Many of these costs may be covered by administrative fees charged to apply for and register patents and trademarks, whereas others may be limited by adherence to international registration agencies such as the Patent Cooperation Treaty (as China does). The largest cost is really the opportunity cost of devoting scarce scientific, engineering, and legal personnel to the complex of IPR administration, a cost that points out the need for maintaining high rates of human capital formation.

Shifting Resources out of Infringing Activities   The most visible aspect of IPR infringement is unauthorized copying of copyrighted materials, such as recorded entertainment and software, and misuse of trademarks.[5] These problems exist in all economies but are endemic in developing nations. For example, table 12.1 shows recent estimates by the International Intellectual Property Alliance of piracy rates (percentage of products sold without authorization) in several countries.[6] These estimates are questionable for many reasons and should be treated with caution. For example, the piracy rates in business applications software are overstated in China because they fail to account adequately for customized applications software, which constitutes about 25 percent of the market and is not easily copied.[7] However, the ranking across countries is probably accurate. It is interesting to note that reported piracy rates generally fall as income rises. Again, therefore, interest in illegitimate copying declines and enforcement improves as incomes rise.

Three other conclusions may be drawn from table 12.1. First, illegal copying rates depend on the strength of local industries that oppose such copying. For example, India has relatively low rates in music recording and business applications software because its local music and software development firms are vibrant sources of employment and activity (though India also has a significant film industry, which suffers from extensive copying). This fact suggests that effective reduction of copyright infringement requires development of legitimate local producing interests. Second, copying rates vary considerably across types of goods, with business applications software experiencing the highest rates and

TABLE 12.1   Estimates of Percentage Piracy Rates for Copyright Goods, 1996–97

Country	Motion pictures		Recorded music		Business application software		Entertainment software	
	1997	1996	1997	1996	1997	1996	1997	1996
Argentina	43	43	35	30	62	73	90	86
Australia	4	4	n.a.	4	32	n.a.	n.a.	n.a.
Brazil[a]	35	38	50	45	70	74	82	82
China	75	85	56	53	96	95	96	97
Egypt, Arab Rep. of	50	25	40	25	85	89	55	51
Hong Kong (China)	20	15	20	20	67	65	70	73
India	80	85	40	30	76	78	82	78
Indonesia	85	85	12	15	93	98	89	82
Italy[a]	35	40	22	33	58	61	55	52
Korea, Rep. of[a]	15	15	10	18	70	76	65	66
Lebanon[a]	99	100	30	n.a.	76	79	n.a.	n.a.
Mexico	55	55	50	50	62	67	82	75
Singapore	15	2	30	n.a.	56	56	68	n.a.
Spain[a]	8	8	2	2	67	74	56	n.a.
Taiwan (China)	10	10	12	8	63	72	65	69
Thailand	50	65	40	40	84	82	85	82
Turkey[a]	95	95	30	30	87	89	89	86

n.a. = not available.
a. First year listed is 1996, instead of 1997, and second year listed is 1995, instead of 1996.
Source: International Intellectual Property Alliance country reports (http://www.iipa.com/countryreports.html).

entertainment software next. One reason for this finding is that software is frequently copied illegally onto the hard disks of personal computers, making it difficult to locate retail sources. In contrast, music recordings and motion pictures have lower copying rates. Third, copying rates in general have declined from 1996 to 1997, reflecting stronger enforcement efforts in many nations—though there were also many increases estimated, pointing out the difficulty of securing copyright compliance. It is likely that the economic troubles in Asia will raise these rates sharply over the next few years.

These high copying rates suggest that there are significant amounts of labor employed in copying and retailing illegitimate products.[8] As enforcement expands, this labor must find alternative employment, meaning that the initial short-run cost of stronger IPRs is labor displacement. Clearly, the associated adjustment costs are minimized in economies that have flexible labor markets and rapid economic growth, making it easier to shift workers and firms into legitimate activities.

Evidence suggests that, because copying is typically done in footloose firms with limited capital requirements, the associated adjustment costs are relatively slight in most circumstances (Maskus 1997; Primo Braga 1996). Indeed, it often happens that former unauthorized factories are licensed to produce by copyright holders because of their expertise.[9] Nonetheless, many displaced entrepreneurs suffer painful losses in profits in the short term, making them powerful political interests against reform.

Monopoly Pricing   The most frequently expressed fear about IPRs is that they create strong market positions, from which firms can raise prices to monopolistic levels. The concern is strongest in developing countries, because applications for IPRs come overwhelmingly from foreign firms, meaning that the associated profits are transferred abroad. This transfer represents a loss in the technology-importing countries' terms of trade, ultimately slowing growth there.

This concern is expressed often regarding introduction of patents for pharmaceutical products. There is evidence that patents support considerably higher prices for protected drugs than for copied and generic drugs (Lanjouw 1998; Watal 1996). However, the extent of these price increases depends on the competitive aspects of markets. The more competitive the local drugs market is before patents are awarded, the larger the share of drug production that consists of copies of patentable drugs will be. Also, the more inelastic demand for medicines is, the higher the price increases caused by patents will be. These conditions suggest that poor countries with extensive drug imitation, including China and India, could experience marked price increases for protected drugs. This prediction is consistent with evidence on recent price trends in uncontrolled pharmacies in China. In this regard, a policy of public procurement at negotiated, controlled prices is sensible for the purposes of providing public health services. It also suggests that imitative drugs firms will come under considerable competitive pressure unless they arrange licenses and technology-transfer agreements with major international pharmaceutical firms.

Another area of concern is computer software. It is often claimed that software would be much more expensive if copyrights were enforced, because the current prices of legitimate copies in developing nations are very high in relation to prices of unauthorized copies. However, software producers prefer to sell in poor countries with high piracy rates at low volumes and significant markups, reflecting small markets with inelastic demand, such as corporate, banking, and government users. For example, Microsoft Office currently sells for RMB 8,000 (approximately US$1,000) in Beijing. Therefore, as markets develop under copyright enforcement, foreign and domestic firms will supply more legitimate copies at considerably lower prices, suggesting that ultimate price increases could be modest.[10]

In sum, there are legitimate causes for concern about monopolization supported by IPRs. However, competitive market realities and well-designed social regulation can mitigate these effects without unduly reducing innovative incentives. Most importantly, IPRs need to be introduced into markets in which other competitive processes, such as firm entry, labor flexibility, distribution systems, and international trade, are strong. It makes little economic sense to protect market positions with both strong IPRs (which raise innovation and growth) and competitive barriers (which reduce them).

Higher Imitation Costs   One essential point of IPRs is to raise the costs of copying and imitating products and technologies in order to safeguard investment returns to creators. Thus, learning technological knowledge through simple imitation becomes more difficult. If simple imitation is the primary source of knowledge diffusion, the result of stronger IPRs could be lower growth.

There is much anecdotal evidence in all countries that firms lose technologies to potential rivals through the defection of technical personnel, misappropriation by input suppliers, copying of blueprints, and the like. In the absence of trade secret protection, these activities are common and help establish competition. However, the practical effects are that firms transfer and use older technologies that they are unafraid to lose, engage in less technical training of workers, take steps to conceal aspects of their technologies from subcontractors and suppliers, and choose not to establish R&D facilities. We have heard these comments frequently from foreign enterprise managers in China, and they affect Chinese enterprises as well.

Thus, there is a balancing act for countries to manage. Stronger IPRs make uncompensated imitation more difficult but improve the quality of technology flows. Countries that wish to become leading technology developers should favor IPRs for that reason.

IPR Abuses   That strong IPRs may be abused by the firms that own them is clear from litigation problems in the United States, the European Union, and elsewhere. Such abuses include bad-faith lawsuits, hidden ownership of intellectual property, restrictive patent-pooling agreements that reduce product competition, refusals to license technologies, tie-in sales to establish dominance in related markets, and insistence on exclusive rights to competing technologies. Thus, it is important for policymakers to develop mechanisms for ensuring the maintenance of competition in markets affected by IPRs.

Overall Effects of IPRs on Growth

Our discussion suggests that strong IPRs could raise or lower economic growth, depending on the circumstances. Thus, the issue is really an empirical one. Fortunately, two recent studies have considered the question carefully in econometric terms. Both find that IPRs generate stronger growth, though they identify different channels by which IPRs do so.

The first study related economic growth rates across many countries to a simple index of patent strength and other variables (Gould and Gruben 1996). The authors found no strong direct effects of patents on growth. But there was a significantly positive effect when the index was interacted with a measure of openness to trade. In particular, the effect of strengthening the patent regime in open economies was to raise growth rates by 0.6 percent on average. Therefore, trade liberalization in combination with stronger IPRs enhances growth, because it improves the competitive nature of markets and increases access to foreign technologies.

The second study performed a similar test but focused on how IPRs affect investment in capital and R&D as well as economic growth (Park and Ginarte 1997). Again, the authors found no direct correlation between patent strength and growth, but patents had a powerful and positive effect on physical investment and R&D spending, which in turn increase economic growth.

Thus, our general analysis supports three major conclusions. First, the relationships between IPRs and economic development are complex, but the evidence supports a positive relationship that operates in both directions. Second, the effectiveness of IPRs in expanding growth and technology development depends heavily on economic circumstances. Policymakers can maximize these effects by promoting an active technology infrastructure, which includes building human capital and skills, developing an innovation system that helps move technologies from laboratories to the market, and establishing a transparent set of IPRs. Other important complementary factors include further structural reform to increase entrepreneurship and flexibility of enterprises; expanded liberalization of restrictions on trade, investment, and technology agreements; and additional steps to ensure competition in domestic markets among firms and across regions. Third, there remains a role for restricting IPRs in achieving social goals—such as limiting the costs of public health care and ensuring an adequate balance of benefits in international technology contracts—but the controls adopted should not unduly limit competitive incentives.

III. The IPR Situation in China

Our analysis of the current situation regarding the use and adequacy of IPRs follows in three parts. First, we discuss the results of interviews conducted in 1997 and 1998 with public officials and university scholars and of an informal survey of enterprise managers. The evidence presented is anecdotal and unsystematic, though it paints a fairly consistent picture. Second, we consider recent patent and trademark statistics in China, looking at trends in their use by domestic and foreign enterprises, broken down by major region of the country. These numbers suggest clearly that the use of formal IPRs is growing rapidly but that there are significant regional disparities associated with differences in regional income levels. Third, we look at some recent data on technology development and inputs, along with some estimated effects on Chinese industrial productivity. Overall, our analysis suggests that the IPR situation for invention and innovation is improving in China but that there are still significant problems associated with inadequate enforcement, regional income differences, insufficient incentives for commercialization of the results of R&D, and relatively low levels of research effort.

Discussion of Interview Findings

Interviews were conducted in Hong Kong (China), Taipei, Shanghai, and Beijing in December 1997 and again in Shanghai and Beijing in July 1998. In Shanghai and Beijing, there were 36 interviews: managers of 14 enterprises, officials of 11 public agencies in the IPR area, scholars from 4 universities, and officials from 7 other organizations, including private associations and law firms. In Taipei and Hong Kong (China), there were 11 interviews: officials from 6 public agencies and 5 other organizations, including enterprises and law firms. In addition, numerous interviews were conducted with respondents familiar with local conditions in Guangdong, Fujian, Jiangsu, Sichuan, and Zhejiang provinces. We uphold confidentiality promises and do not reveal any identifying characteristics of interviewees.

Views of Enterprise Managers   We talked to management officials and intellectual property managers of enterprises from several industries: information technology and software, chemicals and pharmaceuticals, biotechnology and plant genetics, machinery, metals, and consumer goods. The enterprises also represented a mix of state-owned enterprises (SOEs), privately organized Chinese enterprises, joint ventures with international firms, and majority-owned subsidiaries of international firms. Nearly all of these enterprises are engaged in high-technology activities and undertake significant R&D programs, at least in their home countries, if not in China as well. Therefore, these enterprises are not representative of the bulk of Chinese industry at this time; rather, they are in the vanguard of technical change. Accordingly, their managers tend to feel strongly about IPRs and develop defensive strategies to overcome associated problems.

Virtually all enterprise managers believe that the legal structure for IPRs in China is adequate and improving. However, more than half think the overall environment is still weak, and the others find it to be weak but improving. Chinese enterprises tend to view the system as improving more rapidly than do the foreign-owned enterprises and joint ventures.[11]

Three general problems are identified that support the view of weak protection. Overwhelmingly the major problem is inadequate enforcement of trademarks, patents, and copyrights. Enforcement problems are well understood but bear repeating briefly here. There can be lengthy delays in achieving enforcement actions and court rulings. Monetary penalties are small even in cases of significant infringement, and there is a reluctance to impose criminal sanctions for willful and ongoing violations. Limited compensation to victims of infringement and arbitrary and nontransparent enforcement actions (especially at the local level) make enterprises reluctant to proceed. Local authorities may be unfamiliar with the laws. The central government and certain regional and municipal governments are taking a number of steps to reduce these problems, including instituting stronger fines and penalties. For example, in 1997 the criminal law was amended to include some IPR-related violations, placing such matters under the jurisdiction of the Public Security Bureau.

There are several structural sources of weak enforcement, which ultimately must be addressed. First, trademark infringement and illegal copying are profitable activities, which face little opposition in the rural and inland regions owing to low incomes and limited technological capabilities. Indeed, significant regional income disparities present perhaps the greatest structural problem for long-term reform. Second, public awareness of the need to respect intellectual property remains limited. For example, there is little reluctance on the part of poor consumers to buy counterfeit goods, according to survey results mentioned by one interviewee.[12] Furthermore, enterprises engaged in infringement often are significant employers and sources of revenue for local governments, making authorities reluctant to take infringement actions against them. Fourth, low salaries for public officials may reduce officials' effectiveness. Fifth, there remains a considerable scarcity of legal and technical expertise for administrative and judicial work, despite the establishment of special training programs in intellectual property.

Among these problems, so-called regional protectionism in IPRs is regarded as the most difficult to confront by enterprises that suffer infringement. For example, the system suffers from insufficient coordination among regional bureaus of the Administration for Industry and Commerce (AIC). Because each AIC bureau registers trademarks separately, a particular mark may be claimed by competing (and potentially fraudulent) users in different territories. If a trademark is registered nationally, it is supposed to be legally binding, but complaints persist about local protectionism superseding this requirement in practice. Further, the administrative oversight of the regional AIC bureaus is seen to be weak and underdeveloped. This is a result of the decentralized nature of IPR enforcement bureaucracies.

Decentralization permits the power of a municipal government over the municipal AIC bureau to supersede that of the provincial or even the state AIC bureau in the jurisdiction. For many reasons, municipal government officials may have higher policy priorities than IPR enforcement, and some of those priorities may be at odds with safeguarding intellectual property.

Structural problems in enforcement and attitudes lead to at least one distortion in IPR use. Given the structure of the legal and administrative systems in China, many foreign companies find it difficult to pursue patent violation claims. Rather, these companies prefer to take action against patent infringement through trademark enforcement. One person involved in enforcement claimed that although 90 percent of his investigations involve trademark allegations and 10 percent involve patents, up to 60 percent of these cases could be patent violations.[13] However, enforcement is easier if the case is pursued as a trademark violation. One reason for this bias seems to be that, to date, Chinese authorities have been reluctant to entertain patent cases, evidently in the belief that patent infringement embodies technology transfer and helps meet national technology development goals.

It is interesting that managers of foreign enterprises and associations take a more pessimistic view than do managers of Chinese enterprises. The former group tends to see the enforcement situation as worsening or not improving, whereas the latter group sees more improvement. In part, this is an issue of perception; foreign enterprise managers are accustomed to strong enforcement in their home markets. It also stems from sectoral differences among the enterprises represented. Businesses in information technology and software, while still plagued with considerable copying and trademark infringement, detect noticeable improvement in the copyright area. And many new and high-technology Chinese enterprises appreciate the improving climate, which allows them some scope for defending their intellectual property.

A second general problem is that some aspects of Chinese IPR law and practice may favor domestic interests over foreign interests, particularly in administration and enforcement. The most frequent complaint is that all 42 well-known trademarks registered to date are for domestic enterprise names and none are for foreign firms. If China were currently a member of the WTO, this practice could well constitute a violation of national treatment obligations. Other complaints relate to structural problems in legal representation for foreign enterprises and perceived arbitrariness in enforcement actions. It should be noted that Chinese copyright law in some cases actually provides preferential treatment for foreign copyright holders over domestic ones.

The final general complaint on the part of foreign enterprises is that regulations for approval or inspection of technology contracts and investment agreements remain intrusive and costly to comply with. According to one interviewee, this is mainly a "nuisance factor" that delays effective technology transactions and raises negotiation costs but does not significantly deter deals that enterprises find worthwhile for other reasons. However, strong concerns exist about technical secrets (in the form of blueprints and designs) being lost to potential rivals after they are revealed to public design research institutes.

Views of Agency Officials and University Scholars   Officials of public bureaucracies in China share many of the concerns related above but point justifiably to the considerable strengthening of IPR laws as an indicator of progress. Central government officials are committed to improving administration and enforcement as well, despite the structural and regional problems. However, administrative IPR operations are funded insufficiently, and there is not enough technical and judicial expertise in the area.

Public officials are more likely than enterprise managers to raise concerns about the effects of stronger IPRs on prices and competition. For example, in two interviews it was claimed that the recent introduction of pharmaceutical registration and patents has been followed by massive increases in prices of protected drugs on uncontrolled markets. There is also reluctance to liberalize conditions that govern technology-transfer agreements. Some officials also recognize that stronger IPRs should be accompanied by other policy measures to build technological capacities and maintain competition, but this recognition has not resulted in many policy initiatives.

University scholarship in China (and in other countries) in IPRs is overwhelmingly addressed to legal issues. Many scholars are actively involved in assessing shortcomings in the law and in drafting revisions, and they also participate in training new intellectual property lawyers. Few economists study the processes of technical change in China and how they are affected by market structure, competition, and exposure to foreign technologies and investment. Fewer still examine the relationship between IPRs, technical development, and growth. Accordingly, economists in China either remain unaware of IPR issues or are skeptical about the potential for IPRs to increase technological advance and business development.

Effects of Weak Protection   Although the evidence is anecdotal, it seems clear that weak enforcement of IPRs results in widespread infringement that stunts domestic business development. The primary problem is that trademark violations have a profoundly negative impact on innovative Chinese enterprises. Trademarks are really the "front line" of IPRs, because companies that develop copyrighted and patented products market and license them under trademark protection. Many examples were cited of the problems facing Chinese producers of their own brands of consumer goods, such as soft drinks, processed foods, tobacco products, and clothing. It seems that as soon as some brand recognition is established, which requires costly investments in various forms of marketing, enterprises find their trademarks frequently applied to unauthorized products in the same product category or in others altogether. Such goods tend to be of lower quality, damaging the original enterprise's reputation. Negative reputations are extremely costly to overcome. In such cases, enterprises had to shut down, give up on their trademarks and become licensees of better-known enterprises, or undertake extensive private and public enforcement actions. It is impossible to know how much this problem deters the development of new products and enterprises, but the impact is probably significant. Moreover, it effectively prevents interregional marketing that would support economies of scale.

From our interviews, it appears that many Chinese firms are harmed by IPR violations. Enterprises that sell electronics products seemed particularly vulnerable. In consumer goods, such large targets as Hongtashan cigarettes and Maotai liquor experience much counterfeiting, as do many smaller Chinese companies. Counterfeiting of medicines is also widespread, unfortunately. Licensing activities are also a problem. In the mid-1980s, one well-known office supply company with a strong reputation for quality licensed its trademark to a number of factories in neighboring provinces. A decade later, it ended its contacts with these factories. However, both the former licensees and former employees with their own factories now produce inferior versions of the licensed products under the original trademark.

Trademark counterfeiting is particularly acute in sectors that entail low initial capital requirements, allow relatively easy transfer of products and manufacturing facilities among locations, and generate potentially high consumer recognition. Consider the following instructive example from the apparel sector, reported in one interview.

Regarding counterfeit shirts bearing a well-known British brand name, pirates buy the shirts and sell them to peasants, who sew infringing logos onto the shirts in their own homes. There is tremendous incentive for peasants to do this work because in many cases they are workers in factories in Guangdong who get paid once a year. The supplemental income of RMB 400 for sewing the infringing logo, earned upon sale of the shirts to final assemblers, almost doubles their salary. It is virtually impossible to go after these shirts because the factory that produces the shirts is legitimate and because the law forbids raids on people's homes, where the sewing of the counterfeit logo takes place. The manufacturing process is diffused as follows. The shirt is made legitimately in Chaoyang, using buttons made outside Shenzen. The counterfeit logos are sewn on the shirts in Shantou.

The counterfeit labels and boxes are made in southern Zhejiang. The remaining assembly is done in a warehouse either within or just outside Shanghai right before it goes to the retail marketplace in counterfeit goods.

This story is not uncommon. It illustrates both the difficulty of effective enforcement and the significant incentives to counterfeit stemming from poverty. In the short run, such activity is a source of income and local profits. In the long run, it discourages the development of Chinese brands and competition.

Because such infringement is concentrated initially on products with low capital requirements and high labor intensity, products in which China has strong advantages, it tends to reduce incentives for legitimate business development in those industries. However, trademarked products that are custom made or that require extensive after-sales support and communication with designers and engineers at the home office are difficult to copy. These products include items such as customized computer platforms, industrial transformers, elevators, and customized automobile parts—product areas in which foreign enterprises tend to be stronger. It is for this reason that trademark violation is particularly damaging to enterprise development in poor countries.

The discussion so far has focused on trademarks, but inadequate enforcement also results in difficulties with patents and trade secrets. Patent infringement through copying seems to be most common in utility models, which are easy to copy but are overwhelmingly owned by Chinese enterprises. Several foreign enterprises also reported problems with losing patented technologies through unfair means, such as former employees selling protected design specifications and technical manuals or starting a competing business using know-how gained from learning patented processes. According to one industry association, these cases are growing worse and are causing foreign companies to consider carefully their commitment to using technology in the Chinese economy.

Defection of technical and managerial employees was mentioned as a key problem by Chinese enterprises as well. From a policy standpoint, there is a fine line between promoting interfirm mobility of skilled labor, which is procompetitive, and discouraging uncompensated loss of technology through that channel, which is anticompetitive. Both foreign and domestic companies try to cope with the problem through temporary antidisclosure clauses in contracts with key personnel, but these contracts are difficult to enforce in China.

Most respondents agreed that the environment for copyrights is improving in China, although unauthorized copying or use of business software, games, video compact discs (VCDs), and music remains common. Even though illegal production has been reduced markedly by anticounterfeiting campaigns, the production evidently has shifted to Macao and Hong Kong (China) for shipment back to the mainland. Thus, consumption has not fallen much.

Although prominent western firms such as Microsoft, Disney, and Time-Warner claim considerable damages from such copying, it is likely that greater losses are suffered by Chinese entertainment and publishing interests. According to many interviews, the Chinese software industry is growing rapidly, largely because of a substantial base of skilled software engineers and managers. But these firms turn their efforts toward small-scale programs that attract less copying, such as those in business applications or limited-run games. With few exceptions, this strategy will prevent the establishment of Chinese-developed software standards and networking software that provide significant spillover benefits to the economy. On the entertainment side, the Chinese music and film industries are also vibrant, because of an ample supply of creative talent. However, their efforts are also stunted by illegal copying. Moreover, the prevalence of copying promotes the production of low-quality films, limiting China's entry into export markets.

There are significant differences between Chinese and foreign businesses in their abilities to deal with trademark and other IPR-related violations. First, foreign companies have more resources to combat infringement than domestic enterprises have. A private enforcement action costing RMB 16,000 to RMB 21,000 may not be expensive from their standpoint, but it is a significant expense for small or medium-size Chinese operations. Again, therefore, prevailing enforcement difficulties, which push firms toward private solutions, are biased against Chinese business development. Second, foreign companies, particularly western ones, are more inclined to seek legal solutions to IPR problems.

A third and perhaps the most significant difference is that foreign companies always have more choices about business activities in China. At the extreme, they can choose to pull out of the country, and cases were cited of such decisions. Less extreme options are available as defensive strategies against weak IPRs. Managers of most foreign enterprises indicated an extreme reluctance to locate R&D facilities in China. Nearly all indicated that they transfer technologies that are at least five years behind global standards (unless there are other mechanisms for protecting them) in the expectation that those technologies will be lost to local competition, or they bring in technologies that will be obsolete within a specific time period. That lagging technologies are transferred is not necessarily bad for China. These technologies may be more appropriate for local cost conditions and also can serve as springboards for follow-on invention. But as China approaches the technological frontier in several industries, the problem will become more restraining.

Foreign enterprise managers are growing more reluctant to license technologies, preferring instead to move toward joint ventures and even more toward majority-owned subsidiaries in which they can exercise greater control of proprietary secrets. Enterprises are unlikely to integrate their Chinese operations fully, splitting various production processes among facilities so as not to reveal underlying technologies.

There are other defensive measures available to both Chinese and foreign companies to deal with IPR problems. One is to sell only to established customers that need assured quality, such as hospitals, large enterprises, and public agencies. This restriction serves as a barrier to entry of small firms that need the associated products or inputs. A second is to establish strict vertical supply and distribution chains to permit monitoring of quality. Restrictions against market network ownership in China severely limit this possibility and reduce incentives to expand. A third is to use costly technical safeguards, such as software locks and source code that must be decoded to operate software upgrades.[14]

It is impossible to know how much these distortions associated with weak IPRs contribute to economic inefficiency in China, though we suspect the effects are significant. If so, over time stronger IPRs will generate important static and dynamic allocative efficiencies.

Patent and Trademark Activity in China

Despite these problems, the data on patent and trademark use indicate clearly that both foreign and domestic enterprises are applying for more protection. Table 12.2 presents figures on applications for all three types of patents from 1990 to 2000.[15] While domestic enterprises nearly doubled their applications for invention patents between 1990 and 1996, these applications mushroomed in the late 1990s, reaching more than 25,000 by the end of the period. Domestic applications grew

TABLE 12.2   Patent Applications by Type and Nationality, 1990–2000

	Invention patents		Utility models		Design patents		Total patents	
	Domestic	Foreign	Domestic	Foreign	Domestic	Foreign	Domestic	Foreign
1990	5,832	4,305	27,488	127	3,265	452	36,585	4,884
1993	12,084	7,534	47,252	247	8,817	1,342	68,153	9,123
1996	11,471	17,046	49,341	263	21,395	3,219	82,207	20,528
1999	15,596	21,098	57,214	278	37,148	2,905	109,958	24,281
2000	25,346	26,401	68,461	354	46,532	3,588	140,339	30,343
Growth (%) 1990–2000	335	513	149	179	1325	694	284	521

Source: SIPO 1996, 2000; authors' calculations.

by 335 percent over the 1990s, while foreign (nonresident) applications rose by a factor of more than five.[16] The rapid expansion of patent applications for foreign inventions reflects the relatively greater technological content of foreign patents. It is interesting that by 1996 foreign applications were far larger than domestic applications in this category, but by 2000 domestic applications had caught up. In contrast, applications for utility models and design patents, both of which also rose considerably in the 1990s, overwhelmingly are filed by Chinese organizations. The increase in domestic applications for design patents was especially marked. Thus, these rewards for small-scale invention seem to be having their desired effect.

Table 12.3 shows data for patent grants and the aggregate ratio of grants to applications in 2000. Grants to foreign applicants rose by 142 percent, while the number of domestic grants increased by a factor of four. The aggregate grants ratios for invention patents are surprisingly low, perhaps reflecting long examination delays. It is interesting that by 2000 the grants ratios for domestic and foreign applicants were essentially the same. Grant rates are much higher in utility models and design patents, which are easier to examine and carry shorter protection periods. Note the interesting fact that the aggregate grants ratio is higher for foreign applications in all categories but is much lower in terms of total patents. This disparity arises from the huge difference in the number of utility models and design patents that favor China. The expense of such applications is typically not worth undertaking for foreign firms.

TABLE 12.3 Patent Grants by Type and Nationality, 1990–2000

	Invention patents		Utility models		Design patents		Total patents	
	Domestic	Foreign	Domestic	Foreign	Domestic	Foreign	Domestic	Foreign
1990	1,149	2,689	16,744	208	1,411	387	19,304	3,284
1993	2,634	3,922	46,403	236	7,845	1,087	56,882	5,245
1996	1,383	1,593	26,961	210	11,381	2,252	39,725	4,055
1999	3,097	4,540	56,094	274	32,910	3,241	92,101	8,055
2000	6,177	6,506	54,407	336	34,652	3,267	95,236	10,109
Growth (%) 1990–2000	438	142	225	62	23,558	744	393	208
Grants ratio for 2000 (percent)	24.4	24.6	79.5	94.9	74.5	91.1	67.9	33.2

Source: SIPO 1996, 2000; authors' calculations.

**TABLE 12.4 Patenting Indicators for Top 11 Patenting
Regions, 1985–96**

Region	Applications 1985–96	Applications 2000 (rank)	2000 GDP per capita, yuan (rank)	2000 Applications per million people (rank)	2000 Applications per million yuan of GDP (rank)
Beijing	54,348	10,334 (3)	17,936 (2)	3,933 (1)	2,193 (1)
Guangdong	42,159	21,123 (1)	11,181 (6)	488 (5)	436 (7)
Liaoning	38,768	7,151 (7)	11,017 (7)	915 (3)	830 (2)
Shandong	37,082	10,019 (5)	9,409 (8)	408 (8)	434 (8)
Jiangsu	34,983	8,211 (6)	11,539 (4)	470 (6)	408 (9)
Zhejiang	29,197	10,316 (4)	12,907 (3)	624 (4)	484 (5)
Sichuan	27,046	4,496 (8)	4,815 (11)	325 (9)	674 (4)
Hunan	26,400	4,117 (10)	5,733 (10)	410 (7)	715 (3)
Shanghai	21,758	11,337 (2)	27,188 (1)	1,300 (2)	478 (6)
Hebei	20,584	3,848 (11)	7,546(9)	305 (11)	404 (10)
Fujian	11,027	4,211 (9)	11,294 (5)	318 (10)	281 (11)
Correlation with GDP per capita				0.54	0.24

Sources: SIPO, 1996 and 2000; SSBC 1997 and 2001; authors' calculations.

Table 12.4 provides a breakdown of total domestic patent applications for the top 11 patenting regions in China for 1985–96 and 2000. The second column ranks the regions in terms of absolute numbers of patent applications in 2000. Residents of Guangdong applied for more than 21,000 patents, while people in Hebei applied for only 3,848. Better measures of inventive capacity are given in the final two columns as applications per million people and applications per million yuan of regional GDP. In these rankings, Beijing is at the top of the list, with far more applications per capita and per unit of output than any other province. This reflects both Beijing's status as a technology developer and the fact that patent registrations may come through legal offices that are located in the capital. Shanghai has the second-highest number of applications per person but ranks sixth in applications per yuan of GDP. Fujian and Hebei rank low in both categories.

The middle column ranks these regions in terms of average income per capita. The regional disparities in income levels are large, ranging from Sichuan at the bottom to Shanghai at the top. The difference between them is a factor of 5.6, which is extraordinarily high for regions within a country. It reflects the rapid growth in coastal areas relative to inland areas that characterizes China's economic transition.

It is interesting to correlate per capita GDP with the relative patent application figures. We find that there is a strong positive correlation (0.54) between GDP per capita and patent applications per million people. Thus, richer provinces apply for more patents (meaning they develop more products) per person than poor provinces. However, the correlation between GDP per capita and applications per million yuan of GDP is lower (0.24). For example, Shanghai applies for many patents per unit of population owing to its high income level and large skill base. But, in turn, the high number of patents is to some degree a stimulus to economic growth in Shanghai, meaning it has a higher GDP. Thus, from these data it seems that high incomes produce innovations, which in turn raise regional economic growth. It is an interesting question why these growth rates do not spread out across the regions, a question that must await further research.

Tables 12.5 and 12.6 present similar data for trademarks.[17] Trademark applications and registrations have risen quite rapidly, especially those through the Madrid Protocol since 1994. There are far more domestic trademarks than foreign ones, as expected, but foreign applications (directly from abroad and through Madrid Protocol) have risen more rapidly. In table 12.6, we see that Guangdong had the largest absolute number of applications in 1996, followed by Zhejiang and Jiangsu. Scaled by population, however, Shanghai ranks first by a significant margin, followed by Beijing, Zhejiang, and Guangdong. There is a very high correlation (0.81) between per capita GDP and per capita applications, reflecting again that trademark applications rise with income levels. And the correlation with relative output is lower (0.48), suggesting the positive effect of trademarks on development.

TABLE 12.5   Trademark Applications and Registrations

	Applications				Registrations in force			
	Domestic	Foreign	Madrid	Total	Domestic	Foreign	Madrid	Total
1990	50,853	6,419	n.a.	57,272	237,300	42,097	n.a.	279,397
1991	59,124	8,480	n.a.	67,604	271,056	47,859	2,306	321,221
1992	79,837	10,958	2,591	93,386	312,972	53,230	3,486	369,688
1993	107,758	21,014	3,551	132,323	351,695	59,466	5,528	416,689
1994	117,186	20,238	5,193	142,617	398,649	70,216	8,544	477,409
1995	144,610	21,442	6,094	172,146	429,287	76,596	27,896	533,779
1996	122,057	22,615	7,132	151,804	517,167	91,693	39,247	648,107
Total	681,425	111,166	24,561	817,152	2,518,126	441,157	87,007	3,046,290
Growth (%) 1990– 1996	140.00	252.30	175.30	165.10	117.90	117.80	1,602.00	132.00

n.a. = not available.

Source: Trademark Office, SAIC 1996; authors' calculations.

TABLE 12.6   Trademarking Indicators for Top 10 Trademarking Regions, 1996

Region	Applications	1996 GDP per capita, yuan (rank)	1996 Applications per million people (rank)	1996 Applications per million yuan of GDP (rank)
China total	151,804	5,605	124.1	221.3
Guangdong	23,483	9,367 (4)	337.4 (3)	360.2 (2)
Zhejiang	14,516	9,553 (3)	334.5 (4)	350.1 (3)
Jiangsu	10,822	8,445 (5)	152.2 (6)	180.2 (6)
Beijing	8,184	12,823 (2)	649.5 (1)	506.5 (1)
Shanghai	7,218	20,438 (1)	508.3 (2)	248.7 (4)
Shandong	7,139	6,820 (8)	81.7 (8)	119.8 (10)
Sichuan	6,235	3,688 (10)	54.5 (10)	147.9 (7)
Fujian	5,049	7,997 (6)	154.9 (5)	193.7 (5)
Hebei	4,315	5,329 (9)	66.6 (9)	124.9 (8)
Liaoning	3,838	7,664 (7)	93.2 (7)	121.5 (9)
Correlation with GDP per capita			0.81	0.48

Sources: Trademark Office, SAIC 1996, and SSBC 1997; authors' calculations.

It is difficult to sort out why the use of patents and trademarks is rising rapidly in China.[18] One reason is that the laws have improved and application fees are lower, inviting more applications. A second is that, as trademark and patent infringement increase, both domestic and foreign enterprises recognize the importance of establishing intellectual property protection, even in an environment of weak but improving IPRs. A third is that Chinese markets are getting deeper as income grows, despite the substantial barriers to interregional integration. Registration of IPRs is important for exploiting deeper markets. The final reason is that Chinese research organizations and enterprises are engaged in more invention, and Chinese firms are undertaking more innovative activity.

Invention Characteristics in China

We briefly analyze indicators of Chinese technology development and relate them to IPRs. There are several recent and more thorough studies of Chinese innovative activity available.[19] More research into the relationships between IPRs and innovation in China is greatly needed.

There has been a substantial increase in China's expenditure on R&D in the 1990s, rising from RMB 12.5 billion in 1990 to RMB 33.2 billion in 1996. In real terms, this was an increase of 38 percent, or about 6.3 percent per year. However, this expenditure failed to keep up with rapid growth in output, and the share of

**TABLE 12.7   International Comparisons of Science
and Technology Indicators, Recent Years**

	Science and engineering in R&D per 10,000 of labor force	R&D as percentage of GDP	Research institutes	Share of R&D		
				Universities	Enterprises	Other
China	6.8	0.51	41	13	37	9
France	54.8	2.38	21	16	62	1
Germany	61.5	2.27	15	19	66	0
Japan	79.6	2.96	9	20	66	5
Korea, Rep. of	—	2.69	19	8	73	0
Singapore	—	1.12	15	22	63	0
United Kingdom	48.0	2.19	14	16	66	4
United States	74.3	2.45	10	15	71	4

— = not available.
Source: SSTC 1997.

R&D in GDP fell from 0.7 percent to 0.5 percent. The number of scientists and engineers engaged in R&D rose from 419,000 in 1993 to 559,000 in 1996, but the number per 10,000 people in the labor force fell from 6.9 to 6.8.[20] Thus, while absolute resources in R&D are rising, there has been little change in their relative allocation.

Table 12.7 presents some comparative international data. In these data, China is different from high-income economies in two ways. First, it devotes a far smaller share of its labor force and GDP to research. Second, a far smaller share of its R&D is performed by enterprises, with a much larger share undertaken in public research institutes. Thus, in the science and technology field, China has considerable structural transformation to accomplish in order to reach the R&D profiles and levels of technologically advanced countries.

A regional breakdown of 1995 technology data is given in table 12.8. The first part of the table shows expenditures for R&D projects. China in total spent RMB 28.6 billion, amounting to 0.5 percent of GDP. Beijing and Shanghai both spent approximately RMB 3.5 billion, which was 2.6 percent of GDP in Beijing and 1.4 percent of GDP in Shanghai, the largest regional expenditure proportions. Sichuan and Liaoning came next at 0.6 percent, still higher than the Chinese average. Beijing and Shanghai also have by far the largest proportions of their populations allocated to scientists and engineers engaged in R&D. There is a strong positive correlation

TABLE 12.8 Science and Technology Indicators by Region, 1995

Location	R&D expenditure (%)					Scientists and engineers		Patent grants		Invention	
	Total (RMB billion)	Percent of GDP	Research Institutes	Universities	Enterprises	Number (10,000s)	Percent of population	Total	Per RMB billion R&D	Number	Per RMB billion R&D
Total	28.59	0.5	49	5	46	130.08	0.11	41,248	1,442.7	1,471	51.5
Beijing	3.56	2.6	85	6	9	13.27	1.05	4,025	1,130.6	328	92.1
Guangdong	1.59	0.3	47	3	50	5.00	0.07	4,611	2,900.1	56	35.2
Hebei	1.13	0.4	34	2	64	4.42	0.07	1,580	1,398.2	56	49.6
Hunan	0.78	0.4	60	5	35	4.37	0.07	1,515	1,942.3	51	65.3
Jiangsu	2.51	0.5	36	6	58	9.42	0.13	2,413	961.4	72	28.7
Liaoning	1.77	0.6	41	1	58	9.29	0.23	2,745	1,550.8	131	74.1
Shandong	1.59	0.3	33	3	64	6.98	0.08	2,861	1,799.4	84	52.8
Shanghai	3.46	1.4	43	5	52	9.72	0.68	1,436	415.1	72	20.8
Sichuan	2.01	0.6	51	4	45	9.79	0.09	2,019	1,004.4	79	39.3
Zhejiang	0.98	0.3	25	10	65	3.17	0.07	2,131	2,174.5	54	55.1
Correlation with GDP per capita (whole country)	0.59		0.12	0.27	−0.16		0.71		−0.22		
Correlation with GDP per capita (excluding Beijing)			−0.19	0.22	0.15						

Sources: SSTC 1996; SSBC 1997; Liu and White 1998; authors' calculations.

between regional GDP per capita and percentage of GDP spent on R&D (0.59) and between regional GDP per capita and percentage of population in science and engineering (0.71). Clearly, technical skills are drawn to high-income areas, raising technological capabilities there and, in turn, raising local incomes further.

There are large regional differences in the shares of R&D performed by various organizations. In Beijing, 85 percent is performed in state research institutes, 6 percent in universities, and only 9 percent in firms. Research in Zhejiang is organized quite differently, with 25 percent in research institutes, 10 percent in universities, and 65 percent in enterprises. Perhaps surprisingly, Shanghai's proportions are not much different from the national averages. Those regions with the highest proportions of R&D undertaken in enterprises are Zhejiang, Shandong, and Hebei.

It is interesting that the correlation between the R&D percentage conducted by enterprises and regional GDP per capita is slightly negative (−0.16). In fact, this result is due to Beijing's low enterprise share; excluding Beijing leaves a slightly positive correlation (0.15). Thus, there is not much evidence of a relationship between the enterprise share of research spending and regional income levels. One possible explanation is that SOEs conduct a higher percentage of R&D in poorer areas and smaller, more market-oriented enterprises conduct a higher percentage of R&D in richer areas. Thus, there would be no tendency for the enterprise share to rise with GDP levels (although enterprise R&D as a percentage of regional GDP would rise). Unfortunately, the data do not permit looking at R&D by enterprise type.

The last part of the table indicates total patent grants and invention patent grants per billion yuan of regional R&D expenditure. It is interesting that Guangdong received the greatest number of patents overall but a small number of invention patents, despite its low allocation of spending to R&D. Thus, Guangdong's innovative effort is focused heavily on small, incremental innovations that receive utility models and design patents. In contrast, Beijing received fewer patents overall but far more invention patents, with the highest receipt of invention patents per yuan of expenditure. Beijing's research is, therefore, more concentrated on fundamental invention, which is consistent with its high research expenditure in research institutes.

The results for Shanghai are intriguing. Despite a high percentage of R&D and of scientists and engineers, Shanghai ranked last in total patents and invention patents per yuan of R&D. To some extent, this reflects time lags in the granting procedure, which can take up to three years. Recall from table 12.4 that Shanghai currently has a high propensity to apply for patents, meaning that it will receive proportionately more grants in the future. However, these figures suggest that R&D in Shanghai has a low productivity in earning Chinese patent grants. It is conceivable that enterprises in Shanghai tend not to patent, attempting to keep their technical knowledge proprietary within the firm. An additional explanation is that there are diminishing returns to R&D as it rises in proportion to incomes, which would be consistent with the negative correlation coefficients between patent grants per billion yuan and regional income per capita.

Of interest here is what these figures might indicate about commercialization activities in Chinese regions. The data in table 12.8 suggest that, as incomes rise, the structure of R&D spending shifts slightly toward performing more in enterprises and less in research institutions (except in Beijing). This shift has not yet resulted in relatively more patent grants, indicating that both enterprises and research institutions develop patentable inventions and applications, with research institutes accounting for more of this activity at low income levels. However, there is a positive correlation between regional incomes and patent applications, as shown in table 12.4. To the extent that patent applications reflect product innovation and designs, enterprises are more productive at new product development and marketing in the higher-income areas. These findings suggest that both enterprises and research institutes apply for patents, but the products are more likely to be successfully brought to market if developed in richer areas.

It would be interesting to discover whether this process is more common among smaller private enterprises or among SOEs. If it is significantly less common among SOEs, there would be evidence of difficulties in bringing new products to market. In our interviews, we frequently were told that bringing new products to market is a critical problem for technology development in China. Research managers face inadequate incentives to convert the results of their inventive work into marketable products and services, because of unclear rights of ownership to technologies, insufficient links between SOEs and distribution networks, and a capital market that does not sufficiently finance private risk taking. There are reports of similar difficulties in commercializing technologies developed in universities and research institutes.

IPRs play an important and constructive role in overcoming these difficulties. They provide a clearly defined asset over which participants in the research process may bargain for ownership rights. They generate incentives for putting patentable technologies and products on the market under the protection of trademarks and trade secrets. And by raising the certainty of earning economic returns to invention and commercialization, they make these risk-taking activities more attractive to lenders, such as banks and venture capitalists. In turn, financial markets must be sufficiently deep and flexible to be able to allocate lending resources this way. There is an important complementarity between IPRs and financing for innovation.

Growth Effects of Foreign Technology in China

A limited amount of more systematic evidence is available at the industry level and can shed light on the growth effect of enhanced IPR protection. Two recent studies of Chinese productivity found that one of the most salient determinants of productivity change is the interaction between inflows of technology and domestic R&D input.[21] In the more comprehensive of these studies, several models of total factor productivity (TFP) growth are estimated. The model that best explains industry-level productivity is a relatively simple one, where the index of TFP growth is estimated as a function of the share of production in SOEs, FDI, and the interaction between domestic R&D expenditures and foreign technology-transfer contracts (R&D interaction)[22]:

$$\text{TFP Index} = 21.9 - 20.2 \times \text{SOEs} + 39.8 \times \text{FDI} + 8330 \times \text{R\&D interaction}$$
$$R^2 = 0.83 \qquad\qquad (12.1)$$

In this equation, the variable SOEs is the share of production in state-owned enterprises. The effect of the R&D–foreign technology flow interaction is very strong. Thus, foreign technology transfers have significantly positive effects on productivity in sectors that combine them with domestic R&D programs. Moreover, other evidence indicates that, in sectors that do not devote significant resources to R&D, foreign technology transfers do not benefit productivity. Similarly, in sectors that do not take advantage of foreign technology, R&D does not appear to benefit productivity. This outcome suggests that deep synergies exist between innovative efforts and inflows of foreign technology.

As described earlier in the context of developing countries, considerable effort is required to adapt and learn from existing technologies in order to take full advantage of their embodied knowledge. This effort is probably best manifested by R&D expenditures and personnel.[23] Survey evidence from Jiangsu province in the late 1980s indicates that the record of success for technology import projects has been highly uneven, and that the determining factor in project success has usually been the absorptive capacity of an enterprise (Ho 1997). These efforts can be enhanced by IPR protection for incremental innovations, such as utility patents, which further increase the incentives for firms to carry out useful adaptation.

In China, the predominance of SOEs in the import process appears to hinder productivity improvement, albeit in a paradoxical way. As illustrated in the equation above, SOEs are associated with lower productivity growth. Moreover, evidence suggests that the use of technology developed within SOEs does not appreciably raise productivity. However, because these enterprises are the primary importers of technology, they are an important mechanism for funding its acquisition. It is possible that technology imports by SOEs and perhaps also their R&D efforts spill over into productivity gains by nonstate firms in SOEs' own industries. With enhanced IPR protection, the financial benefits of these import and indigenization efforts could be partly realized by the SOE, perhaps through licensing.

From the standpoint of productivity enhancement, technology transfer through licensing is a more attractive option for technology acquisition than foreign investment, because of the higher level of disclosure involved. However, foreign providers of technology are undoubtedly hesitant to transfer their best technologies to outside firms, especially if IPR protection is inadequate. Thus, a dual strategy is preferable, taking advantage of the straightforward productivity-enhancing effects of FDI and the more complex and interactive effects of technology licensing. From either perspective, a stronger IPR system increases the level and quality of technology provided through both licensing and FDI, and, therefore, increases productivity.

A remaining question is the extent to which Chinese innovation (independent of foreign technology) affects productivity, and what effect enhanced IPR protection might have on it. Defining innovation is extremely difficult in the context of a developing country. Many forms of adaptation, absorption, and even creative imitation can be legitimate manifestations of innovation. In the study described above, virtually all of the measured effects of R&D on productivity could be attributed to R&D's interactive effects with foreign technology. The result is not surprising when considered in the light of a recent product innovation survey, which found that about 90 percent of the Chinese firms in the sample classified their innovations as unique only at the domestic or regional level—not the international level.[24]

More studies of IPRs and innovation are necessary, but some preliminary conclusions may be drawn from the evidence provided above. Although stronger IPR protection may make imitation more costly, real productivity benefits are likely to be realized through higher quality and levels of foreign technology inflows (ideally by transfer, but alternatively through direct investment). These inflows, in turn, are critical to the nourishment of domestic innovation efforts. Finding an appropriate IPR system that can attract foreign technology and simultaneously enhance and protect domestic incremental innovation is the key challenge.

IV. Conclusions and Recommendations

Our analysis of economic development and IPRs in China points to a number of tentative conclusions. In general, economic theory indicates that IPRs could either enhance or limit growth and development. Our review of the evidence supports a positive relationship, consistent with the microeconomic foundations of IPRs. In particular, IPRs are effective devices for handling particular market failures associated with cultural creation and invention and technology use. These market failures become more acute as economies grow, meaning that the need for effective patents, trademarks, trade secrets protection, and copyrights increases over time. China has made significant progress on the legislative end but continues to experience severe enforcement problems.

China is beginning a long process of increasing sophistication in technology use and technology development. Three critical problems face China in undertaking this technological transition. First, inadequate enforcement of IPRs limits incentives to develop products and brand names, especially on the part of small and medium-size enterprises. This problem limits the entry of new firms and the development of entrepreneurial skills. It also restricts the ability of enterprises to market nationally and to take advantage of economies of scale, and it deters significant investment in quality improvement and maintenance. In turn, this situation will make it increasingly difficult to break into export markets for high-quality and high-technology goods. China's access to top-quality international technologies will continue to be limited.

Second, even though Chinese enterprises and research organizations are engaging in more innovation, the country remains well behind global standards in allocating resources to R&D and science. Moreover, our interviews indicated that there are structural difficulties in commercializing the results of invention, and the data are somewhat consistent with this view. This situation points out the importance of continuing to develop a coherent technology innovation system. The state has important roles to play in promoting precompetitive research and removing disincentives to commercialization. China has made considerable progress toward these goals, with support programs in information technology, biotechnology, and other important areas, along with efforts to raise the flow of knowledge from institutes and universities to producing enterprises. Nonetheless, ambiguities remain about intellectual property ownership and the financial system is ill equipped to support risk taking. It will become increasingly difficult for the state to promote such activities as the economy develops along more entrepreneurial lines. This is another reason that continued strengthening of IPRs is an important component of the evolving innovation system.

Third, stronger IPRs alone are not sufficient to establish effective conditions for further technology development and growth. Rather, they must be embedded in a broader set of complementary initiatives that maximize the potential for IPRs to be dynamically procompetitive (see Maskus 1998a for a more detailed discussion). One such initiative is an active technology innovation system, as discussed earlier. Another is to strengthen the development of human capital through education in science, technology, and law and also to encourage the acquisition of skills through training in enterprises. Note that enterprises will be more willing to undertake such training under an improved IPR regime. These programs help Chinese enterprises raise their technological capabilities, which is critical for the adaptation of foreign technologies and innovation of new products. Such capabilities are enhanced if enterprise managers are empowered to act flexibly in cutting costs and improving organizational structures.

A third such initiative is to raise the degree of competition on domestic markets to promote innovation and ensure that stronger IPRs do not become a damaging source of market power. Additional enterprise reform and deregulation, substituting price signals and market incentives for centralized control, is important in this context. So is further liberalization of foreign trade and investment regulations. In terms of technology-transfer controls, the Chinese government asserts a legitimate right to ensure that China gains from the transfer and diffusion of technology. However, it is likely that foreign enterprises react to rigid transfer requirements, to arbitrary application of those requirements, and—especially—to weak protection of patents and trade secrets by markedly limiting both the amount and quality of technology transferred. Thus, a considered relaxation of those controls and a shift to a simple approval process could beneficially raise competition in China. In particular, it could assist pharmaceutical enterprises in establishing technology licenses with foreign firms as they come under great competitive pressure from stronger drug patents.

Finally, like other countries, China has the right to safeguard its interests in competition and social objectives through effective regulation of IPRs as those rights become stronger. Thus, the government should think through the appropriate form of pricing regulations in its drug procurement programs, as medicines receive stronger protection. More fundamentally, an opportunity arises for China to consider what form of competition regime it will implement as it shifts further toward the market. Currently, China tries to maintain competition through centralized regulation of market structure, ownership, and innovation, a system that will become increasingly incompatible with needs for technological change. Thus, a shift toward antimonopoly regulation of IPR abuses such as monopoly pricing, restrictive licensing arrangements, and refusals to deal is important. Such regulation needs to be well defined, nondiscriminatory, and professionally applied by the competition authorities and courts in order to be effective. This points again to the need for building legal expertise in IPRs over the long term.

Notes

1. For extensive reviews see Evenson and Westphal (1997), Maskus (1998b), and Primo Braga, Fink, and Sepulveda (1998).

2. Maskus (1997) describes this process in detail based on research in Lebanon. A version of that paper is included as chapter 11 in the current volume.

3. See Evenson and Westphal (1997). These distances depend on many factors, including geographical separation, factor endowments, domestic technical capabilities, and restrictions on technology trade.

4. UNCTAD (1996) presents estimates of such costs in several developing countries.

5. It is interesting that economists pay little attention to this issue, despite its political prominence. The reason is that straightforward piracy is inefficient (in that the resources could be better used elsewhere in the economy) but does not entail many economic subtleties. In contrast, dynamic issues of technology development make patents and trade secrets a more interesting subject of inquiry.

6. There are no comparable estimates of rates of product sales under trademark misappropriation, though such sales are clearly large and damaging to both foreign and domestic trademark holders. The difference is that there are far fewer major U.S. companies selling copyrighted goods, making it easier to organize them for reporting and lobbying purposes, than U.S. companies selling under trademarks (which would, of course, be all U.S. firms operating abroad).

7. Anonymous interview conducted by the authors in Beijing, July 1998.

8. Maskus (1997) details this situation in the case of Lebanon; the description is in chapter 11 of the current volume.

9. For example, according to an anonymous interview conducted by the authors in Hong Kong (China) in 1997, two major American entertainment companies have done this in China.

10. According to an anonymous interview conducted by one of the authors in Taiwan, (China) in 1997, prices of copyrighted goods have fallen sharply in Taiwan (China) since the aggressive crackdown on counterfeiting in the mid-1990s, in part because of additional competition from legitimate local developers.

11. This view is consistent with evidence from the *World Competitiveness Report*, published by the World Economic Forum. In 1995, managers of multinational enterprises ranked China 22nd of 26 developing economies in the strength of IPRs. However, China had the fourth largest rise in this index between 1994 and 1995, attesting to its improvement. See also Tackaberry (1998) for an extensive anecdotal discussion of enforcement problems.

12. However, in our field research, we are discovering that, although poor consumers are sensitive to large price margins in VCDs and software, they increasingly resent finding markets saturated by counterfeit consumer goods and foodstuffs, causing legitimate goods and fakes to sell for nearly the same prices.

13. We cannot verify the accuracy of these figures, but recent interviews with managers of joint ventures in Chongqing support the general point.

14. Revealingly, representatives of one major software firm indicated that China is the only market in which it operates where it requires a technical software lock.

15. The original version of this paper contained data from 1990 to 1996, but the figures were updated to 2000 at the request of a manuscript reviewer.

16. Readers who consult patent statistics from the World Intellectual Property Organization (WIPO) may note that those data indicate far greater numbers of foreign patent applications by the mid-1990s for China than those reported here, which come directly from China's Intellectual Property Office. The difference is that the WIPO data include applications through the Patent Cooperation Treaty, and WIPO's convention is to include any Patent Cooperation Treaty application as an application in all Patent Cooperation Treaty member states, including China, even if the applicant has no intention ultimately of acquiring protection in those states. Thus, by the mid-1990s, WIPO's patent applications data for foreigners, especially in developing countries, are greatly overstated and should not be used for analytical purposes.

17. Data were not readily available to update these figures to 2000.

18. It should be noted that such applications are rising rapidly in many other developing nations as well.

19. See Dougherty (1997); Gao and Fu (1996); Gao and Liu (1990); Jiang (1996); Liu and White (1997, 1998); Ma and Gao (1998). Some updates of this literature on technological change may be found in the chapters in Bhattasali, Li, and Martin (forthcoming).

20. See SSTC (1997).

21. Dougherty (1997) looks at the period from 1980 to 1995 for all enterprises at the township level and above, whereas Liu and White (1997) look at the period from 1989 to 1993 for large and medium-size enterprises.

22. These results are adapted from Dougherty (1997). The TFP Index is an ordinal ranking of industry performance, with a higher score reflecting higher TFP growth. FDI, R&D, and technology transfers are measured as a share of an industry's total investment.

23. Liu and White (1997) favor R&D personnel as their measure.

24. Ma and Gao (1998) describe the 1994–95 pilot survey.

References

Bhattasali, Deepak, Shantong Li, and William J. Martin, eds. 2004. *China and the WTO: Accession, Policy Reform, and Poverty Reduction Strategies* (Oxford, U.K.: Oxford University Press).

————. 2000. *Annual Report 2000*. Beijing.

Coe, David T., Elhanan Helpman, and Alexander W. Hoffmaister. 1997. "North-South R&D Spillovers." *The Economic Journal* 107: 134–49.

Contractor, Farok J. 1980. "The Profitability of Technology Licensing by U.S. Multinationals: A Framework for Analysis and an Empirical Study." *Journal of International Business Studies* 11: 40–63.

Dahab, Sonia. 1986. "Technological Change in the Brazilian Agricultural Implements Industry." Ph.D. dissertation, Yale University, New Haven, Conn. Processed.

Dougherty, Sean M., 1997, "The Role of Foreign Technology in Improving Chinese Productivity," MIT Science and Technology Initiative, Beijing. Processed.

Evenson, Robert E., and Larry E. Westphal. 1997. "Technological Change and Technology Strategy." In Jere Behrman and T.N. Srinivasan, editors, *Handbook of Development Economics: Volume 3*. Amsterdam: North-Holland.

Gao, Jian, and Fu Jiaji. 1996. "The Key Problems of Technological Innovation in Business Firms." *Science and Technology International* 1: 24–33.

Gao, Jian., and Liu Xielin. 1990. "The Regional Characteristics of Innovation in China." *China Science and Technology Forum* 1:42–45.

Gould, David M., and William C. Gruben. 1996. "The Role of Intellectual Property Rights in Economic Growth." *Journal of Development Economics* 48: 323–50.

Ho, Samuel. 1997. "Technology Transfer to China during the 1980s—How Effective? Some Evidence from Jiangsu." *Pacific Affairs* 70: 85–106.

Jiang, Liu 1996. "Technological Innovation in Business Strategy." *Science and Technology International* 1: 60–63.

La Croix, Sumner. 1992. "The Political Economy of Intellectual Property Rights in Developing Countries." In James A. Roumasset and Susan Barr, eds., *The Economics of Cooperation: East Asian Development and the Case for Pro-Market Intervention*. Boulder, Colo.: Westview Press.

La Croix, Sumner, and Denise Konan. 1998. "Intellectual Property Rights in China: American Pressure and Chinese Resistance." University of Hawaii. Processed.

Lanjouw, Jean O. 1998. "The Introduction of Pharmaceutical Product Patents in India: 'Heartless Exploitation of the Poor and Suffering'?" Working Paper 6366, National Bureau of Economic Research, Cambridge, MA.

Lee, Jeong-Yeon, and Edwin Mansfield. 1996. "Intellectual Property Protection and U.S. Foreign Direct Investment." *Review of Economics and Statistics* 28: 181–86.

Liu, Xielin, and Steven White. 1997. "The Relative Contributions of Foreign Technology and Domestic Inputs to Innovation in Chinese Manufacturing Industries." *Technovation* 17:119–25.

————. 1998. "An Exploration Into Regional Variation in Innovative Activity in China." *International Journal of Technology Management* 21: 114–129.

Ma, Chi, and Gao Chang Lin. 1998. "Technological Innovation in China's Manufacturing." State Science and Technology Commission, Beijing. Processed.

Mansfield, Edwin. 1985. "How Rapidly Does Industrial Technology Leak Out?" *Journal of Industrial Economics* 34:217–23.

————. 1995. "Intellectual Property Protection, Direct Investment, and Technology Transfer." Discussion Paper 27. International Finance Corporation, Washington, D.C.

Maskus, Keith E. 1997. "Intellectual Property Rights in Lebanon." International Trade Division, World Bank, Washington, D.C. Processed.

————. 1998a. "The International Regulation of Intellectual Property." *Weltwirtschaftliches Archiv* 134: 186–208.

————. 1998b. "The Role of Intellectual Property Rights in Promoting Foreign Direct Investment and Technology Transfer." *Duke Journal of Comparative and International Law* 9: 109–161.

Maskus, Keith E., and Christine McDaniel. 1999. "The Impacts of the Japanese Patent System on Post-War Productivity Growth." *Japan and the World Economy* 11: 557–574.

Maskus, Keith E., and Mohan Penubarti. 1995. "How Trade-Related Are Intellectual Property Rights?" *Journal of International Economics* 39: 227–48.

Mikkelsen, K. W. 1984. "Inventive Activity in Philippine Industry." Ph.D. dissertation. Yale University, New Haven, Conn. Processed.

Park, Walter G., and Carlos Ginarte. 1997. "Intellectual Property Rights and Economic Growth." *Contemporary Economic Policy* 15: 51–61.

Primo Braga, Carlos A. 1996. "Trade-Related Intellectual Property Issues: The Uruguay Round Agreement and Its Economic Implications." In Will Martin and L. Alan Winters, eds., *The Uruguay Round and Developing Countries*. Cambridge, U.K.: Cambridge University Press.

Primo Braga, Carlos A., Carsten Fink, and Claudia Paz Sepulveda. 1998. "Intellectual Property Rights and Economic Development." World Bank, Washington, D.C. Processed.

Rapp, Richard T., and Richard P. Rozek. 1990. "Benefits and Costs of Intellectual Property Protection in Developing Countries." *Journal of World Trade* 24: 75–102.

Ryan, Michael P. 1998. *Knowledge Diplomacy: Global Competition and the Politics of Intellectual Property.* Washington, D.C.: Brookings Institution.

Scotchmer, Suzanne. 1991. "Standing on the Shoulders of Giants: Cumulative Research and the Patent Law." *Journal of Economic Perspectives* 5(Winter): 29–42.

Sherwood, Robert M. 1990. *Intellectual Property Rights and Economic Development.* Boulder, Colo.: Westview Press.

Siebeck, Wolfgang E. 1990. *Strengthening Protection of Intellectual Property in Developing Countries: A Survey of the Literature.* Discussion Paper 112.World Bank, Washington, D.C.

Smith, Pamela J. 1998. "Are Weak Patents a Barrier to U.S. Exports?" *Journal of International Economics* 48: 151–177.

SIPO (State Intellectual Property Office). 1996. *Annual Report 1996.* Beijing.

————. 2000. *Annual Report* 2000. Beijing.

SSTC (State Science and Technology Commission of China). 1996. *China Science and Technology Indicators, 1996.* Beijing.

————. 1997. *China Science and Technology Statistics, Data Book 1997.* Beijing.

SSBC (State Statistical Bureau of China). 1997. *China Statistical Yearbook 1997.* Beijing.

————. 2001. *China Statistical Yearbook 2001.* Beijing.

Tackaberry, Paul. 1998. "Intellectual Property Risks in China: Their Effect on Foreign Investment and Technology Transfer." *Journal of Asian Business* 14: 1–24.

Trademark Office, State Administration for Industry and Commerce of China. 1996. *Annual Report on China's Trademarks 1996.* Beijing.

UNCTAD (United Nations Conference on Trade and Development). 1996. *The TRIPS Agreement and Developing Countries.* Geneva.

Watal, Jayshree. 1996. "Introducing Product Patents in the Indian Pharmaceutical Sector: Implications for Prices and Welfare." *World Competition* 20:5–21.

World Economic Forum. 1997. *World Competiveness Report 1997.* Geneva: World Economic Forum.

Yang, Guifang, and Keith E. Maskus. 1998. "Intellectual Property Rights, Licensing, and Economic Growth." University of Colorado at Boulder. Photocopied.

INDEX